for Sarah in
mutual voluminous
Lydgate-reading!

Fiona

W9-CBG-564

John Lydgate

John Lydgate

*Poetry, Culture,
and Lancastrian England*

edited by

Larry Scanlon *and* James Simpson

University of Notre Dame Press

Notre Dame, Indiana

Library of Congress Cataloging-in-Publication Data

John Lydgate : poetry, culture, and Lancastrian England /
edited by Larry Scanlon and James Simpson.
p.   cm.
Includes index.
ISBN 0-268-04115-6 (alk. paper)
ISBN 0-268-04116-4 (pbk. : alk. paper)
1. Lydgate, John, 1370?–1451?—Criticism and interpretation.
2. Literature and history—Great Britain—History—To 1500.
3. Great Britain—History—Lancaster and York, 1399–1485.
4. Civilization, Medieval, in literature.   I. Scanlon, Larry.
II. Simpson, James, 1954–
PR2037.J64   2005
821'.2—dc22
2005029345

Contents

Introduction

Larry Scanlon and James Simpson

Literary scholarship has increasingly come to appreciate the power and authority of the marginal. John Lydgate presents the peculiar challenge of being marginal and central at once. The central English poet of his own century, he was consigned to the margins by the end of the next century and has remained there ever since. Efforts at recuperation have all been obstructed, in small ways and large, by his original centrality. The dominant modern conception of Lydgate is that of the minor poet. Although the dominance of that conception has now begun to fade, it still retains considerable influence; more importantly, it hinders attempts to reach more productive views.

On the face of things, there is little minor about Lydgate. He was the author of more lines of poetry than any other figure in the Anglophone tradition, and his work was known by nearly all segments of the contemporary reading public. "Minor poet" was the status imposed on him to a large extent, *faute de mieux,* by the imperatives of Victorian philology. In its broadest outlines, Middle English literature as we now have it is largely the product of the great editing projects of the later nineteenth century, which were able to organize the unruly remnants of medieval manuscript culture by imposing on them modern ideals of authorship. Victorian philology saw its charge as twofold: enhancing the scientific field of historical linguistics and, guided by that knowledge, recovering the Middle English canon. In their pursuit of the first of these goals, an authoritative history of the English language, late-nineteenth- and early-twentieth-century editors were concerned to produce reliable texts, regardless of perceived aesthetic value. Thanks to the catholic energies of the Early English Text Society and to no less energetic German philologists, many of the texts of Lydgate on which we still rely were produced between 1882 and 1932.[1] However, recovering the Middle English canon was as much a matter of careful aesthetic discrimination as it was of historical reconstruction. In spite of his massive output and his undeniable importance to his own contemporaries, Lydgate was consigned to the ranks of lesser figures because his poetry could not be made to fit nineteenth-century aesthetic ideals. Thus scholarly accounts of Lydgate were long marked by a peculiar doubleness: careful philological expositions of his language, the extant manuscript evidence of his poems, and his possible influences and audiences were punctuated by denunciations of his poetic failings. The energy with which Lydgate scholarship marshaled its erudition was matched by the energy with which it belittled the object of that erudition, usually in contrast with Chaucer's achievement.

To an extent that may not always be appreciated at present, this peculiar aesthetic hostility contradicted nineteenth-century philology's paramount ideal, that of scientific neutrality and detachment. This contradiction was the product of a much longer history. Because Middle English literary history was formed out of the radical rupture of the Reformation, it had to contend, from its sixteenth-century beginnings, with potential dismissal by those hostile to the Catholic centuries, particularly those between the twelfth and the fifteenth inclusive, *en bloc*. From the 1530s forwards, the immense significance of ecclesiastical history has exerted an ineluctable undertow on literary history. Many Protestant cultural historians nevertheless resisted the outright rejection of the "Catholic" centuries of the later Middle Ages; they did so by isolating a few very exceptional and prophetic figures from the later medieval period who foresaw the brilliant new present of sixteenth-century Reformation and humanism. These select few proved the negative medieval rule by exception. Precisely because Chaucer was consistently isolated as the exception, the monastic Lydgate, his closest and very definitely Catholic competitor, was taken to prove the medieval rule. This historical logic has been reformulated across four centuries of literary history, according to the demands of different historical interests.[2]

Already in the sixteenth century bibliographers and editors had formulated the concept of Lydgate as Chaucer's foil: Lydgate is "the verye perfect disciple and imitator of the great Chaucer, the onelye glorye and beauty of [our tunge]." But even as Lydgate imitates Chaucer, he does not understand him: "[A]s it hapned the same Chaucer [lost] the prayse of that tyme wherin he wrote beyng then when in dede al good letters were almost aslepe, so farre was the grossenesse and barbarousenesse of that age from the vnderstandinge of so devyne a writer."[3] With the development of systematic literary history in the later eighteenth century, the position was restated, positing Lydgate's oeuvre as evidence of a medieval revanche, after the bright but short-lived new start represented by Chaucer. In his influential *History of English Poetry* (1774–81), for example, Thomas Warton says that after the spring of Chaucer, we expect summer, but "winter returns with redoubled horrors. . . . Most of the poets that immediately succeeded Chaucer, seem rather relapsing into barbarism, than availing themselves of those striking ornaments which his judgment and imagination had disclosed."[4]

For the most part, Warton's nineteenth-century successors accepted this view without exception. And it passed without much explicit notice into modern literary studies, as that field essentially reinvented itself after the First World War. In certain respects, the twentieth century's passive transmission of the Reformation's view of fifteenth-century literature is even more contradictory than that of the nineteenth. At its inception modern literary studies embraced the ideal of scientific rigor even more vigorously than its Victorian predecessors; its desire for a radical break with previous forms of literary scholarship was one of its most prominent themes. One of the founders of New Criticism declared in 1929 that "the history of criticism . . . is a history of dogmatism and argumentation rather than a history of research."[5] Yet it was precisely because of this desire for a radical break that New Criticism and the other modern formalisms failed to rethink the challenges posed by Middle English literature. Defining themselves in stark opposition to philology, they often put philology's most frequent object of study into question as well. They were only too happy to accept philology's own verdict on the negligibility of the fifteenth century. Moreover, in a couple of extremely influential cases, the principle of Chaucer's singularity became expendable as well.

Although Chaucer is treated sympathetically in William Empson's *Seven Types of Ambiguity,* he becomes the object of a symptomatic exclusion in one of the most influential essays of 1930s, John Crowe Ransom's "Criticism, Inc." This essay capped an important debate and solidified the opposition between historical "scholarship" and literary "criticism" that would become a fundamental fault line well into the 1970s. (Indeed, one could argue the opposition persists *mutatis mutandis* in current juxtapositions of traditional "historical periods" to "theory" or "cultural studies.") Ransom aggressively promotes the contemporary as the proper object of criticism. He treats Chaucer as the epitome of the *ancien régime,* "the familiar locus of the 'hard' scholarship, the center of any program of advanced studies in English which intends to initiate the student heroically and once for all, into the historical discipline," and he concludes dismissively, "[T]he official Chaucer course is probably over ninety-five per cent historical and linguistic, and less than five per cent aesthetic or critical."[6]

In retrospect, it is clear that the demise of the study of medieval literature was nowhere near as imminent as either its opponents expected or its practitioners sometimes feared. Nevertheless, medievalists found themselves on the defensive during much of the middle of the twentieth century. Those studies that would become most influential, such as C. S. Lewis's *Allegory of Love* or J. R. R. Tolkien's "The Monster and the Critics," had to manage complicated negotiations between the traditional requirements of philology and the powerful new tools of formalism. In the 1950s and 1960s, many of these negotiations concentrated on the recovery of Chaucer himself, especially among the leading medievalists of North America. Thus one can find them in the work of E. Talbot Donaldson, Charles Muscatine, and even, in a more paradoxical fashion, D. W. Robertson. At the same time, Middle English studies' abrupt shift from the center of the discipline to a much more marginal position had an especially exclusionary impact on already "minor" figures like Lydgate. By 1932, most of Lydgate's oeuvre had been published. The next few decades saw a continuing stream of philological notices, brief mentions in literary histories, and a sympathetic, if measured, treatment in C. S. Lewis's *Allegory of Love,* but little else.[7] The first monograph on Lydgate did not appear until 1952: Walter Schirmer's *John Lydgate: Ein Kulturbild aus dem 15 Jahrhundert.* Still working largely within a philological framework, Schirmer presented Lydgate as a humanist and avoided the question of his literary value by concentrating mainly on questions of intellectual history.[8]

Two decades later Derek Pearsall, whom Maura Nolan has aptly described as "the reluctant hero of Lydgate studies," produced the first fully "modern" response to Lydgate.[9] *John Lydgate* remains the single most complete and most authoritative treatment of Lydgate. One can see in it the same split between careful, precise erudition and aesthetic hostility that marks the older philological work. Pearsall's critique of Lydgate's poetic failings is often delivered with great wit and panache. Nevertheless, if generally dismissive, Pearsall is often more measured, and his aesthetic evaluation is comprehensive and coherent in a way that the older accounts were not. There is no doubt that *John Lydgate* rearticulates—and at some length—the venerable Reformation topos of Lydgate's negative exemplarity in relation to Chaucer.[10] But in the very comprehensiveness of the rearticulation we can also see a characteristic, if paradoxical, response to the demands of modern formalism. Aesthetic reevaluations of older poets constituted one of formalism's earliest impulses, which offered a crucial support of its polemic against the aesthetic insensitivity of its philological predecessors. As instances we might cite Pound and Eliot's attacks on Milton, Empson's trashing of the Romantics in the opening pages of *Seven Types of Am-*

biguity, and John Crowe Ransom's critique of Shakespeare's sonnets. From this perspective, Pearsall's strictures on Lydgate's poetics were modern and traditional at once, part of the book's claim to participate in the discourse of literary criticism as formalism had reshaped it. Indeed, an insistence on the primacy of the poetic is a hallmark of Pearsall's own distinguished career. It has been particularly evident in Pearsall's influential, if not foundational, engagement with textual studies, where he has often taken to task less aesthetically minded textual scholars in terms quite reminiscent of the New Critical critiques of "historical scholarship."[11]

New Criticism was displaced as the governing paradigm of literary study in the 1970s. By that time, Middle English scholars had devised immensely fertile ways of applying New Critical perspectives to the specificities of medieval texts. From Chaucer, they moved on to other texts that were susceptible to New Critical treatment, looking to those that manifested, preferably in combination, a high level of stylistic complexity; structural tension between the different parts of a given work; and a thematized, often ironic narratorial presence. They looked mainly to other late-fourteenth-century texts from the reign of Richard II (1377–99), notably *Sir Gawain and the Green Knight* and, with greater difficulty, *Piers Plowman.* As the field began to respond to feminist, Marxist and other theoretical trends reshaping literary studies as a whole, it still tended to concentrate on Ricardian texts. However, by the end of the 1980s, the field's usual chronological focus had broadened dramatically. The impetus for this shift was internal as well as external. New Historicism was chief among the external influences: its concentration on social context catalyzed an even more general suspicion of the category of the "major author" (under pressure from the 1960s, if not before). As a field to which New Criticism had grudgingly granted one (Chaucer) or at most two major authors (i.e., Chaucer and Langland), Middle English studies had the most to gain from this shift.

At the same time, the textual recovery of the large archive of Lollard texts activated both the study of Lollardy and, perforce, a more generally applicable set of questions concerning vernacular cultural movements and their official sponsors or resistance. Work on Lollard texts led ineluctably to phenomena that many earlier schools of criticism had either taken as given (e.g., the use of the vernacular) or dismissed as unliterary. That is, the project of reading deliberately anonymous texts, produced under hostile institutional and legal conditions, in a vernacular whose content and very use was polemical, all led ineluctably to institutional and discursive history. Study of "literary" texts was reinserted into a broader, richer textual environment in such a way as to answer broader cultural questions, notably concerning the structures of power relations pertaining between writers, readers, texts, and institutions. The category of "minor author" has fallen away, and an unprecedented amount of scholarly attention has been granted to a wide range of writers, many of them scarcely noticed before: John Gower, Thomas Hoccleve, Julian of Norwich, Margery Kempe—to name only the most prominent. Lydgate has certainly taken his place among this group, yet even so scholarly attention has still lagged, especially in comparison to Gower and Hoccleve. Despite another excellent monograph in 1985,[12] two excellent bibliographical guides,[13] and a number of significant newer, historicist treatments,[14] Lydgate's poetry (and prose) remains, quite simply, the largest, most underexplored area of Middle English studies. Until it faces the challenge of this corpus of texts, Middle English literary history must remain fragmentary and inchoate. There are no doubt a variety of reasons for this lag. One might be the sheer size of the opus. But certainly another is the continuing power even now of the Reformation topos of his negative exemplarity. Certainly that topos has haunted even some of the most influential of recent reconsiderations.[15]

John Lydgate: Poetry, Culture, and Lancastrian England attempts to remedy this continuing problem. We believe it offers something almost entirely new in Lydgate studies. We propose to take Lydgate seriously as a major poet, and offer some account of the truly remarkable range and variety of his work. At the same time, this volume is not a "Companion to Lydgate," offering a conspectus of Lydgate's oeuvre. The editors projected this volume by commissioning essays not on the basis of coverage but rather on the basis of readiness to think well beyond the worn clichés of Lydgate criticism.

A single-author anthology may strike some as itself an outdated approach to this problem. This volume does after all depend, at least provisionally, on the very category of "major author" that in practice has operated so much to Lydgate's detriment. Yet from our perspective, that contradiction is precisely why this volume must focus solely on Lydgate. We offer two justifications, each from alternate sides of the problem. The first is to note that in practice the death of the author has proved much exaggerated. Author study may some day become obsolete. Nevertheless, that day has not arrived; nor does its arrival seem imminent. More particularly, to deny Lydgate all treatment as a major author, no matter how provisional, would ultimately mean reinforcing the trap in which we currently find him. The only way to get him out of the shadow of Chaucer, to accord to the many texts he produced a specificity of their own, is by considering them, at least initially, as part of a corpus of which he is the author. To move now solely to a contextual or cultural approach, in which his texts are considered only as part of the larger cultural formations of their historical moment, or even as part of the transmission of the Chaucerian tradition, would in effect constitute a return to the days when he rated only brief mentions in comprehensive literary histories.

The second justification is that any initial survey of Lydgate's vast corpus will quickly come to the recognition that the study of Lydgate's textual corpus is itself necessarily "field focused." Lydgate's poetry is more thoroughly imbricated in explicitly public concerns of given regimes than the work of any other major insular and/or British poet writing between, say, Wace (d. ca. 1180) and Spenser (d. 1599). Consideration of this field, then, raises, and promises to answer, precisely those questions of historical import mentioned above. No medieval British poet is so clearly linked with specific institutional interests as Lydgate, and none is involved with such a wide range of such interests. Unlike any previous post-Conquest English kings, Lancastrian monarchs all fostered explicit relations with poets writing in English, prime among whom was Lydgate. Monarchs were not the only powerful patrons to see advantage in the cultivation of vernacular poetry: Lydgate's patrons also included aristocrats, London bureaucrats and merchants, monastic foundations, and parish communities. His addressed and/or actual readership included all of the above plus gentry readers. His generic range is, accordingly, wider than that of any medieval poet: the genres in which he wrote include elegiac love lament; mercantile romance; animal fable and political allegory; urban satire; anti-Lollard polemic; epithalamium; Marian lyric and narrative; *roman antique*; spiritual allegory; political, mercantile, and ecclesiastical performance scripts; *de casibus* tragedy; psalm translation; varieties of hagiography; pseudo-Aristotelian political advice literature; and spiritual autobiography.

If Lydgate was in some ways an official poet, the powerful institutions for which he wrote were not, however, serenely secure. He wrote for a dynasty whose power was grounded on the illegitimate coup d'état of 1399 and whose continuing but fragile viability depended on immensely ambitious claims to France. These claims became potentially unsustainable with the death of Henry V in 1422, leaving the throne subject to civil dissension, occupied as it was by an eight-month-old infant, the future Henry VI (1422–61, 1470–71), who in maturity was incapable of taking decisive control of the unmanageable inheritance left him by his father. In the reigns of Henry IV (1399–1413) and Henry V (1413–22), the regime was also threatened by, or rather created a threat out of, a heretical movement. Different works by Lydgate explicitly (or all but explicitly) address each of these treacherous historical conjunctures. Neither was the dynasty by any means consistent in its practice across the forty or so years of Lydgate's poetic career: Lydgate adroitly wrote within and across the specific and even conflicting constraints of three Lancastrian monarchs (Henry IV, Henry V, and Henry VI). He also wrote from at least three centers of English cultural or military power (London, Paris, and Bury, the site of the great monastic foundation to which Lydgate belonged).

"Lydgate," then, represents less a single authorial consciousness in the traditional sense of a solitary genius than a point of transmission between often-powerful institutions and their readers. Those institutions did not form a coherent, seamless bloc but were themselves clearly divided; Lydgate, indeed, often served as the mediating voice between one institution and another. He wrote within and across different literary systems, and he wrote from very different historical situations, whether he addressed the dangers of heresy, international conflict with France, or civil war, and whether he addressed a militaristic king (Henry V) or a king experiencing military failure (Henry VI).

Lydgate's activity in this wide variety of institutional fields illuminates his contributions to literary history. He is Chaucer's first great impresario and competitor. He presents, deploys, and occasionally rebuffs Chaucer's works in a vernacular with newly emergent authority and, thanks primarily to Lydgate's praise and use of Chaucer, an emergent sense of its own poetic tradition. Lydgate transmits to English the great secular narratives of disastrous city-state conflict (i.e., those of Troy and Thebes), derived from twelfth-century French humanist texts in the vernacular, just as he imports newer forms of Italian, Latin humanism with his translation, via a French intermediary, of Boccaccio's *De casibus virorum illustrium*. These and other secular works fulfilled a Lancastrian project of promoting an English vernacular tradition of high literary status that could stand beside a long French, and a more recently established Italian, tradition.

If on the one hand official Lancastrian institutions fostered the vernacular for secular poetry, on the other they strictly delimited its use for theological subjects. Lydgate also responded to this contrary exigency. Lollard use of the vernacular, in plain style, for biblical translation and theological discussion was judged dangerous by the Lancastrian Church. Apparently in response to this conjuncture, Lydgate developed an ornate, highly mannered rhetorical mode for religious, especially Marian, verse. (His often-derided cultivation of such an "aureate" style awaits historicization.)

The essays here (all commissioned and freshly written for this volume, except for Rita Copeland's 1992 essay on rhetoric) certainly fulfilled the editors' expectations of new paths into Lydgate's writing. The opening essay (Hardman) broaches the fundamental question of his syntax. Its notorious "failures" are revealed to derive from the need of modern editors to make what is in fact a coherent and meditated syntactic practice conform to modern standards. No less fundamental are the aesthetic presuppositions with which we come to Lydgate's poetry, and the deep-set resistances to the lack of novelty always implicit in translational practice (Scanlon).

Many essays broach the question of Lydgate's "official" poetry. New Criticism and New Historicism have both, for related reasons, been suspicious of such writing. For the New Critic, poetry had to incorporate and balance conflicting and deeply felt personal perspectives, while for the New Historicist poetry was either wholly collusive with an always oppressive and single source of power or wholly subversive. Because New Historicists generated their scholarly mode out of the experience of sixteenth-century texts, they discussed political poetry in the terms of a much more centralized political and courtly culture. The alternatives for political poetry were either total collusion and identification with the operations of power or subversive intent. A third possibility was apparently subversive intent whose subversive nature turned out to be a mirage, no more than a conduit for and condition of impersonal Power.

Inspired by the historicist turn, many essays here consider previously marginalized official forms, such as the royal entry, the mumming, the epithalamium, and the royal pedigree. Other essays discuss Lydgate's self-presentation or enterprise in higher-profile commissioned texts, such as *Troy Book,* the hagiographies, and *The Fall of Princes,* but do so with an eye to the cultural politics of these texts. If, however, many of these essays practice a broadly historicist scholarship on official poetry, they all do so in a nuanced way, avoiding the flattening and often inappropriate antinomies imported from sixteenth-century models. There is no unanimity of view among these essays regarding Lydgate's collusion with or critical distance from sources of authority. They argue for different distances between patron and poet. What, however, unites all these essays (by Meyer-Lee, Straker, Simpson, Benson, Nolan, Summit, Copeland, Somerset, and Nisse) is a much more nuanced account of the modalities of this official poetry: its sophisticated self-consciousness about its laureate status (Meyer-Lee); its precision of address, as it mediates between different centers of power, either metropolitan and courtly (Benson, Nolan) or monastic and courtly (Nisse, Somerset); its skill in raising the awareness of its readers about the cultural capital they accrue from this poetry (Nolan); its difference from "propaganda" (Straker); its rhetorical self-consciousness about, and confidence in, addressing the powerful (Simpson); its importation of republican rhetorical modes and political ideas into English monarchical conditions (Copeland,

Summit); its parallels and material overlaps with other cultural projects, such as Duke Humphrey's library (Summit); its use of hagiographical materials for the expression of monarchical representation in new circumstances (Somerset); and its capacity to repudiate itself (Nisse).

The essays presented here offer, in short, new paths into an exceptionally fertile and large poetic territory, which promises any number of further opportunities for fresh exploration.[16]

Notes

1. For a list of these texts, see James Simpson, *Reform and Cultural Revolution, 1350–1547* (Oxford: Oxford University Press, 2002), chap. 2.

2. A more expansive and more fully documented form of the argument in the next few paragraphs can be found in Simpson, *Reform and Cultural Revolution,* 39–40.

3. Citations taken from Robert Braham's preface to the 1555 edition of Lydgate's *Troy Book.* Braham's preface is reproduced in *Lydgate's Troy Book,* 4 vols., ed. Henry Bergen, EETS, e.s., 97, 103, 106, 126 (London: Kegan Paul, Trench, Trübner, 1906, 1908, 1910, 1935), 4:60–65; quote on 63.

4. Thomas Warton, *The History of English Poetry from the Close of the Eleventh to the Commencement of the Eighteenth Centuries,* 3 vols. (London: Dodsley et al., 1774–81), 2: 51.

5. I. A. Richards, *Practical Criticism: A Study of Literary Judgment* (New York: Harcourt, Brace & World, 1929), 7.

6. William Empson, *Seven Types of Ambiguity,* rev. ed. (New York: New Directions, 1947), 58–64; John Crowe Ransom, "Criticism, Inc.," in *The World's Body* (New York: Charles Scribner's Sons, 1938), 339, 341. Earlier contributions to this debate include R. S. Crane, "History vs. Criticism in the Study of Literature," *English Journal (College Edition)* 24 (1935): 645–67; Howard Mumford Jones, "Literary Scholarship and Contemporary Criticism," *English Journal (College Edition)* 23 (1934): 740–58; and J. L. Lowes, "Presidential Address," *PMLA* 48 (1933): 1399–1408. One of the ironies of the hostility of the American New Critics to medieval literature is that it was a medievalist, Hector Chadwick, who engineered the first institutional home for literary studies in its modern form with the creation of a new English curriculum after 1918 at Cambridge. See E. M. W. Tillyard, *The Muse Unchained: An Intimate Account of the Revolution in English Studies at Cambridge* (London: Bowes & Bowes, 1958); and Francis Mulhearn, *The Moment of "Scrutiny"* (London: New Left Books, 1979), 3–4, 15–34.

7. C. S. Lewis, *The Allegory of Love: A Study in Medieval Tradition* (London: Oxford University Press, 1936), 234–44.

8. Walter F. Schirmer, *John Lydgate: Ein Kulturbild aus dem 15 Jahrhundert* (Tübingen: M. Niemeyer, 1952); trans. Ann E. Keep as *John Lydgate: A Study in the Culture of the*

Fifteenth Century (London: Methuen, 1961). Alain Renoir would also treat Lydgate as a humanist in his monograph *The Poetry of John Lydgate* (Cambridge, MA: Harvard University Press, 1967).

9. Maura Nolan, "Virtuous Prolongation: Lydgate's Canacee" (paper presented at the Thirteenth Biennial Congress of the New Chaucer Society, Boulder, CO, July 19, 2002); Derek Pearsall, *John Lydgate* (London: Routledge & Kegan Paul, 1970).

10. On this point, see Simpson, *Reform and Cultural Revolution,* 46–47.

11. See, for instance, Pearsall's response to T. A. Shippey in "Texts, Textual Criticism, and Fifteenth Century Manuscript Production," in *Fifteenth-Century Studies: Recent Essays,* ed. R. F. Yeager (Hamden, CT: Archon Books, 1984), 129–30. Ralph Hanna remarks, not entirely sympathetically, on this tendency in Pearsall's work in "Analytical Survey 4: Middle English Manuscripts and the Study of Literature," *New Medieval Literatures* 4 (2001): 244. For the same critique, aimed this time at recent historicist, feminist, and theoretically inflected Chaucer scholarship, see Derek Pearsall, "The Future of Chaucer Studies," *Poetica* 50 (1998): 17–27.

12. L. A. Ebin, *John Lydgate,* Twayne's English Author Series 407 (Boston: Twayne Publishers, 1985).

13. See Alain Renoir and C. David Benson, "John Lydgate," in *A Manual of the Writings in Middle English, 1050–1500,* 7 vols., ed. J. Burke Severs and A. E. Hartung (New Haven: Connecticut Academy of Arts and Sciences, 1967–), 6:1809–1920, 2071–2175; and Derek Pearsall, *John Lydgate (1371–1449): A Bio-Bibliography,* English Literary Studies 71 (Victoria, BC: University of Victoria, 1997).

14. Notably David Lawton, "Dullness and the Fifteenth Century," *ELH* 54 (1987): 761–99; Seth Lerer, *Chaucer and His Readers: Imagining the Author in Late-Medieval England* (Princeton, NJ: Princeton University Press, 1993); Larry Scanlon, *Narrative, Authority, and Power: The Medieval Exemplum and the Chaucerian Tradition,* Cambridge Studies in Medieval Literature 20 (Cambridge: Cambridge University Press, 1994); Paul Strohm, *England's Empty Throne: Usurpation and the Language of Legitimation, 1399–1422* (New Haven, CT: Yale University Press, 1996), and "Hoccleve, Lydgate and the Lancastrian Court," in *The Cambridge History of Medieval English Literature,* ed. David Wallace (Cambridge: Cambridge University Press, 1999), 640–61.

15. Simpson, *Reform and Cultural Revolution,* 47–50.

16. Two new books in particular are already beginning such exploration: Nigel Mortimer, *John Lydgate's "Fall of Princes": Narrative Tragedy in Its Literary and Political Contexts* (Oxford: Oxford University Press, 2005), and Maura Nolan, *John Lydgate and the Making of Public Culture, 1422–32* (Cambridge: Cambridge University Press, 2005).

I

Lydgate's Uneasy Syntax

Phillipa Hardman

My title is borrowed from a recent critical assessment of Lydgate's reputation by Derek Pearsall: "He was much admired in his day, but his verbosity, the inflation of his diction, *the uneasiness of his syntax,* and the unevenness of his metre are obstacles to pleasure."[1] While Lydgate's prolixity and elaboration may be attributed to a medieval aesthetic now alien to most readers, who would find Geoffrey de Vinsauf's advice on the employment of *amplificatio* in fine writing a recipe for literary disaster, and while some of the perceived defects in Lydgate's meter may be open to further negotiation between philology and paleography, the question of Lydgate's uneasy syntax seems to be one on which modern critics are all in agreement and for which there is no obvious excuse. The distressing characteristics of the poet's syntax are more fully described in Pearsall's earlier monograph, *John Lydgate*: "His sentences often ramble on, accommodating any stray thought or allusion that may occur to him. . . . Instead of selecting and subordinating he accumulates detail laboriously in a profusion of parentheses." His use of "unrelated participles instead of finite verbs . . . contributes more than anything to the effect of formlessness and irresolution, especially in couplet writing." His "loose attitude to conjunctions (especially 'for'), sudden changes of tense, and from indirect to direct speech, the frequency of inversion, . . . the very distinctive habit of using *as* + personal pronoun instead of the relative pronoun" are all traits that are said to "cause distress to the reader."[2] Indeed, Lydgate's faulty syntax has become a critical commonplace, reinforced by dismissive judgments in literary handbooks such as J. A. Burrow's dictum: "His writing has all the faults one would expect of a one-hundred-thousand-line poet. It is diffuse and often, especially in its syntax, negligent."[3]

The most frequently cited example of Lydgate's syntactical ineptitude is the opening of the *Siege of Thebes,* where the poet has apparently pitted himself against his master Chaucer in an attempt to outdo the inimitable opening sentence of the *Canterbury Tales* and has suffered the inevitable humiliation of merely exposing his own inferiority. Not only does he not know when to stop; he seems unaware how to stop the flow of temporal clauses with a properly placed main clause. Pearsall notes with exasperation that "there is still no main verb in sight when the desperate editor has to call a halt after forty-five lines."[4] Axel Erdmann's nerve held out a little longer: his edition for the Early English Text Society places a somewhat arbitrary full stop at line 64 and another at line 65.[5] Rosamund Allen, in a discussion of the significance of the *Siege of Thebes* in relation to the *Canterbury Tales,* offers a colorful image for Lydgate's syntactical performance as "apt to wobble off course and collapse like someone on a monocycle," but though she sternly criticizes this outstandingly bad example ("The all-important missing verb in Lydgate's opening to the *Siege* is an error"), her description of the effect of this lengthy nonsentence is very interesting:

> It sinks away like sugar down a funnel and leaves nothing behind except an after-image of bustling activity: Lydgate has taken us from the spring setting, sun, showers, flowers (1–17), through the recapitulation of the varieties of the tales which were told on Chaucer's original pilgrimage (18–38), to a slotted-in allusion to Chaucer, "Chief Registrer of þis pilgrimage," who "Al þat was told forȝeting noght at al" (48–49) recorded everything, rejecting only "the chaff" (39–57), as the tales were told during the entire journey from Southwark under the direction of the Host. (58–64)[6]

This seems to me a perfect account of just the effect Lydgate needed to achieve in order to establish his position in relation to Chaucer and the *Canterbury Tales:* a certain degree of humble self-effacement, but an illusion of having mastered the material, the whole being dazzlingly encompassed in a single breath before he passes on to his own entry into the narrative. For the listener or reader, this "after-image" is precisely what remains in the mind; it is only the editor who agonizes about the missing verb and the placing of the full stop. As Erdmann and Ekwall note of the experience of reading the *Siege,* "The logical connection of the sentences being decidedly superior to the syntactical, there is generally not the slightest difficulty in following and appreciating the ideas presented."[7]

But is it acceptable just to agree to overlook Lydgate's inferior syntax in this way? It is not as if the poet were incapable of writing verse in standard syntactical sentences. For example, following the prologue, Lydgate begins the first part of the *Siege of Thebes* with this complex sentence of seventeen lines, in which he adroitly makes the transition from the pilgrimage frame to the ancient tale:

> Sirs / quod I: sith of ȝour curtesye
> I entred am / in-to ȝour companye,
> And admitted / a tale for to telle
> By hym þat haþ pouer to compelle,
> I mene our hoste, gouernour and guyde
> Of ȝow echon / ridyng her be-side;
> Thogh that my wit / barayn be and dul,
> I wol reherce / a story wonderful,
> Towchinge the siege / and destruccioun
> Of worthy Thebees / the myghty Royal toun,
> Bylt and begonne / of olde antiquite,
> Vpon the tyme / of worthy Iosue,
> Be dyligence / of kyng Amphioun,
> Chief cause first / of his fundacioun,
> For which his fame / which neuere shal away,
> In honure floureth / ȝit vnto this day,
> And in story / remembred is and preised.
>   (1.177–93)[8]

Four subordinate clauses cover the narrator's acceptance into the pilgrim company, the authority of the Host, and Lydgate's modest apology, despite which, he declares, in the simple main clause that falls in the middle of the sentence, "I wol reherce a story wonderful," followed by an elaborate series of explanatory phrases to establish the importance and antiquity of Thebes, and the final subordinate clauses asserting the everlasting memorial of its founder "in story." Lydgate as storyteller thus acts as the fulcrum in the sentence while the balance shifts from the here and now of Canterbury and pilgrimage to the "wonder and merveil" (1.195) of "olde antiquite." The syntactical control of the sentence affords a modest but genuine example of what John Norton-Smith has praised in other of Lydgate's works as his "more Latinate, periodic, sentence structure."[9] He picks out for special praise in this respect the anti-Lollard poem *A Defence of Holy Church,* in which "the rime-royal stanza pattern is subordinated to expanded and suspended syntax," and regrets that "the beneficial tightness of periodic syntax" was never extended to "the repetitious flow of his usual narrative style." Although the sentence quoted above from the *Siege of Thebes* does not display all the virtuoso effects of "expanded and suspended syntax," it suggests nonetheless that Lydgate's interest in experimenting with periodic syntax did extend into his narrative poems.

Apart from elaborate stylistic effects involving periodic syntax, Lydgate was also a competent master of a plain narrative style, typically using sentences of four to eight lines with uncomplicated syntactic structures, examples of which can readily be found throughout the *Siege of Thebes,* the *Troy Book,* the *Fall of Princes,* and his other narrative works: a point conceded by Erdmann and Ekwall, who note, "[T]here are unimpeachable sentences in all of them."[10] After the lengthy arguments for and against Paris's expedition in the *Troy Book,* for instance, Lydgate narrates the beginning of his voyage in book 2 with a series of short simple clauses that makes the whole undertaking seem deceptively easy:

> Þei hale vp ankir, and by þe large se
> Þei gan to seile, and haue þe wynde at wille,
> Þe water calme, blaundischyng, and stille,
> With-oute trouble of any boystous wawe.
>
> (2.3386–89)[11]

More extended use of simple syntax gives Lydgate a flexible tool for narrating sequential action, as in his account of Paris and Helen's fatal acknowledgment of their passion:

> Þei kepte hem clos, þat no worde a-sterte;
> Þer was no man þe tresoun myȝt aduerte
> Of hem tweyn, ne what þei wolde mene;
> But at þe last, Paris and þis quene
> Concluded han, with schort avisement,
> Fully þe fyn of her boþe entent,
> And sette a purpos atwix hem in certeyn,
> Whan þei cast for to mete ageyn.
>
> (*Troy Book,* 2.3735–42)

Addressing the reader, Lydgate can write an expansive yet short and plain sentence:

> Now have I told / vnto ȝou / ground of al,
> That ȝe wel knowe / be Informacioun

Cleerly the pith / and exposicioun
Of this mater / as clerkes can ȝou telle.
(*Siege of Thebes,* 1.316–19)

Sentence construction in his stanzaic narratives can be equally lucid, as in his account of the death of Virginia in the *Fall of Princes:*

Whan Appius hadde youe his iugement
Ageyn this maide, which aforn hym stood,
Hir manli fadir, most knyhtli off entent,
Took hir appart, as he thouhte it good,
And with a knyff shadde hir herte blood:
Dempte it bettre to slen hir in clennesse,
Than the tiraunt hir beute sholde oppresse.
(2.1380–06)[12]

The question therefore is, if Lydgate was capable of writing good syntax of both simple and complex kinds, why did he apparently choose to write in a way that has drawn such hostile and exasperated criticism from so many modern readers? It is important to note that this hostile judgment is a comparatively recent phenomenon: in the eighteenth century Thomas Warton was able to write that Lydgate's "naturally verbose and diffuse" manner "contributed in no small degree to give a clearness and a fluency to his phraseology," so much so that Warton could state: "He is the first of our writers whose style is clothed with that perspicuity, in which the English phraseology appears at this day to an English reader."[13] The difference in reading habits now, over two hundred years later, may mean that the "copiousness" Warton admired in Lydgate is more likely to be judged tedious; but it is not so easy to explain why there should have been such a change of opinion as regards his language that the last thing most readers would now attribute to Lydgate's style is perspicuity.

One major difference between Warton's experience of reading Lydgate and ours, however, is in the editions from which the texts are read. Early prints, like many manuscripts, tend to mark midline caesuras but otherwise leave the couplets or stanzas to speak for themselves, only rarely placing a stop at the end of a long section of text or at the completion of the whole work. This openness would have allowed the virtues of fluency and copiousness to be appreciated by Warton in long uninterrupted sequences, following the logical development of Lydgate's ideas, as noted by Erdmann and Ekwall, without intrusion from added punctuation. As Mary Hamel points out, "[M]edieval syntax was generally speaking paratactic rather than hypotactic," and the necessity of adding modern punctuation to medieval texts sets up false expectations of regular syntax "according to modern (or classical) standards."[14] It seems possible that critical dissatisfaction with Lydgate's syntax derives in large part from the frustrations of nineteenth- and twentieth-century editors trying to produce acceptably punctuated editions for modern readers. Lydgate's first editor for the Early English Text Society, Josef Schick, complained of the difficulty he had punctuating, with harsh criticism for the poet's interminable sentences: "His sentences run on aimlessly, without definite stop, and it is often difficult to say where a particular idea begins or ends."[15]

A similar experience when working on the *Life of Our Lady* was the stimulus for this study: I had difficulty in finding a place to stop that would allow me to quote a complete sense-unit of reasonable length, despite the fact that the *Life of Our Lady* is in rhyme-royal stanzas, and that Lydgate's stanzaic poems have been thought less likely than his couplet works to suffer from his notoriously loose syntax, given the more tight-knit structure of the stanza.[16] In fact, in long stretches of the *Life of Our Lady* the stanza pattern is more or less ignored as an organizing sense-unit, and the use of enjambment frequently links not only lines but stanzas in an unbroken sequence, overflowing the confines of the elaborate rhyme scheme in an often highly effective way. This fluid style of writing is particularly characteristic of the first three books of the poem, but there are also numerous examples in books 4 to 6, despite the notably simpler narrative structure of these shorter last three books.[17] The editors of the 1961 critical edition of the poem chose not to provide any punctuation at all for books 1 and 2, beyond reproducing the kind of midline caesura marks found in the manuscripts, thus avoiding the difficulties they encountered in punctuating books 3 to 6. The long first sentence of book 3, for example, though the meaning is not in doubt, is quite hard to unravel syntactically and is correspondingly difficult to punctuate successfully, as can be seen from this quotation, where the editorial punctuation cannot be said to aid the reader (it is particularly misleading in lines 3–4):

> Whanne al was hust and al was in silence,
> And in his course the longe sterry nyght
> Was passed half and fresche of aperaunce,
> Lucyne shone on hevyn fayre and bryght;
> Thy worde, oo lorde, that is moste of myght,
> Whiche ay abydythe and partyth not from the,
> Sent and discended from thy Royall see,

Hathe sodenly upon all the erthe
Shed his light for our saluacion,
As I shal synge or maies dai the ferthe;
If ye lust here of humble affection, –
How in the yere by computacion
Fourty and two of Octouian;
Ferthermore, aftir the worlde beganne, [etc.]

(3.1–14)[18]

The key to the problem seems to be the way Lydgate makes the transition into the story of the Nativity, moving from the Old Testament vision of the Word of God bursting upon the world to the precise historically documentable moment when Caesar Augustus issued his decree for a universal census. Just as he did in the opening sentence of the first book of the *Siege of Thebes,* Lydgate makes himself and his function as poet the bridge into the new narrative subject, but in this case the syntax is less regular. The first nine lines paraphrase the biblical verses used in one of the masses of Christmas week: "Cum enim quietum silentium contineret omnia, et nox in suo curso medium iter haberet, | omnipotens sermo tuus de caelo a regalibus sedibus . . . prosilivit" (Wisdom 18.14–15). "While all things were in quiet silence, and the night was in the midst of her course, | Thy almighty word leapt down from heaven from thy royal throne" (Douai). Lydgate claims this as his poetic subject now as he speaks: "As I shal synge"; but he also makes this same promise act as introduction to the historical event of the census that follows immediately: "As I shal synge . . . | If ye lust here . . . | How in the yere by computacion | Fourty and two of Octouian," which was also (and here I give a skeleton précis of Lydgate's next forty-five lines) 5,199 years after the Creation, when there was universal peace, and when Augustus sent out his decree, every person was enrolled in the town of his birth. The promise "I shal synge . . . | If ye lust here" thus reads in relation to both the clauses preceding it and those following it: Janus-like, it is facing both ways. In terms of Lydgate's material here this is very appropriate, as it looks back to the Old Testament past of prophecy and forwards, forging a connection with the historical events of the New Testament.

For Lydgate, I would suggest, in this work at least, the peculiarity of his syntax can create effects that contribute importantly to the purpose of the poem as a whole. His habit of running sentences on, as Schick puts it, without definite stops—that is to say, with stops that have less than the finality of a full stop but can sometimes be represented by a colon, semicolon, or dash—does indeed make it "difficult to say where a particular idea begins or ends"; but this is precisely what I take Lydgate's purpose here to be. The *Life of Our Lady* brings together Old Testament prophecy and classical portents, gospel and apocryphal narrative, scholastic exegesis and affective devotional response, all held together by the conviction that Mary is central to the whole history of humanity, from the Fall to the end of time.[19] The ease with which Lydgate moves from past to present to future, from narrative to commentary to prayer, without definite stops between, can be seen as enacting this conviction, stressing the continuity of prophecy, revelation in time, and faithful response.[20] A striking example of Lydgate's mobile style of composition is his sensitive rendering of the moment of Epiphany, when the three kings enjoy the divine presence after offering their gifts to the child Jesus (5.295–329). Their delight in the infant's physical beauty leads to their personal experience of spiritual desire and consolation in a single fluid movement that provides an implied model for the passage later in the book when Lydgate involves readers in replicating the experience of epiphany in our own contemplation of Mary and Jesus "in picture" (5.631–83). The passage is quoted here without the confusing punctuation of the 1961 edition (in which, for example, a full stop is inexplicably placed at the end of each stanza), though it is difficult to see how its various indefinite stops might successfully be conformed to modern expectations of formal punctuation.

> And of these yefteȝ passyng Reuerent
> Full of mysterrye and hevenly privete
> Whan thay had made her presente
> Vnto the childe ay sittyng on her knee
> With grete avyse thay gan be-holde and se
> To fore that thay Remevyde fro that place
> His godely chere and his fayre face
>
> Considryng his feturs by and by
> With grete insight and humble entencion
> And ay the more thay loke bysyly
> The more thay ioyen in her inspection
> And thought all as in her reason
> Though kynde and god had sette in o fygure
> The beaute holy of euery creature
>
> It myght not in sothenesse haue be liche
> To his fayrnesse nor peregall
> For he that is above nature ryche

Hath made this childe fayrest in speciall
For in his face they byholden all
The hole beaute and fayrnesse eke also
Of hevyn and erthe to-gydre bothe twoo

Wherefore no wondre though thay hem delyte
Most passyngly vpon hym to see
For thay in hert reioysen hem not a lyte
On hym to loke that thay haue liberte
For ay the more playnely that thay be
In his presence the parfyte hote fyre
Of hertly Ioye hem brent by desyre

And of o thyngh full gode hede thay toke
How that the chylde demurely cast his sight
Tawardes hem and godely gan to loke
On her face3 with his eyne bryght
And how that he put his Arme3 right
Godely to hem makyng a manere signe
To hem of thankyng with chere full benigne.

As is obvious from the opening line, however, this "sentence" is in fact attached by conjunction to the previous passage describing and interpreting the gifts of gold, incense, and myrrh; and the following passage celebrating Mary as the Madonna of Humility is also connected by "And" and leads without a definite stop through the account of the three kings' return to their country, to an interpretation of the meaning of *epiphany,* and finally to the prayer and meditation on "this high feste" that conclude the book. The historical narrative is thus made indivisible from a personal response to the revealed mystery of divine truth.[21]

The idea that Lydgate's apparently imperfect syntax might in some cases be a deliberate choice intended to produce a particular effect seems worth exploring in relation to other of his works. If we approach the much-cited case of the prologue to the *Siege of Thebes* without any preconceptions on the correct or ideal length of an opening sentence, but just read it with an appreciation of its function in summarizing all the actions of Chaucer's pilgrims prior to Lydgate's meeting them, then we find that it does indeed contain a main verb. The whole opening sentence extends to ninety-one lines, the first sixty-seven all amplifying the adverbial time-clause of the opening line: "Whan bri3te phebus passed was the ram," continuing "whan . . . the tyme whan . . . the tyme whan . . . and this while that," encompassing all the "bustling activity" of the pilgrimage from Southwark and the pilgrims' safe arrival and lodging in Canterbury. Only then does Lydgate stabilize the sentence with the main clause:

> I not in soth / what I may it call,
> Hap / or fortune / in Conclusioun,
> That me byfil / to entren into toun,
> The holy seynt pleynly to visite
> (68–71)

and he goes on to fill out the circumstantial detail of his vow, his clothes, horse, and servant, his chancing on the same inn as the pilgrims, and his welcome from the Host. Thus, as we have seen before, Lydgate places himself at the center of meaning in the sentence, and here the sentence is prolonged until Lydgate the pilgrim has been fully incorporated into the narrative of Chaucer's company, complete with his own characterizing description imitating the portraits in the General Prologue.

Mary Hamel describes an interestingly similar problem in the alliterative *Morte Arthure,* in a passage "that has been criticized on more than one occasion because 'it is impossible to punctuate according to our ideas of clause and sentence.'"[22] This is the catalog of Arthur's conquests that follows the narrator's introduction, which consists of a "when"-clause extended by a large number of variations, including independent clauses, over twenty-two lines before arriving at the main clause (26–51). Its organization, as Hamel explains, is best understood as "a rhetorical rather than a syntactical structure," whose purpose is to focus directly on the specific moment in narrative time and to subordinate to it the previous history contained in the temporal clauses. This description exactly fits the structure and purpose of Lydgate's opening sentence in the *Siege of Thebes.* Although subordinated, in each case the elaborately extended "when"-clause is essential to the rhetorical design, in order to convey the full greatness of Arthur's past deeds at a moment in time and, for Lydgate, to establish the literary importance and cultural currency of the masterpiece to which he is (fittingly) attaching his own work.

Many of the faults for which Lydgate's style and syntax have been criticized, in fact, characteristically occur in introductory passages such as this (though not always of such great length) and can perhaps best be explained as functions of their situation in the text. The accumulation of parallel adverbial clauses and absolute constructions serves to recapitulate past events and to place the new ensuing action in relation to them. In the prologue, Lydgate's narrative is thus placed in the context of prior "facts" (the pilgrimage to Canterbury; Henry V's commissioning the *Troy Book*), while in the openings of books or major sections within the narrative such syntactical features can be understood as devices serving the purpose of helping the reader or listener to navigate a long and complicated narrative. For example, in the *Troy Book,* the introductory passage at the beginning of book 4 displays the method in brief (without Lydgate's customary amplification of temporal detail):

> Hector þus ded, as ȝe han herd me seid,
> And Achilles in his tent I-leid,
> With his woundis mortal, freshe, & grene,
> Vp-on a morwe, whan þe sonne shene
> Enchasid had a-way þe dirke nyȝt,
> Agamenoun, þe wyse worþi knyȝt,
> In his werkis passingly prudent,
> Hath in al haste for his lordis sent.
>
> (4.1–8)

As the narrator in the *Siege of Thebes* continues the account of his acceptance into the pilgrim company, Lydgate's next sentence displays another irregular syntactical feature that critics have censured: a sudden switch from indirect to direct speech and from past to present tense. Again, however, this is really a problem only when one tries to edit the text and has to decide where to open the inverted commas. Reading it aloud, one hears the voice of the narrator slipping into character, re-enacting the part he played opposite the Host:

> I answerede my name was Lydgate,
> Monk of Bery, nyȝ fyfty ȝere of age,
> Come to this toune to do my pilgrimage
> As I haue hight : I haue therof no shame.
>
> (92–95)

While this clearly starts with indirect speech and ends with direct speech, the two lines between can be read in either mode. As with so much in Lydgate's output, a precedent for this permeable style of writing can be found in the work of his master Chaucer, where, for example, the voice of the narrator in *Troilus and Criseyde* can slip easily from reporting Pandarus's thoughts in the past tense to speaking them directly, as if in his persona (3.523–32).[23] Apart from this distinctive practice, both direct and reported speech in Lydgate's works are usually syntactically regular, as in this passage of brief, forceful dispute:

Than Polymyte / of malys / and hegh pride
Tolde hym shortly / he shulde not abide,
Nor logge ther / thogh he hadde it sworn.
"For I," quod he / "toke it vp to-forn
And wil it kepe / during al this nyght,
I seie the platly / maugre al thy might."
Quod Tydeus / "that is no curtesie
Me to deuoyde / but rather vileynye,
ʒif ʒe take hede / that seme a gentil knight."
                    (*Siege of Thebes*, 2.1323–31)

The four lines from the prologue to the *Siege of Thebes* (92–95) quoted above demonstrate a habit of Lydgate's versification that is particularly interesting in this discussion, where it is becoming evident that in a number of ways Lydgate's writing actively resists the limits inherent in normal syntax and verse structures. Instead of exploiting the epigrammatic potential of the couplet form and its tendency to encourage closure and the separation of ideas by making sentence endings coincide with couplet endings, Lydgate, on the contrary, often chooses to conclude a sentence in the first line of a couplet, thus ensuring that the couplet rhyme will connect the two adjacent sentences. So, here, the first line of Lydgate's speech completes the couplet left unfinished at the end of the Host's address, and the Host then answers Lydgate's rather defensive conclusion, "I haue therof no shame," by completing the rhyme: "'Daun Iohn,' quod he, 'wel broke ʒe ʒoure name!'" Thus the newcomer is integrated into the established structure of the tale-telling frame, in just the same way that Chaucer effects the Canon's Yeoman's entry into the pilgrim company, splitting couplets between him and the Host until he begins his tale.

Connectedness is a quality Lydgate must have valued highly. This is apparent not only in the linking of sentences by rhymes and the overflowing of stanza bounds but in the frequency with which his sentences start with a conjunction: *and, but,* or *for.* When selecting passages to demonstrate Lydgate's ability to write competent syntax, I deliberately avoided quoting sentences beginning with these words, tarred as they are with Pearsall's brush of distressful "looseness," and this meant having to pass over the vast majority of examples. Indeed, one can read long passages of Lydgate's narratives in punctuated editions and find that almost every full stop is followed by one of these words, or by a clause beginning with a relative word or phrase, all contributing greatly to the perceived effect of an unstoppable narrative flow, of the running on of ideas without definite stops noted by Schick. This should not, however, be taken as proof of aimless, rambling, or formless sentence structure; it simply signals that Lydgate was organizing his material in units larger than the normal sentences and paragraphs that modern readers are used to. If we take the *Troy Book* as an example and look at the narrative sections into which the book naturally falls, many of which coincide with the textual subdivisions marked in manuscripts by large capitals, we find a high level of connectedness within every section, achieved by Lydgate's systematic use of initial conjunctions, frequent relative adjectives, and indefinite stops. The boundaries between sections, by contrast, are clearly indicated by narratorial conclusions—for example, "anoon as ʒe schal here" (1.622), "ʒiffe þat ʒe liste, anoon ʒe schal it here" (1.1344), "As ʒe schal here, ʒif ʒe liste abide" (1.1512)—with decisive stops. These endings are followed by equally clear signals of a new beginning with no use of initial conjunctions, involving a change of time, place, or subject, precisely according to one's normal expectation of subdivision in medieval narrative.[24]

The large scale of Lydgate's narrative units seems proportionate to the length and expansive style of his major narrative works. But did Lydgate have a particular reason for choosing so often to use conjunctions (especially *for*) to achieve the connectedness he wanted within the units? To an ear accustomed to the English Bible in either the Douai or King James version, the repeated use of *for, and,* and *but* in initial positions sounds very familiar: in the Gospels, many verses begin with one or another of these three words, while in the first chapter of Genesis, for example, almost every verse begins with the word *and,* and in the first chapter of the Book of Wisdom nearly all verses begin with *for.* In the Latin Vulgate Bible that Lydgate knew, he would have read the same verses beginning with *et,* or *sed,* or an *enim* construction (all of which were literally translated into English in the Wycliffite Bible).[25] Was this perhaps the model he took for his own composition of long works subdivided into clearly marked sections but with conspicuous verbal signals of continuity holding together the constituent elements (sentences/verses) within each section? At any rate, with such a prestigious model available, it is hard to maintain the position that Lydgate's practice in this respect is idiosyncratically faulty.

We may distinguish from all the preceding examples of Lydgate's syntactical practice three general models employed by the poet for different rhetorical purposes. In the first place, there is a greatly extended sentence structure, characterized by multiple subordinate clauses, absolute constructions, and delayed main clause, typically used in prologues and at the openings of major new sections of narrative in order to encompass all the preliminary material in a single, loosely constructed past-time unit before commencing the new narrative action. Second, there is a concise style with use of regular syntax that characteristically appears in dialogue, where it serves to give a dramatic immediacy to the exchange, and in passages of pithy proverbial commentary (see, e.g., *Siege of Thebes,* 1.1014–16: "Of Cursid stok / cometh vnkynde blood, | As in story / ʒe may rede her to-forn; | Al be the Roose / grow / out of a thorn"). Third, there is what may be thought of as an intermediate pattern: that found throughout Lydgate's narrative verse, in which simple syntactical structures are connected by conjunctions and relative phrases in order to form much larger narrative units, suggesting that Lydgate's syntactical purpose is not the clear separation of ideas into discrete sentences and paragraphs, as modern readers expect, but the bringing into continuous relation of all connected material.

It is quite difficult for modern readers now to experience the true fluidity and connectedness of Lydgate's writing, obscured as these qualities are by the punctuation decided on by nineteenth- and twentieth-century editors. As shown in the example of the prologue to the *Siege of Thebes,* there was a tendency to insert a full stop at the earliest perceived opportunity, and this felt need for definite stops often destroys the balance of Lydgate's larger-scale narrative syntax.[26] For instance, after the lengthy prologue to the *Troy Book,* Henry Bergen presents the first four lines of book 1 as a complete sentence:

In þe regne & lond of Thesalye,
The whiche is now y-named Salonye,
Ther was a kyng callyd Pelleus,
Wys & discrete & also vertuous.

(1.1–4)

The apparent simplicity of this sentence is increased by the couplet structure of the verse, the emphasis falling on the first line with its stressed initial syllable and the third with its obvious main clause, while the descriptive clause and phrase in lines 2 and 4 sink naturally to a subordinate level, altogether making a satisfyingly compact introduction to the story. However, the lines do not really constitute a self-contained short sentence, despite the full stop at the end of line 4. The sense of the passage runs on: "The whiche, as Guydo lyst to specefie, | Helde the lordeschipe and the regallye | Of this yle" (5–7), explaining how Pelleus's people were all destroyed by the gods, "Excepte the kyng, þe whiche went allone | In-to a wode for to make his mone" (27–28), where he saw the ants and prayed the gods "To turne this amptis in-to forme of man" (45) to repopulate his kingdom, which prayer the gods granted, thus producing the Myrmidons, famed for their antlike virtues, which (supposes Lydgate euhemeristically) were the source of this fable (74–75). Bergen has inserted several full stops in the course of this passage, but none is indisputable and all impede the clear structure of the narrative, with its focus on the king's solitary survival and desperate prayer, and the flow of ideas from narrative to commentary. Reading Lydgate's text in manuscript, on the other hand, makes it evident that the inherent punctuation of metrical verse, visibly presented by lineation and in many cases caesura marks as well, with small colored capitals sometimes added to indicate minor narrative subdivisions, is perfectly adequate for understanding the flexible construction of the poet's syntax and for enabling a reader to deliver the text intelligibly to a listening audience.[27]

As critics have often observed, Lydgate tends to suffer unduly from the almost inescapable comparison with Chaucer, and in this matter of the effects of editorial punctuation the contrast is enhanced by the fact that while Lydgate's works have for the most part been edited only once, Chaucer's have received the attentions of many different editors. Had Lydgate's poems been as widely read and as frequently edited as Chaucer's, no doubt his texts would now benefit from more refined presentation.[28] But conversely too, the phenomenon noted by James Simpson, that Chaucer is thought of as speaking directly to modern readers whereas Lydgate's voice is dismissed as typical of medieval obscurity,[29] may perhaps owe something to the "modernization" of Chaucer's punctuation and its effect on the perception of his syntax. A comparison of the closing sequence of the General Prologue in the Ellesmere MS and *The Riverside Chaucer* (715–858), for example, reveals that most of the six major syntactical divisions in the passage, marked in the printed edition by paragraph indentations, are already indicated by two-line capitals in the manuscript. Almost all the other editorial punctuation, which produces thirty-eight separate sentences of varying length, is more or less open to question: Are the full stops really signaling "definite" points of syntactic completion, or could they equally well be replaced by "indefinite" punctuation within larger continuing structures? As with Lydgate's works, reading Chaucer's text, with its use of paratactic syntax and frequent initial conjunctions, in a manuscript copy gives a greater impression of the fluency and connectedness of his writing; but a "sentence" of thirty-two lines (715–46) in a modern printed edition does not look reader-friendly.

Lydgate's style and syntax have sometimes been unfavorably compared with the practice of his contemporary Thomas Hoccleve. John Burrow, for example, comments: "He [Hoccleve] tends to be rambling and repetitive; but his syntax (unlike Lydgate's) is energetic and controlled";[30] and Pearsall praises the "fluent informality and conversational quality of his [Hoccleve's] verse, especially in dialogue," adding that the "easy command of his verse makes him a much more endearing poet than Lydgate."[31] These differences in style and appeal to some extent reflect differences in the kind of poem for which each writer is best known. Unlike Lydgate, Hoccleve did not undertake lengthy historical narratives, and, as I have tried to show, some peculiarities of Lydgate's syntactical style are directly attributable to the needs of his narratives; on the other hand, Lydgate does not deal with engagingly personal material of the kind that plays a major role in Hoccleve's poems, and relatively little of his work is cast in the form of dialogue. Nevertheless, a comparison from the two poets' works of passages serving similar specific functions can show some similarities in their practice. For instance, Hoccleve's opening lines in the prologue of his *Series* (1–21) may be set beside Lydgate's seasonal openings in the *Life of Our Lady* (1.1–21; 4.1–16). Again, although modern editions of Hoccleve's poem variously place full stops after lines 7, 9, 10, 12, 14, and 16,[32] these represent conclusions of different and less than "definite" force, for his paratactic clauses could equally well be separated by colons, semicolons, or dashes. I quote the text here without punctuation.[33]

> After that hervest inned had his sheves
> And that the brown sesoun of Mihelmesse
> Was come and gan the trees robbe of her leves
> That grene had ben and in lusty freshnesse
> And hem into colour of yelownesse
> Had dyed and down throwen under fote
> That chaunge sank into myn herte rote
>
> For freshly broughte it to my remembraunce
> That stablenesse in this world is there non
> There is no thing but chaunge and variaunce
> How welthy a man be or well begon
> Endure it shall not he shall it forgon
> Deth under fote shall him thrist adown
> That is every wightes conclusioun
>
> Which for to waive is in no mannes might
> How riche he be strong lusty fresh and gay
> And in the ende of November upon a night
> Sighing sore as I in my bedde lay

For this and other thoughts which many a day
Before I took sleep cam non in myn ye
So vexed me the thoughtful maladye.

The sinewy, energetic quality of Hoccleve's verse that rightly earns critical admiration is, it seems to me, enhanced here by reading the passage as a flexible, continuous syntactic whole, and his style is thus brought into closer comparison with Lydgate's, writing at the height of his powers in the prologue to the *Life of Our Lady*.[34]

O thoughtfull herte, plunged in distresse
With slombre of slouthe, this long winters nyght
Oute of the slepe of mortall hevynesse
Awake anoon, and loke upon the light
Of thelke sterre that with hir bemys bright
And withe the shynyng of hir stremys merye
Is wonte to gladde all our Emysperye

And to oppresse the derkenesse and the doole
Of hevy hertes that soroen and syghen ofte
I mene the sterre of the bright poole
That with hir bemys whan she is alofte
May al the trowble aswagen and asofte
Of worldely wawes which in this mortall see
Have vs byset withe grete aduersitee

The Rage of whiche is so tempestyuous
That whan the calme is moste blandyshyng
Then is the streme of dethe moste perylous
If that we wante the light of hir shynyng
And but the syght, allas of hir lokyng
From dethes brinke make us to escape
The haven of lif of us may not be take.

(1.1–21)

The elaboration of temporal clauses and delayed main clause in Hoccleve's first stanza resembles Lydgate's typical practice in prologues, and the opening lines of the *Life of Our Lady,* book 4, provide a restrained example where, like Hoccleve, Lydgate is setting the seasonal scene in order to provoke an access of "remembrance" in the poet-figure. The passage quoted above from book 1, on the other hand, shows at the beginning of the third stanza a characteristic habit of Lydgate's, as he uses a relative clause to surge forward into a new connected thought after a line ending that would otherwise come to a natural close, and Hoccleve performs precisely the same maneuver in the opening line of his third stanza.

Of course, it is not my purpose to suggest that Lydgate's syntax never deserves the criticism it has constantly received over the last hundred years. However, I do think that the harsh judgments of early editors tend to have been repeated without sufficient reexamination of the evidence. For example, the opening sentence of Lydgate's *Guy of Warwick* was claimed by Julius Zupitza in 1873 to be the worst possible case of an anacoluthon, in which "not only the predicate of the sentence is wanting, but the subject as well,"[35] and the same assertion was still being made a century later, even after H. N. MacCracken had edited the text.[36] The truth is that like so many of Lydgate's introductory sentences, this one merely delays the main clause for twenty lines while extended adverbial phrases and absolute constructions set the scene. The first two stanzas give the general picture, and in the third stanza Lydgate comes to the point: 927 years after Christ's birth, in King Ethelstan's reign, during the persecution by the Danes who slaughtered and burned people indiscriminately, destroyed ecclesiastical and secular buildings, and laid all waste as far as Winchester—

> In this brennyng, ffurious cruelte,
> Two Denmark pryncis, pompous & elat,
> Lyk woode lyouns, void of all pite,
> Did no favour to louh nor hih estaat.
>
> (17–20)

Lydgate's attempt at sardonic understatement here may be thought misguided, but he is certainly not guilty as charged of gross violation of syntax: there is nothing wrong with his main clause from a functional point of view. Even the ironic use of litotes makes sense when it is read in the light of the whole sentence. The indiscriminately pitiless behavior of these two particular Danes has been incrementally prepared for by the cruelty of the Danes in general, who in their slaughter "made noon excepcioun" (7), "Spared nouther hih nor louh degre" (9), and even "Spared nat women greet with chylde" (16). After the climax of this catalog of cruelty, Lydgate switches straight to complaint, before

characteristically eliding back into the narrative without a syntactical break and
with no stop at the end of the stanza:

> Allas! this lond stood so dysconsolaat,
> Froward Fortune hath at hem so dysdeyned,
> Mars & Mercurie wer with hem at debaat,
> That bothe þe kyng and pryncis wer distreyned
>
> By froward force to take hem to the fflyght,
> Thes Danyssh pryncis ageyn hem wer so wood.
>
> (21–26)

In this brief study my aim has been primarily to suggest that, in some cases
at least, the so-called faulty construction and uneasiness of Lydgate's syntax in
his narrative poems may in fact be the result of stylistic devices, intended to create specific effects. Lydgate's grammatical syntax, I would argue, makes more
sense when it is understood as serving the larger narrative syntax of his works:
articulating the various parts of complex histories such as the *Troy Book;* linking together narrative and non-narrative material into a seamless whole in the
Life of Our Lady; and effecting the transition from the world of the poet and his
audience, in prologue or frame, into the world of the narrative. From this argument, however, has grown a sense of the limitations of modern readings of Lydgate's verse when constricted by the demands of printed punctuation. Of course,
one major purpose of the editions of Lydgate's works (as of all texts) for the
Early English Text Society was to provide material for the Oxford English Dictionary, and firm decisions on syntax and punctuation are very helpful in deciding questions of semantics. But if Lydgate is liberated from such demands, the
fluent, expansive rhythms of his narrative poems can more easily be appreciated, especially if the frequent references to a listening audience are taken not as
wholly formulaic but as referring to a probable mode of reception for his texts.[37]
The connectedness of Lydgate's style has much in common with habits of oral
speech, and an interesting parallel with his habit of linking successive sentences
together by conjunctions can be seen in the written texts that represent two
fifteenth-century oral self-presentations: Margery Kempe's *Book* and William
Thorpe's *Testimony,* in both of which long strings of sentences are linked with
repeated *and*s and other conjunctions.[38] Equally, the tendency to repeat material with variation (a feature of Lydgate's writing that has often earned him
critical censure) is a device particularly well suited to public or shared reading.[39]
A combination of the current interest in manuscript studies with recent con-

cerns to recover the material conditions of the reception of literature in the medieval period gives reason to hope that this may be a good time for Lydgate's poetry to be candidly heard on its own terms and for worries about his "uneasy syntax" to be finally laid to rest.

Notes

1. Derek Pearsall, ed., *Chaucer to Spenser: An Anthology of Writings in English, 1375–1575* (Oxford: Blackwell, 1999), 343.

2. Derek Pearsall, *John Lydgate* (London: Routledge & Kegan Paul, 1970), 58–59. The use of unrelated participles that Pearsall here terms "almost a Lydgate signature" is exemplified in the *Siege of Thebes,* Pro.86–87 ("Besechinge you that ye wil me telle | First youre name") and 98 ("Preiyng you soupe with us tonight"), on which he comments: "Such loosely related participial constructions are characteristic of Lydgate's often tiresome syntax" (Pearsall, *Chaucer to Spenser,* 347). However, both these instances, prefaced by the Host's naming and welcoming the narrator, are probably following the pattern of polite address found in contemporary letter writing. See also Erdmann and Ekwall's additional example in lines 3316–17 of the *Siege*; *Lydgate's Siege of Thebes,* 2 vols., ed. Axel Erdmann and Eilert Ekwall, EETS, e.s., 108, 125 (London: Kegan Paul, Trench, Trübner, 1911, 1930), 2:21 (all further citations are to this edition). To be fair to Erdmann and Ekwall, it should be noted that their catalog of Lydgate's "loose syntax," while comparable to Pearsall's, does not necessarily brand every feature a fault.

3. J. A. Burrow, "Old and Middle English (c. 700–1485)," in *The Oxford Illustrated History of English Literature,* ed. Pat Rogers (Oxford: Oxford University Press, 1987), 54. Burrow turns to Hoccleve for contrast, who "wrote less and wrote better. Though he cannot be called concise, his English is generally plain and sinewy, and he displays a real command over the poetic syntax of the rhyme-royal stanza." Interestingly, the same adjective was used by C. S. Lewis of Wyatt, a poet he saw as shaking off "medieval habits": "For those who like their poetry lean and sinewy and a little sad, he is a capital poet. His fame is in the ascendant." C. S. Lewis, *English Literature in the Sixteenth Century Excluding Drama* (Oxford: Clarendon Press, 1954), 224, 230. One may discern Burrow's implicit privileging in Hoccleve of those characteristics most akin to the admired features of early modern writing and least "medieval."

4. Pearsall, *Chaucer to Spenser,* 345.

5. The full stop in line 64 may be a misprint, however: Eilert Ekwall's introductory account of Lydgate's "loose syntax" instances "the passage ll. 1–65, in which no full-stop is marked in the printed text" (*Lydgate's Siege of Thebes,* 2:20).

6. Rosamund S. Allen, "*The Siege of Thebes*: Lydgate's Canterbury Tale," in *Chaucer and Fifteenth-Century Poetry,* ed. Julia Boffey and Janet Cowen (London: King's College London Centre for Late Antique and Medieval Studies, 1991), 133–34.

7. Introduction to *Lydgate's Siege of Thebes*, 2:15.

8. Throughout this chapter, poetry is cited parenthetically in the text by line number or by book and line numbers.

9. *John Lydgate: Poems*, ed. John Norton-Smith (Oxford: Clarendon Press, 1966), 151.

10. Introduction to *Lydgate's Siege of Thebes*, 2:15.

11. *Lydgate's Troy Book*, 4 vols., ed. Henry Bergen, EETS, e.s., 97, 103, 106, 126 (London: Kegan Paul, Trench, Trübner, 1906, 1908, 1910, 1935). All further citations are to this edition.

12. Lydgate's *Fall of Princes*, 4 vols., ed. Henry Bergen, EETS, e.s., 121, 122, 123, 124 (London: Oxford University Press, 1924–27). Either Lydgate omits the pronoun subject in a paratactic main clause here: "[He] demte," or *demte* is a past participle used absolutely, "[having]" being understood.

13. Thomas Warton, *The History of English Poetry from the Twelfth to the Close of the Sixteenth Century*, ed. W. Carew Hazlitt (London: Reeves & Turner, 1871; orig. pub. 1774–1781), 3:59, 54. An earlier critical comment about Lydgate occurs in John Skelton's *Phyllyp Sparowe* (in *John Skelton: The Complete English Poems*, ed. John Scattergood [New Haven, CT: Yale University Press, 1983]):

Also Johnn Lydgate
Wryteth after an hyer rate;
It is dyffuse to fynde
The sentence of his mynde,
yet wryteth he in his kynd,
No man can amend
Those maters that he hath pende;
Yet some men fynde a faute,
And say he wryteth to haute.

(804–12)

However, although this looks like an early criticism of Lydgate's syntax on similar lines to nineteenth- and twentieth-century strictures, it is important to note that (i) it is in the voice of young Jane, and the same word *diffuse* (not meaning the same as when modern critics use it, but "difficult") is used of all the ancient poets that Jane cannot imitate (767–68); (ii) it is really Lydgate's high style, not his poor syntax, that makes it hard to understand his meaning; accordingly, one editor places a colon, not a semicolon, at the end of line 805 (Pearsall, *Chaucer to Spenser*, 551).

14. Mary Hamel, ed., *Morte Arthure: A Critical Edition* (New York: Garland, 1984), 22–23.

15. Introduction to *Lydgate's Temple of Glas*, ed. Josef Schick, EETS, e.s., 60 (London: K. Paul, Trench, Trübner, 1891), cxxxiv. He continues: "He [Lydgate] knows little

of logic connection, or distinct limitation of his sentences, and the notion of artistic structure, by which all ideas form, in mutual interdependence, an organic whole, is entirely
foreign to him." He seems uninterested in discovering what alternative notions of style or
structure might have informed the poet's work. Schick's criticism sets the agenda for the
majority view of Lydgate's writing in the next hundred years.

16. Pearsall, *John Lydgate,* 58.

17. See my discussion in Phillipa Hardman, "Lydgate's *Life of Our Lady*: A Text in
Transition," *Medium Ævum* 65 (1996): 248–68.

18. *A Critical Edition of John Lydgate's Life of Our Lady,* ed. Joseph A. Lauritis,
Ralph A. Klinefelter, and Vernon F. Gallagher (Pittsburgh: Duquesne University, 1961).
All further citations are to this edition.

19. Pearsall gives as one reason for the higher incidence of loose syntax in Lydgate
than in Chaucer that "Lydgate's thought-patterns are characteristically associative and
encyclopaedic, and much of his poetry therefore is allusive, accumulative and descriptive,
where the problems of syntax are more acute than in straightforward narrative" (*John
Lydgate,* 59). Whether they result from thought-patterns or stylistic choice, for these characteristic effects Lydgate's syntax can perhaps be seen as a solution, not a problem.

20 In a perceptive brief account of the *Life of Our Lady,* Norton-Smith describes the
structure of the work in terms of its "delayed and suspended narrative movement" (*John
Lydgate: Poems,* 155), a description that highlights the parallel between the macro- and
micro-structures of the text, narrative and syntactic.

21 For further examples of Lydgate's fluid syntax in this text, see Hardman, "Lydgate's
Life of Our Lady," 250–51.

22. Hamel, *Morte Arthure,* 22, quoting Ronald A. Waldron, "Oral-Formulaic Technique and Alliterative Poetry," *Speculum* 32 (1957): 800–801.

23. Come if hem list, hem sholde no thing faille;
    And for to ben in ought aspied there,
    That, wiste he wel, an impossible were.

    Dredeles, it cler was in the wynd
    Of every pie and every lete-game;
    Now al is wel, for al the world is blynd
    In this matere, bothe fremde and tame.
    This tymbur is al redy up to frame;
    Us lakketh nought but that we witen wolde
    A certeyn houre, in which she comen sholde.

The Riverside Chaucer, 3rd ed., ed. Larry D. Benson (Oxford: Oxford University Press,
1988), 520. Pearsall notes, "These lines [528–32] could be given to Pandarus or they could
be regarded as the narrator's enthusiastic participation in Pandarus's plans" (*Chaucer to
Spenser,* 44). As well as validating Lydgate's practice by reference to Chaucer's, one might

question the grounds of this particular critical complaint. Most literary critics would now take such playful transgression of narrative "boundaries" to signal a writer's artistic skill rather than incompetence.

24. See my discussion of narrative divisions in Phillipa Hardman, "Fitt Divisions in Middle English Romances: A Consideration of the Evidence," *Yearbook of English Studies* 22 (1992): 63–80.

25. See *King Henry's Bible: MS Bodley 277: The Revised Version of the Wyclif Bible*, vols. 1 and 2, ed. Conrad Lindberg (Stockholm: Almqvist and Wiksell, 1999, 2001); *MS. Bodley 959: The Earlier Version of the Wycliffite Bible*, 8 vols., ed. Conrad Lindberg (Stockholm: Almqvist and Wiksell, 1959–97).

26. Mary Hamel describes similar results of editorial impatience in previous editions of the *Morte Arthure* (85 n. 56). Her skepticism on the need for punctuation is salutary: "Such punctuation marks, however, are essentially crutches required by modern perceptions of language; they are not required by the poem itself, which makes its syntactical and rhetorical structures clear by the management of half-lines" (23).

27. In "'To show our simple skill': Scripts and Performers in Shakespearean Comedy" (paper presented at the International Shakespeare Conference, Stratford-upon-Avon, 2002), Michael Cordner pointed to the growing practice of using unpunctuated alongside edited texts in preparing productions and noted that actors find the simple lineation of verse sufficient punctuation (as seen in contemporary practice in the possibly holograph page of *Sir Thomas More*). This suggests that the joke about punctuation in Peter Quince's prologue (*A Midsummer Night's Dream*, 5.1.107–18) partly depends on a recognition that the manuscript text would have provided lineation and rhyme as guides to delivery, with an occasional caesura/comma in the middle of the line that Quince takes as a full stop: "Our true intent is. All for your delight | We are not here. That you should here repent you" (114–15).

28. Between the publication of the first volume of his text of the *Troy Book* in 1906 and his fourth volume, consisting of an introduction and commentary, in 1935, Bergen had second thoughts about the punctuation of several passages, which are recorded as if errata in the notes on the text.

29. James Simpson, "Bulldozing the Middle Ages: The Case of 'John Lydgate,'" in *New Medieval Literatures: 4,* ed. Wendy Scase, Rita Copeland, and David Lawton (Oxford: Oxford University Press, 2001), 224–28.

30. John Burrow, ed., *English Verse, 1300–1500* (London: Longman, 1977), 266.

31. Pearsall, *Chaucer to Spenser*, 319.

32. See *Thomas Hoccleve's Complaint and Dialogue,* ed. J. A. Burrow, EETS, o.s., 313 (1999), 3; Burrow, *English Verse,* 266; Pearsall, *Chaucer to Spenser,* 335; Douglas Gray, ed., *The Oxford Book of Late Medieval Verse and Prose* (Oxford: Clarendon Press, 1985), 56.

33. Quoted from Burrow, *English Verse,* 266. The autograph manuscript of the *Series* (Durham University Library, MS Cosin V.iii.9) lacks the first quire containing the prologue and Complaint: these are supplied in the hand of John Stowe. Stowe's copy simply has a stop at the end of every stanza, but the remainder of the text in Hoccleve's hand,

like manuscript copies of Lydgate's poems, has none of these stops, though it has virgules within the majority of lines. See *Thomas Hoccleve: A Facsimile of the Autograph Manuscripts,* ed. J. A. Burrow and A. I. Doyle, EETS, s.s., 19 (Oxford: Oxford University Press, 2002); Burrow, *Thomas Hoccleve's Complaint,* liii–lv.

34. Pearsall praises Lydgate's "disregard [of] the stanza" and "running on freely" in this prologue, which he argues is "one of the high points in English religious writing" (*John Lydgate,* 289–90).

35. As quoted in Schick, introduction to *Lydgate's Temple of Glas,* cxxxvi.

36. Pearsall, *John Lydgate,* 58. For *Guy of Warwick,* see *The Minor Poems of John Lydgate,* ed. Henry Noble MacCracken, EETS, o.s., 192 (London: Oxford University Press, 1934), 2:516. All further citations are to this edition.

37. See Joyce Coleman, *Public Reading and the Reading Public in Late Medieval England and France* (Cambridge: Cambridge University Press, 1996).

38. See *The Book of Margery Kempe,* ed. Sanford B. Meech and Hope Emily Allen, EETS, o.s., 212 (London: Oxford University Press, 1940); Anne Hudson, ed., *Two Wycliffite Texts,* EETS, o.s., 301 (Oxford: Oxford University Press, 1993).

39. This point is made by Pearsall, *John Lydgate,* 9. It is interesting that critics note positive aspects of Lydgate's fluid style or (as here) explanatory details of contemporary cultural context but still return to the same standards of "classical" sentence structure by which to judge his syntax.

2

Lydgate's Laureate Pose

Robert J. Meyer-Lee

One is persuaded that his morality is official and impersonal—
a system of life which it was his duty to support—and it is perhaps
a half understanding of this that has made so many generations
believe that he was the first poet laureate,
the first salaried moralist among the poets.
—W. B. Yeats[1]

In his seminal *Self-Crowned Laureates,* Richard Helgerson singles out this remark of Yeats's about Spenser to illustrate the modern antipathy toward laureate self-representation. In the anachronistic assumption that Spenser was England's first poet laureate, Yeats detects an attempt to explain the shallow and
artificial nature of the Elizabethan poet's authorial pose. Yet from a wider perspective, this anachronism is simply a misplaced point of origin. The first "salaried moralist among the poets"—if one counts a royal annuity as a salary—did
not postdate Spenser but predated him by nearly two hundred years, arriving in
the form of the monk of Bury St. Edmund's. Chaucer and Hoccleve received
annuities earlier, but these were *prima facie* for their work as civil servants
rather than as poets. Because the work Lydgate performed for the crown, as far
as we know, consisted solely of his verse, it seems fair to assume that his long-
awaited annuity was a belated recognition of his decades-long service as poet to

Lancastrian kings and princes.[2] In this work Lydgate expressed a morality that was indeed both "official" and (from a modern perspective) "impersonal," and Spenser, who would have had at his disposal the mid-sixteenth-century prints of the *Troy Book* and the *Fall of Princes*,[3] perhaps there discovered a precedent for the pose that Yeats found so off-putting. Although the laureateship in its present form came into being only with Dryden's appointment in 1668, the epithet "Laureate Lydgate"—the title of a chapter in Derek Pearsall's authoritative monograph on the poet—is no anachronism.[4]

In making this claim, I do not mean to imply simply that, in practical terms, Lydgate's poetic career resembles those of the nineteenth-century laureates for whom Yeats and his contemporaries held little regard—although, indeed, more than just Lydgate's annuity sets him apart from his predecessors in this respect.[5] Rather, my claim pertains to the (always unrealized) idealizations of the poet and poetry that underlie the modern institution of poet laureate—and to the beliefs, conventions, and techniques that together seek to bring into being the grandest possibilities for poetry as public discourse. This is the laureateship, not as Dryden and his successors practiced it, but as Petrarch imagined it. The extent to which modern laureates are frequently the targets of the scorn of their fellow poets indicates just how much Petrarch's dream remains a potent influence as a guiding ideal. This ideal's vitiated approximations help both to articulate it and to confirm its power, and in English literary history Lydgate sits prominently, without embarrassment, at the head of a long list of laureate dreamers whose practice ultimately fails to coincide with what the poet desperately wishes it to be.[6]

In this essay, I focus on a single aspect of Lydgate's poetic practice, one that occupies a particularly central place in his efforts to fashion himself as laureate. Specifically, I argue that Lydgate not only produced the kind of work one expects from a laureate but also brought into English a mode of authorial self-representation that serves as the ground of laureate performance—now as well as then. To this end I first examine one of Lydgate's most characteristic poetic voices, an authoritative first-person persona necessarily associated with his empirical person; I show how he forges this persona from his relationship with Chaucer and an idealizing poetics deriving from devotional epideixis. Next, I discuss how, in the watershed moment of the *Troy Book,* he invents a notional English laureateship by blending this persona with that of the monastic historian and putting the resulting authorial pose into a reflexive relationship with power. I conclude by exploring briefly some of the inherent tensions within this laureate pose and suggesting that this pose and its vitiating tensions persist, at some level of sedimentation, in the English poetic tradition to this day.

Lydgate, Chaucer, and the Praising Poet

In the prologue to his *Tale of Sir Thopas,* Chaucer the Pilgrim provides his famous indirect self-portrait through his report of the Host's answer to his own question, "What man artow?":

> He in the waast is shape as wel as I;
> This were a popet in an arm t'enbrace
> For any womman, smal and fair of face.
> He semeth elvyssh by his contenaunce,
> For unto no wight dooth he daliaunce.
>
> (7.700–704)[7]

By referring to himself indirectly as a "popet" and "elvyssh," the narrator has left us with an indelible impression of a mischievous but wise personality. Yet he nowhere indicates that this personality must be *necessarily* attached to Geoffrey Chaucer, Esquire. Indeed, this self-portrait is remarkable for the extent to which it avoids any index of social identity. It individualizes the speaker, but it does not invoke his historical specificity.

In the prologue of the *Siege of Thebes* (c. 1421), which Lydgate stages as a continuation of the *Canterbury Tales,* the Host asks the pilgrim narrator a similar but much more specific question than "What man artow":

> daun Pers,
> Daun Domynyk / Dan Godfrey / or Clement,
> ȝe be welcom / newly into kent,
> Though ȝoure bridel / haue neiþer boos ne belle;
> Besechinge ȝou / þat ȝe wil me telle
> First ȝoure name / and of what contre
> With-oute more shorte-ly that ȝe be,
> That loke so pale / al deuoyde of blood,
> Vpon ȝoure hede / a wonder thred-bar hood,
> Wel araied / for to ride late.
>
> (82–91)[8]

As in Chaucer's passage, this indirect self-portrait emphasizes physical description, but here the point is to reinforce the already tendered image of poverty (73–75) appropriate to a monk's social station—an image that, as has been frequently noted, stands as Lydgate's self-conscious differentiation of his actual, *personal* practice of monasticism from that of the General Prologue's worldly but fictional monk.[9] Along these same lines, in contrast with Chaucer's oblique presentation of his alter ego, Lydgate places great emphasis on his poet-figure's name—that is, on the specific signifier that would decisively identify the narrator with an extraliterary person. And unlike Chaucer's reticent *popet,* Lydgate's narrator does not hesitate to respond to the host's question:

I answerde, "my name was Lydgate,
Monk of Bery / ny3 fyfty 3ere of age,
Come to this toune / to do my pilgrimage,
As I haue hight / I haue therof no shame."
(92–95)

Here the speaker provides his surname, his social identity, the town of his abbey, his age, and a polite insistence on the propriety of his being away from the cloister. This blunt self-identification has often received comment, but for the most part critics dismiss it as evidence of Lydgate's poetic incompetence. In his clumsy attempt to imitate a Chaucerian persona, Lydgate, according to these critics, confuses fact with fiction and thereby dramatically dilutes the aesthetic power of the latter.[10]

Such charges of incompetence are frequently leveled against fifteenth-century poets in general and Lydgate in particular. But if we instead defer these charges and search first for a thematic purpose behind Lydgate's revisions of Ricardian precedents, we must ask why Lydgate, if he simply meant to imitate Chaucer, would so unlike his master firmly identify the narrator not only as pilgrim and poet but also as "man"—the empirical, historically specific monk of Bury. A full answer to this question in respect to the *Siege* I leave to another occasion; here, I suggest only that Lydgate indeed confuses fact with fiction but that this confusion is both necessary and strategic. By the time he began work on the *Siege,* he had, through such efforts as the *Troy Book,* established himself as notional as well as de facto poet laureate of the Lancastrian regime. The politically fraught *Siege,* as it seems to have had no patron and includes no mention of its source, rests all its claims to authority—and it possesses some considerable ones—on the living *auctor* it introduces in its prologue. To put it simply, Lydgate enters his text to bestow upon it the authority that he possesses outside of it. The agon with Chaucer that he stages through his imitation of the *Canterbury Tales*—as well as through his accompanying eulogy of his master—aims not so much to depict himself as an authentic disciple and heir as to transform Chaucer into a flesh-and-blood laureate who retroactively defines the role that Lydgate implicitly claims to occupy.

Lydgate's *A Balade in Commendation of Our Lady* deploys, in comparison, a more subtle agon with Chaucer, yet in a helpfully compact form it exemplifies much of the poetics that underlies such mammoth works as *Troy Book* and *Siege of Thebes*. In this lofty panegyric to the Virgin, we wait three stanzas for the commendation proper to begin, during which we encounter the poet talking about himself and, in the process, supplying a telling allusion:

> A thowsand storiis kowede I mo reherse
> Off olde poets touchyng this matere:
> How that Cupide the hertis gan to perse
> Off his seruauntis, settyng tham affer.
> Lo here the fin of th'errour and the weere,
> Lo here of loue the guerdoun and greuaunce
> That euyr with woo his seruaunts doth avaunce.
>
> (1–7)[11]

In foregrounding an "I" who could rehearse, but does not (here, at least), a "thowsand storiis" of "Cupide" from the "olde poets," these opening lines establish a great deal: the thematic importance of the first-person speaker, that speaker's poetic knowledge and authority, the fact that the speaker is rejecting secular erotic verse, and—through the allusion of the last three lines to the *Troilus and Criseyde* narrator's suddenly Christian disgust with his narrative—a complex interpoetic relationship that aims to depict Lydgate as a spiritually correct successor to his lay predecessor. Lydgate in fact earlier alludes to these lines of *Troilus* in his *Complaynt of a Lovere's Lyfe*, a reworking of the *Book of the Duchess* in which his version of the Black Knight laments the fate of love-struck men using Chaucer's anaphora.[12] The implication of what is thus a double allusion is that Lydgate, as he has demonstrated in the *Lovere's Lyfe*, could, if he wished, supply yet another poem in the mode of Chaucer's courtly work, but he has already attained a level of spiritual insight that Chaucer reaches only at the end of *Troilus*.

The point of this stanza is not that Lydgate is advertising his actual rejection of a prior career as poet of secular, amorous verse. (Indeed, we are not even certain when either poem was written, although an early date has traditionally been assumed for the *Lovere's Lyfe*, if only by analogy with the chronology of Chaucer's oeuvre.) The point is rather that Lydgate is making a claim, vis-à-vis his poetic relationship with Chaucer, that he, specifically, is qualified to produce a more exalted form of poetry. And in the immediately following stanza, he makes this claim almost explicit:

> Wherefore I wil now pleynly my stile redresse,
> Of on to speke, at nede that will not faile.
> Allas, for dool I ne can nor may expresse
> Hir passand pris, and that is no mervaile.
> O wynd of grace, now blowe into my saile,
> O auriat lycour of Clyo, for to wryte
> Mi penne enspire of that I wold endyte.
>
> (8–14)

By paronomastically affirming that he will his "stile redresse," he is saying, on the one hand, simply that he will redirect his "penne" from the "thowsand" rejected "storiis" (of, implicitly, unfaithful women like Criseyde) to the Virgin, who, rather than advancing her servants "with woo," "will not faile" "at nede." On the other hand—and more significantly—he is saying that he will make the *style* of his writing more suitable to this divine rather than erotic object of praise.[13] In particular, he will write in the ostentatiously lofty style he names here and elsewhere "auriat." Next, by insisting that he "ne can nor may expresse" the "passand pris" of his object, he is—given the 119-line panegyric that follows—calling attention to his qualification, as wielder of aureate language, for doing just this. Revealingly, it is "Clyo," the muse of history, on whom he calls for aid. This invocation may at first seem both generically and (given the antipagan allusion of the previous stanza) thematically inappropriate, until we realize that its function is self-referential. It is a reminder that the speaker is a monastic writer who, given the histories and chronicles for which monasteries were famous, would be identified with this muse more than any other.[14]

This pair of stanzas in particular and this poem in general exemplify two aspects of Lydgate's poetics that prove crucial in his laureate performances. The first, more straightforward aspect is the specificity of the poem's first-person pronoun, such that it may be occupied only by a unique authorial speaker.[15] Although this is a characteristic feature of the *dit,* in devotional works it is much more common for the "I" to be generic and hence occupiable by any reader who wishes to use the poem in his or her devotions. The most pertinent example of such a work is Chaucer's *An ABC,* a translation of a prayer to the Virgin in Deguileville's *La pelerinage de la vie humaine* that has been said to have influenced Lydgate's *Commendation.* In Chaucer's poem the first-person pronoun is wholly generic, the "I" being that of a public prayer. If Lydgate had left off the first three stanzas of his *Commendation,* his first person would have been similar; or, to put this point another way, with his strategically placed metapoetic exordium, he has made the poem's "I" unoccupiable by design.

The second aspect of Lydgate's poetics exemplified by this poem is its deployment of epideictic address, which is in one sense its most obvious feature, the fourth stanza beginning, "O sterne of sternys with thi stremys clere" (22). The epideictic mode (i.e., verse that possesses the aim of praise or blame) was a natural avenue of expression for Lydgate; Curtius has documented how important this mode was for the Latin poetry with which he would have been familiar, and O. B. Hardison has shown how in the late Middle Ages, through Averroes's paraphrase of Aristotle's *Poetics,* poetry was widely understood as fundamentally epideictic discourse.[16] Yet in another sense, epideixis becomes for Lydgate his special and most powerful method of poetic personalization. With this mode he leverages a complex set of relays among poet, addressee, and poem in order to raise the stakes of the thematic valence of his specific person.

In its encomiastic register, an epideictic poem expresses the ideality of its praised object through some effect of heightening. Whether through style, rhetoric, or matter, the poem must in some way supply a verbal analogue for the extraordinary nature of that which it praises. The poem must, as Joel Fineman has said, "add something to merely mimetic description,"[17] the hyperboles of this heightening being attempts to hypostatize the object's transcendental quality. In short, the great claim of the epideictic poet is that he or she brings into being a verbal double of the ideal nature of that which he or she praises. And in the extreme, this claim goes beyond analogy and insists that the poem has made manifest ideality per se. The most authentic poem of praise, in this sense, becomes an instance of the same ideal nature that makes the object praiseworthy in the first place. This understanding of poetic praise would have been quite familiar to Lydgate; when he writes in his verse commentary on Psalm 88 that the "Fynal intent of euery creature / Shulde resounne to Goddys hih preysing,"[18] he articulates what amounts to the same theory through the theological commonplace that a human being becomes most fundamentally Godlike when praising God. To the extent that poetry has been singled out— since at least the time of David if not from its very beginnings—as the privileged medium of praise, it becomes a place par excellence where a human being may reveal the divinity of his or her spirit.

What is more, for Lydgate poetry—and aureate poetry in particular—is itself a worthy object of praise, and the terms in which he expresses this praise shed light on the crucial role that epideixis plays in his poetics. On the one hand, poetry for Lydgate translates the ideal into the human sphere by a process of illumination. As he puts it in the paean to poets and writing that opens book 4 of the *Fall of Princes* (completed c. 1438), "God sette writyng & lettres in sentence, / Ageyn the dulnesse of our infirmyte, / This world tenlumyne be crafft of elloquence" (4.29–31).[19] The "crafft of elloquence," in other words, is a mode of illuminating bestowed by God on writers so that they may make manifest eternal truths not otherwise available in our state of "infirmyte." On the other hand, this illumination not only describes what poetry provides but also, as the following passage from the *Life of Our Lady* illustrates, describes the process of its own inspiration:

> Now, fayre sterre, O sterre of sterres all—
> Whose light to see angelleȝ delyte—
> So late the golde dewe of thy grace fall
> Into my breste like skales, fayre and white,
> Me to enspyre of that I wolde endyte—
> With thylke bame sent downe by myracle
> Whan the hooly goost the made his habitacle—
> And the licour of thy grace shede
> Into my penne, tenlumyne this dite,
> Throrough thy supporte þat I may procede
> Sumwaht to saye in laude ande preys of the.
>
> (1.50–60)[20]

Here, both poet and poem receive divine inspiration through the illumination of the "fayre sterre" in the same way that the Virgin is impregnated by the "hooly goost"; so illuminated, the poet "may procede" to reflect back that very divine light, in the "laude and preys" that will illuminate his readers. For Lydgate, poetry both divinely illuminates and is divinely illuminated. And by figuring this illumination as the falling of "golde dewe," he all but names his aureate style as both the instrument for illuminating and the manifestation of his poetry's illuminated state—the "licour of [the Virgin's] grace" of this passage being one and the same as the "auriat lycour of Clyo" that he invokes at the beginning of the *Commendation*. Crucially, he supplements his description of this double illumination by supplying an instance of that which he speaks—the lofty, ornate nature of this very passage. Through its aureation it radiates the divine inspiration for which it asks, and in this way it exemplifies what Fineman calls the autological quality of epideictic representation: in pointing toward something else, it is always also pointing back at itself.[21]

When combined with the specificity of Lydgate's "I," this autological dynamic takes in the historically specific poet as well as the poem. Not only does an equivalence obtain between the praised object and the praising medium, but the praising subject must likewise be elevated; to be adequate to the poetry that is in turn adequate to the ideal nature of that which it describes, this subject becomes symmetrically idealized. When a poem's first-person speaker is occupiable, as is typical of devotional poetry, this idealization is an instrument for the formation of a spiritual community; the poet and the readers, in the moment of experiencing the poem, are all joined in communion with God. In contrast, the precise denotation of the "I," as in much of Lydgate's work, restricts this elevation to the specific poet, relegating to the reader the role of vicarious poet rather than participant subject.

In the *Commendation,* when Lydgate claims in the third stanza to be "vnworthi . . . to loue such on [i.e., the Virgin]" and requests "hir grace" to enable his "laude and presyng," he is at once requesting and demonstrating the same sort of illumination as in the *Life of Our Lady,* in which he makes present "the licour of [the Virgin's] grace" through his "laude and preys." He is asserting that, once so illuminated, he is in fact no longer "vnworthi," and, not coincidentally, he begins his praise proper in the fourth stanza with the same image of stellar superabundance that dominates the prologue of the *Life of Our Lady*: "O sterne of sternys with thi stremys clere." (As Fineman observes, the ideal in epideictic poetry is traditionally figured as brilliant specularity.)[22] Leveraging the well-established conventions of the humility topos, Lydgate characteristically points the epideictic finger back at himself by claiming that he has not (successfully) pointed at all.[23]

One may justifiably wonder why Lydgate, as a monk, would have indulged in such coded self-aggrandizement. The first three stanzas of the poem are plainly inessential to its devotional function. Surely from a monk—whose most basic selfhood ought to be a homogeneous *imago dei*—we expect the specificity of the poet to be emptied into a universalized, Spitzerian lyric ego.[24] Of course, Lydgate was to some extent encouraged to depart from this convention by the precedent of the Ricardians. But his eclipse of even his English predecessors in this regard requires a fuller explanation, for which we must turn to Lydgate's interactions with the Lancastrians at the beginning of the fifteenth century.

The First English Laureate

We know that quite early in his career Lydgate had some form of contact with the most illustrious of the Lancastrians, known at that time as heir apparent

Henry of Monmouth, and most scholars believe that this contact had far-reaching effects on his subsequent poetry. A letter survives, probably written sometime between 1406 and 1408, from the Prince of Wales to the abbot of Bury St. Edmund's requesting that Lydgate be allowed to remain at Gloucester College to pursue his studies.[25] Whatever level of interaction this letter documents, given subsequent events we can say with some confidence that the Prince of Wales saw in the monk a potential means for royal intervention into high culture. In particular, the prince, with his later commissioning of the *Troy Book*, pursued such intervention to legitimate himself both in the eyes of the public and in those of his father. After having virtually ruled the country in his sick father's stead during 1410–11, he had been summarily dismissed by the latter in November 1411. At the end of September 1412, he had entered London with a large group of supporters and held his famous tête-à-tête with the king. Although they reconciled, the prince's position was still shaky: he had no role in government or in affairs overseas. He turned, therefore, to restoring his image as military hero and epitome of English chivalric culture. As Lydgate tells us in the *Troy Book*'s prologue, the prince commissioned the poet on October 31, 1412 to render into English verse the most authoritative version of the most important narrative of ancient history, the *Historia destructionis Troiae* of Guido delle Colonne.[26]

The series of invocations with which Lydgate begins the poem is revealing. Initially, the opening of the prologue works the same way as does the above passage from the *Life of Our Lady,* only in this case it is Mars rather than Mary who is the object of epideictic address, who emanates the illuminating "sterne lyght," directs Lydgate's "stile," and fills his "penne" with "aureat lycour" (Pro.1, 29, 31).[27] But then Lydgate abruptly turns to address instead a series of goddesses, beginning with "Othea, goddesse of prudence," who serves as an intercessor, a means to "make[n] Clyo for to ben [his] muse" (Pro.38–40). At the end of the series, it is one of Clio's "sustren," Calliope, whom he finally asks "tenlumyne . . . þis wirk" (Pro.41, 59). Clio, as muse of history, is, as I have already mentioned, a marker for Lydgate's specific person; Mars, as "myghty lorde" (Pro.4) and "souereyn and patrown" (Pro.7) of chivalry, must be, at least in part, a marker for the prince. Othea, an allusion to the *Epistre Othea* by Christine de Pizan—a text, I believe, the prince had earlier shown Lydgate[28]—appears as the medium that relates the two; and the outcome of this relationship is Calliope, who, as muse of epic, stands for the work that follows. To put this formulaically, Mars joined with Clio by means of Othea produces Calliope, which is equivalent to saying that the Prince of Wales brought together with Lydgate by means of the *Epistre Othea* produces the *Troy Book*.

Invocations to Mars, Clio, and Calliope are, of course, appropriate in this context and hence do not by themselves imply anything special; but the presence of Othea, which cannot so easily be explained, disrupts the conventionality and flags the more specific meaning of this series of names. Already at this point, Lydgate has begun to fashion an epideictic circuit involving the prince, himself, the style and matter of the poem, and the authority of both the antique poetic tradition and an eminent contemporary poet. And it is within this framework that he next turns to the circumstances of the prince's commissioning. At the beginning and end of this following passage stands the author, who initially asserts the purity of his motives ("For God I take hyȝly to wyttenesse / That I this wirk of hertly lowe humblesse / Toke vp-on me" [Pro.69–71]) and concludes by announcing his intention to begin the work the prince has commissioned ("The whyche emprise anoon I gynne schal / In his worschip for a memorial" [Pro.119–20]). Between these poles the passage is all about the prince, and its primary end is to document his twofold rationale for the project and suggest the relationship between his royal person and that rationale. First, the prince understands the Troy story to be filled with narratives of exemplary aristocratic martial behavior—to express, that is, the "worthynes" of "verray knyȝthod" and the "prowesse of olde chiualrie" (Pro.76–78). Readers of the *Troy Book* should, as the prince himself does in respect to his "bokys of antiquite," pursue "vertu" by "example" of the ideal knights that the work depicts (Pro.80–82). Second, England ought to have this "noble story" available in its own "tonge"; if England is to realize its imperial ambitions, then it may no longer be culturally and linguistically dependent on "latyn" and, especially, "frensche" (Pro.113–16). In relation to these two aims, on the one hand the prince represents a living ideal knight—as indicated by the twenty-line panegyric of him sandwiched between the accounts of the aims. On the other hand, as the one "To whom schal longe by successioun / For to gouerne Brutys Albyoun" (Pro.103–4), he is an embodiment of the nation that lays claim to an equal share of the "trouthe" (Pro.116) of the Troy story. With this double valence, the historically specific person of the prince hypostatizes the very raison d'être of the *Troy Book:* he is at once a living instance of its exempla and a personification of its political claims. Hence, when Lydgate says he will begin the "emprise . . . In his worschip for a memorial," the poet is quite concisely describing the essence of (at least what the prince wanted from) the project: an authoritative and moralistic historical narrative that is also a memorial to a living prince, his massively amplified encomium.[29]

In the immediately subsequent passage, Lydgate supplies an exceedingly ornate, twenty-six-line astronomical dating of the moment at which he is beginning his translation. Although jarring in its sudden appearance, this passage or something akin to it, in the context of the dialectic governing the epideictic aims of this prologue, is precisely what we should expect. Through his elevated diction and lavish rhetoric, Lydgate idealizes the moment at which he sets out on his great work. Along with being a "memorial" to Henry, the poem will be a memorial to itself, the passage operating to this end as an inaugurating auto-panegyric, raising the poem and poet to the same status its patron.

The *Troy Book* thus has two idealized agents at its center: the prince who commissions it, who exemplifies its ideals, and who will presumably recover in the future what it describes as lost in the past; and the translator who fulfills the commission and thereby effects the first stage of the recovery. It is, tellingly, to the second of these agents that the last two-thirds of the prologue is devoted. In this space, Lydgate describes the ideal practice the *poet* ought to exemplify—namely, the conveying of "trouthe"—and, as he makes clear, in this context *trouthe* means historical veracity. Without "writyng" that records "[w]ith-oute feynynge" and "[w]ith-oute fauour," no models of "grete prowes" would remain, and we would be "begyled / Of necligence thoruʒ forʒetilnesse" (Pro. 154–83). If, in contrast, the past is rendered truthfully, the "lack or prys" apportioned by "clerkis" will be authoritative directives for the behavior of future "conquerouris" (Pro.174–88).

This formulation of literary truth, although it largely derives from Guido's concerns in his prologue, also conveniently conforms to the tradition of monastic history writing.[30] Lydgate, having earlier suggested this tradition with the figure of Clio, here ushers it into the foreground, since a social identity as monastic historian proves, for two principal reasons, crucial to his strategies of authorization. First, this tradition possesses a (putatively) autonomous authority vis-à-vis the specific political regime in the context of which it happens to operate. Precisely because of this apparent autonomy, the historian may effectively operate as legitimizer of this regime.[31] As long as the historian gives the impression that he distributes "lak or prys" only as "men disserue" (Pro.187) and not according to political interest, then his praise of a sovereign—whether explicitly given or coded via the manner in which events are recorded—carries the authoritative weight of both church and history. Second, this social identity supplies a wholly traditional precedent for drawing attention to Lydgate's empirical person. In contrast with devotional poetry's generic first person, monastic history writing uses the biographical element of the traditional academic preface as an authenticating analogue for the veracity of the history it reports.[32] The factuality of a historical account receives confirmation via the self-evident factuality of a named, historically specific author. In his pose as monastic historian, then, Lydgate carries in his specific person the authority of a tradition that has Venerable Bede as its forefather. He bestows praise from the standpoint of an embodied, independent authority that goes back as far as the English royalty itself.

Lydgate, moreover, is fully aware of the mutually corroborating exchange between these two sources of authority. After stating once again the maxim of objective history writing—"Clerkis wil write, and excepte noon, / The playne trouthe whan a man is goon" (Pro.193–94)—he (unlike Guido) goes on to argue for the political utility of this supposedly politically neutral writing. The "writing trewe" of historical poets ought to be "cherisched" and "hounoured gretly" by "lordes" because it is this writing that advertises those lords' "manhood and prowes . . . and her worthynes" (Pro.195–200)—i.e., that establishes the intrinsic merit that legitimates their status as lords. Importantly, clerks have not simply "enacted" the "renoun" of lords (and here the verb *enacten* means to record in a chronicle)[33], but also "gilte" it (Pro.198–99). To gild, as its more common denotation suggests, means for Lydgate to put into aureate language or, more generally, to heighten panegyrically. He is therefore insisting that historical poetry, just like its devotional counterpart, should not simply record the "worthynes" of the object it describes but should imitate that worthiness in the loftiness of its style. It should not merely rehearse "al þe trouthe / With-oute fraude" about "her manhood and prowes" (Pro.199–204) but *manifest* martial glory in an act of stylistic prowess.

There is a potential contradiction here, which has been present from the beginning of the *Troy Book* prologue, and which is best phrased as a question: How may one create in a single text both factual history and encomium without the history becoming mere flattery or the encomium patently disingenuous? Lydgate opens himself to this contradiction because the conflation of historian and panegyrist offers him the most potent authorial pose for the task at hand. As suggested by the immediately subsequent passage, with this conflation he reaches toward a sociopolitical identity as poet that would enable the implicit claims of the dating passage to be realized; he seeks to establish the poet as possessing a literary authority akin to the prince's political one so that the poet serves the prince but is not a servant of the prince:

> For elles certeyn [without writing] the grete worthynesse
> Of her [i.e., lords'] dedis hadde ben in veyn;
> For-dirked age elles wolde haue slayn
> By lenthe of ȝeris þe noble worthi fame

Of conquerours, and pleynly of her name
For-dymmed eke the lettris aureat,
And diffaced the palme laureat,
Whiche þat þei wan by kny3thod in her dayes,
Whos fretyng rust newe and newe assayes
For to eclipse the honour and the glorie
Of hi3e prowes, which clerkis in memorie
Han trewly set thoru3 diligent labour,
And enlumyned with many corious flour
Of rethorik, to make us comprehende
The trouthe of al, as it was kende[.]
                                        (Pro.206–20)

In this passage there is a seamless transition from the epideictic object's "grete worthynesse" to the "enlumyned" nature of the epideictic poet's language, a transition accomplished by the double duty performed by the couplet "aureat"/ "laureat." This couplet refers backward syntactically and figuratively to the praised object's "worthynesse" and in the same gesture refers forward—via the standard Lydgatean connotations of *aureat*—to the "many corious flour / Of re- thorik" of "clerkis." The claim is that poets, as conquerors of time, deserve as much fame—and, implicitly, as much autonomy—as the conquerors whose "worthi fame" they "[h]an trewly set."

Lydgate at this point has laid the groundwork for his later explicit designa- tion of this claim as that of a poet laureate, the rhyme pair "aureat"/"laureat"— one of his favorites, as Seth Lerer has shown—more or less revealing his hand.[34] He devotes much of the remainder of the prologue to a measurement of the literary past according to the historian's ruler, running through a catalog of Troy story *auctores* from Homer to the very source for this passage, "Guydo" (Pro.360), and holding each up to the standard of "cronyculeris" (Pro.246). Yet what he does not locate in this catalog is an English precedent for his laureate pose, which is crucially needed, since in early-fifteenth-century England liter- ary decorum, especially when addressing a prince, did not allow a living author directly to claim an authority equivalent to his patron's. This claim instead had to be made through a proxy, a past *auctor* whose intellectual and cultural au- thority was self-evident and whose ancestorlike relationship to the present au- thor was apparent. In Lydgate's case, the most suitable such *auctor* would be one who wrote vernacular poetry in the high style and who, moreover, had only recently died, so that he could be both eulogized and imagined as a living, empirical person rather than as merely an authoritative name. The obvious candidate for such an *auctor* was, of course, Chaucer, the father of Lydgate's and Henry's common friend Thomas Chaucer, and the man who left behind his own Trojan tale, *Troilus and Criseyde*.[35]

In the prologue of the *Troy Book,* perhaps finding it inappropriate to mention Chaucer within a list of Latin and Greek *auctores,* Lydgate only alludes to his predecessor through the latter's own famously elusive *auctor,* "Lollius" (309). In book 2 he finds a better opportunity, when confronting the moment at which he must supply an epideictic description of Criseyde. But his use of Chaucer becomes most explicit in book 3, when he reaches that notoriously fraught moment of Criseyde's abandonment of Troilus. This passage, beginning as a simple reference to Chaucer's much more detailed account of the event, develops into a quite intricate eulogy of his poetic master. Here, as in book 2, Lydgate's Chaucer, having "gilte" (3.4237) the English language, exemplifies Lydgatean poetics. But in this case, Chaucer's achievement qualifies him for the "laurer of oure englishe tonge," and Lydgate insists that Chaucer is to England what the paradigmatic poet laureate "Petrak Fraunceis" is to "Ytaille" (3.4246–51). In turn, Lydgate conveys the nature of his own relationship with this English laureate by means of the key term *magnifie,* which appears here both in respect to what Chaucer does to the English language (3.4242) and in respect to what Lydgate does to Chaucer (3.4261). In this context, the verb means at once "to adorn," "to make famous," "to praise," and "to make great or powerful"; hence, by asserting that he will "magnifie" his predecessor through his writing in the same way that Chaucer has magnified English, Lydgate claims an epideictic equivalency that all but explicitly names himself as heir to the "laurer."[36] At this point, Lydgate has retroactively reconfigured his predecessor into an English poet laureate, and, since Chaucer is dead and the seat vacated, he has opened up a space for himself in the present for precisely this role.[37]

Lydgate waits to name himself, however, until near the end of the *Troy Book.* Having finished the narrative, Lydgate records in verse the date of the poem's completion. This he gives in respect to both the birth of Christ and the reign of his patron, now Henry V and recent conqueror of France, and this second dating naturally leads into another panegyric for Henry, a rather longer and more aureate one than that of the prologue. After digressing pointedly into a call for peace (with Henry as emperor over both realms, of course), this panegyric concludes, conventionally, in a prayer for its object of praise. But in the immediately following lines, Lydgate, as by now should be expected, turns back to himself, briefly recounting the poem's commissioning, and this time naming himself and explicitly providing his social identity:

Thus shal I ay—ther is no more to seye—
Day & nygt for his [i.e, Henry's] expleit y-preye
Of feythful herte & of hool entent,
That whylom gaf me in commaundement,
Nat yore a-go, in his faderes tyme,
The sege of Troye on my maner to ryme,
Moste for his sake, to speke in special.
Al-thoug that I be boistous and rual,
He gaf me charge this story to translate,
Rude of konnynge, called Iohn Lydgate,
Monke of Burie be professioun[.]

(5.3459–69)

In this passage, what may at first seem to be the throwaway tag "Moste for his sake" stands for the essential epideictic strategy of the entire project. It binds together the poem, "The sege of Troye"; the patron for whose "sake" Lydgate began in his "maner to ryme"; and the specific poet doing this rhyming, "called Iohn Lydgate, / Monk of Burie be professioun." Significantly, following this act of self-naming we encounter a rather involved insistence on the poet's inadequacy as both monk and versifier, which runs for nearly fifty lines, culminating in a conventional plea for "correccioun" (5.3516) and a final eulogy for his "maister Chaucer" (5.3521). Yet in naming himself in his own, authorial voice and providing along with this name his extrapoetic social identity, Lydgate has done here what his "maister" never does—and, indeed, what very few poets writing in English have done before him.[38] And in this instance, when he does finally name his master, he figures him not so much, as in the prior eulogies, as a proxy for his own poetic authority but as an ideal reader, who "liste nat poinche nor gruche at euery blot . . . but seide alweie þe best" (5.3522–24). The elaborately amplified humility topos separating his self-naming from his naming of Chaucer thus serves as a signpost for what is in fact a moment of self-aggrandizement. The implication is that Chaucer has given ground to his successor, and now that the disciple has gone beyond his master, he may respectfully declare for his precursor that there "Was neuer noon to þis day alyue . . . Þat worþi was his ynkhorn for to holde" (5.3528–30).

More important, however, than whatever anxiety of influence it may rechannel, this act of self-naming ushers Lydgate's notional laureateship into being. More than any other gesture, it brings together and embodies in his empirical person the instrumental aims of his royal patronage and the ethereal claims of the high-culture literary tradition. With this compound embodiment, the idea of an English laureateship is invented. The poet laureate—the site of intersection between politics and culture, the king's double in the realm of the aesthetic—need not possess an actual, institutionalized title. In fact, as I implied at the opening of this essay, such institutionalization spells the demise of the laureateship in its most potent form, as once it possesses concrete sociopolitical existence, the mystification it relies upon for its authority becomes much more difficult to maintain. Lydgate—as we have noticed, for example, in the elaborate self-dating of the *Troy Book*—effects this mystification by elevating the occasionality of his works from the timebound to the timeless, from something by definition historically contingent to something standing above history.[39] In the process of this elevation, the specificity of the occasion is not evaporated but rather idealized: the reasons for a poem's composition, the time at which it was begun, and, most important, the person writing it are all in the same moment both contingencies and ideals. Textualized in this manner, in a poem of the most authoritative matter written for a king, Lydgate indeed becomes a practicing laureate, albeit one whose notional post must be reinvented with each poem, and whose laureate dream of unity between political utility and cultural apotheosis cannot possibly be realized.

Epilogue: "Al-thoug that I be boistous and rual . . ."

Before ending this essay I must briefly return to a topic that I have admittedly explained away too easily—the humility topos, which appears everywhere in Lydgate's work and especially at those moments in which he is calling attention to his historically specific person. Gestures of humility are for Lydgate no empty convention but serve a variety of essential functions, only one of which I have mentioned thus far—namely, by conveying precisely the opposite of what they literally communicate, they are a means of tactful self-aggrandizement. This function cannot be overemphasized, and not only because so many readers have simply taken Lydgate's self-abnegation at his word and agreed that yes, he certainly is a dim star in the sunlight of Chaucer, and, indeed, the "defaute ys in Lydegate."[40] But even more important is the fact that this inverted self-aggrandizement, given the notional nature of Lydgate's laureateship, forms this laureateship's very fiber. Without an official status as laureate, Lydgate, as I have said, must reinstall himself in that office with each poem, and one of his most powerful rhetorical strategies for doing so is to proclaim ostentatiously his unsuitability for it. Lydgate's laureateship, produced and perpetuated by the manner in which he represents himself, receives its being by being denied.

Two other functions of the humility topos, moreover, have at least equal bearing on the nature and practice of this laureateship. First, as David Lawton has argued, the humility topos allows fifteenth-century poets to utter some-times-unwelcome truths to those in power.[41] In respect to Lydgate specifically, scholars have argued that the monk voices a veiled but consistent critique of militaristic royal policy, even within such monuments to royal power as the *Troy Book*.[42] As voicing criticism *in propria persona*—even coded criticism—can be dangerous, Lydgate's self-abnegations help to dampen the force of the pos-sible affront to his patrons. One may fairly wonder why Lydgate would even risk such an affront, but in fact he had no choice: such a risk is entailed by the very mutual legitimation that both he and his patrons seek. Lydgate, as I have claimed, is only able to be an effective agent of legitimation because, in his iden-tity as a monastic writer, he in theory possesses an authority independent of that of his patrons. To maintain this identity and therefore also his efficacy as a legitimizer, he must, so to speak, stay in character. He must take positions and voice concerns consistent with this identity, drawing on a set of interests distinct from—and therefore at times in conflict with—those of his patrons. Like all dialectical relationships, this one contains a paradox, which is that to be an ef-fective propagandist, Lydgate must also be a stern critic. Faced with this neces-sity, Lydgate at the end of the *Troy Book* couches the declaration of his name, his social identity, and the fact that his sovereign gave him "charge this story to translate" in an equally pronounced insistence that he is "boistous and rual." He must, to be the monkish laureate Henry wants him to be, utter unpleasant truths of, for example, the horrors and fruitlessness of royal militarism, but he is smart enough to deliver these truths with a large dose of self-deprecation.

The other crucial function of the humility topos possesses a much less inten-tional nature, operating like a nervous tic that relieves the pressure created by theoretical and practical tensions within laureate poetics. In theory, the poet is both a self-determining analogue of the prince and somehow also a monumen-talizer of that prince; in practice, his intent to speak the truth is severely cir-cumscribed by his economic and political dependence on those to whom he speaks. In respect to these tensions, the humility topos operates as an acknowl-edgment of the profound asymmetry between patron and poet—the vast gulf in social status, wealth, and power that separates them. It is, simply put, the ap-propriate manner in which to address one's superiors, and, as such, it is a bald admission of inferiority. While this admission does serve in turn as a *via negativa* toward self-aggrandizement, it does so only at the cost of also indicating the notional basis of laureate authority and hence that authority's ultimate subjection to the more concrete political and economic power of the prince.

The ineluctable advertisement of the laureate's subjection, and the necessity that he maintain an at least partially oppositional stance toward his patron, are more or less what Louis Montrose, writing about Spenser, terms the "resistance" inhering within laureate self-representation:

> [Resistance] is a matter of the text registering the felt but perhaps not consciously articulated contradiction between Spenser's exalted self-representation as an Author and his subjection to the authority of an other, the contradiction between a specific authorial ideology—that of "the Laureate"—and the social conditions of literary production with which that ideology may be realized in Spenser's historical moment and from his social position within it. In Spenser's text, the refashioning of an Elizabethan subject as a laureate poet is dialectically related to the refashioning of the queen as the author's subject.[43]

The "exalted self-representation" as laureate and the ambivalent, dialectical relationship between poet and sovereign that Montrose describes are precisely what we have seen to be fundamental to Lydgate's self-representation. Once they are noticed, such similarities between Spenser's and Lydgate's poetic projects seem too striking to be accidental. With virtually homologous structures of cultural and political posturing, the two poets' respective laureate poetics are close cousins.

The tradition begun by Lydgate, despite the tremendous blow it received from the Reformation's obliteration of its monastic base, has not so much waned as found occult avenues of persistence. Just a half-century after its apparent dissolution, this tradition has an unmistakable rebirth in Spenser; and from him onward, one can trace in English poetry an unbroken line of laureate poses, reaching as far as to Wordsworth (and hence to us) by way of his reading of Milton's reading of the Tudor poet. Even the most paradigmatic of English romantics finds himself, in his old age and soon to become England's official laureate, writing verse the nature of which would easily win the approval of Lydgate and his patron Henry V:

> Speaking through Law's dispassionate voice the State
> Endues her conscience with external life

And being, to preclude or quell the strife
Of individual will, to elevate
The groveling mind, the erring to recall,
And fortify the moral sense of all.[44]

Only an authoritative poet who embodies state power—that is, a postfeudal laureate, whether notional or actual—could write such lines. That this poet is the same one who wrote *Tintern Abbey* suggests that, in English poetry, one should never be surprised to find a laureate lurking behind a singer of subjectivity. Although Lydgate is not an elemental figure of English literary history in the same way that Chaucer or Wordsworth is, he permanently altered its course, putting into place a relationship between power and self-representation that haunts, even to this day, poetry's greatest claims to being something other than mere words.

Notes

I owe thanks to Lee Patterson, Traugott Lawler, Pericles Lewis, Matthew Giancarlo, Ramie Targoff, and Maura Nolan, all of whom offered invaluable advice on drafts of some or all of these pages. I would also like to thank the editors of this volume, whose thoughtful questions at the 2000 New Chaucer Society Congress and subsequent assistance have proved greatly helpful. Early formulations of this essay's argument presented at the Yale Medieval-Renaissance Colloquium and at Kalamazoo received encouraging feedback.

1. W. B. Yeats, *Essays* (New York: Macmillan, 1924), 458–49, quoted in Richard Helgerson, *Self-Crowned Laureates: Spenser, Jonson, Milton and the Literary System* (Berkeley: University of California Press, 1983), 48. I was led to Helgerson's book by Seth Lerer, *Chaucer and His Readers: Imagining the Author in Late-Medieval England* (Princeton, NJ: Princeton University Press, 1993), to which study this present essay—although not always in agreement—owes a general debt.

2. For Lydgate's annuity, see Derek Pearsall, *John Lydgate (1371–1449): A Bio-Bibliography,* English Literary Studies 71 (Victoria, BC: University of Victoria, 1997), 36–39, and, for the pertinent documents, appendix nos. 14–29.

3. See ibid., 71 and 80.

4. Derek Pearsall, *John Lydgate* (Charlottesville: University Press of Virginia, 1970).

5. For example, one thinks of his remarkably broad patronage, his many politically motivated productions, and the impressive circulation of manuscripts in his own lifetime.

6. For a somewhat less abridged account of the influence of the idea of the laureate on fifteenth-century English poetry, see Robert J. Meyer-Lee, "Laureates and Beggars in Fifteenth-Century English Poetry: The Case of George Ashby," *Speculum* 79 (2004): 688–726.

7. Cited from *The Riverside Chaucer*, ed. Larry D. Benson (Boston: Houghton Mifflin, 1987). Throughout this chapter, poetry is cited parenthetically in the text by line number or by book (or, as here, fragment) and line numbers.

8. *Lydgate's Siege of Thebes,* 2 vols., ed. Axel Erdmann and Eilert Ekwall, EETS, e.s., 108, 125 (London: Kegan Paul, Trench, Trübner, 1911, 1930); all further citations are to this edition. Here and in all citations of EETS editions, I do not reproduce editorial diacritics, emendation brackets, or indications of expansion.

9. For a recent, penetrating discussion of this differentiation, see Scott-Morgan Straker, "Deference and Difference: Lydgate, Chaucer, and the *Siege of Thebes*," *Review of English Studies,* n.s., 52 (2001): 1–21.

10. For example, see John M. Ganim, *Style and Consciousness in Middle English Narrative* (Princeton, NJ: Princeton University Press, 1983), 104. For a discussion of this moment in the *Siege* more congruent with mine, see Stephanie Trigg, *Congenial Souls: Reading Chaucer from Medieval to Postmodern* (Minneapolis: University of Minnesota Press, 2002), 94–95.

11. All citations of this poem are from *John Lydgate: Poems,* ed. John Norton-Smith (Oxford: Clarendon Press, 1966). I have in some cases modified the punctuation. The poem's date is unknown.

12. The pertinent lines of *Troilus and Criseyde* are 5.1849–55, and those of the *Complaynt of a Lovere's Lyfe,* 400–406 (see *John Lydgate: Poems,* 143; all citations are to this edition).

13. For *redresse,* see the three meanings for *redressen* v. given in the *Middle English Dictionary (MED)*. For *stile,* see *stile* n.(2) meanings (a), (b), and (c), which cover denotations from "writing instrument," to "subject matter," to "elaborate, ornamented style," and for each of which the *MED* provides an example from Lydgate's *Troy Book.*

14. Norton-Smith finds another echo of *Troilus and Criseyde* (viz., 2.1–10: see *John Lydgate: Poems,* 144) in this invocation. If this is the case, it not only makes the tie to Chaucer so much the firmer but also—as Lydgate has then displaced the invocation from the more appropriate context of a historical romance to the inappropriate one of a devotional panegyric—makes its self-referential quality so much more unmistakable.

15. I do not mean to claim here that this first-person specificity is uniformly characteristic of Lydgate's poetic practice. Lydgate in fact often deploys a more generic first person. In addition—as David Lawton, *Chaucer's Narrators* (Cambridge: D. S. Brewer, 1985), reminds us—one cannot assume that a poetic "I" is used in a consistent manner even in the same work. Nonetheless, as the instances cited in this present essay suggest, Lydgate makes use of first-person specificity so frequently—and especially in his most prominent works—that it is fair to cite this feature as a central element of his poetics.

16. See Ernst Robert Curtius, *European Literature and the Latin Middle Ages*, trans. Willard R. Trask (Princeton, NJ: Princeton University Press, 1990), esp. 154–59, and O. B. Hardison Jr., *The Enduring Monument: A Study of the Idea of Praise in Renaissance Literary Theory and Practice* (Chapel Hill: University of North Carolina Press, 1962), 34–36 and passim.

17. Joel Fineman, *Shakespeare's Perjured Eye: The Invention of Poetic Subjectivity in the Sonnets* (Berkeley: University of California Press, 1986), 5. Cf. Hardison, *Enduring Monument*, 30.

18. *Misericordias domini in eternum cantabo*, 5–6, in *The Minor Poems of John Lydgate*, ed. Henry Noble MacCracken, EETS, o.s., 107 (London: Oxford University Press, 1911), vol. 1.

19. *Lydgate's Fall of Princes*, 4 vols., ed. Henry Bergen, EETS, e.s., 121, 122, 123, 124 (London: Oxford University Press, 1924–27). As Bergen points out in his notes (4:205), this entire passage on writing and writers is original to Lydgate.

20. *A Critical Edition of John Lydgate's Life of Our Lady*, ed. Joseph A. Lauritis, Ralph A. Klinefelter, and Vernon F. Gallagher (Pittsburgh: Duquesne University, 1961). The date of this work is uncertain; Pearsall favors 1415–16 (*Bio-Bibliography*, 19–20). For the notion of illumination in these two passages, see Lois Ebin, *Illuminator, Makar, Vates: Visions of Poetry in the Fifteenth Century* (Lincoln: University of Nebraska Press, 1988), 24.

21. I do not mean to suggest here that Lydgate, as is sometimes thought, supplements his verse with aureation as a rule. He is instead relatively selective in this regard, deploying this style typically only when it is thematically relevant, as in this passage from the *Life of Our Lady*. In comparison, he renders vast stretches of such works as the *Troy Book* in an unadorned middle style appropriate to the purposes of narration.

22. See Fineman, *Shakespeare's Perjured Eye*, 13.

23. For a brief history of this very old convention, see Curtius, *European Literature*, 83–85.

24. I refer to the infamous formulation of the medieval lyric ego in Leo Spitzer, "Note on the Poetic and the Empirical 'I' in Medieval Authors," *Traditio* 4 (1946): 414–22. The notion of the occupiable "I" that I have been using derives from the refinement of Spitzer's formulation in Judson Boyce Allen, "Grammar, Poetic Form, and the Lyric Ego: A Medieval *A Priori*," in *Vernacular Poetics in the Middle Ages*, ed. Lois A. Ebin (Kalamazoo, MI: Medieval Institute Publications, 1984), 199–226. For the ideal monastic selfhood as an *imago dei*, see Caroline Bynum Walker, *Jesus as Mother: Studies in the Spirituality of the High Middle Ages* (Berkeley: University of California Press, 1982), 87.

25. Pearsall prints this letter in *Bio-Bibliography*, appendix no. 8, and discusses its implications on 15–17.

26. For the events of 1410–13, see Christopher Allmand, *Henry V* (London: Methuen, 1992), 43–58. For the relationship of the *Troy Book* to Lancastrian politics, see,

among other studies, Alan S. Ambrisco and Paul Strohm, "Succession and Sovereignty in Lydgate's Prologue to *The Troy Book*," *Chaucer Review* (1995): 40–57; Lee Patterson, "Making Identities in Fifteenth-Century England: Henry V and John Lydgate," in *New Historical Literary Study: Essays on Reproducing Texts, Representing History,* ed. Jeffrey N. Cox and Larry J. Reynolds (Princeton, NJ: Princeton University Press, 1993), 69–107; and Christopher Baswell, "*Troy Book*: How Lydgate Translates Chaucer into Latin," in *Translation Theory and Practice in the Middle Ages,* ed. Jeanette Beer (Kalamazoo, MI: Medieval Institute Publications, 1997), 215–37.

27. *Lydgate's Troy Book,* 4 vols., ed. Henry Bergen, EETS, e.s., 97, 103, 106, 126 (London: Kegan Paul, Trench, Trübner, 1906, 1908, 1910, 1935); all further citations are to this edition. I have also consulted *John Lydgate: Troy Book: Selections,* ed. Robert R. Edwards (Kalamazoo, MI: Medieval Institute Publications, 1998).

28. I cannot here present the evidence for this contention; I outline the facts and their significance in Robert J. Meyer-Lee, *Poets and Power from Chaucer to Wyatt* (Cambridge: Cambridge University Press, forthcoming). The most important studies on this topic are J. C. Laidlaw, "Christine de Pizan, the Earl of Salisbury and Henry IV," *French Studies* 36 (1982): 129–43, and C. David Benson, "Prudence, Othea and Lydgate's Death of Hector," *American Benedictine Review* 26 (1975): 115–23.

29. That this is not exactly what the prince received from the *Troy Book,* when its sentiment is considered as a whole, has been well argued by James Simpson in *Reform and Cultural Revolution*, vol. 2 of *The Oxford English Literary History* (Oxford: Oxford University Press, 2002), 77–103, with reference to the somewhat earlier alliterative *Destruction of Troy.*

30. For a thorough discussion of Lydgate's historicism in the *Troy Book,* see C. David Benson, *The History of Troy in Middle English Literature: Guido delle Colonne's "Historia destructionis Troiae" in Medieval England* (Woodbridge: D. S. Brewer, 1980), 97–129. For Guido, see *Historia destructionis Troiae,* ed. Nathaniel Edward Griffin (Cambridge: Mediaeval Academy of America, 1936), trans. by Mary Elizabeth Meek as *Historia destructionis Troiae* (Bloomington: Indiana University Press, 1974).

31. For this prerequisite of a legitimizing agent's distinction from those whom he legitimizes, see Larry Scanlon, *Narrative, Authority, and Power: The Medieval Exemplum and the Chaucerian Tradition* (Cambridge: Cambridge University Press, 1994), 311.

32. For the discursive roles of the academic preface, see the groundbreaking book by A. J. Minnis, *Medieval Theory of Authorship: Scholastic Literary Attitudes in the Later Middle Ages,* 2nd ed. (Philadelphia: University of Pennsylvania Press, 1988). For discussions of the pose of the historian in particular, see Andrew Galloway, "Writing History in England," in *The Cambridge History of Medieval English Literature,* ed. David Wallace (Cambridge: Cambridge University Press, 1999), 225–83; Christiane Marchello-Nizia, "L'historien et son prologue: Forme littéraire et stratégies discursives," in *La chronique et l'histoire au Moyen Age: Colloque des 24 et 25 mai 1982,* ed. Daniel Poirion (Paris: Presses de l'Université de Paris-Sorbonne, 1986), 13–25; and Peter Damian-Grint, *The New Historians of the Twelfth-Century Renaissance* (Woodbridge: Boydell Press, 1999).

33. See *MED enacten* v. meanings 2 and 3.

34. See Lerer, *Chaucer and His Readers,* 45–49.

35. Lydgate himself documents his relationship with Chaucer's son Thomas in the poem known as *On the Departing of Thomas Chaucer*; see the edition in *John Lydgate: Poems.*

36. See *MED magnifien* v. 4, 1 (a), 1 (b), and 2 (a), respectively. Baswell comes to similar conclusions about this passage in *"Troy Book,"* 230. See also Nicholas Watson, "Outdoing Chaucer: Lydgate's *Troy Book* and Henryson's *Testament of Cresseid* as Competitive Imitations of *Troilus and Criseyde*," in *Shifts and Transpositions in Medieval Narrative: A Festschrift for Dr Elspeth Kennedy,* ed. Karen Pratt (Cambridge: D. S. Brewer, 1994), 95.

37. The strategic manner in which Lydgate deploys his eulogies of Chaucer has been much noticed. See, in particular, John H. Fisher, "A Language Policy for Lancastrian England," *PMLA* 107 (1992): 1168–80; Lerer, *Chaucer and His Readers,* 22–56; A. C. Spearing, *Medieval to Renaissance in English Poetry* (Cambridge: Cambridge University Press, 1985), 59–120; Daniel T. Kline, "Father Chaucer and the *Siege of Thebes:* Literary Paternity, Aggressive Deference, and the Prologue to Lydgate's Oedipal Canterbury Tale," *Chaucer Review* 34 (1999): 217–35 (especially for the Bloom-inflected phrasing in the next paragraph); and Scanlon, *Narrative, Authority, and Power,* 299–349.

38. For example, the appearance and thematic function of Lydgate's act of self-naming here stand in some contrast with Langland's in *Piers Plowman.* While Lydgate names himself bluntly in a manner that telescopes the work's narratorial voice down to a specific, concrete individual, Langland refers to his historical specificity ambiguously in manner that always retains, ultimately, a paradigmatic function. See the masterful analysis of Langland's signatures in Anne Middleton, "William Langland's 'Kynde Name': Authorial Signature and Social Identity in Late Fourteenth-Century England," in *Literary Practice and Social Change in Britain, 1380–1530,* ed. Lee Patterson (Berkeley: University of California Press, 1990), 15–82. See also James Simpson, "The Power of Impropriety: Authorial Naming in *Piers Plowman*," in *William Langland's Piers Plowman: A Book of Essays,* ed. Kathleen M. Hewett-Smith (New York: Routledge, 2001), 145–65.

39. For a similar view of Lydgate's pervasive occasionality, see Lois A. Ebin, *John Lydgate* (Boston: Twayne Publishers, 1985), 91.

40. *Virtues of the Mass,* 88, in *Minor Poems of John Lydgate,* vol. 1.

41. David Lawton, "Dullness and the Fifteenth Century," *ELH* 54 (1987): 761–99.

42. James Simpson and Scott-Morgan Straker, in a series of studies, have been at the forefront of those who argue for Lydgate's consistently critical stance toward his patrons. For example, for this stance in the *Troy Book,* see Straker, "Rivalry and Reciprocity in Lydgate's *Troy Book*," *New Medieval Literatures* 3 (1999): 119–47. Simpson's and Straker's positions may be contrasted with those of Pearsall and Ambrisco and Strohm, who understand Lydgate's laureate performances as for the most part propagandistic in intent, if not always in execution. For a view somewhere between these poles, see Colin Fewer, "John Lydgate's Troy Book and the Ideology of Prudence," *Chaucer Review* 38 (2004): 229–45.

43. Louis Adrian Montrose, "The Elizabethan Subject and the Spenserian Text," in *Literary Theory/Renaissance Texts,* ed. Patricia Parker and David Quint (Baltimore: Johns Hopkins University Press, 1986), 323.

44. Lines 9–14 in the ninth of the *Sonnets upon the Punishment of Death,* in *Wordsworth: Poetical Works,* ed. Thomas Hutchinson and Ernest de Selincourt (Oxford: Oxford University Press, 1936). Wordsworth composed this set of sonnets during 1839–40. He accepted the laureateship in 1843.

3

Lydgate's Poetics

Laureation and Domesticity in the *Temple of Glass*

Larry Scanlon

What We Talk about When We Talk about Lydgate

In a word: aesthetics. The proverbial badness of Lydgate's poetry has been a truth universally acknowledged for so long that even those who would like to talk about something else usually find themselves talking about aesthetics first. Newer, critically self-aware, politically sophisticated forms of historicism have opened up Middle English authors and traditions that previous scholarship had found largely illegible or unimportant. But these historicisms have proceeded more slowly with Lydgate than with others. (The comparative profusion of work on Gower or Hoccleve offers an instructive contrast.) Moreover, as such work has sought to reevaluate Lydgate by recovering the political complexities of his historical situation, it has still defined that situation in aesthetic or affective terms: as a "dullness," a "narrowing," an "*aetas puerorum.*" It is true that each of these terms has some historical warrant; it is also true that each term introduces an argument that will go on to complicate it. There may even be a kind of elegance in the simplicity of these terms that enables their arguments to get a hearing.[1] Nevertheless, this common impulse to sum up the best part of a century in a single, pejorative trait remains rather more poetic than historical. It consigns the period to the role of bit player, a flat character in the familiar historiographical epic whose heroes are Chaucer and the rounded glories of the late fourteenth century. A related line of argument has looked to some version of the anxiety of influence to explain Lydgate's abasement before Chaucer.[2] All of these explanations retain a certain functionalism, haunted by the aesthetic dismissals they are attempting to displace. Whatever the plausibility of the various political, cultural, and ideological reasons advanced to explain Lydgate's dependence on Chaucer, no one has succeeded in offering a compelling poetic explanation for it. Indeed, the very fact of offering political, cultural, or ideological explanations requires that Lydgate's aesthetic be taken as in some way a given.

These explanations also remain hostage to one of the central tropes of older Lydgate criticism. Even the harshest condemnations of Lydgate's poetic faults invariably end with the concession that he simply shares the limitation of his age. Moreover, Lydgate's cultural and historical significance is precisely the justification his detractors have always offered for the study of what they understand to be such bad poetry. Josef Schick, editor of the *Temple of Glass* for the Early English Text Society, and possibly the most dyspeptic of Lydgate's modern commentators, declares that "the verdict passed" upon the work's "poetic value . . . should be: 'Very small, almost nil.'" Laying out many of the themes that will dominate Lydgate scholarship for most of the twentieth century, Schick goes on to describe "the monk's" style as "drawled out and incompact." The "sentences run on aimlessly" and

> it is often difficult to say where a particular idea begins or ends. One certainly has the impression that the monk never knew himself. . . . He knows little of logic connection, or distinct limitation of his sentences, and the notion of artistic structure, by which all ideas form, in mutual interdependence, an organic whole, is entirely foreign to him.

Schick grudgingly notes Lydgate's facility in "long sermons and moralizations" but then adds, "[S]howers of commonplaces, proverbs, and admonitions rain down upon us." Nor does Lydgate handle dialogue well, "direct and indirect speech" flowing together "in a very careless manner." In two places in the *Temple of Glass,* "our monk apparently . . . at first intended to give only a few words of reply, for which indirect speech might conveniently be employed; but he changed his mind, and when once in full swing, it is no easy matter to stop him." Finally, "this carelessness in language" parallels "the monk's inconsistency in depicting his ideas."[3] Yet in spite of all this evident annoyance Schick still finds Lydgate's poems worthy of serious study:

> [T]hey afford a rich hunting-ground for the Chaucer-scholar, the archaeologist and the student of language and early typography. . . . Furthermore they form a vast storehouse of mediaeval lore, many of the most popular sources

of the knowledge being, in a greater or lesser degree, incorporated in them; and as they are mainly translations or compilations made evidently for the best-educated of his nation, they furnish ample illustration of what was then considered as the highest literary culture.[4]

Derek Pearsall's 1970 critical biography, still the most important and influential piece of Lydgate scholarship ever written, recapitulates many of Schick's objections, albeit with much better humor. In his recent "bio-bibliography," Pearsall also offers a concise version of Schick's rationale for studying the poet in spite of his failings: "Lydgate is probably more important for his place in the literary and political culture of his day than as a poet in the traditional literary-critical sense."[5] Pearsall does not share the presentist complacency of Schick's aesthetic judgments, but he does share the same basic assumption: that historical questions can be easily separated from purely poetic ones.[6] On the one hand, this assumption privileges the poetic, setting it apart as a constant impervious to historical vicissitudes. On the other hand, the privilege is also an impoverishment. While Pearsall's distinction invites further historical inquiry so far as Lydgate's "literary and political culture" is concerned, it suggests that inquiries into the possible historicity of purely poetic assumptions and categories are pointless, perhaps even unwelcome. Poetry of the past can teach us about the past, but, paradoxically, it can't teach us about poetry—or at least it can't teach us anything we don't already know.

This essay seeks a fuller historicism. It takes as a likelihood the possibility that Lydgate may indeed have something to teach us about poetry—not just fifteenth-century poetry but poetry as we ourselves understand it. I have chosen as my text Schick's particular bête noire, the *Temple of Glass*. Poetry and poetic authority are the central concerns of this poem. It defines these concerns through the discourse of laureation, one of the major preoccupations of Lydgate's entire career. Though this topic is hardly new to Lydgate scholarship, many of its facets remain unexplored, including the crucial question of its historical trajectory. Laureation is very much a product of the later Middle Ages specifically, and it straddles the divide between the medieval and the early modern. The discourse was revived, if not invented, by Petrarch and introduced to the English tradition by Chaucer in the brief elegy to Petrarch in the prologue to the *Clerk's Tale.* As we shall see, the *Temple of Glass* draws directly on the *Clerk's Tale,* and in particular on the ironic connection Chaucer implicitly establishes between Petrarch's laureation and the tale's incipient cult of domesticity. Rightly considered by many Lydgate scholars to be an imitation of the *Parliament of Fowls,* the poem is also, in more literal terms, a rewriting of the

House of Fame. In fact, Lydgate constructs his poem out of material drawn from the rest of Chaucer's corpus as well. His deployment of Petrarch and the *Clerk's Tale* consolidates the Chaucerian material, giving us an unusually direct view of Lydgate's reconstruction of a poetic past almost entirely out of materials which that past itself provides.

Lydgate's poetic is durative and radically diachronic. It stakes its own authority almost entirely on adumbrating the superior authority of a dominant predecessor. It is not simply that Lydgate depends on Chaucer but that he continually advertises that dependence, makes it central, celebrates it, exfoliates it in great detail, and at every possible point identifies his own authority with it. Few Middle English scholars are now content to view Chaucer's dominance over his fifteenth-century successors as effected in some magical way by the sheer force of his genius. Nevertheless, we still lack the conceptual tools to produce a convincing alternative. The problem is twofold. First, while postmodernity has forsaken Romantic ideals of organic unity, individual genius, and artistic originality, it still has difficulty imagining any aesthetic value in continuity with or in submission to the authority of the past. In spite of all the lessons deconstruction and other forms of postmodern thought have taught us about the impossibility of the purely original, or purely individual, we continue to equate aesthetic value with the break, the new, the resistant, and the subversive.

The persistence of these associations is symptomatic of an even deeper problem. Modernity takes its aesthetic convictions to be at the core of its own privileged rationality, a crucial source of its epistemological superiority over the premodern. (This assumption may explain why newer historicisms are not necessarily any better at examining their own aesthetic predilections than older ones: doing so would require giving up the very epistemological edge over past work that they are trying to claim.) Philosophers and intellectual historians conventionally associate the origin of aesthetics with Plato. However, as a philological matter the aesthetic is as modern a category as one can find. A neo-Greek coinage of eighteenth-century German idealism, which enters English as a learned borrowing on the eve of the nineteenth century, the aesthetic is an Enlightenment ideal through and through. It seeks a rationality independent of all the preconceptions of the past. In Kant's classic formulation in the *Critique of Judgement*, aesthetic judgments originate in subjective experience but presuppose a *sensus communis*.[7] They thus necessarily operate in the eternal present of the a priori. Indeed, in his exposition of this sense in the *Critique*, Kant returns momentarily to the iconoclastic zeal of his broadside "An Answer to the Question: 'What Is Enlightenment?'" The most important requirement of the *sensus communis* is to "think for oneself," to escape prejudice and achieve that "eman-

cipation from superstition" which "is called *enlightenment*."[8] The aesthetic is
the product of genius, "the innate mental aptitude *(ingenium) through which
nature gives the rule to art*." Originality is genius's "primary property," and
"everyone is agreed on the point of the complete opposition between genius and
the *spirit of imitation*."[9]

There is no denying the influence or continuing power of this ideal—nor do
I have any interest in denying it. I wish only to point out that because this ideal
depends upon a rigid opposition between genius and imitation, it accommo-
dates with difficulty more diachronic versions of aesthetic experience. The
model ignores the constitutive role the past may play in aesthetic productions
of the present. Nor is the problem by any means confined to late medieval
instances, like Lydgate. It is present from the dawn of the Western tradition,
in the very first words of one of its two earliest poems: "Ἄνδρα μοι ἔννεπε,
μοῦσα. . . ." When a poem begins by invoking the Muse, the voice that speaks
is neither the poet's nor the Muse's alone but hovers between the two. Modernity has generally deflected the very difficult questions raised by such conver-
gences between past and present by treating them as defining features of the
premodern, now forever lost. In conservative versions of this view, the distinction between poet and tradition is superficial or illusory. Premodern culture
speaks in a single voice. It expresses a unity that modernity has lost and can
never recover. More progressive versions of this view posit the same unity but
define it in less benevolent terms. Tradition is repressive, a repository of dead
conventions; those few, singular authors still worth reading are the ones whose
genius enabled them to transcend tradition. This notion is one of modernity's
most characteristic convictions. Although it owes its vigor largely to the Enlightenment, its expression then was anticipated by the Renaissance in its attempts to distance itself from the Middle Ages. Indeed, one of the earliest versions of this to be found in Anglophone tradition is Sidney's famous appropriation
of Chaucer, with its implicit dismissal of Lydgate and his other disciples: "Chaucer, undoubtedly, did excellently in his *Troilus and Cressida;* of whom, truly, I
know not whether to marvel more, either that he in that misty time could see so
clearly, or that we in this clear age walk so stumblingly after him."[10] Sidney is
certain in his conviction both of Chaucer's authority and of the superiority of
his own "clear age" to the "misty time" of Chaucer. It is a wonderful feature of
this twofold conviction that what would seem to be a tension between these two
claims actually serves as mutual reinforcement. Chaucer's excellence is made
more marvelous by the mistiness of the time from which it emerges. The marvel rubs off on Sidney as well. For he takes his recognition of Chaucer's excellence not to mitigate the mistiness of Chaucer's age but, on the contrary, to

confirm the superiority of Sidney's own. In spite of such contradictory logic, this sort of temporal confidence underwrites many modern readings of the great premodern poets. Modern exegetes confirm the authority of such poets precisely by investing it with the superiority of the modern to the premodern, which is taken as a given.

Postmodern thought often repeats this pattern as well. Many postmodern theorists have rejected the notion of individual genius and are suspicious of aesthetic categories generally. Yet such categories continue to operate sub rosa in postmodern readings of premodern poetry. Such poetry is still treated as a privileged anticipation of the present, although now the themes are postmodern and include deconstructions of the very category of agency on which the conception of individual genius depends. This dilemma and others like it have no doubt played a large role in the resurgence of the aesthetic as an urgent topic of current theoretical debate. The resurgence began with appearance of Terry Eagleton's *Ideology of the Aesthetic* in 1990, a book that sets out to explain "the *theoretical* persistence of the aesthetic." Eagleton views the aesthetic as "an eminently contradictory phenomenon," both the "secret prototype of human subjectivity in early capitalist society, and a vision of human energies as radical ends in themselves which is the implacable enemy of all dominative or instrumentalist thought."[11] Predictably, he grounds this contradiction in the loss of the premodern. He argues that the aesthetic offers an ideal of internalized self-control that bourgeois culture felt it needed as it did away with the external constraints of what he calls "feudal absolutism."[12] This argument is a highly functionalist one, as Eagleton readily concedes.[13] Nevertheless, its functionalism is less of a problem than its dependence on the very idealist tradition that it is attempting to deconstruct. For Eagleton's argument offers a political version of the common and widely influential modern notion given in its classic formulation by Matthew Arnold: that culture offers modern society a source of cohesion it can no longer find in religion.

It is probably symptomatic of the aesthetic's unresolved relation to the diachronic that although Eagleton's work was motivated by a desire to move beyond the category's political contradictions, the debate his work has initiated has been more concerned with reexamining the category itself. Some participants in this debate present the renewed attention to the aesthetic as a much-needed corrective to what they view as the current field's excessive interest in the theoretical and the political. But the more dominant—and in my view, more promising—approach treats this return to the aesthetic as unfinished business, an issue that has been rendered newly urgent precisely because of the theoretical and political breakthroughs the discipline has seen in the past thirty years. Surprising as it may seem, the *Temple of Glass* speaks most directly to this strand, as we will discover by examining a leading instance.

Isobel Armstrong's *The Radical Aesthetic* seeks to recover the "democratic and radical potential of aesthetic discourse" by refiguring its relation to loss.[14] She argues that Eagleton's Marxist critique, as well as the deconstructive critiques of Paul De Man and Jacques Derrida, "undermine aesthetic discourse but refuse to remake it."[15] Returning to oppositions that animate the aesthetics of both Kant and Hegel—the sublime and the beautiful, reason and the passions, taste and disgust, symbol and identity—she demonstrates that "giving up on" the aesthetic "as an obsolete hierarchical category expressive of the bourgeois individual self" actually collapses the tensions between these oppositions that Kant and Hegel work so hard to maintain.[16] She advocates instead a return to the Hegelian category of mediation, redefined by the philosopher Gillian Rose as "a broken middle." That is, in contrast to Althusserian and deconstructive readings of Hegelian mediation as the collapse of opposed categories into a false unity, she argues with Rose that mediation works precisely by "working over" the oppositions even as it holds them in place.[17] The artwork has a synecdochic relation to this working over: "embedded in the ordinary processes of being alive," it is "a representation of mediation, a form of thinking, a request for knowledge, rather than . . . a privileged kind of creativity cut off from experiences everyone goes through."[18] In its translation of the broken middle, the aesthetic's most salient feature is its power of transformation. Moreover, the translation is itself synecdochic, embedded. What postmodern thought should concentrate on in the aesthetics it receives from Kant and Hegel is this potential for transformation rather than the categories by which that potential is constrained. Feminism and issues of gender have a particularly crucial role to play, for a variety of reasons, the most constitutive of which is the recourse to a gendered logic within Kantian aesthetics itself. "The zone of the sublime is the head, from which Kant and Burke explicitly excluded women," while the beautiful is associated with the sexual and female.[19]

Without really addressing the diachronic directly, *The Radical Aesthetic* nevertheless restores diachrony to the aesthetic. To understand the artwork as transformative, as a working-through, and as mediating processes in which it is itself embedded is necessarily to understand its effect as occurring across time. The aesthetic no longer originates in its own pure resistance. Founded on loss, across the fissures of the broken middle, the artwork necessarily enacts continuity by speaking to the loss that founds it. Indeed, without such continuity, the artwork could never offer up its loss for recognition.[20] Armstrong enacts this fractured continuity in her method. She returns to Kant and Hegel to recover what is missing from current theoretical discussions, yet what she recovers is not some buried truth but a promise yet to be fully realized. However, in defining that promise, she appeals to the ideal of the absolute break that everywhere else her argument complicates.

Early on, she declares, "[I]t is the aesthetics of Enlightenment Europe . . . which first made gender apparent, first made the feminine visible, as a topos in philosophical discussion."[21] Even when restricted to the field of "philosophical discussion," this claim is so preposterous it is barely worth refuting. Indeed, the purpose of the claim is less to locate the actual moment when philosophy first noticed women than to strengthen the case for rehabilitating Kant and Hegel. It invokes modernity's settled conviction of its own uniqueness with a shopworn claim as banal in its form as it is variable in its substance. There is probably not a single category of importance to modern culture—individuality, race, nationalism, secularization, indeterminacy, what have you—that has not at some time been declared to originate with it. Armstrong herself will effectively refute the claim in the book's final chapter. As it comes time to find the appropriate figural vocabulary for summing up, she reaches back well past the Enlightenment to Ovid, a writer to whom gender and the feminine were quite apparent, in their philosophical as well as poetic valences. She rewrites the Narcissus story, making Echo the real hero. Narcissus's gaze is male and synchronic; Echo's speech is female and diachronic. While his "reflection may be in excess of its object, it can never be different, never can be other than simultaneous. . . . [A]n echo does not have this simultaneous and immediate manifestation. There is a gap between its manifestation and originary sound." Articulated as a repetition around this gap or "caesura," Echo becomes the figure for the fractured continuities Armstrong has been pursuing and enacting throughout. As she notes a bit later, "In transit, an echo multiplies its flight across the sky and turns back to a different sound, but not quite, and another sky, but not quite."[22] This not-quite-difference can describe Armstrong's relation to the previous theorists her book assembles, and to Ovid himself. She often reads them against the grain, and even when she does not, their repetition in her text is at once hers and theirs. Thus Armstrong's Echo suggests the same relation between past and present I have already noted more conventionally expressed in another female figure, the Muse. As the concluding point of Armstrong's argument, this classical figure also demonstrates that the current reexaminations of the aesthetic cannot confine themselves to the category's modern moment of origin or its aftermath. On the contrary, we will never fully understand the aesthetic's rejection of the past until we understand what it owed the very past it was so confident it had transcended.

For all of her interest in mediation and transformation, Armstrong's convictions about the liberating politics of the aesthetic ultimately operate according to a ruptural and presentist logic of invisibility—that is, exactly the sort of logic her rereading of Ovid is meant to disavow. Kant and Hegel make women and gender relations visible without fully recognizing what they have done; the feminist theorist reading them against the grain can reorient their discovery of the aesthetic so that it will actually do the liberating work it promises but does not deliver. Equipped with this notion now properly oriented, the theorist can read a premodern text like Ovid even more profoundly against grain, recovering a voice like Echo's never properly heard until now. But what if these voices were actually heard all along, not simply as the feature of a few isolated and privileged texts but as a matter of traditional practice?

From the beginning the discourse of laureation was a poetics of loss. Moreover, as Chaucer brought it to England he defined it in part in gendered terms. In his *Collatio laureationis,* Petrarch presents his acceptance of the laurel in part as recalling the lost customs of antiquity when poets were better respected.[23] Chaucer's association of laureation with loss is even starker. Even as he celebrates Petrarch as "the lauriat poete / . . . whos rethorike sweete / Enlumyned al Ytaille of poetrie," he also insists that Petrarch is "now deed and nayled in his cheste." His envoy defines Griselda as a lost ideal in almost the same words, albeit in a somewhat more ironic context: "Griselde is deed, and eek hire pacience / And both at ones buryed in Ytaille" (4.29, 30–33, 1177–78).[24] In the *Temple of Glass,* Lydgate will exfoliate this connection and use it to gloss the conflation between the poetic and erotic he effects in broader ways with his combined deployment of the *Parliament of Fowls* and the *House of Fame.* In this way the poem offers a particularly literal confirmation of Armstrong's notion of the aesthetic as transformative, "working over" the Chaucerian materials out of which it is constructed and amplifying their already elaborate explorations of gender relations and loss. The literality of the confirmation also makes it a challenge. Here is a premodern text whose interest in gender and loss comes out of the continuities with the tradition it helps construct rather than out of resistance.

Raptus, Laureation, and Loss

As it happens, we can find a material illustration of Lydgate's transformative, mediating poetic in some of the details of the *Temple of Glass*'s textual history. The poem's earliest extant exemplar of the *Temple of Glass* occurs in Cambridge UL MS Gg. 4.27(1) (fols. 490v–516r). This manuscript has been dated to the decade 1420–30 and is best known as a major Chaucer collection. One of the "seven primary manuscripts of the *Canterbury Tales*,"[25] it is unique among all extant Chaucer manuscripts in providing an account of his entire career, "the only surviving example of a fifteenth-century attempt to collect Chaucer's major poetical works in one volume."[26] The manuscript contains in order: a number of lyrics, *Troilus and Criseyde,* a mostly complete version of the *Canterbury Tales* (Ellesmere order), the *Legend of Good Women,* the *Parliament of Fowls,* the *Temple of Glass.*[27] Its versions of the *Legend* and the *Parliament* are also the earliest extant. The placement of the *Temple of Glass* (explicitly ascribed to Lydgate) clearly indicates that the compiler of this collection viewed Lydgate's poem as a continuation of the *Parliament,* one that might properly be included in a collection otherwise devoted to mapping the integrity of Chaucer's full corpus. Thus, even as the compiler is engaged in the establishment and demarcation of that corpus, he is at pains to emphasize its permeability, its productive enabling of future work. Moreover, pointedly ignoring the directions of Chaucer's *Retraction,* he displaces the finality of this last word with both the *Legend* and the *Parliament.* The transmission of Chaucer's poetic authority to his leading disciple that this manuscript sketches occurs across three dream visions, two by Chaucer, one by Lydgate, all three of them centrally concerned with the problem of female agency and female erotic choice. The arrangement also contrasts sharply with the teleology that modern Chaucer scholarship has assigned to the chronology of Chaucer's career, the "French" period of the early dream visions succeeded by the Italian period of his maturity, the *Troilus* and the Canterbury collection. The outward and linear thrust of this teleology strongly suggests that Chaucer's goal was to transcend his own medieval moment toward the glories of the Renaissance as revealed in the Italian *quattrocento.* The arrangement in this manuscript is more circular and suggests that Chaucer's goal was to return to the literary culture of his time and reshape it, instead of escaping. The arrangement works backward from the end of his final work toward the beginning of his career, through the *Legend* first, an "Italian" work to the extent that it was inspired by Boccaccio's *De claris mulieribus,* and then to the more "French" *Parliament* (which of course also contains much Italian material). While such a conception certainly can be viewed as a typical fifteenth-century "narrowing" in its return to the French from the Italian, it is actually much closer to Chaucer's own practice. The influence of Italian tradition is evident from the *House of Fame* forward, but Chaucer was always much more interested in integrating the two influences than in subordinating the one to the other. The *Clerk's Tale* itself provides a particularly telling example of this tendency. Clearly a response to Boccaccio and Petrarch, it also draws heavily on the Parisian *Li livre Griseldis.*

A. S. G. Edwards and Derek Pearsall have astutely observed that "the evidence of Lydgate's *Temple of Glass* (with extensive echoes from the *House of Fame*)" indicates that copies of the *House of Fame* "were circulating in the early years of the fifteenth century, earlier than surviving copies."[28] Indeed, the poem's echoes of many of Chaucer's other works might be taken not only as evidence of their circulation but also as evidence of notions of an integral Chaucerian corpus predating the attempt to establish it in Cambridge UL MS Gg. 4.27(1). Inasmuch as it seems likely that the *Temple of Glass* itself also predated this manuscript, its inclusion and position suggest not simply that the compiler recognized it as an imitation of the *Parliament* but that he was also responding to its attempt to rearticulate Chaucer's entire corpus in miniature. In reconfiguring the *Parliament,* Lydgate substitutes the more explicitly erotic Venus for the *Parliament*'s more philosophical Nature, but he also makes the poem as much a continuation of the *House of Fame* and its more strictly poetic concerns. He draws his title from the *House of Fame,* and the poem's setting—that is, a temple rather than a garden—from book 1 of the *House of Fame.* The *Temple of Glass* reiterates the *House of Fame*'s invocation of previous European tradition, reading back to Virgil and Ovid and up through more immediate predecessors, although here Lydgate replaces Dante with the *Roman de la Rose* and Petrarchan discourse of laureation. But the poem also makes Chaucer's work the new center of that tradition. Long-established topoi like Virgil's Temple of Venus or Ovid's metamorphoses serve largely as accents to a distinctively Chaucerian vocabulary, as Lydgate supplements the plot of the *Parliament* and the setting of book 1 of the *House of Fame* with a variety of citations of Chaucer's other works, including the *Book of the Duchess,* the *Knight's Tale,* the *Franklin's Tale,* and, as I have already noted, the *Clerk's Tale.* The *Temple of Glass* effects a magisterial synthesis of these materials worthy of Chaucer himself. Lydgate emplots his exploration of poetic authority by returning to the structure of the *Parliament.* Instead of the daring series of ekphrases that constitute the *House of Fame* (that is, the descriptions of architectural structures, pictures, and other decoration), there is a single opening ekphrasis followed by a love *débat.* At the same time, as we shall see, the movement from the ekphrasis to *débat* is driven by a Chaucerian concern for marginalized voices. Moreover, Lydgate anticipates that concern in the ekphrasis itself with an extraordinarily dense and diverse range of reference.

The poem opens with a series of Chaucerian echoes, which, if anything, enable an even fuller evocation of the ambiguous authority of the dream vision as a genre. Like the *House of Fame,* the *Temple of Glass* is set in mid-December, "when of Ianuarie / Ther be kalendes of þe newe yere" (67), ominously close to

Christmas. In the *House of Fame,* Chaucer's dreamer falls asleep almost immediately. The *Temple of Glass* opens with a moment of insomnia and psychic distress that is more generically characteristic. This opening partially recapitulates
the *Parliament*'s dreamer, "Fulfyld of thought and busy hevynesse" (89), and it
enables Lydgate to present the onset of his vision as a spiritual rebirth:

> Wiþin my bed for sore I gan me shroude,
> Al desolate for constreint of my wo,
> The long[e] nyȝt waloing to and fro,
> Til at[te] last, er I gan taken kepe,
> Me did oppresse a sodein dedeli slepe
> Wiþin þe which me þouȝt[e] þat I was
> Rauysshid in spirit in [a] Temple of Glass—
> I nyst[e] how, ful fer in wildirnes—
> That foundid was, as bi lik[ly]nesse,
> Not open stele, but on a craggy roche,
> Like ise ifrore.
>
> (10–20)

Enshrouded as if for burial, overtaken by a "sodein dedeli slepe," Lydgate is
"rauyisshid in spirit." The lines invoke the profound passivity of the Christian
contemplative, but they do so as part of a virtuosic deployment of intertexts.

   This passage tersely conflates the first book of the *House of Fame* with the
third. Chaucer sets book 1 in a temple of Venus, "a temple ymad of glas" (120).
Lydgate sets his vision in the same place, but he transforms the desert that surrounds Chaucer's temple in book 1 into a "wilderness," and reveals the setting
at the beginning. (Chaucer waits till the end of book 1.) Moreover, Lydgate also
adds to this temple the most salient feature belonging to the House of Fame. As
Chaucer explains at the beginning of book 3, the House of Fame is built on "A
roche of yse and not of stel" (1130); accordingly, Lydgate founds his temple "not
opon stele, but on a craggy roche, / Like ise ifrore." The ostensibly redundant
epithet *ifrore,* "frozen," reminds us of a point Chaucer makes at greater length.
Ice is at once more refulgent and less permanent than glass (*House of Fame,*
1120–46). This paradoxical quality makes it an appropriate metaphor for the
durability of poetry, precisely when it is conceived in the shadow of Christian
revelation.

   Chaucer is more anxious about this issue than Lydgate, even though he is
the one who originates the metaphor. In both the *House of Fame* and the *Parliament,* he uses the generic premise of the dream vision as another level of mediation, addressing the authority of poetry by adumbrating the authority of dreams.

The *Parliament* also adds the precedent of the *Roman de la Rose,* opening with a summary of Macrobius's *Somnium Scipionis.* The *House of Fame* expresses its anxiety more directly. Its first line is a prayer at least as old as the *Dream of the Rood:* "God turne us every drem to goode" (1). The dangers inherent in the dream's ambiguous simulation of authentic visionary experience haunt the entire first book, from its quicker summary of Macrobius, through the invocation of Morpheus, to the book's conclusion, where the Dreamer repeats the opening prayer. After surveying the desert surrounding Venus's glass temple, he exclaims, "O Criste . . . that art in blysse / Fro fantome and illusion / Me save!" (492–94). Lydgate's clerical position may have given him a bit more confidence in the face of these ambiguities. But, paradoxically, he could also draw confidence from Chaucer's authority itself. In less than two lines, Lydgate transforms Chaucer's temple into a site where the revelatory, the poetic, and the erotic all directly converge. From his deadly sleep, "me þou3t[e] þat I was / Rauysshid in spirit in a Temple of Glass." *Ravished* was a verb often used to describe the revelatory transport of specifically religious visions. Thus the *Pearl*-poet, just before his actual vision of Christ, declares, "felde I nawþer reste ne travayle, / So watz I ravyste with glymme pure."[29] The line also recalls the passage from Virgil's third *Georgic,* which Petrarch takes as the text for his laureation address, *Sed me Parnassi deserta per ardua dulcis raptat amor* (But a sweet love ravishes [transports] me to the desert heights of Parnassus).[30] The elegy from the prologue to the *Clerk's Tale* suggests that Chaucer may have known this address. Whether it inspired his conception of the *House of Fame* is less clear. Nevertheless, that is exactly what Lydgate's citation would have us believe, that Virgil's *deserta ardua* lie behind the ice cliffs supporting both his Temple and Chaucer's House. The citation also subsumes the entire House of Fame tradition—a tradition that will endure well into the eighteenth century—into the broader discourse of laureation.[31]

Petrarch himself is concerned with the relation between poetic authority and divine revelation. Throughout his address he asserts both that poetry is divinely inspired and that it is distinct from theological discourse. His exposition of Virgil's line suggests the genres of biblical commentary or the sermon. He describes the line as *propositionem meam,* chosen from "poetic scripture" *(poeticis scripturis),* and then, even as he distinguishes his address from "theological declamations," he prays to the Virgin that it win divine favor (13). He stakes his claim for poetry's divine warrant on authoritative but distinctly pagan sources, Cicero, Juvenal, and Lucan, and through Cicero, Varro, and Ennius. These citations establish the poet as sacred and inspired by a divine spirit, notions that will come back later in more personal terms (15–16). Petrarch will claim that

God granted a "certain agility of imagination" *(agilitatem quandam ingenii),* as he is, according to the Roman satirist Perseus, "Master of the arts and grantor of genius" [Magister artis ingeniique largitor] (20).

The *Georgics* are nominally a guide to farming, addressed to Virgil's patron Maecenas. Yet throughout the series, Virgil views his subject in macrocosmic terms. Constantly alert to the figural possibilities of the minutiae of agricultural lore, he frequently uses them as a pretext for moralizing, and he is eager to demonstrate the interdependence between the fate of an individual estate and the larger Roman *imperium* and culture. This tendency is particularly evident in the third Georgic, which concerns the breeding of horses, cattle, and sheep. The poem begins with Virgil's desire to write a poem in praise of Caesar, an enterprise he imagines as a conquest. He will bring the Muses back from the Aeonian peak; build a temple to Caesar, who will become the deity to Virgil's poet-conqueror; and then supervise a procession that brings all of the empire to admire this deity. His advice on breeding emphasizes the importance of cattle and horses to Rome's martial enterprises and the farmer's responsibility in managing their sexual desire, the "frenzy and fire" *(furias ignemque)* into which all races rush (3:242–44). The poem thus presents Virgil's desire for poetic achievement mediating between the farmer's supervision of breeding animals and Roman quest for empire. The lines Petrarch quotes directly follow the discussion of the "frenzy" *(furor)* of mares, the greatest frenzy of all, inspired by Venus herself (3:266–68), while the desert heights toward which Virgil's *amor* drives recall somewhat ironically the mountain meadow where the bull is isolated to safeguard his potency (3:212–14). Petrarch leaves the erotic connotations of Virgil's *amor* entirely implicit and stresses instead its transcendent political dimensions. The poet will not ascend Parnassus without a desire for study, and the "efficient causes" of such a desire: "the honor of the state" [honor rei publicae] (7), personal glory, and inspiration of others. Whether Lydgate knew the third Georgic, his phrase "rauisshed in spirit" restores Virgil's link between the poetic and the erotic. The glass temple to which his dreamer has been ravished is the temple of Venus; the vision he will see turns throughout on the problem of erotic choice.

Odd as it seems, this return to the erotic may also owe something to *ravish* in its mystic or contemplative sense. By the fifteenth century, *ravishing,* like *raptus,* which it translated, could be applied to Christian visionary experience and could attract some of the erotic connotations more generally associated with the contemplative lexicon. Thus, even as cautious and centrist a figure as Walter Hilton could describe the visionary experience as a "ravischinge of lufe."[32] The specifically erotic content in such phrases remains elusive, as does their relation to the earliest meanings of *rapere*, "rape" and "plunder." The earliest influential Christian use of *raptus* to mean divine vision occurs in the Vulgate, 2 Corinthians 12:2–4, where Paul declares he knows "hominem in Christo . . . raptum . . . usque tertium caelum" (a man in Christ . . . transported . . . to the third heaven). No erotic associations are explicit here, and they may not have arisen until the time of Bernard of Clairvaux, the single thinker of the later Middle Ages most responsible for the turn of the Christian contemplative tradition toward explicitly erotic language. In his *Sermons on the Ascension,* Bernard associates this passage from Paul with the Canticles, and in his *Sermon on the Canticles* themselves he employs *rapere* and its derivatives with some frequency.

Moreover, this appeal to the contemplative lexicon, however ambiguous, may underwrite another aspect of Lydgate's reworking of Chaucer, his response to Chaucer's daring equation of poetic authority with female agency. Lydgate draws his opening ekphrasis from the one which dominates book 1 of the *House of Fame.* Chaucer draws that from a moment in book 1 of the *Aeneid* (itself drawn from a key moment in the *Odyssey).* After their shipwreck, Aeneas and Achates, concealed by Venus in a thick mist, make their way to the temple that Dido "was founding" *(condebat)* to Juno. There Aeneas suddenly sees brass plates depicting Troy's fall. Weeping, he asks Achates,

> What place . . .
> What region on earth is not full of our struggles?
> Behold Priam! Here also are virtue's rewards
> Here are tears for human happenings and mortal sufferings touch the heart
> Dissolve your fears; this fame will bring you some salvation.
> [quis iam locus . . .
> quae regio in terris nostri non plena laboris?
> en Priamus! Sunt hic etaim sua praemia laudi,
> sunt lacrimae rerum et mentem mortalia tangunt.
> solve metus; feret haec aliquam tibi fama salutem.][33]

This temple, commemorating the founding of a city, turns poetry into architecture—pictures cast in brass and set on temple walls. In spite of this enhanced durability, Aeneas's weeping confirms that poetic continuity is still founded on loss. At the same time this scene focuses on what can be rescued. The Trojans' *labores* have been so monumental that every land seems full of them. Somewhat ironically, this very monumentality constitutes the possibility of deliverance:

"this fame will bring you some salvation." If the tears these pictures depict and elicit prefigure Aeneas's abandonment of Dido, the solidity of their preservation in Juno's temple prefigures Rome's foundation.

Chaucer retains Virgil's fascination with the solidity and transformative power of poetic continuity. Yet he also finds a new way to illustrate its foundation in loss. The temple of Juno becomes the temple of Venus, the narrative on the walls becomes the *Aeneid* itself, and Aeneas's sorrow gives way to Dido's. Enshrining Virgil's own poem in this version of the temple to poetic continuity first produced by Virgil himself makes the *Aeneid* a shrine to itself. That is, Chaucer wittily acknowledges the role that Virgil's poem plays in creating its own posterity. But the other two changes render the duration of Virgil's authority more contingent. Making Venus its tutelary deity takes Aeneas's lineage literally, but in an ironic way. The heroic becomes a subsidiary of the erotic, deprived of its transcendent, quasi-divine claims, restricted instead to the realm of purely human desire, and classed with the more banal and universal forms of human continuity. Moreover, the shift to Dido insists on a loss that is irremediable. "Through yow is my name lorn" (346), she declares in her apostrophe to Aeneas, and the fame that transforms his loss to salvation brings her no such thing.

> O wikke Fame!—for ther nys
> Nothing so swift, lo, as she is!
> O, soth ys, every thing ys wyst,
> Though hit be kevered with the myst,
> Eke, though I myghte duren ever
> That I have don rekever I never . . .
> (349–54)

Chaucer underlines the point, commenting directly after the conclusion of her complaint,

> But that is don, is not to done;
> Al hir compleynt ne al hir moone,
> Certeyn, avayleth hir not a stre.
> (361–63)

What is done cannot be undone: the finality of history is its severest form of loss. Dido, the archetypal woman betrayed, becomes the voice of that loss. By placing her in the center of the temple, by making her the originary witness to the historicity of the poetic authority, Chaucer insists on the centrality of a question as unanswerable as it is unescapable: If poetry is a form of continuity drawn out of loss, what is its relation to that which it cannot preserve? Chaucer seeks to locate his own version of Virgil's temple, his own version of poetic authority, in the aporia of this question. And he dramatizes the question as a desire to hear Dido speak. Although as a matter of fact he draws Dido's speech from Ovid's *Heroides,* it is part of his fiction that it comes directly from her. He interjects at the beginning of her lament:

> In suche wordes gan to pleyne
> Dydo of hir grete peyne,
> As me mette redely—
> Non other auctor alegge I.
>
> (311–14)

At this point Chaucer's text becomes co-extensive with Dido's complaint—which he claims to have invented. His voice gives way to hers; it becomes hers. The poetic past becomes masculine, the poetic present, feminine; poetic authority is given an uncertain future that converges on the past it could not or would not salvage. The rest of the poem is concerned with recovering the irrecuperable. Chaucer makes Virgil's temple its governing conceit, defining poetic authority in a series of edifices with increasingly ephemeral fabrics. Permeated by history in all its contingency, the House of Fame is built of beryl but stands on an ice cliff continually melting and refreezing, yet it still cannot fulfill the dreamer's desire "somme new tydinges for to lere" (1886). The House of Tydings, a ramshackle labyrinth, is barely an edifice at all, turning about constantly "as swyft as thought" (1924). Here in the form of all human speech, the dreamer confronts historical contingency at its fullest and most ephemeral. Nevertheless, inasmuch as it emerges as speech, even here such contingency is still not accessible as an absolute immediacy. Moreover, the house cannot contain it. The poem ends in this impasse, irresolute and unfinished, with the enigmatic appearance in its last line of an unidentified "man of gret auctorite" (2158).

The *House of Fame* articulates an interest in the marginal and excluded that lasts throughout Chaucer's career and is the hallmark of the *Canterbury Tales.* Not everyone will agree with David Wallace's claim that no later work of English literature surpasses the Canterbury collection in this respect.[34] Nevertheless, it is difficult to name another major author so interested in not just the variety but also the dignity of lower-class, female, or otherwise marginalized voices before the advent of the novel—and that includes Shakespeare.[35] The point is worth stressing, for detractors of Lydgate generally ignore it. Even if Lydgate's poetic interests are less capacious than Chaucer's, this is a fault he shares with all of his successors, from Skelton to Milton, and beyond. The point is particularly relevant to the *Temple of Glass,* which, in its broadest and most neutral outlines, does constitute a narrowing of the interests expressed in the *House of Fame.* Where the *House of Fame* moves through three edifices, the *Temple of Glass* confines itself to one, an amalgam of Chaucer's temple of Venus and House of Fame. Lydgate eliminates the House of Tydings entirely. Yet even in this constriction, he is anticipated by Chaucer himself, whose dreamer focuses on the man of great authority after hearing "gret noyse" from the corner of the hall: "Ther men of love-tydinges tolde" (2140–44). Moreover, the constriction is precisely what enables Lydgate to concentrate on Chaucer's equation of poetic authority and feminine agency.

Lydgate pursues this Chaucerian interest in the feminine first of all by making the gallery of wall paintings more encyclopedic.

> Of sondri lovers lich as þei were of age,
> Isette in ordre after þei were true
> Wiþ lifli colours wondir fressh of hue
> (46–48)

The *Aeneid* still has pride of place, but the poem's full narrative has given way to Dido alone, and an abbreviated version of her complaint, "Hov she deceyued was of Eneas" (58). Lydgate makes erotic betrayal a subcategory of the larger problem of *trothe,* or fidelity.[36] Chaucer had appended to Dido's complaint a brief catalog of other classical betrayals: Phyllis by Demophon, Briseida by Achilles, Oenone by Paris, Isiphile and Medea by Jason, Hercules by Dianira, and Ariadne by Theseus. Lydgate incorporates this catalog into his gallery and substantially expands it. He follows Dido with Jason and Medea but then broadens his focus. The next pair is Venus and Adonis, an instance not of betrayal but of desire overcome by circumstance, and that is followed by two paragons of marital fidelity, Penelope and Alcestis. These are also instances of circumstance thwarting desire, but in these cases a heroic feminine constancy, a steadfast devotion to husband and marital obligation, enables desire to transform circumstance. Fifteen more instances follow, filling out Lydgate's attempt to sketch the vicissitudes of erotic desire in all their variety. He retains some of Chaucer's instances of betrayal, such as Demophon and Phyllis, and Theseus, but adds star-crossed lovers like Pyramus and Thisbe, and cases like Paris and

Helen, or Tristan and Isolde, that demonstrate a fidelity paradoxically born out of infidelity. He also adds three famous rapes: Tereus and Procne, the Sabine women, and Lucretia. Thus his expansion of betrayal to *trothe* cannot be read as a simple idealization. On the contrary, the shift to *trothe* constitutes a deidealization. It expunges a certain sentimentality latent in Chaucer's exemplification of historical loss in the figure of Dido, the woman who loves the man who betrays her past the point of her own self-destruction. In Lydgate's gallery, desire meets loss in all its materiality, whether for better or for worse. He features its durability and transformative power, not simply in the heroic achievements of figures like Penelope or Alcestis, but in the institution of marriage that gives their self-sacrifice its particular meaning. At the same time, the invocation of rape reminds the reader that such social structurations of desire are at least partly underwritten by violence.

Marriage also underlies another crucial feature of Lydgate's gallery: his four postclassical instances. They occur in two pairs, and all four are surprising, both in themselves and in their pairings. The first pairing is Griselda with Tristan and Isolde, which he invokes directly after Penelope and Alceste. The second pairing constitutes the last instances, Martianus Capella's Mercury and Philology, and Canacee, the heroine of the *Squire's Tale.* The citation of the *Marriage of Mercury and Philology* returns the dream-vision to one of its foundational texts, and its central allegorical equivalence between poetry and marriage. The juxtaposition of this text with the *Squire's Tale* implicitly offers Chaucer as Martianus's peer. That is, it makes Chaucer a defining authority for the genre, a move anticipated by Lydgate's selection and arrangement of the gallery's classical instances. Many of these can be related to the *House of Fame.* Many of the others can be related to other Chaucerian texts: Alcestis to the *Legend of Good Women* and (through her analog Alcione) the *Book of the Duchess,* for example, or Paris and Helen to the *Parliament* and *Troilus and Criseyde,* or Palamon to the *Knight's Tale.* Some, like Theseus, can be related to both the *House of Fame* and other texts. The citation of the *Squire's Tale* sums up these associations. Lydgate singles out Canacee's magical ring, which allows her to understand the language of birds, part of Chaucer's own remarkable rewriting of the *Parliament of Fowls* within that tale. The first morning Canacee wears the ring she encounters a peregrine falcon, lamenting at length her betrayal by a tercelet. Lydgate will follow this link to the *Parliament* with some personifications drawn from that poem's version of the garden wall from the *Roman de la Rose:* Jealousy, Danger, and Disdain. Moreover, as Lydgate's citation is itself a rewriting of a tale Chaucer ostentatiously left unfinished, the citation associates

Chaucer's authority with incompletion and an imperative to rewrite, and it authorizes Lydgate's rewriting of Chaucer's corpus as a whole through the erotic concerns of the *Parliament*.

However, as daring and subtle as this concluding instance is, the intertextual trajectory ultimately directing Lydgate's revisions comes from the first of the postclassical instances. Griselda is easily the most unexpected figure in the entire gallery. She is a peasant girl among queens and a Christian among pagans. Though her story may ultimately derive from a folktale, in its written form it is specifically a late medieval invention, at a distance generically as well as chronologically from the world of romance, and its *translatio studii*. A self-sacrificial heroine who concentrates her spiritual energies within the confines of marital duty, Griselda brings to erotic literature an impulse that approaches the hagiographical. It is this spiritualization that makes her crucial to Lydgate. The Griselda story first appears as the final tale in Boccaccio's *Decameron,* but Petrarch's ostentatiously humanist rewriting of Boccaccio's version gives it the form that will produce the tale's dispersion across northern Europe. In the *Decameron* the tale is a sort of antiexemplum, a tale of a petty tyrant, which Dioneo offers in contradiction to the day's theme of munificence. Petrarch transforms it into a tale of good governance by making Griselda its protagonist and offering her as an exemplar of Christian patience. Thus, in translating Boccaccio's vernacular into Latin, Petrarch also finds virtue where Boccaccio saw only venality. Paradoxically, Petrarch's Latin makes the tale more accessible to other vernacular traditions, and his transformation of Griselda obviously made the tale seem worth further translation. Griselda is important to Lydgate both as a bearer of vernacular authority and as an example of female virtue. Her pairing with Isolde, the most constant of Arthurian heroines, may be meant to mark the distinction between her story and the adulterous world of romance. But Griselda also enlarges the connection between Lydgate's poem and the discourse of laureation, effecting a conflation between female agency and poetic authority that will carry into the love debate. To understand this connection, we will need to return once more to Chaucer.

Griselda to the Rescue

The pivotal role Petrarch played in the dispersion of the Griselda story may well have inspired Chaucer to associate it with his laureateship. In any case, Chaucer clearly exploits the connection to dramatize once again the relation between poetic authority and loss. The Clerk names Petrarch as the story's source and offers a brief elegy.

> I wol you telle a tale which that I
> Lerned at Padowe of a worthy clerk,
> As preved by his wordes and his werk.
> He is now deed and nayled in his cheste;
> I prey to God so yeve his soule reste!
> Fraunceys Petrak, the lauriat poete,
> Highte this clerk, whos rethorike sweete
> Enlumyned al Ytaille of poetrie,
> As Lynyan dide of philosophie,
> Or lawe, or oother art particuler;
> But Deeth, that wol nat suffre us dwellen heer
> But as it were a twynkling of an ye,
> Hem bothe hath slayn, and alle shul we dye.[37]

The Clerk offers Petrarch's credentials as laureate tersely and in a subordinate clause. Petrarch's "rethorike sweete"—presumably the product of his clerical learning—illuminated all Italy "of poetrie"—a phrase that admits of at least three complementary readings. Petrarch's rhetoric poetically unites all of Italy; it makes this united Italy illustrous by virtue of his poetic achievement; and it reveals to Italy the illumination of his learning. In spite of this richness, the Clerk frames his adumbration of Petrarch's laureate achievement with the irremediable loss of his death. First, the Clerk defines that loss in the individual terms of Christian eschatology: "He is now deed and nayled in his cheste / I preye to God so yeve his soule reste!" Then he concludes with a more classical declaration of its banality, "alle shul we dye," a banality that, in this context, makes the particular loss of Petrarch the more devastating.

The connection between Petrarch's laureateship and the Griselda story is not immediately obvious, yet Chaucer insists upon it. In the tale's envoy, he subjects the ideal Griselda embodied to the same language of loss, albeit in a more parodic context. "Griseld is deed, and eek hire pacience / And both atones buryed in Ytaille," the envoy begins, before ironically urging "archewyves" to stand "at defence" and offer their husbands "no reverence" (4.1177–78, 1195–1205). Modern Chaucerians have not paid much attention to this trajectory framing the *Clerk's Tale*. When they have, they have concentrated almost exclusively on the irony, subsuming the elegy in the prologue to the parody of the envoy. The envoy then becomes a dismissive comment on either Petrarch's celebration of Griselda or Griselda herself. Thus we have here a crucial point in Chaucer's reception history where, in contrast to Lydgate's reading, which takes both laureation and Griselda seriously, it is the modern reading that is narrow. The Clerk ends the tale with a translation of Petrarch's moral:

> This storie is seyd nat for that wyves sholde
> Folwen Grisilde as in humylitee,
> For it were inportable, though they wolde,
> But for that every wight, in his degree,
> Sholde be constant in adversitee
> As was Grisilde; therfore Petrak writeth
> This storie, which with heigh style he enditeth.
>   (4.1142–48)

Like Petrarch, the Clerk generalizes Griselda's virtue, denying its literal application to wives alone. Yet after two more stanzas of exposition he abruptly shifts into an antifeminist register, ironically returning to the literal application he has just disavowed. Warning "lordynges" that Griselda's virtue is a rarity— "It were ful hard to fynde now-a-dayes / In al a toun Grisildis thre or two" (4.1164–65)—the Clerk playfully pays homage to the Wife of Bath "and al hire secte" (4.1170–71). In the envoy that follows, Chaucer extends the irony in his own voice, endorsing "archewyves" and encouraging them, "Ne suffreth nat that men yow doon offense" (4.1195–97).

If this irony undercuts the moral, it does so precisely by insisting on Griselda's status as ideal wife. In this way it rejoins contemporary French treatments of the tale. Both Philippe de Mézières and *Le ménagier de Paris* offer more straightforward affirmations of Griselda as a feminine and domestic ideal— the significance that, without displacing Petrarch's more general moral, would become the overriding one in the Griselda story's long and extensive dispersion through the next several centuries.[38] Indeed, as Chaucer's ironic lapse into the literal brilliantly demonstrates, any figural reading of Griselda, no matter how general, must ultimately depend on the letter of her exemplarity. That is to say, such readings can never ultimately escape or repress the very particular specificities of her marital status and the domestic sphere where her trials are played out. David Wallace has convincingly argued that Chaucer's treatment of Griselda must be read against the ideal of "wifely eloquence" he offers in the figure of Prudence from the *Tale of Melibee*.[39] I would take this point a step further and argue that Griselda constitutes an intermediary stage between Prudence and the Wife of Bath.[40] The Wife—her very identity the product of the clerical tradition of antifeminism—speaks for experience against authority. This project is an inherently negative one; without some form of authority to give it shape, experience cannot recognize or identify itself. The clerks have written all the stories. The Wife must attempt to make sense of her experiences in a language inherently hostile to them—a profound disadvantage that makes it difficult, if not impossible, for her resistance to achieve positive form. As the envoy to the *Clerk's Tale* reminds us, where the Wife resists, Griselda submits. Yet, paradox of paradoxes, out of that submission Griselda invests the domestic sphere, and more particularly, the office of wife, with enduring moral weight and spiritual authority. She thus anticipates the central conceit of the *Tale of Melibee*: that companionate marriage offers the best model for morally upright, spiritually informed lay governance.

In treating marriage as an arena of spiritual struggle, the Griselda story also participates in an even broader cultural trend of the later Middle Ages: the church's sacralization of marriage. Indeed, insofar as its narrative turns on the promise Walter extracts from Griselda, the story depends specifically on the doctrine of marriage formation first propounded in the decretals of the latter half of the twelfth century and dominant by the end of the thirteenth. This doctrine held that the central element defining the validity of a marriage was the consent of the two parties. Even more strikingly, the story's advent in the latter half of the fourteenth century coincides exactly with the period that James Brundage and other historians have identified as the moment when lay authorities began to reclaim the regulation of marriage from the church.[41] To be sure, this reappropriation was a slow, almost glacial, process, and even slower in England than it was on the Continent.[42] (Indeed, jurisdiction over marriage was not completely removed from English ecclesiastical courts until 1753.)[43] In any case, the actual proportion of jurisdictional control seems less important in itself than it is for its illustration of lay acceptance and assimilation of canonical doctrine. There is one, fairly spectacular instance from fourteenth-century England of lay authority venturing into marriage regulation: the 1352 parliamentary Statute of Treason. In addition to proscribing acts against the crown, it also defines as treasonous a wife's murder of her husband. As Paul Strohm points out, the peculiar logic of this categorization assumes an analogy between domestic and sovereign political authority.[44] But it assumes that analogy in a more positive way as well. The statute's main intention was to clarify the crime of treason and expand its application to the royal family, including under its purview acts against the queen and the king's heirs and their spouses, as well as household officers. Thus, the statute was part of the crown's successful effort to sharpen the distinctions between itself and the rest of the aristocracy in the fourteenth and fifteenth centuries. As another part of that effort, the crown also proliferated "noble styles and titles" specific to the royal family. The most obvious of these was the Prince of Wales, the title that Edward III bestowed for the first time on Edward the Black Prince. But he also anticipated that title by making the prince the Duke of Cornwall in 1337, making him the first duke in English history. Over the next two centuries fifty-two dukedoms would be created, almost all of them "for the benefit of the royal family."[45] At the same time, to compensate for "the decline and deinstitutionalization of queenly power in the later twelfth and thirteenth centuries," queens were drawn more tightly into the domestic orbit of their husbands. They became "intercessors" in relation to the king.[46] In both cases, the royal household became a nuclear family "commensurable" with any other domestic unit in the kingdom.[47] Royal power was enhanced, but only through the prior assumption of this analogy. Princes became dukes because they were the king's sons, and the queen became an intercessor because she was his wife. Finally, such commensurability featured prominently in the broader carnivalesque inversions characteristic of royal entertainments. As Susan Crane has recently demonstrated, the charivari, which "took remarriages or unsuitable marriages as their occasion," had a specifically aristocratic form frequently seen at royal courts, which involved courtiers assuming lower-class dress and manners.[48] Lydgate himself participated in this trend. The *Mumming at Hertford,* performed before Henry VI on the Christmas of 1427, is written in the antifeminist register of Chaucer's envoy and consists, according to Shirley's rubric, "of þe rude upplandisshe people compleynyng on hir wyves, with the þe boystous aunswere of hir wyves."[49] It also explicitly invokes Chaucer's envoy. In their answer the wives proclaim "oure partye þe worthy Wyff of Bathe" and declare that the "pacyence" of wives "was buryed long agoo, / Gresyldes story recordeþe pleinly soo."[50]

Lydgate's recourse to Griselda in the *Temple of Glass* is less explicitly ironic. However, as a signifier at once of laureation, domesticity, and repressed female agency, her introduction into this dreamscape of erotic loss enables Lydgate to enact a striking transformation of his own. The stories of unrequited love that dominate his gallery depend simultaneously on two distinct forms of durability, the durability of poetry and the durability of desire, and on keeping them separate. For desire can remain unrequited only if it cannot finally be converted into poetry. Lydgate's appeal to Griselda enables him to fuse these two forms of durability. Griselda, with her indomitable exertion of feminine constancy and patience, displaces Dido's loss, transforming that irrecuperable experience into a kind of authority. Moreover, Lydgate will extend this transformation from the static realm of his ekphrasis into the love-debate and across the full trajectory of his poem. In many respects the love-debate is utterly conventional: in its diction, its allusions, its imagery, and even its envoy, which, with the hyperbolic modesty of courtly compliment, reduces the whole poem to nothing more than a small tribute to its female protagonist. Nevertheless, by focusing this conventional performance through the issue of female agency that Griselda highlights, Lydgate simultaneously makes it something new.

The lovers are anonymous and their love is mutual. In spite of the pride of place Lydgate has given to Dido, as he moves into the rest of the poem he shows little interest in unrequited royal love with world-historical consequences. Although both of his lovers will work through the fears and conflicting desires of courtly lovers, the relation between desire and social class has grown purposely blurred. There is no clear tension between lover as desiring subject and lover as monarch or courtier, that insoluble dilemma of private desire and public responsibility that renders courtly love impossible but also peculiarly exalted. Lydgate's concern is the transcendent impulse that erotic desire retains as it is appropriated by the quotidian. The dreamer discovers the female lover first. As the ekphrasis ends, he finds her kneeling before Venus's statue. She is, conventionally enough, transcendentally beautiful. As the dreamer remarks, "I gan mervaile hou God or werk of Kynd / Miȝten of beaute such a tresour find / To yeven hir so passing excellence" (279–81). At the same time, she is also an "exemplarie" of honesty,

> . . . and mirrour eke was she
> Of secrenes, of trouth, of faythfulnes,
> And to al oþer ladi and maistres,
> To sue vertu, whoso list to lere.
>
> (294–97)

This exemplarity corresponds to the lady's transcendent beauty, yet its pedagogical function, the moral obligation it places on every "ladi and maistres" who "list to lere," shifts us almost imperceptibly from the courtly to the domestic, as does her anonymity. That is to say, while her beauty simply gives her a singularity that is unapproachable, this moral exemplarity makes her a standard to be imitated. That is especially true if we take seriously the class distinction implicit in the pairing "ladi and maistres": *ladi* strictly speaking means a noblewoman at court; *maistres* could mean any female head of household—as the *Middle English Compendium* explains, "as a polite mode of reference to a woman," the term "is less deferential than *ladie*."[51]

The male beloved will enter the poem in a parallel scene. Yet there the dreamer will discover him in a rewriting of Chaucer's dreamer's entrance into the House of Tydings. They both emerge from the "Gret pres of folk with murmur wondirful," who are rushing and shoving in the now crowded temple. That later scene will make it even clearer that this lady and her beloved, despite all her virtues and the full attention they get from Venus, are nevertheless one pair among innumerable others. In this earlier scene, as Lydgate's concentration on the lady's privilege gives way to her exemplarity, he also endows her with an agency that the older traditions of love poetry had largely denied to women. Noting that her garment was embroidered with the legend "De Mieulx en Mieulx," the dreamer explains:

> This is to sein þat she, þis benigne,
> From bettir to bettir hir herte doþ resigne
> And al hir wil to Venus þe goddes,
> Whan þat hir list hir harmes to redresse.
> For, as me þou3t, sumwhat bi hir chere,
> Forto compleyne she hade gret desire:
> For in hir hond she held a litel bil
> Forto declare þe somme of al hir wil
> And to þe goddes hir quarel forto shewe.
>
> (310–20)

Out of submission comes self-assertion. The Lady's resignation of "al hir wil" is actually constituted by her "gret desire" to complain and formalized in the "litel bill," which enables her to declare "þe somme of al hir wil." In contrast to the aloof and capricious heroines of romance, this protagonist is from the beginning the source of her own desire rather than a reflection of someone else's. With her entreaty to Venus, it is she who makes the first move. While not unprecedented, this portrayal by Lydgate is highly unusual. It is not just that he endows his lady with erotic agency. In giving her desire narrative priority, he also gives her the capacity of suffering to the full the agonies of the courtly lover, that mark of sublime privilege almost entirely reserved to male figures. As indicated by such paradigmatic cases as Amans from *Le Roman de la Rose* or Chaucer's Troilus, courtly love begins when the male lover, hitherto footloose and fancy-free, suddenly beholds his beloved in all her transcendent beauty. The intense psychic distress that immediately follows demonstrates the inherent nobility of the lover's desire. Thus, when Lydgate's Lady declares, "þou3 I brenne with fervence and with hete, / Wiþin myn hert I mot complein

of cold," her oxymoron and the psychic state it expressed are both utterly conventional. Yet she also essentially remakes these conventions because it is she
who speaks them.[52]

The Lady's complaint has usually been read as indicating that she is already
married to someone else. In fact, the indication is minimal and ambiguous.[53] It
rests entirely on a single, inexplicit line, "I am bounde to þing þat I nold" (335),
from which her married state must be inferred. Moreover, this already uncertain inference is rendered even less certain by the very next line (I quote both
for clarity):

> For I am bounde to þing þat I nold:
> Freli to chese þere lak I liberte . . .
>
> (335–36)

Freedom of choice is precisely what someone who is married lacks: that person
has already made his or her choice and is under a sacred obligation to maintain
it. The line applies much more closely to an unmarried woman confronting the
somewhat contradictory features of medieval marriage doctrine. Ultimately,
marriage depends on the free election of the two prospective partners, yet most
medieval thinkers who advocate such freedom argue almost as vociferously that
partners should also respect the wishes of their families. A young woman who
loved someone her father rejected would indeed have been free to choose where
she lacked liberty. There is very little else in the poem to indicate that the Lady's
desire is adulterous. On the contrary, Lydgate's continual focus on constancy
and honest virtue, from the Lady's initial description to Venus's reply, and the
later exchanges between Venus and the lovers strongly suggest that marriage is
what the Lady seeks and what Venus will promise. If line 355 is meant to suggest adulterous desire at all, it can only be as an ambiguous extension of the
honest desire that concerns the poem everywhere else, to make the point that
even desire that is less than honest can profit from similar discipline.

Venus will promise the Lady

> That ȝe shal have ful possession
> Of him þat ȝe cherissh nou so wel
> In honest maner wiþoute offencioun,
>
> (427–32)

but only after explicit appeals to the virtues of marriage. Venus begins her reply
with a promise of relief merited by the Lady's "sadde trouþe," "feiþful menyng,"

and "innocence" (377–83), a promise she then repeats in terms that clearly recall the *Clerk's Tale:*

> And for þat ȝe ever be of oon entent
> Withoute chaunge or mutabilite,
> Have in ȝour peynes ben so pacient
> . . . .
> Your wo shal nou no lenger be contuned.
>
> (384–87, 390)

Two stanzas later she invokes Griselda by name along with two other exemplary wives:

> Griselde was assaied atte ful
> That turned aftir to hir encrese of ioye,
> Penalope gan eke for sorowis dul
> For þat her lord abode so long at Troie.
> Also þe turment þere coude no man akoye
> Of Dorigene, flour of al Britayne:
> Thus ever ioy is ende and fine of paine.
>
> (405–11)

The last line of this stanza recalls a variety of lines from Chaucer that characterize the contingencies of Fortune (for example, from the *Nun's Priest's Tale:* "For evere the latter ende of ioye is wo" [8.3205]). This insistence on joy as the inevitable end of erotic pain might seem to demonstrate little more than philosophical naïveté. In fact, Venus's apparent denial of historical contingency has a more complex purpose. It is meant to emphasize, not the inevitability of happy endings, but the transformative power of suffering. In the next stanza she even appeals for proof to the authority of Christianity.

> And trusteþ þus, for conclusion,
> The end of sorrow is ioi ivoide of drede.
> For holi saintis þuruȝ her passioun
> Have heven iwonne for her soverain mede. . .
>
> (412–15)

This abrupt shift in register might seem to make the philosophical confusion even worse. But its very abruptness underlines the dependence that has been there all along. Medieval romance offers erotic love as a secular equivalent of Christian transcendence. Venus rewrites the impossibility conventionally framing this correspondence by offering Griselda as a mediating term. Griselda's transcendence is morally authentic, yet still ultimately secular: she directs her quasi-saintly forbearance toward the secular institution of marriage. By classing her with Penelope and Dorigen, Venus insists that all erotic forbearance is spiritual and that all erotic desire can be made subject to spiritual discipline. This insistence simply completes the transcendent ambitions that the conventions of courtly love continually proclaim. If the suffering of the courtly lover demonstrates a spiritual privilege, then it must behave like properly spiritual suffering in other ways as well. As Venus's imperative to the Lady indicates, the ultimate joy she promises is a matter of trust. What she offers is less a guarantee than an invitation to be tested and endure. Indeed, it is a reminder to the Lady that her exemplarity must be continually re-earned. The response to the dilemma of being free to choose where one lacks liberty is simply to choose anyway. By holding steadfastly to her choice, the Lady trusts that ultimately the obstacles to her liberty will give way. Paradoxical as it may seem, she will overcome the contradictory forces she faces precisely by submitting to them fully.

Venus's advocacy of submission is also conventional. Yet because in deploying it she conflates the erotic and the religious, she enables submission to become self-assertion and transforms moral submission into a peculiarly efficacious form of erotic agency. The Lady will get all she desires. Venus promises not only to deliver the beloved in an honest manner but that "with my brond I have him set afire" (436). The love affair will follow a conventional course in every respect. True to Venus's promise, the male beloved will be abruptly plunged into psychic distress. In his very first words he laments, "Allas, what þing mai þis be?" He is now "bound þat whilom was so fre"; while before he felt

> . . . riȝt nouȝt of loves peine:
> But nou of nwe within his fire cheyne
> I am embraced, so þat I mai not strive,
> To love and serve whiles þat I am on lyve
> The goodli fressh in þe tempil yonder
> I saugh riȝt nou—þat I had wonder
> Hou ever God, forto reken all,
> Myȝt make a þing so celestial,
> So aungellike on erþe to appere.
>
> (573–81)

The fire of love comes precisely as a vision of transcendent, indeed angelic, beauty. The male beloved will make his own entreaty to Venus. Venus will grant it and instruct him to woo the Lady without revealing that the Lady has already declared her love for him. Thus, as he moves through the conventional stages of courtly love, at each step he simply reflects the Lady's prior desire. This delicate irony shadows his subsequent protestations, threatening to expose as entirely illusory the conventional assumption that love affairs begin with male speech. Curiously, the Lady's initial response is also utterly conventional: a violent blush.

> Hir bloode astonyed so from hir hert it ran
> Into hir face, of femynynite:
> Thuruȝ honest drede abaisshed so was she.
> (1044–46)

Yet once she accepts his suit, it is she who then entreats Venus on behalf of them both. And Venus replies to her first. When Venus turns to the male beloved, she makes one last appeal to the *Clerk's Tale:*

> And first of al, my wil is þat þou be
> Feiþful in hert and constant as a walle
> Trwe, humble and meke, and þerwithal secre,
> Withoute chaunge in parti or in al.
> (1152–53)

"Constant as a walle" is the figure Chaucer uses to describe Griselda at the moment when her constancy finally overwhelms Walter's desire to test it. During his final outrage, the mock marriage to their daughter, he asks Griselda for her opinion of his new bride. Griselda answers mildly, warning him only not to test "this tendre mayden" so severely,

> And whan this Walter saugh hire pacience,
> Hire glade chiere, and no malice at al,
> And he softe had doon to hire offence,
> And she ay sad and constant as a wal,
> Continuynge ever hire innocence overal,
> This sturdy markys gan his herte dresse
> To rewen upon hire wyfly stedfastnesse.
> (4.1039, 1044–50)

"Constant as a wal" signifies Griselda's steadfast passivity at its most transformative. When Lydgate's Venus enjoins the same constancy to the male beloved, she takes literally the Clerk's Petrarchan moral—that Griselda's example applies to "every wight, in his degree" (4.1145). She takes it literally in another way as well. It is no now longer a simple exhortation for spiritual forbearance in the abstract. Venus has returned it to the domestic sphere from which Griselda's example originates and has made it the basis for an entirely mutual erotic contract, as binding on men as on women. Moreover, the figure also resonates with the poem's central conceit. The poem dramatizes the constancy, the durability, of poetry by transforming it into the temple's transparent walls. Lydgate uses Griselda's constancy to rewrite the erotic, which, thus rewritten, makes poetry's incomplete and unending transformation of loss at once more accessible and more ethical. His domestication of the erotic, his subjection of it to Griselda's quasi-sacral spiritual discipline, is less a means of policing it than of dissolving its privilege. In similar fashion, his domestication of the poetic is not a defense against Chaucer's authority, still less a failure to respond to Chaucer's work in all of its magisterial complexity. Instead it is an affirmation of that complexity in the attempt to extend and preserve it. There is no doubt that this poetics of continuity can never be fully recuperable in modern terms. But that is hardly the point. If we are willing to take seriously the labile relation it proposes between past and present, we are no more obligated to take it as the remedy for what is lacking in our current aesthetic dilemmas than we are justified in rejecting it as unenlightened or repressive. We can take it instead as clear historical evidence that there is no inevitable link between aesthetic value and discontinuity and that the aesthetic is not necessarily condemned to be the sole property of the present.

Notes

1. David Lawton, "Dullness and the Fifteenth Century," *ELH* 54 (1987): 761–99; Paul Strohm, "Chaucer's Fifteenth Century Audience and the Narrowing of the 'Chaucer Tradition,'" *Studies in the Age of Chaucer* 4 (1982): 3–32; and Seth Lerer, *Chaucer and His Readers: Imagining the Author in Late Medieval England* (Princeton, NJ: Princeton University Press, 1993), 13–21. Lawton argues that the dullness with which fifteenth-century poets have been charged "is a willed, self-conscious and ostensible dullness. It is the social mask of a Renaissance poet" (791). The stance drew its philosophical authority from Boethius, and it enabled Hoccleve, Lydgate, and others to offer forceful advice to patrons on whom they were dependent. Strohm argues that "Chaucer's fifteenth-century

followers neglect his mature works of greatest formal and thematic complexity, in favor
of a comparatively narrow range of *dits amoureux* and visions in the manner of continental France" (5). Strohm connects this narrowing to the substantial broadening of Chaucer's readership from the small of group of like-minded knights and esquires connected
to the royal court that constituted his immediate audience. This homogeneous group
gave way to a much larger and diverse group, consisting especially of "urban merchants
and country gentry," whose "interest in consolidating their class positions might well
have inclined away from stylistic and thematic experiment"(31). Lerer argues Lydgate
and his contemporaries were infantilized by both the figure of father Chaucer and their
dependence on princes and child kings through period's many dynastic uncertainties and
that they developed discourses of laureation to compensate for this disadvantage. Strohm's
more recent treatment of Lydgate, in his magisterial *The Empty Throne: Usurpation and
the Language of Legitimation, 1399–1422* (New Haven, CT: Yale University Press, 1998),
returns to Lawton's central trope, the "public posture of dullness," and offers a more complicated account of the trope's ideological deployment. He writes that

> beneath the deceptively placid surface of Lancastrian letters roils a veritable ocean of
> unacknowledged aberration . . . . Hoccleve's and Lydgate's aspiration to full com-
> plicity was unwavering, but the impossibility of Lancastrian requirements drove even
> the most resolutely loyal texts into a morass of embarrassing half-acknowledgments
> and debilitating self-contradictions. (194–95)

A certain residual image of Lydgate the incompetent hack hovers over these remarks; yet
at the same time Strohm's very specific connection of the poets' textual instabilities to the
"impossibility of Lancastrian requirements," also opens some space for the questions I
want to pursue in this essay. In Strohm's account, ideological imperatives have begun to
operate like poetry—that is, through ambiguity, contradiction, and other forms of textual complexity. If that is true, if even ideology has the density of poetry, then any simple
dichotomy between the two becomes impossible. Ideology and poetry are no longer mutually exclusive, and there are choices even the most ideologically motivated poet will
make on grounds that are primarily poetic. For this reason, I see my present endeavor as
a complement to ideological investigations like Strohm's (and indeed my own previous
work on Hoccleve and Lydgate).

  2. This argument originates with A. C. Spearing, *Medieval to Renaissance in English
Poetry* (Cambridge: Cambridge University Press, 1985), 59–120, and can also be found in
Larry Scanlon, *Narrative, Authority and Power: The Medieval Exemplum and the Chauce-
rian Tradition* (Cambridge: Cambridge University Press, 1994), 322–50; Nicholas Wat-
son, "Outdoing Chaucer: Lydgate's *Troy Book* and Henryson's *Testament of Cresseid* as
Competitive Inheritors of *Troilus and Criseyde*," in *Shifts and Transpositions in Medieval
Narrative: A Festschrift for Elspeth Kennedy,* ed. Karen Pratt (Cambridge: D. S. Brewer,
1994), 89–108; and Lerer, *Chaucer and His Readers,* 72–56. Though quite distinct, these

readings each derive with varying degrees of directness from Harold Bloom's highly gendered, psychoanalytic account of poetic influence, and they are united in taking Lydgate's frequent recourse to humility *topoi* as rhetorical disguises for his rivalry with Chaucer. I continue to find these readings convincing so far as they go. However, they are necessarily partial, for they still take Chaucer's dominance as already established. In viewing the relation between the two poets in largely instrumental terms they do not explain what attracts Lydgate to Chaucer in the first place, nor what Lydgate thought he might learn from Chaucer, nor why Lydgate was so convinced that Chaucer was entitled to the overarching authority Lydgate wanted to concede to him.

3. *Lydgate's Temple of Glas,* ed. Josef Schick, EETS, e.s., 60 (London: K. Paul, Trench, Trübner, 1891), xiv, cxxxiv–cxxxvi.

4. Ibid., xii.

5. Derek Pearsall, *John Lydgate* (London: Routledge & Kegan Paul, 1970), and *John Lydgate (1371–1449): A Bio-Bibliography,* English Literary Studies 71 (Victoria, BC: University of Victoria, 1997), 9.

6. In addition to equating "artistic structure" with the specifically Romantic ideal of organic unity, Schick also complains that Lydgate's sentences are impossible to punctuate (*Lydgate's Temple of Glas,* cxxxvi).

7. Immanuel Kant, *The Critique of Judgment,* trans. James Creed Meredith (Oxford: Clarendon Press, 1952), 41–42, 82–89.

8. Ibid., 152; emphasis in original. Cf. "What Is Enlightenment," in *Kant: Political Writings,* 2nd enl. ed., ed. Hans Reiss, trans. H. B. Nisbet (Cambridge: Cambridge University Press: 1991), esp. the opening paragraph (54):

> *Enlightenment is man's emergence from his self-incurred immaturity. Immaturity* is the inability to use one's own understanding without the guidance of another. This immaturity is *self-incurred* if its cause is not lack of understanding, but lack of resolution and courage to use it without the guidance of another. [emphasis in original]

9. Kant, *Critique of Judgment,* 168–69 (emphasis in original).

10. Sir Philip Sidney, *An Apology for Poetry,* ed. Geoffrey Shepherd (London: Thomas Nelson, 1965), 133.

11. Terry Eagleton, *The Ideology of the Aesthetic* (Oxford: Blackwell Publishers, 1990), 2–9, emphasis in original.

12. Ibid., 13–30.

13. Ibid., 4.

14. Isobel Armstrong, *The Radical Aesthetic* (Oxford: Blackwell Publishers, 2000), 2.

15. Ibid., 1–5.

16. Ibid., 79.

17. Ibid., 44–81.

18. Ibid., 79–80.

19. Ibid., 1. Armstrong also offers a more tortuous and conditional argument for the centrality of feminism and gender, based on Cora Kaplan's argument that "girls enter into language circuitously, with more complex negotiations with repression and absence than do boys." As a result of their "heightened sense of contradiction," women are in a particularly privileged position to engage in the "linguistic experiment" necessary for re-shaping the aesthetic (41–43). In what may be the book's most original chapter, Armstrong presents her case for "thinking affect," deconstructing the privileged association of reason with the sublime. Arguing that postmodernity's "fascination" with the sublime is founded on "the conviction that emotion and reason can never belong to each other," she responds with "two desiderata . . . first, to reconnect emotion and reason and to affirm the epistemic status of emotion and knowledge; second, to reclaim the social function of emotion" (108–48).

20. Ibid., 69.

21. Ibid., 30.

22. Ibid., 245, 256.

23. Francesco Petrarca, "La 'Collatio Laureationis' del Petrarca," ed. Carolo Godi, *Italia Medioevale e Umanistica* 13 (1970): 16, 23–27. The *Collatio* is most easily available in translation, as the "Coronation Oration" in Ernest Hatch Wilkins, *Studies in the Life and Works of Petrarch* (Cambridge: Medieval Academy of America, 1955), 300–313. Hatch's translation is based on an earlier edition: *Scritti inediti di Francesco Petrarca,* ed. Attilio Hortis (Trieste, 1874), 311–28. Subsequent citations are to the Godi edition; page numbers are given in the text. Translations are my own, though I have been guided by Hatch.

24. *The Riverside Chaucer,* ed. Larry Benson (Boston: Houghton-Mifflin, 1986); all further citations are to this edition. Throughout this chapter, all poetry is cited parenthetically in the text by line number or by book (or, as here, fragment) and line numbers.

25. M. C. Seymour, *A Catalogue of Chaucer Manuscripts,* vol. 2, *The Canterbury Tales* (Aldershot, Hants.: Scolar Press, 1997), 7–11.

26. *The Poetical Works of Geoffrey Chaucer: A Facsimile of Cambridge University Library MS GG.4.27,* 3 vols., ed. M. B. Parkes and Richard Beadle (Norman, OK: Pilgrim Books, 1980), 3:1. As Parkes and Beadle note, only two other manuscripts even come close. British Library MS Harley 1239 contains *Troilus and Criseyde* and five Canterbury Tales, while British Library MS Harley 7333 contains the *Canterbury Tales,* the *Parliament of Fowls,* and a number of Chaucer's shorter poems. The latter is best considered a miscellany, as it contains a wide variety of work by other poets. See M. C. Seymour, *A Catalogue of Chaucer Manuscripts,* vol. 1, *Works before the Canterbury Tales* (Aldershot, Hants.: Scolar Press, 1997), 21–23.

27. In this manuscript the poem includes the 628-line *Complaint,* which follows the envoy. Modern scholars have universally held the *Complaint* to be spurious, in all probability added, as Pearsall explains, "by a literal-minded scribe to fulfill the promise of a 'litel treatise in prais of women'" (*John Lydgate,* 109).

28. A. S. G. Edwards and Derek Pearsall, "The Manuscripts of the Major English Poetic Texts," in *Book Production and Publishing in Britain, 1375–1475,* ed. Jeremy Griffiths and Derek Pearsall (Cambridge: Cambridge University Press, 1989), 258.

29. Malcolm Andrew and Ronald Waldron, eds., *The Poems of the "Pearl" Manuscript* (Berkeley: University of California Press, 1978), p. 105, 1088–89.

30. Virgil, *Georgics* 3.291–92.

31. Lydgate may have drawn additional encouragement from the Invocation to book 3 of the *House of Fame.* Playfully addressed to Apollo, it ends with Chaucer's promise to kiss "the nexte laure y see" (1107).

32. Walter Hilton, *The Scale of Perfection,* 1.8.5a. In this passage Hilton is concerned to define the "perfect loving of God." In Evelyn Underhill's slightly modernized edition, the context is as follows:

> And that is when a man's soul first is reformed by fullhead of virtues to the image of Jhesu; and after when he is visited, is taken from all earthly and fleshly affections, from vain thoughts and imaginings of all bodily creatures, and as it were mickle is ravished out of the bodily wits and then by the grace of the Holy Ghost is illumined for to see by understanding Soothfastness, which is God, and ghostly things, with a soft sweet burning love in Him, so perfectly that by ravishing of love the soul is oned for the time and conformed to the image of the Trinity.

Walter Hilton, *The Scale of Perfection,* ed. Evelyn Underhill (London: John M. Watkins, 1923), 14.

33. Virgil, *Aeneid* 1.459–63.

34. David Wallace, *Chaucerian Polity: Absolutist Lineages and Associational Forms in England and Italy* (Stanford, CA: Stanford University Press, 1997), 65.

35. As Wallace demonstrates with a trenchant analysis of Shakespeare's treatment of the rude mechanicals in *Midsummer Night's Dream (Chaucerian Polity,* 119–24).

36. Here I am following Norton-Smith's reading of this passage; *John Lydgate: Poems,* ed. John Norton-Smith (Oxford: Clarendon Press, 1966), 181. Schick, in *Lydgate's Temple of Glas,* argues that the lovers are arranged according to physical age, but that reading cannot be sustained.

37. *Riverside Chaucer,* 137.

38. Thus the most widely distributed version of the tale in early modern England was a chapbook that first appeared in 1619. Entitled *The Ancient True and Admirable History of Patient Grisel,* it bears the engaging subtitle *How Maides, By Her Example, In Their Good Behaviour, May Marrie Rich Husbands; and Likewise Wives By Their Patience and Obedience May Gain Much Glorie.* The figure of Griselda remains a living part of Anglophone literature up to the present moment. For instance, she figures prominently Caryl Churchill's 1982 play, *Top Girls*; for further discussion, see my "What's the Pope Got to Do With It? Forgery and Desire in the *Clerk's Tale,*" *New Medieval Literatures* 9 (2003): 129–65.

39. Wallace, *Chaucerian Polity*, 261.

40. Cf. ibid., 226.

41. James Brundage, *Law, Sex, and Christian Society in Medieval Europe* (Chicago: University of Chicago Press, 1987), 3–4. As Brundage notes, "[M]odern states appropriated much medieval canonistic doctrine. A substantial part of legal doctrine about sexual activity and about matrimony in the Western world remains bound by its medieval Christian origins to this day."

42. Cf. ibid., 404–16.

43. Lawrence Stone, *The Family, Sex and Marriage in England, 1500–1800*, abridged ed. (New York: Harper & Row, 1979), 32.

44. Paul Strohm, *Hochon's Arrow: The Social Imagination of Fourteenth-Century Texts* (Princeton, NJ: Princeton University Press, 1992), 121–49.

45. Ralph A. Griffiths, "The Crown and the Royal Family in Later Medieval England," in *Kings and Nobles in the Later Middle Ages: A Tribute to Charles Ross*, ed. Ralph A. Griffiths and James Sherborne (New York: St. Martin's Press, 1986), 18–19.

46. Strohm, *Hochon's Arrow*, 95–119.

47. I take the term *commensurable* from David Herlihy, *Medieval Households* (Cambridge, MA: Harvard University Press, 1985). Herlihy argues that as early as the eighth century, medieval society began to move definitively away from the asymmetric "household system of antiquity," in which "different sectors of society possessed fundamentally different domestic units," toward a domestic system "commensurable and comparable" across "all levels of the social hierarchy" (v). Although Herlihy identifies a number of factors driving this change, he names chief among them the church, which "sought to impose a common rule of marriage upon all the faithful in all social classes. Two of its commands had a powerful impact upon marriages and the formation of households: exogamy and monogamy" (61).

48. Susan Crane, *The Performance of Self: Ritual, Clothing, and Identity during the Hundred Years War* (Philadelphia: University of Pennsylvania Press, 2002), 143–55. Crane argues that the "inferior elements" in the courtiers' costumes "transform identity, if only for the moment, in substantial compensation for the ritual's inability to transform the irregular marriage itself" (155).

49. John Lydgate, "A Mumming at Hertford," in *The Minor Poems of John Lydgate*, ed. Henry Noble MacCracken, EETS, o.s., 192 (London: Oxford University Press, 1934), 2:675.

50. Ibid., 2:679, lines 168–76. It is worth noting that Lydgate's other rewriting of Chaucer's envoy, "Bycorne and Chychevache," commissioned by "a werþy citeseyn of London," also presents itself as a dramatic piece. The running title in one of its three extant manuscripts, Trinity College, Cambridge, R. 3.19, describes it as a mumming (*Minor Poems of John Lydgate*, 2:433). If Maura Nolan is right to argue that Lydgate's mummings were a court form that he popularized by bringing to wealthy urban audiences, then this text offers a particularly interesting and complex instance of the symbolic commensura-

bility of marriage: the court's transposition of itself to a sphere of rustic domesticity now reappropriated by an upwardly mobile urban bourgeoisie.

51. *Middle English Dictionary,* in the *Middle English Compendium*, ed. Frances Mc-Sparren, http://ets.umdl.umich.edu/m/mec/index.html, sense 4 of *maistres(se* (n.).

52. Cf. Alain Renoir, *The Poetry of John Lydgate* (Cambridge, MA: Harvard University Press, 1967), 93: "In the *Temple of Glass* . . . Lydgate's preoccupation with the individual human being allows him to express what earlier poets of courtly love have failed even to suspect. He shows us the woman suffering"; and Lois Ebin, *John Lydgate* (Boston: G. K. Hall, 1985), 28–29: "Lydgate introduces a double complaint in the *Temple of Glass,* so that the poem embodies both the masculine and feminine perspectives." Lydgate effects a similar reversal in *A Gentlewoman's Lament.* As the rubric explains, this short poem is "a balade seyde by a gentilwomman which loved a man of gret estate." *Minor Poems of John Lydgate,* 2:418.

53. This reading seems to have begun with C. S. Lewis, *The Allegory of Love: A Study in Medieval Tradition* (London: Oxford University Press, 1936), 239–42. See also Pearsall, *John Lydgate,* 104–8, and *John Lydgate: Poems,* 178, 183.

4

Propaganda, Intentionality, and the Lancastrian Lydgate

Scott-Morgan Straker

Ask any Middle English scholar about John Lydgate, and the answer will probably include some of the following critical commonplaces: Lydgate was tedious, prolix, and devoted to Chaucer, although nowhere near as good. He produced an enormous array of texts for diverse occasions and patrons. He also "performed a semi-official role as apologist for the Lancastrian government";[1] he was a producer and disseminator of pro-Lancastrian ideology, asserting the legitimacy of the dynasty to rule over England and France in ways that conform to other royally sponsored discourses. He was, in other words, a propagandist. So entrenched in scholarly literature has the notion of the Lancastrian Lydgate become that it is rarely questioned, an oversight that in my view leads to a misunderstanding of Lydgate's relationship with his patrons, and consequently of the function of public poetry in the fifteenth century. Lydgate was capable of adopting a wide array of attitudes toward his patrons and of making complex statements to and about them. The familiar notion of the Lancastrian Lydgate imposes a false uniformity and simplicity onto those statements, preventing us from correctly assessing Lydgate's importance as a political writer.

I wish to reexamine some of the statements Lydgate makes to his Lancastrian patrons; in particular, I will take issue with critics who explicitly label Lydgate a propagandist. This label is misleading for two reasons. First, it is imprecise: it implies continuity between modern and medieval forms of political persuasion, whereas modern propaganda analysis defines propaganda as the product of twentieth-century technologies of communication. Second, it is based upon assumptions about the intentions behind the poems, assumptions that are not supported by the poems themselves. The texts I have chosen are three short poems that Lydgate produced between 1422 and 1432: *On Gloucester's Approaching Marriage, The Title and Pedigree of King Henry VI,* and *King Henry VI's Triumphal Entry into London.* Nothing in Lydgate's oeuvre seems to bear out charges of propaganda better than these poems: they shamelessly glorify royal dynasts and portray as immanent and legitimate a sovereignty that was in fact highly contingent. Nevertheless, I shall argue that the label "Lancastrian propaganda" applies to none of them: the first is not propaganda at all, the second is ambiguous, and the third, although propaganda, is in no meaningful sense Lancastrian. I will begin by outlining the consensus that Lydgate's poetry in some way supported the Lancastrian dynasty.

Several scholars argue that the Lancastrians adopted a deliberate policy of cultivating support among the middle classes by fostering the use of English in the nation's legal, political, and cultural institutions; one component of this policy was the patronage of vernacular poets such as Chaucer, Hoccleve, and Lydgate.[2] None of these poets is more firmly connected with royal policy than Lydgate. His historiographical narratives have been tied to royal interests: several critics link the *Troy Book,* commissioned by Henry V, to royal legitimation,[3] and the *Siege of Thebes* has been shown to rely on rhetorical strategies that originate in diplomatic documents and other royally sponsored discourse.[4] However, the occasional poems that Lydgate wrote during the 1420s and 1430s are most consistently associated with royal propaganda. J. W. McKenna has shown how several of Lydgate's poems participated in a systematic campaign by the council to muster support for England's overlordship of France, a campaign that encompassed numismatics, visual art, and public spectacle as well as literary texts.[5] Most decisive of all, Derek Pearsall insists that Lydgate's propagandistic activity is one of his few innovations: Lydgate is "the first English poet . . . to fashion his poems as instruments of royal policy."[6] Dissenters to this consensus are few.[7] For the majority of scholars, Lydgate provided ideological support for his Lancastrian patrons, and this propagandistic role provides one of the best reasons to read him. We who work on this maligned poet dispense with such reasons at our peril.

Earlier critics are the most likely explicitly to call Lydgate a propagandist. For example, V. J. Scattergood states, "One would expect dynastic propaganda from Lydgate, who . . . had assumed a sort of unofficial laureateship."[8] Richard Firth Green refers to Lydgate's "role as a Lancastrian propagandist."[9] Derek Pearsall's *John Lydgate: A Bio-Bibliography* contains the following heading: "Lancastrian Propagandist and Laureate Poet to Crown and Commons, 1426–32";[10] headings are particularly effective in reifying interpretations into facts. Subsequent writers tend to speak of Lydgate's political engagement in more general terms.[11] For example, Rita Copeland does not argue that specific poems by Lydgate support specific royal policies; rather, his entire concept of rhetoric serves to reify royal hegemony. Fifteenth-century poets such as Lydgate and Hawes pay lip-service to the scientific model of rhetoric promoted by vernacular intellectuals such as Brunetto Latini, Dante, and Gower; however, their association of rhetoric purely with verbal ornamentation deprives it of its deliberative function and renders it purely epideictic, suited to aggrandizing the power of political patrons.[12] Lee Patterson subscribes to a widespread view of Lydgate as a poet not fully in control of his utterance. In the *Siege of Thebes,* Lydgate "took it upon himself both to exemplify and to promote his role as the monastic supporter of Lancastrian rule" by basing his poem on political ideologies evident in royal diplomacy.[13] However, Lydgate's pro-Lancastrian ideology is undermined by his intractably antifoundationalist Theban subject matter.[14] Finally, Ambrisco and Strohm argue that the quest for literary legitimacy in the prologue to Lydgate's *Troy Book* resonates with the Lancastrian dynasty's quest for political legitimacy. However, this resonance occurs not because of Lydgate's intention but because of the symbolic function of fifteenth-century kingship: "The uneasy Lancastrian throne may, in other words, be seen as a place of collection *and* projection of legitimacy-fears, an exceptionally charged site, but by no means the only significant one, for the expression of deep unease about symbolic guarantees."[15] Instead of associating Lydgate with propaganda, these accounts delimit Lydgate's relationship with political authority in terms of his culture: that relationship lies beyond Lydgate's conscious control, determined by either his understanding of the literary tools at his disposal, his subject matter, or the sign system in which he operates.

The critics who avoid the term *propaganda* seem to me to be on safer ground, but they are also hedging their bets. The Lancastrian Lydgate must be either a flatterer or a propagandist, and the discursive acts that these critics attribute to Lydgate go beyond simple flattery. Although it can have public consequences, flattery is essentially a private relationship whereby the flatterer manipulates his sovereign to achieve some personal benefit. Lydgate certainly derived personal benefit in the form of patronage from his literary output, but the emphasis of these critics is on Lydgate's attempt to justify or glorify his patrons to a larger audience. Flattery and propaganda are actually quite different types of utterance: the former is addressed to the individual who forms its subject, while the latter is addressed to a group that is not its direct beneficiary. The nature of the utterance is therefore dependent upon its context, which comprises both audience and intention. If you tell a king that he is great, it is flattery; if you tell a king that he is great within earshot of someone else and with the intention of being overheard, it is propaganda. All of the critics I have cited share three assumptions about Lydgate's relationship with his Lancastrian patrons, assumptions that imply propaganda even when critics avoid this term. First, Lydgate speaks on behalf of power to some larger public. Second, whereas flattery is inimical to true sovereignty,[16] Lydgate is complicit in promoting the ideological goals of his patrons. Third, the defining characteristic of Lydgate's political utterances is their falsity, a characteristic that is explained with reference either to Lydgate's intention or to the culture in which he operates. The term that best encapsulates these assumptions about addressee, complicity, and falsity is *propaganda;* the critics who openly use this term express a consensus that many others tacitly accept. To assess the validity of this consensus, it is necessary to investigate what propaganda entails and how it might apply to a medieval author.

Propaganda and Intention

Researchers into historical uses of propaganda must first determine whether propaganda can even exist in premodern societies. Many modern attempts to theorize political persuasion define propaganda in terms of modern technologies of mass communication.[17] Indeed, one of the most influential theorists views propaganda exclusively as the product of modern technology: "[P]ropaganda must be conducted within the context of the technological society. Propaganda is called upon to solve the problems created by technology, to play on maladjustments, and to integrate the individual into a technological world."[18] There are historical surveys of political persuasion that accept the existence of premodern propaganda; unfortunately, they tend to treat the Middle Ages only superficially, and sometimes inaccurately.[19] These surveys operate within the analytical parameters laid down by studies of twentieth-century propaganda, which fall into two groups: those that treat propaganda as a distinct use of language that differs from normal communication and those that view propaganda merely as a subsection of the general category of persuasive rhetoric. Analysts falling into the first group aim to inoculate readers against propaganda by identifying its manipulative strategies. In the 1930s, the American Institute for Propaganda Analysis formulated seven techniques that propagandists use to distort the truth, all of which are designed to foster immediate, emotional responses.[20] Subsequent scholarship brought the tools of linguistics or General Semantics to bear on the problem of propaganda.[21] These techniques share a commitment to formalism: they treat language as an autonomous system that is subject to scientific analysis. Just as a physicist can define the mechanical laws of motion, the linguist can establish the normative rules for communication and identify propaganda by its violation of those rules. Propaganda is thus a dangerous simulacrum of communication, designed to penetrate its hearers' defenses and distort their perception of the truth.

These formalist approaches will not help us to understand the Lancastrian Lydgate. There is an obvious problem of anachronism: definitions of propaganda in terms of modern discourses cannot easily be transposed to any political statement that Lydgate might make. However, what concerns me more are the assumptions of falsity and complicity implicit in these approaches, which arise from predetermined ideological positions: propaganda always manipulates its hearers for sinister or at least selfish purposes, the power that it sustains is always harmful, and the propagandist is always complicit. Formalist methods pose as objective analysis that helps the vulnerable to identify harmful discourse but in fact offer a taxonomy of decision that has already been made on political grounds. These ideological assumptions prevent us from seeing that some propagandistic lies are useful. For example, the myth of the melting pot, by which people of diverse origins are theoretically forged anew as Americans, equal in worth and privilege, is not in any sociological sense true, but it is an extremely useful myth for promoting tolerance of immigration and assimilation. Some propaganda is even true, or situated between truth and falsity. Consider a Soviet May Day parade, in which a display of military hardware is linked to an ideology of Soviet strength and progress through unity: the ideology may be questionable, but the bombs are real. To analyze a spectacle such as this, it is not enough to determine the degree of truth it expresses; the analyst must also examine its purpose, or the effect it is intended to have on its audience. Jacques Ellul divides propaganda into two categories: agitative, which urges people to do something, and integrative, which urges them to believe something, to accept some political or economic structure. According to Ellul, all communities require integrative propaganda to survive, because it is through propaganda that they incorporate individuals into themselves, unify the behavior of their members, and disseminate their values to other communities.[22] This requirement is nowhere stronger than in modern technological society, in which so much of the information that we need in order to function comes at second hand. Because all information must persuade us to accept it as valid even when we cannot verify it against our experiences, the distinction between information and propaganda is in practice impossible to maintain.[23] Owing in part to Ellul's influence, the trend in recent studies of propaganda has been to treat it as a subsection of public relations, one that is not formally distinct from other persuasive uses of rhetoric, such as advertising.[24] These studies are perhaps on safer methodological ground than those of the formalists but are no more applicable to the Middle Ages; Lydgate is certainly not drawing on commercial discourses to sell his patrons.

To understand Lydgate's political statements, we need a method for linking them to social action that takes account of the different tasks such utterances can perform, that avoids the ideologically motivated assumption of falsity, and that does not attribute unverifiable motives to Lydgate. One possible alternative is Quentin Skinner's use of speech act theory to distinguish between intention and motive. According to speech act theory, an utterance's meaning comprises three components: locution, or the message its words denote; illocution, or the speaker's intentional state in uttering the message;[25] and perlocution, or the effect the message causes. Skinner illustrates these components with the following example: a policeman shouts to a skater, "The ice over there is thin." The statement's locutionary force communicates to the skater that the ice is liable to break, and its illocutionary force issues a warning.[26] Illocutionary acts such as warning, praising, blaming, thanking, apologizing, and so forth do not necessarily tell us anything about the speaker's motive. The policeman may be motivated by sincere concern for the skater's well-being, but perhaps he is indifferent to the skater and is simply doing his job. Without more context, we cannot tell. Illocution or intention is thus the task that a speaker performs in making a meaningful utterance; motive is antecedent to and causative of the utterance but lies outside of it and is therefore irrelevant to its meaning.[27] Whereas intention is a property of the utterance and can be interpreted within a given social context, motive is a property of the speaker and cannot necessarily be extrapolated from intention.

I will now propose some criteria for analyzing Lydgate's political discourse, criteria that I hope will show that the label "Lancastrian propagandist" obscures the range of statements that Lydgate's poems make. Previous discussions of Lydgate's political discourse are based on two methodologically unsound assumptions: first, they imply Lydgate's complicity in the agenda of his Lancastrian patrons to assert their legitimacy (an assumption of motive), and second, they treat that agenda as spurious (an assumption of falsity). Both assumptions may be true in some cases, but they overlook important statements that Lydgate is making and not making in the poems I have chosen to examine. As an alternative, I propose to begin by examining the audience to which these poems are addressed. Thanks to the mass media, modern propaganda can appear to originate with authority figures themselves, as is the case with a parliamentary speech to the throne or a presidential address. In contrast, the medieval propagandist's voice is interposed between the authority about which it speaks and the audience that is the target of its perlocutionary aim. This middle position requires propaganda to perform two speech acts at once. Toward authority it must appear to be constative, not doing anything but simply describing an immanent reality that exists regardless of the propagandist's utterance. Toward the audience it must be performative, producing the unity, abstract support, or concrete action that perhaps would not exist without it.[28] Of course, this appearance is an illusion: propagandistic discourse is performative on all levels, especially in what it says about authority. However, it must appear to describe, not produce, the reality of that authority. The discursive position of a propagandistic utterance, then, is as important as the content of the utterance; in addition to considering what it says, we must ask where an utterance originates and at whom it is aimed.

Propaganda must also obscure the gap between motive and intention. For a given illocutionary act there can be a number of motives, but the propagandist must appear to be fully invested in his utterance; in other words, he must appear to be complicit.[29] It follows that irony has a very limited role to play in propaganda: a propagandist can employ irony to ridicule his opponents, but his speech act must otherwise betray no hint of distance between his locution, or what his words appear to say, and the illocutionary act that makes the most sense for that locution. If any irony is discernible in Lydgate's words about his patrons, then we need to reconsider the nature of his illocutionary act. Finally, deciding whether Lydgate's political utterances can be called propaganda is only part of my task. Scholars who call Lydgate a propagandist have shown that his representations of individual Lancastrian dynasts and of the dynasty's legitimacy correspond to similar representations in other royally sponsored discourses. Certainly, it is important to know how Lydgate's poems fit into a larger public relations exercise. However, it is equally important to specify the sort of action to which they impel the audience. Does Lydgate urge readers to agitate or integrate, to do or to believe? The answer again pertains to intentionality: I hope to show that Lydgate performs a wider array of illocutionary acts toward specific but diverse audiences than scholarship has hitherto recognized. Change the audience and you change the illocutionary act; rather than focusing on whether Lydgate's poems are propaganda, I prefer to analyze the intentional states Lydgate manifests toward specific audiences.

I hope to demonstrate with these criteria the necessity of intentionality as an interpretative category in discussions of Lydgate's political discourse: any attempt to analyze this discourse must recognize intentionality as a factor in textual meaning. To that end, I will approach three of Lydgate's supposedly propagandistic poems by asking the following questions: Where does this discourse originate, and at what audience is it aimed? What speech acts does it appear to perform? What is its intention, by which I mean, what social act does it perform in a given context? Finally, what claim does it make on its audience? That is to say, if we determine that it is propaganda, is it agitative or integrative?

Before turning to Lydgate, I will apply these criteria to the *Gesta Henrici Quinti* to highlight the difference between Lydgate's poems and a more overtly propagandistic work. The *Gesta* is a Latin prose chronicle written in 1417 by an unidentified royal chaplain who accompanied Henry on his invasion of France in 1415. Thus it originates in the middling position of propaganda, mediating between the king and his subjects who were not present on his campaign. The *Gesta* quite specifically meets the needs of royal policy: in 1417, Henry V was preparing his second invasion of Normandy and had to justify the coming campaign at home and abroad, in particular at the Council of Constance, the gathering of European clergy that had convened in 1414 to heal the Great Schism. The French delegates and their allies disputed England's right to represent Scotland and Wales and even to participate in the conference at all; they also resented the controversial partisanship shown by the council's secular patron, Emperor Sigismund, to the English cause.[30] To support the English position, the *Gesta* portrays Henry as a devoutly pious Christian prince who does his utmost to avoid shedding Christian blood; his campaigns are attributable purely to the willful arrogance of the French, who refuse to accede to Henry's just demands, and his victories furnish proof that God is on his side. The following passage is representative:

> [T]he French council (cleaving inordinately to its own will, which it treats as though it were law) could not, by any equitable course or just means, be induced to accept such a peace without immense injury to the crown of England and perpetual disinheritance of the same in certain of the most noble parts of it belonging to us in that kingdom, although to procure that peace the king had been willing to make concessions noble and notable enough. At length, not perceiving any other remedy or means by which he might attain his right, he hastened to seek a ruling from the Supreme Judge, deciding to wield, with His help, the power of his just sword and by use of this blameless sword to exact what the French, by their blameworthy and

unjust violence, have for so long a period of time striven to usurp and with-hold. (15)

Henry appears not as an aggressor but as a benevolent but exasperated king who is compelled by rebellious subjects to fight for what is rightfully his.

The *Gesta*'s representation of Henry is fully consonant with other royally sponsored statements about Henry's objectives, such as diplomatic documents or parliamentary sermons.[31] Moreover, the *Gesta* itself refers to other documents and pronouncements originating with the king and his council that substantiate the same position; in other words, it acknowledges its status as one component of a complex, centrally orchestrated propaganda campaign. For instance, the *Gesta* refers to a dossier of documents that Henry ordered to be compiled to illustrate his title to the duchy of Aquitaine; he ordered copies of this dossier to be sent to Sigismund and the delegates at Constance so "that all Christendom might know what great acts of injustice the French in their duplicity had inflicted on him, and that, as it were reluctantly and against his will, he was being compelled to raise his standards against rebels" (17–19). Elsewhere, the *Gesta* summarizes the sermon about England's military victories preached by Henry Beaufort, bishop of Winchester and chancellor of England, at the opening of Parliament in March 1416: "he referred to the triumphs of our king which God had afforded him against the obstinacy of the French, . . . and he concluded from this that the title of the crown of England to the kingdom of France had been divinely made plain" (123). Far from exhibiting any resistance to this claim, the *Gesta* author interjects a fervent statement of support: "O God, why does this wretched and stiff-necked nation not obey these divine sentences, so many and so terrible, to which, by a vengeance most clearly made manifest, obedience is demanded of them?" (125).

The *Gesta* author's statements about Henry appear to be constative, simply declaring the plain truth that is amply attested in other documents and even in the playing out of historical events. However, the writer's illocutionary act is clearly directed not toward Henry but toward Henry's subjects or potential allies at the Council of Constance. To this audience, the writer's speech act is not constative but performative because it seeks to bring a state of affairs into being by expressing it. Its function is integrative, uniting readers in the belief that Henry enjoyed divine support, that his cause was just, and that his foes were themselves responsible for their suffering, and vindicating Sigismund for his partisanship. This belief could be translated into concrete action by the other, more agitative components of this coordinated campaign.[32] I will now turn to Lydgate's poetry to show how unlike the *Gesta* it is.

An Exemplary Couple

On Gloucester's Approaching Marriage[33] praises Jacqueline of Hainault and Humphrey, Duke of Gloucester, rejoices at their coming nuptials, and expresses the wish that their union should benefit England in the way that Henry's marriage to Katherine of Valois unified England and France. The poem must have been written in 1422, probably before the death of Henry V on 31 August of that year.[34] Although the envoy is addressed to Jacqueline, most scholars accept the possibility that the poem was commissioned by Humphrey.[35] Lydgate's epithalamion has hitherto impressed no one with its political acumen: Derek Pearsall states, "Nothing could better illustrate Lydgate's lack of contact with political realities," but grudgingly admits that "if it had to be done it is hard to know how it could have been done better."[36] Paul Strohm's brief discussion claims that the poem is rife with inconsistencies but rejects the possibility that they might be deliberate:

> [Lydgate] develops his poems in terms so inherently flawed, contradictory, and unsusceptible of belief as to pose an interpretative problem in their own right. Whether because of the inherent impossibility of his descriptive mandate, or the promptings of his own imp of the perverse, Lydgate constantly veers toward the very things that cannot be said, and the very images that discredit or destabilize his enterprise.[37]

Because we know a priori that Lydgate was congenitally subservient and a bit thick, we must attribute any inconsistencies in his work not to his volition but to the intractability of his task: "Lydgate's aspiration to full complicity was unwavering, but the impossibility of Lancastrian requirements drove even the most resolutely loyal texts into a morass of embarrassing half-acknowledgements and debilitating self-contradictions."[38] Lancastrian poetics becomes nothing but an extended parapraxis. Strohm overlooks the possibility that Lydgate's procedure was deliberate; once we admit this possibility, Strohm's "debilitating self-contradictions" become a coherent strategy for balancing political criticism with the decorum of addressing powerful patrons. I will argue that Lydgate's epithalamion reveals a poet who is profoundly aware of the political danger that his patron's actions pose.

The centerpiece of English diplomacy during the 1420s was the fragile Burgundian alliance. English ambitions in France were greatly abetted in 1419 by the murder of John the Fearless, Duke of Burgundy, who was lured into an ambush at Montereau by the Dauphin Charles. Burgundy's successor, his son

Philip the Good, allied with Henry V: Philip agreed to support Henry's claim to the French throne in return for Henry's undertaking to bring the dauphin to justice.[39] In 1420, Henry pressed home his advantage by marrying Katherine of Valois, daughter of Charles VI, and forcing Charles to sign the Treaty of Troyes: the terms of this treaty dispossessed the dauphin and named Henry as Charles's heir. Despite Henry's diplomatic success, his victory was far from secure; when he died unexpectedly on 31 August 1422, leaving an infant son as his heir, the English faced a difficult task in maintaining their hold on northern France against the dauphin's supporters. Without the alliance with the Duke of Burgundy, this task would have been impossible.[40] The flight of Jacqueline of Hainault to England dealt that alliance a critical blow.

Jacqueline was heir to Hainault, Holland, and Zeeland, counties that bisected the Burgundy estates and that hence were coveted by successive dukes. In 1418, John the Fearless arranged for Jacqueline to marry his nephew, John IV, Duke of Brabant. However, Jacqueline's uncle, John of Bavaria, bishop of Liège, also claimed title to her inheritance and tried to prevent the marriage. The result was civil war in Flanders, with the Duke of Burgundy taking John of Brabant's side and Emperor Sigismund supporting John of Bavaria. Jacqueline's marriage went ahead, but the incompetent Duke of Brabant alienated her affections in 1420 by mortgaging Holland and Zeeland to John of Bavaria. Soon afterwards, Jacqueline left his court and sought refuge in England, where Henry V welcomed her and even agreed to pay her expenses.[41] This welcome was a cause of concern to Philip the Good, since it suggested that Henry was taking an interest in Burgundian affairs. Philip's concern increased when Henry's youngest brother, Humphrey, Duke of Gloucester, began to take an interest in Jacqueline. Humphrey was not a happy man in 1422: his attempts to extend his authority in England after Henry V's death and to claim the right of guardianship of the infant Henry VI were both rebuffed by Parliament.[42] On finding his political ambitions thwarted at home, Humphrey turned his attention to the international stage: he married Jacqueline of Hainault in 1422 and declared his intention to recover Jacqueline's inheritance from the Duke of Burgundy's vassal. England was drifting toward a war with its crucial ally.

Lydgate's task of celebrating the marriage of Humphrey and Jacqueline required him to find a way to praise one of the worst diplomatic blunders of the century. The marriage was disastrous for three reasons. First, it alienated the ally on whom England's cherished French holdings depended: by 1424, an English army under Humphrey was openly at war with the Duke of Burgundy, and only the exertions of Humphrey's older brother John, Duke of Bedford, prevented the Burgundian alliance from collapsing years earlier than it ultimately did. Second, the legality of the marriage was doubtful, since Jacqueline was already married to the Duke of Brabant. Jacqueline and Humphrey obtained a dispensation to marry from the anti-Pope Benedict XIII, but the authority of his dispensation was dubious; it took the other pope, Martin V, six years to reach a decision about the marriage, during which time it languished in legal limbo.[43] Finally, the marriage deepened divisions within England. Humphrey's relations with his fellow councilors were not cordial: his hostility toward his arch-rival Henry Beaufort, bishop of Winchester, flared into armed conflict in 1425, and Humphrey's ham-fisted intervention into domestic and foreign politics strained his relationship with John, Duke of Bedford. It is impossible to determine how much of this future dissension Lydgate could foresee in 1422, but it was probably apparent to most observers that Gloucester's marriage would not foster political harmony. Lydgate's awareness of these problems explains certain strategies that he adopts in his poem. The manifest danger posed by the marriage required Lydgate to adopt a meticulously apolitical rhetoric of praise; however, his carefully deployed literary, biblical, and historical references covertly restore the political context and hence expose the danger.

Lydgate begins his poem by asserting the power of marriage to unite nations and links that power to a providential order:

> The heven aboue disposethe many thinges
> Which witt of man can not comprehende:
> The faatal ordre of lordes and of kynges
> To make somme in honnour hye ascende,
> And somme al-so ful lowe to descende,
> And in loue eeke to lacen and constreyne,
> Hertes tenbrace in Iubiters cheyne.
>
> Thus cam in first the knotte of allyaunce
> Betweene provynces and worthy regyouns,
> Folkes to sette in pees and acordaunce,
> To beon alloone in theyre affeccouns [sic]
> And to exclude alle devysyouns.
>   (8–19)[44]

Lydgate alludes to Chaucer's *Knight's Tale,* which concludes with Theseus's Boethian speech likening the cosmic order to a "faire cheyne of love" (1.2988).[45] However, Lydgate uses this image quite differently from Chaucer. Theseus posits an eternal and immutable "Firste Moevere" from whom all things derive:

"Nature hath nat taken his bigynnyng / Of no partie or cantel of a thyng, / But of a thyng that parfit is and stable, / Descendynge so til it be corrumpable" (1.3007–10). To each element of this hierarchically arranged universe the Creator has assigned a fixed span of time: Theseus lists some of these elements, beginning with the natural world (an oak, a stone, a river), proceeding to human creations (great towns), and finally to humans themselves (men and women, kings and pages), concluding that although their spans differ, all must eventually pass away (1.3017–30). Theseus thus incorporates humanity into a natural order governed by a celestial design. The only correct response to the universal fact of death is one of Stoic acceptance:

> Thanne is it wysdom, as it thynketh me,
> To maken vertu of neccessitee,
> And take it weel that we may nat eschue,
> And namely that to us alle is due.
> And whoso gruccheth ought, he dooth folye,
> And rebel is to hym that al may gye.
>   (1.3041–46)

The apolitical, universalizing text that Theseus utters has a very political context: Theseus seeks to bring about the marriage between Palamon and his sister-in-law Emelye, definitively incorporating Theseus's former Theban adversary into the Athenian polity that he rules. Theseus's speech thus underwrites exactly the sort of political marriage to which Lydgate refers, but it conceals its political nature behind a universalizing cosmology.[46] Lydgate's appropriation of Jupiter's chain renders explicit the politics that Theseus's rhetoric tries to conceal. Whereas Theseus portrays the marriage of Palamon and Emelye as a pious act of submission to the divine ordinance that governs the entire natural world, Lydgate links marriage to the human world of politics, the "faatal ordre of lordes and of kynges" (10). This order is neither eternal nor stable but is characterized by endemic competition for honor: it makes "somme in honnour hye ascende, / And somme al-so ful lowe to descende" (11–12). Marriage is therefore a tool of political rivalry in a system in which one lord's success entails another's defeat. Although this system is under divine control, it is one of "many thinges / Which witt of man can not comprehende" (8–9), and its process of rising and falling fortunes seems incompatible with the harmonious political relations in which the poem places so much hope. Lydgate's opening lines oppose ideal to actual; this opposition intensifies when he provides examples of political marriages.

Lydgate's first example is drawn from ancient history: "Recorde I take of Calydoyne and Arge, / Howe thoo landes so broode, so wyde, so large, / Were maked oon . . . / By maryage, wheeche a-fore were tweyne" (32–35). The reference is to the marriage between Tydeus, son of Oeneus, King of Calydon, and Deipyle, daughter of Adrastus, King of Argos. The consequences of this marriage are well known to readers of Lydgate's *Siege of Thebes,* a work that dates to the same period as *On Gloucester's Approaching Marriage.*[47] Adrastus's other daughter is married to Polyneices, who is feuding with his brother Eteocles over the kingship of Thebes. As a result of these marriages, Adrastus, Tydeus, and the kings of nearly every other Greek city state become embroiled in a fratricidal war that consumes the lives of all the Greek heroes who participate, save only Adrastus, who returns to Argos to die prematurely of sorrow. The events that begin with a political marriage culminate in two calamities:

The worthy blood of al grece spilt,
And Thebes ek, of Amphion bylt,
With-oute Recur brought vnto Ruyne
And with the soyle made pleyn as a lyne,
To wildernesse turnyd and desert,
And Grekys ek falle into pouert,
Both of her men and also of her good;
For fynaly al the gentyl blood
Was shad out ther, her woundys wer so wyde,
To los fynal vnto outher syde.

(4636–44)[48]

Clearly some realms are best not united. Lydgate's citation of this marriage in his epithalamion is straightforward irony: the passage implies that the marriage was politically constructive, but anyone familiar with the myth would know that it was exactly the opposite.

The irony involved in Lydgate's second example is more complex. This example is taken from recent history: it was the marriage of Henry V and Katherine of Valois that "here to-forne, as made is remembraunce, / The werre stynt of England and of Fraunce" (41–42). No sooner does Lydgate place the union of these realms in the past—the war ended "here to-forne"—than he projects it once more into the future: "And, as I hope, of hert and menyng truwe / The mortal werre ceese shal and fyne, / Betweene thoo boothe, and pees ageyne renuwe" (43–49). The celebrated union of England and France is both past and future, both a historical event concluded and consigned to memory and a fervent hope for an indefinite future. It is everywhere but here and now. In a sense, Lydgate is historically accurate: the Treaty of Troyes officially ended the war, but by 1422 it was apparent that peace was as far from reach as ever. Within weeks of marrying Katherine, Henry was once more fighting the dauphin; in 1421 he lost his brother Thomas to an ambush at Baugé and mounted a protracted siege of Meaux that proved costly in both money and lives.[49] However, Lydgate is surely also voicing skepticism over the potential of marriages to resolve wars. Immediately after putting off Anglo-French peace to the future, Lydgate claims that marriage will enable "oure Brettaygne / To fynde a wey wherby we may atteyne / That Duchye of Holand by hool affeccoun [*sic*] / May beo allyed with Brutus Albyoun" (53–56). By linking the two marriages, Lydgate makes the first a precedent for the second. When Lydgate claims that Humphrey's marriage will unite England and Holland in the way that Henry's united England and France, what exactly is he saying?

From the outset of the poem, Lydgate's strategy is ironically to undermine the attentive reader's faith in political marriages. Lydgate's fair chain of marriage is not a principle of cosmic harmony but a tool of political struggle; it is not voluntary but serves "in loue to lacen and constreyne" the hearts of lords and kings (13). The historical examples he cites show that political marriages do not always bring about "pees and vnytee" and that unification has sometimes led to calamity. These examples are all the more pointed because they both concern disputed inheritances: like the thrones of Thebes and France, Jacqueline's inheritance was disputed by a close relative. One interpretation of Lydgate's historical examples is that getting involved in such disputes through marriage can lead to further violence. In the rest of the poem, Lydgate uses similarly pointed references to cast further doubt on Humphrey and Jacqueline's marriage. Lydgate turns his attention to the personal qualities of the bride and groom, which he extols using platitudes that appear to be disconnected from any specific circumstances; he can do little else without acknowledging that the marriage is likely to cause an international incident. Nevertheless, intimations of danger slip in through a series of comparisons that Lydgate draws between the bride and groom and exemplary figures from the Bible and classical myth.

Lydgate praises Jacqueline as follows:

As Hester meeke, and as Iudith saage,
Flouring in youthe lyke to Polixseene,
Secree feythful as Dydo of Cartage,
Constant of hert lyche Ecuba the qweene,

And as Lucresse in loue truwe and cleene,
Of bountee, fredame, and of gentylesse,
She may be called wel lady and maystresse.

Feyre was Heleyne, liche as bookes tellethe,
And renommed as of seemlynesse;
But sheo in goodnesse fer aboue excellethe.

(71–80)

Several of the stories behind these women bear an eerie resemblance to the political circumstances of Jacqueline's marriage. Both biblical women use their influence over men to score a victory for their nation. Esther manipulates her husband, King Ahasuerus, to procure the murder of her political opponent Aman and to enable the Jews to slaughter their enemies throughout the realm. Judith capitalizes on Holofernes' lust to gain an opportunity to murder him and thus liberate her nation from a foreign conqueror. Jacqueline is likewise engaged in a struggle to free her nation from an overbearing conqueror, the Duke of Burgundy. Furthermore, these comparisons cast her relationship with Humphrey in an unflattering light, implying that he is being seduced into assisting a foreign people.

The remaining women to whom Jacqueline is compared all intensify conflict in some way, usually at high personal cost. They are all victims of male violence or perfidy, which would hardly reassure Jacqueline, but their implications are even more sinister for Humphrey. Lydgate's *Troy Book,* completed in 1420, recounts the sacrifice of Polixena by the victorious Greeks before their homecoming; this homecoming leads to a sequence of civil wars that exterminate all the survivors of Troy. The *Troy Book* also describes how Hecuba lures Achilles into an ambush that costs him his life, an association that Humphrey cannot have found appetizing; Hecuba subsequently goes mad from grief when all of her offspring are slaughtered or enslaved. Lucrece is raped by Tarquin and commits suicide, which precipitates the permanent expulsion of the Roman kings. Lucrece's martyrdom sparks the birth of a republic, an accomplishment that Humphrey, a member of the royal family, would doubtless not want his wife to emulate. Dido is another seductive foreigner, but she is also a distraction: she represents the temptations of Aeneas's oriental past that threaten to deflect him from his nation-building mission.[50] Likening Jacqueline to Dido casts Humphrey in the role of Aeneas and therefore implies that the foreign adventure to recover Jacqueline's inheritance distracts him from his own nation-building responsibilities as a member of England's governing council.[51] Finally, while it is reassuring that Jacqueline's goodness exceeds that of the notorious Helen, this comparison is the most pointed of all. Helen was carried off from her husband Menelaus and married to her foreign captor Paris. The resulting Trojan War was a disaster for the nations of both her husbands. Jacqueline already had a husband, the hapless Duke of Brabant, when she married Humphrey, and her second marriage likewise heralded a war between her two husbands' nations. Even a superficial knowledge of the stories behind the women to whom Lydgate compares Jacqueline should cause the reader to doubt Lydgate's assertion that Jacqueline's arrival in England will cause "A nuwe sonne to shynen of gladnesse, / In boothe londes, texcluden al derknesse / Of oolde hatred and of al rancour" (60–62).

Turning to Humphrey, Lydgate links him to the knightly ideals of *sapientia et fortitudo:* he is "best pourveyed of manhood and of might, / . . . And is also of wisdam and prudence" (124–26). Humphrey then receives his own set of exemplary comparisons:

> For with Parys he hathe comlynesse,
> In trouth of loue with Troyllus he doothe shyne,
> And with Hectour he hathe eeke hardynesse,
> With Tedeus he hathe fredam and gentylesse,
> Wal of Bretayne, by manly vyolence,
> Ageyne hir foomen to standen at defence.
> . . . .
> With Salamoun hathe he sapyence,
> Faame of knighthoode with Cesar Iulius,
> Of rethoryk and eeke of eloquence
> Equypollent with Marcus Tulius,
> With Hanubal he is victorious,
> Lyche vn-to Pompey for his hyeghe renoun,
> And to gouuerne egale with Cypyoun.
> (134–54)

Some of these allusions pick up on references that Lydgate has already made: Humphrey is the Paris to Jacqueline's Helen, and the comparison to Tydeus reminds us that the union by marriage of Calydon and Argos involved both nations in the disastrous civil war between the Theban brothers Polyneices and Eteocles. Tydeus is not the only figure linked to civil war. Julius Caesar's "knighthoode" was employed in the civil war with Pompey; it also led to his murder, which sparked the civil war that claimed the life of Marcus Tullius

Cicero. These intimations seem pointed given Humphrey's notable talent for civil strife: his lifelong habit of quarrelling with fellow councilors brought England close to civil war in the 1420s and led to his arrest and death in 1447.[52] There is a further link between the men to whom Humphrey is compared: most of them are emblems of futility. Solomon is legendary for his wisdom but also for his decline into dotage and idolatry: his wisdom could not save him any more than Cicero's eloquence could prevent his murder. Hannibal's initial victories culminate in defeat and suicide. Hector's "hardynesse" cannot prevent his death in battle; indeed, in Lydgate's *Troy Book,* his wife's intervention inflames Hector's hardihood, causing him to abandon his accustomed prudence and resulting in his death (3.4896–5399).[53] Finally, Troilus's "trouth of loue" is not matched by his lover Criseyde, who abandons him for the enemy soldier Diomede. Jacqueline had also abandoned one husband to take up with a foreign warrior, who would shortly be besieging her first husband's strongholds. These grim associations betray anxiety over Humphrey's conduct: they certainly confirm the "manly vyolence" that Lydgate attributes to him (139), but they also demonstrate that this violence can have socially disastrous results. Only the example of Scipio seems untinged by irony.

The comparisons that Lydgate draws between the happy couple and their unhappy historical counterparts identify the intended audience of the poem: although the envoy addresses Jacqueline, the poem is really aimed at Humphrey. Jacqueline's associations are simply sinister while Humphrey's are tragic, both in the medieval sense that they entail a reversal from greatness to disaster and in the Aristotelian sense that the very quality that distinguishes the hero can lead to his downfall. Jacqueline's comparisons make her out to be a scheming, foreign seductress and a victim, and there is nothing much to be done about that. Tragedy, however, can be averted if only the tragic hero can recognize the qualities that render him vulnerable: if Humphrey could but recall the histories of the men he is said to resemble, he might be motivated to try to avoid their tragic fate. When Lydgate asserts Humphrey's learning, he lists the intellectual disciplines in which his patron excels: "he doothe his witt applye / To reede in bookis, wheeche that beon moral, / In Hooly Writt with the allegorye, / He . . . [is] expert in poetrye, / With parfounde feeling of phylosofye" (141–47). This reading list omits an important category of writing, one with which Lydgate was much preoccupied: history. If Humphrey was as learned in history as he is said to be in other disciplines, he would have understood the poem's references, and Lydgate might have had to do some fast talking.

Lydgate claims that because of Humphrey's "knyghtly fame," he is worthy "To beo regystred in the Hous of Ffaame" (132–33). Paul Strohm rightly observes that Lydgate offers "no explicit recognition of the scandal such recognition would imply for any careful reader of Chaucer's poem."[54] I would argue that this recognition is implicit, and that just as Chaucer exposes the arbitrariness and superficiality of fame, Lydgate's catalog of massacred worthies criticizes the martial masculinity that is so important a part of Humphrey's public identity. When "This Martys sone" is married to Jacqueline, Lydgate assures us, "Thane were this lande in ful sikurnesse / Ageyns thassaute of alle oure mortell foone" (155–63). But who are these "mortell foone" who threaten the union of England and Holland? The obvious candidate is the Duke of Burgundy, the ally upon whom England's prior union with France depends. One union can be achieved only at the expense of another, and the political coup that Humphrey hopes to achieve by marrying Jacqueline threatens to undo what his older brother Henry V achieved in marrying Katherine. Lydgate's epithalamion thus does not make a clear, constative statement about Humphrey; instead, it uses irony to raise a series of questions. Can political marriages unite nations? If so, should the newer union displace the older? Lydgate's depoliticizing strategy of concentrating on the couple's personal qualities surreptitiously reminds us of the political context: If Jacqueline is so free from vengefulness (94–95) and Humphrey is so prudent, why are they transforming England's one-time ally into a mortal foe? The poem so completely undermines its celebration of the marriage that Lydgate must be either monumentally stupid or actually rather clever. In my view, the consistency with which Lydgate's irony points the reader toward the political context favors the latter conclusion.

By associating Humphrey and Jacqueline with figures responsible for the outbreak or escalation of violence, Lydgate encourages his readers to reflect upon the relevance of these tragic historical episodes to the present situation. However, the poem's illocutionary force is directed not toward an audience of subjects but toward Humphrey. Lydgate uses irony to admonish Humphrey's conduct: he links political marriages not to peace but to conflict, reminds Humphrey of the dire consequences such marriages have had in both the classical and the recent past, and surrounds Humphrey and his bride-to-be with a network of sinister associations that expose the risks that the couple is incurring. The poem's illocutionary act, then, is one of warning. I am making no claim about Lydgate's motive: perhaps he privately wished to expose Humphrey as a dangerous political imbecile, or perhaps he was sincerely devoted to Humphrey and wanted him to mend his ways to avert disaster. Neither motive can be extrapolated from the poem. What can be seen clearly is the ironic gap between Lydgate's utterance about his patron and his intentional state. It is therefore wrong to categorize *On Gloucester's Approaching Marriage* as Lancastrian propaganda: it admonishes the authority figure about which it speaks, and if it has any integrative function, it urges its readers to integrate by questioning the actions of a prominent Lancastrian dynast.

Disclaiming and Mediating

The Title and Pedigree of Henry VI is a translation of a French poem written by Laurence Calot at the Duke of Bedford's instigation; Calot's poem was intended to assert Henry VI's legitimacy to a French audience and was accompanied by a genealogical diagram demonstrating the boy-king's descent from St. Louis on both his mother's and father's side.[55] The poem's effectiveness has been questioned: Lee Patterson argues that it "bespeaks by the very ardor of its commitment the tenacity of the doubts it means to remove."[56] I think that its propagandistic valence is undermined in a less roundabout manner and that its commitment to its position is less firm than it appears.

First, we must distinguish between the part of the poem that Lydgate attributes to Calot and the parts in which he discusses his task as translator. Calot's poem is enclosed within two sections of discourse by Lydgate, a 74-line prologue that is set off from the rest of the poem in the manuscript and a 68-line epilogue that is not separate but that contains a clear shift in subject. Lydgate's enclosure thus comprises nearly half of the poem's 329 lines and sits in an uneasy relationship to the rest. Calot's component is propaganda in very much the way that the *Gesta Henrici Quinti* is. The poem signals its status as part of a larger campaign by referring to the genealogy.[57] It is clearly addressed to an audience of subjects, sending an integrative message by urging them to believe in Henry VI's legitimacy and to offer him their support. We can be more specific about this intended audience: it is clearly French. The poem claims that the dauphin's treacherous murder of John, Duke of Burgundy, "Caus[ed] in soth his vnabilite / For to succede to any dignite, / Of knyghtly honure to regne in any lond" (103–5). Because the dauphin had disqualified himself, God provided an alternative heir in Henry VI (109–33). The implication is that if the dauphin had not committed the murder, there would have been no need for Henry to succeed; this is not the English position, according to which the English kings were always the legitimate kings of France, regardless of the dauphin's conduct.[58] The rest of Calot's poem outlines the protocol surrounding the Treaty of Troyes and describes in detail the marriage ceremony between Henry V and Katherine of Valois (156–207). This focus on legalism and ceremony is clearly designed to distinguish Henry V from his rival: whereas the dauphin scorns the law, Henry "in no wise list not be exempte; / From poynt to poynt list no thing withdrawe, / The bonde filowyng of Holy Chirche lawe" (199–201). Calot resorts to a standard propagandist's technique of deflecting our attention from something that is at issue to something that is not. Presumably, no one doubted that Henry VI's parents were lawfully married; they doubted that he was King of France. However, Calot is also drawing on his audience's loyalty to the Valois dynasty. Does Henry's legitimacy derive primarily from his father or mother? French and English readers would answer this question differently.

Calot's poem is a straightforward example of integrative propaganda, albeit one whose message does not correspond to the official English position. Lydgate's enclosure complicates matters. He begins by praising the Earl of Warwick, citing the earl's victorious campaigns and devotion to Henry VI, and stating that Warwick commanded him to translate Calot's poem (1–34). He then states that the Duke of Bedford, equally victorious and devoted to Henry, commissioned Calot's original (35–54). Finally, he turns to his own role: "I, as he that durst not withsey, / Humbly his biddyng did obey, / Ful desirous him to do plesaunce" (55–57). This familiar persona of the fearful and subservient poet eliminates any responsibility for his utterance that he might otherwise have to bear: he disclaims any intention beyond that of flattering his patron. In other words, he shows his propagandistic utterance to have been wholly instigated by interested parties. What I am calling Lydgate's epilogue is equally noncommittal: he describes how Calot "toke on him the laboure of this werk" (269) and reminds the reader that the Earl of Warwick "Gaf me precept in conclusioun / To make therof a playn translacioun" (284–85). He ends by telling us the date on which he began it and describes at length the astronomical conjunctions that attended this event (287–323). The only purpose for this passage that I can imagine is to evoke the astrological determinism that invariably accompanies reference to celestial movements. In effect, Lydgate's enclosure of Calot's poem attributes responsibility for the poem to Warwick, to Bedford, to Calot himself, perhaps even to the stars—everywhere, in fact, but to Lydgate. I have claimed that one of propagandistic features of the *Gesta Henrici Quinti* is its alignment with other officially sponsored documents; however, the *Gesta* author stops short of identifying the king or his supporters as the cause of his writing and declares his unwavering belief in the claims he propagates. No such declaration is present in Lydgate's *Title and Pedigree*.

Calot's propagandistic message is directed toward a French audience; Lydgate's message is clearly directed toward a different audience, an English one. About Henry VI's legitimacy the poem's speech act appears to be constative, as one would expect of propaganda, but one seeks in vain for a message aimed toward an audience of subordinates in Lydgate's section of the poem. We cannot attribute Calot's utterance to Lydgate, since Lydgate himself disclaims responsibility for it. The speaker neither aligns himself with his utterance nor ironically distances himself from it. His illocutionary force is directed toward his patron (he aims to please), but toward any other audience no intentional state is discernible. We have, then, a piece of integrative propaganda embedded within a framework that exposes its propagandistic origin but that makes no propagandistic claim of its own. *The Title and Pedigree of Henry VI* fails as propaganda, but not because it protests too much. Rather, it protests too little: it smothers a positive message within an utterance that is almost purely phatic.

At least one of Lydgate's poems, *King Henry's Triumphal Entry into London*,[59] is unambiguously propagandistic, although not in a way that one might expect. This poem describes a royal entry made by Henry VI on 21 February 1432; it was probably commissioned by the mayor of London, since its envoy is addressed to him (531–37) and the poem praises him on several occasions (e.g., 57–63, 342–48). This poem functions as propaganda for the mayor, and more importantly for the city of London, asserting its close relationship with the king and its blessed status as the site of Henry's return from France (510–23). What it is *not*, however, is Lancastrian propaganda, in the sense of justifying the king's actions or legitimacy or asserting the reality of his power. Instead, it asserts the tractability of Lancastrian power, portraying the king in a state of potentiality and as an object of instruction. The degree to which Lydgate's poem circumscribes Henry VI's power becomes clear if the 1432 pageant is contrasted with the a prior royal entry on which it is clearly modeled, namely the entry that Henry V made into London on 23 November 1415, following his victory at Agincourt.[60] One obvious difference is that Henry V genuinely was a victorious king, returning home after inflicting a crushing defeat on his enemies; the triumph in the title of Lydgate's poem is purely notional. Henry V is an active presence in his pageant, not in the sense of what he does, but in the way that he provides a focus for the pageant's Christological imagery: "Henry V is indisputably the centre of the pageant: meanings crystallise around him. He is the Christ figure who fulfills the trope of the New Jerusalem, whose entry accompanied by the polyvalent Benedictus qui venit rewrites all the Old Testament signs and Old Testament kings. . . . [H]e is the point where meanings converge, the transcendental signified."[61] The king's genuine accomplishments facilitate his identification with the victorious biblical king David and the Messiah whom David typifies; this identification in turn integrates London and the whole nation into a biblical model of kingship in which the king and his victories are authorized by God.

Henry VI was ten years old at the time of his 1432 London entry, and his youth requires Lydgate to adopt a different strategy. Instead of receiving worship, as Henry V does, the younger Henry receives an array of intangible gifts. These gifts take many forms: the mayor offers him welcome, the "sturdy champeoun" on London Bridge offers him protection from his foes (85–91), and a series of allegorical female figures (Dame Sapience, Mercy, Trouthe, and so forth) offer him the ethical and intellectual attainments over which they preside. Where Henry V is a king in actuality, Henry VI is a king in potential, and the spectators witness an elaborate schoolroom allegory in which he starts in a state of blankness and has the attributes of kingship progressively inscribed upon him. His power is not immanent like his father's; rather, the logic of the pageant places him in a subordinate position to all of the real and allegorical agents who participate in his formation. This subordination is most apparent in a striking instance of doubling. At the climax of Henry V's 1415 pageant, Henry encounters a figure enthroned in the form of the sun; the logic of this pageant identifies this solar king with God the Father, thereby casting Henry as God the Son coming to take up his dominion in the New Jerusalem. In Henry VI's pageant, when the boy king arrives at London's Conduit, he sees the following spectacle: "myddys above in ffull riche array, / Ther satte a childe off beaute precellyng, / Middis off the throne rayed like a kyng" (276–78). This pantomime king is "governe[d]" by three women—Mercy, Trouthe, and Clemens—who are necessary to keep "His myhty throne ffrom myschieff and ffallyng" (289), and by two judges and eight sergeants, who remind us that "kyngis, princes, shulde aboute hem drawe / Folke that be trewe and wel expert in lawe" (305–6). Henry is confronted by a vision of himself as a child, not yet governing but governed, dependent on female virtues for his inner character and on male expertise for his public office. The 1415 pageant situates Henry V at the symbolic center of an apocalyptic kingship; Henry VI's pageant places him in the nursery. The fact that the child is positioned above him displaces him from this spectacle of mediated power: Henry VI is subordinate even to this simulacrum of himself.

Although Henry VI's pageant draws on the features of his father's London entry seventeen years before, its orientation toward the mayor and London and its transformation of the spectacle of kingship scatters and deflects the Christological focus of the earlier pageant. Lydgate's poem is propaganda; more specifically, it is an allegory of proprietorship. Part of this allegory is aimed at Henry, showing him the attributes that he must attain to be a king. However, the passive role into which he is cast, and his dependence on a kaleidoscopic sequence of allegorical parent figures for the attributes that he requires, emphasize not the immanence but the contingency of his kingship. A true king knows that it is better to give than to receive. Built upon this educative allegory is an additional one that incorporates the city of London into the process of the king's construction. London's geography is mapped onto the king's psyche: he receives the seven liberal arts at Cornhill, his sense of justice at the Conduit, and the blessing of the Trinity at St Paul's. (At Westminster he receives £1000.) London becomes indissolubly part of the king's identity, creating for the city and its inhabitants a powerful proprietorship over the king: he is beholden to them not only for his welcome and his gifts both tangible and intangible but also for his very self. So while it is quite accurate to view *The Triumphal Entry* as propaganda, it is not in any simple sense Lancastrian.[62]

The standard view of Lydgate's subservient Lancastrianism is simply false with regard to *On Gloucester's Approaching Marriage* and conceals important truths about the other poems under discussion. Like the parts of the *Troy Book* that are addressed to Henry V, *On Gloucester's Approaching Marriage* offers veiled criticism of its patron's militarism and performs the illocutionary act of warning. *The Title and Pedigree of Henry VI* embeds integrative propaganda within a framework with no discernible intention toward its audience. Only *King Henry VI's Triumphal Entry into London* seems to me to be unequivocally propagandistic; however, its direct beneficiary is not Lancastrian power, and certainly not Henry VI, but rather the city of London as a community and the mayor that presides over it. It is integrative propaganda of the sort that communities use to define, unite, and promote themselves; it is essential to the very existence of communities. It is tempting here to reach the simple conclusion that there is good and bad propaganda and that Lydgate wrote the good kind; however, I do not think that this conclusion is warranted. All varieties of propaganda, whether agitative or integrative, are equally spurious, and equal in their potential to lead to constructive or destructive action. In his massive oeuvre, Lydgate constructs communities out of many planks, only some of which are admirable: prudence, pacifism, and knowledge of history, but also xenophobia and hostility toward women. A more satisfactory reason for insisting upon the integrative function of Lydgate's political discourse rests not upon an evaluation of different types of propaganda but upon precise understanding of the nature of Lydgate's social engagement. It is a fundamental misunderstanding of Lydgate to assert his complicity in his patrons' self-interested and aggressive agendas, because such an assertion overlooks his willingness to criticize those agendas. Instead, I would align Lydgate's illocutionary acts with the public poetry that Anne Middleton situates in the late fourteenth century.[63] Public poetry, with its devotion to the common weal and its mandate to offer advice to princes, enables Lydgate to balance the roles of loyal subject and political critic. My claim that Lydgate is a public poet does not attribute to him the liberal human-ism of formalist attempts to inoculate modern society against the dangers of propaganda: just as propaganda is not automatically false, communitarian rhet-oric is not automatically free from violent exclusions and oppressive ideologies. It does, however, categorize Lydgate's political discourse more accurately than the label of propagandist.

To interpret Lydgate's public poetry we must define the nature of his illocu-tionary acts and the audience at which they are aimed; in other words, we re-quire the category of intentionality to assess the social function that these texts perform. A grasp of intentionality shows why the standard assumptions of fal-sity and complicity explain these poems so badly. Readers who are committed to the established view of Lydgate may simply conclude that he was as incompe-tent at propaganda as he was at everything else. Although this is not a view I share, it is perhaps preferable to the alternative of categorizing him as some-thing that he was not. If readers turn to Lydgate seeking propaganda, that is to say an alliance between political authority and culture to harness a community in pursuit of that authority's ends, they will in almost all cases be disappointed. Let us instead read Lydgate for what he was: a historian, a writer of religious verse, a popularizer of learned culture, a misogynist, and a pacifist.

Notes

1. R. F. Green, *Poets and Princepleasers: Literature and the English Court in the Late Middle Ages* (Toronto: University of Toronto Press, 1980), 189.

2. The case for a royally sponsored language policy is most forcefully stated—in my view, overstated—by John H. Fisher, "A Language Policy for Lancastrian England," *PMLA* 107 (1992): 81–100; see also John M. Bowers, "The House of Chaucer & Son: The Business of Lancastrian Canon-Formation," *Medieval Perspectives* 6 (1991): 135–43. Christo-pher Baswell, "*Troy Book*: How Lydgate Translates Chaucer into Latin," in *Translation Theory and Practice in the Middle Ages,* ed. Jeanette Beer, Studies in Medieval Culture (Kalamazoo: Medieval Institute Publications, Western Michigan University, 1997), 215–37, argues that Lydgate attempts to transfer the cultural authority of his Latin source (Guido delle Colonne's *Historia destructionis Troiae*) to vernacular Troy books such as Chaucer's *Troilus and Criseyde* and his own.

3. According to Alan S. Ambrisco and Paul Strohm, "Succession and Sovereignty in Lydgate's Prologue to the *Troy Book*," *Chaucer Review* 30 (1995): 40–57, the prologue sup-ports the dynasty's legitimacy. Nicholas Watson, "Outdoing Chaucer: Lydgate's *Troy Book* and Henryson's *Testament of Cresseid* as Competitive Imitations of *Troilus and Cri-*

seyde," in *Shifts and Transpositions in Medieval Narrative: A Festschrift for Dr Elspeth Kennedy,* ed. Karen Pratt (Cambridge: D. S. Brewer, 1994), 89–108, sees in the poem a reflection of Henry's rigorous personal morality (101). Baswell, "*Troy Book,*" finds support for Henry's imperialist agenda in France: the *Troy Book* "bodies forth a poem of England's imperial and genealogical origin—Troy—in which is implicit an argument for England's current imperial claims on the Continent" (217).

4. Lee Patterson, "Making Identities in Fifteenth-Century England: Henry V and John Lydgate," in *New Historical Literary Study: Essays on Reproducing Texts, Representing History,* ed. Jeffrey N. Cox and Larry J. Reynolds (Princeton, NJ: Princeton University Press, 1993), 69–107.

5. J. W. McKenna, "Henry VI of England and the Dual Monarchy: Aspects of Royal Political Propaganda, 1422–1432," *Journal of the Warburg and Courtauld Institutes* 28 (1965): 145–62.

6. Derek Pearsall, "Lydgate as Innovator," *Modern Language Quarterly* 53 (1992): 15. See also the chapter entitled "Laureate Lydgate" in Derek Pearsall, *John Lydgate* (London: Routledge & Kegan Paul, 1970), 160–91.

7. David Lawton, "Dullness and the Fifteenth Century," *ELH* 54 (1987): 761–979, asserts Lydgate's pacifism (779); James Simpson, "'Dysemol daies and Fatal houres': Lydgate's *Destruction of Thebes* and Chaucer's *Knight's Tale,*" in *The Long Fifteenth Century: Essays for Douglas Gray,* ed. Helen Cooper and Sally Mapstone (Oxford: Clarendon Press, 1997), 15–33, demonstrates Lydgate's rejection of the chivalric ethos of his aristocratic patrons. I have argued elsewhere that Lydgate's *Troy Book* criticizes Henry V's martial or marital practices; Scott-Morgan Straker, "Rivalry and Reciprocity in Lydgate's *Troy Book,*" *New Medieval Literatures* 3 (1999): 119–47.

8. V. J. Scattergood, *Politics and Poetry in the Fifteenth Century* (London: Blandford Press, 1971), 73.

9. Green, *Poets and Princepleasers,* 190.

10. Derek Pearsall, *John Lydgate (1371–1449): A Bio-Bibliography,* English Literary Studies 71 (Victoria, BC: University of Victoria, 1997), 28.

11. There are exceptions, though. Linne B. Mooney, "Lydgate's 'Kings of England' and Another Verse Chronicle of the Kings," *Viator* 20 (1989): 255–89, identifies Lydgate's "Kings of England sithen William Conqueror" as "not only a prototype but a paragon of English propaganda" (263). This claim is especially important because it situates Lydgate at the beginning of a national tradition of propaganda. Similarly, Seth Lerer, *Chaucer and His Readers: Imagining the Author in Late Medieval England* (Princeton, NJ: Princeton University Press, 1993), writing about the period from 1429 to 1436, states, "Lydgate . . . comes off as a vigorous propagandist for the Lancastrian house during these years" (14). Lerer argues that Lydgate's poetic fictions are always predicated upon a fiction of patronage: "[H]is construction of an 'aureate' past peopled by 'laureate' poets . . . suggested that the definition of a poet is to be found, in part, in the nature of his patron, and further, that the ideal patron for a poet is the state itself" (61). Lerer is quite right to emphasize Lydgate's investment in idealized portrayals of literary patronage; however, I

question his characterization of Lydgate's relationship with "the state," a characterization that makes propaganda fundamental to Lydgate's poetics.

12. Rita Copeland, "Lydgate, Hawes, and the Science of Rhetoric in the Late Middle Ages," *Modern Language Quarterly* 53 (1992): 57–82, reprinted as chapter 9 of the present volume.

13. Patterson, "Making Identities," 74.

14. The "Theban story inevitably called into question both the commitment to purposive action and the rectilinear transmission of value from the past that underwrite medieval monarchy" (ibid., 97).

15. Ambrisco and Strohm, "Succession and Sovereignty," 53–54.

16. All medieval political theorists see flattery as a threat to political order, either because it subordinates the sovereign's will to that of his subjects or because it fosters the unbridled sovereign will that leads to tyranny. John of Salisbury, *Policraticus,* ed. and trans. Cary J. Nederman (Cambridge: Cambridge University Press, 1990), treats flattery as a form of usurpation: "You believe that service is meted out; you are actually subjected to an extreme and distressing servitude" (20–21).

17. E.g., Leonard W. Doob, *Propaganda: Its Psychology and Technique* (New York: Henry Holt, 1935), 333–404; William Castle Hummel and Keith Gibson Huntress, *The Analysis of Propaganda* (New York: Dryden Press, 1955), 5–14.

18. Jacques Ellul, *Propaganda: The Formation of Men's Attitudes,* trans. Konrad Kellen and Jean Lerner (New York: Knopf, 1965), p. xvii. In *Histoire de la propagande* (Paris: Presses Universitaires de France, 1967), Ellul discusses instances of medieval propaganda but insists that modern definitions and analytical techniques will not work for earlier periods: "La propagande actuelle présente des caractères qui ne se retrouvent dans aucun des phénomènes politiques du passé. On est alors obligé ou de choisir une définition très vague qui ne correspond pas vraiment au fait actuel, ou bien, si l'on part de la situation contemporaine, de considérer qu'il n'y a jamais eu de propagande dans le passé" (5).

19. For an overview of propaganda in English history, see Bertrand Taithe and Tim Thornton, "Propaganda: A Misnomer for Persuasion?" in *Propaganda: Political Rhetoric and Identity, 1300–2000,* ed. Bertrand Taithe and Tim Thornton, Themes in History (Thrupp, Stroud, Gloucestershire: Sutton Publishing, 1999), 1–24. For individual instances, see Robert Brentano, "Western Civilization: The Middle Ages," in *The Symbolic Instrument in Early Times,* ed. Harold D. Lasswell, Daniel Lerner, and Hans Speier (Honolulu: University Press of Hawaii, 1979), 552–95; and Philip M. Taylor, *Munitions of the Mind: A History of Propaganda from the Ancient World to the Present Era* (Wellingborough: Stephens, 1990). Oliver Thomson, *Easily Led: A History of Propaganda* (Thrupp, Stroud, Gloucestershire: Sutton Publishing, 1999) links the nature of specific instances of medieval propaganda to the institutions (such as the papacy, the cult of saints, and religious orders) that spawned them; the most important institutions in the late Middle Ages were national monarchies, which patronized and exploited literary texts to suit their purposes (120–65). Unfortunately, Thomson's discussion is marred by errors and untenable assertions: he cites Lydgate as the author of "The Libel of English Policies" *(sic)* (158) and claims that Malory's *Morte Darthur* "bolstered" Edward IV's rule (159).

20. Institute for Propaganda Analysis, "How to Detect Propaganda," *Propaganda Analysis* 1 (1937): 1–4. The techniques are name-calling, glittering generality, transfer, testimonial, plain folks, card-stacking, and the band wagon.

21. Charles A. Fleming, "Understanding Propaganda from a General Semantics Perspective," *Et Cetera* 52 (1995): 3–12, shows that the institute's seven discursive techniques violate the six principles of General Semantics. Terence P. Moran, "Propaganda as Pseudocommunication," *Et Cetera* 36 (1979): 181–97, lists techniques by which propagandists deprive the audience of control. Suzanne C. Schick, "Propaganda Analysis: The Search for an Appropriate Model," *Et Cetera* 42 (1985): 63–71, takes all of these methods to task for neglecting the context in which propaganda occurs.

22. Ellul, *Propaganda,* 62–70.

23. Jacques Ellul, "Information and Propaganda," *Diogenes* 18 (1957): 61–77.

24. J. A. C. Brown, *Techniques of Persuasion: From Propaganda to Brainwashing* (Baltimore: Pelican Press, 1963), offers a psychoanalytic comparison of propaganda and persuasion in general communication. James E. Combs and Dan D. Nimmo, *The New Propaganda: The Dictatorship of Palaver in Contemporary Politics* (New York: Longman, 1993), and Anthony R. Pratkanis and Elliot Aronson, *Age of Propaganda: The Everyday Use and Abuse of Persuasion,* rev. ed. (New York: W. H. Freeman, 2001), study propaganda alongside other forms of persuasion, including advertising.

25. John R. Searle, *Intentionality* (Cambridge: Cambridge University Press, 1983), details the relationship between intentional states and speech acts. Chapter 1, "The Nature of Intentional States," defines intentionality as "that property of many mental states and events by which they are directed at or about or of objects or events in the world" (1). If I assert, deny, believe, or doubt that Henry VI is the legitimate king of France, these statements exhibit both propositional content ("Henry VI is the legitimate king of France") and an intentional state. In the first two cases, this intentional state is the illocutionary force of the speech act that presents the statement (asserting, denying); in the latter two, it is the psychological mode in which the propositional content is held (believing, doubting). Searle distinguishes between intentionality and intentions: "[I]ntending to do something is just one form of Intentionality along with belief, hope, fear, desire, and lots of others; and I do not mean to suggest that because, for example, beliefs are Intentional they somehow contain the notion of intention or they intend something or someone who has a belief must thereby intend to do something about it" (3). When I state that illocutionary acts are intentional, I am using the general sense of intentional states rather than the specific sense of intending to do something.

26. Quentin Skinner, "'Social Meaning' and the Explanation of Social Action," in *The Philosophy of History,* ed. Patrick Gardiner, *Oxford Readings in Philosophy* (Oxford: Oxford University Press, 1974), 106–27.

27. Quentin Skinner, "Motives, Intentions and the Interpretation of Texts," in *On Literary Intention: Critical Essays,* ed. David Newton de Molina (Edinburgh: Edinburgh University Press, 1976), 210–21.

28. For these two basic categories of speech act, see J. L. Austin, *How to Do Things with Words,* ed. J. O. Urmson (Oxford: Oxford University Press, 1962): a constative utter-

ance describes a reality that preexists the utterance, while a performative creates by the act of utterance the condition to which it refers. Austin himself undermines this distinction by suggesting that all utterances are performative: even description performs a socially consequential act.

29. Most definitions of propaganda emphasize the self-interested motivation of the propagandist: see, e.g., Garth S. Jowett and Victoria O'Donnell, *Propaganda and Persuasion,* 2nd ed. (Newbury Park, CA: Sage Publications, 1992), 6. The propagandist's task is to make his hearers believe that his motives are in alignment with their interests.

30. For the chronicle's date, authorship, and purpose, see the introduction to the excellent edition by Frank Taylor and John S. Roskell, eds., *Gesta Henrici Quinti: The Deeds of Henry the Fifth* (Oxford: Clarendon Press, 1975), xviii–xxviii.

31. Ibid., xxix–xxxii; Patterson, "Making Identities," 78–87.

32. In identifying the *Gesta* as propaganda, I am in no way impugning its value as a historical source; its description of Henry's invasion of Normandy is one of the best surviving accounts of a medieval English military campaign. The fact that the *Gesta* can be both thoroughly propagandistic and an invaluable witness to historical events illustrates why the assumption of falsity can be so unhelpful to our understanding of medieval political persuasion.

33. *The Minor Poems of John Lydgate,* ed. Henry Noble MacCracken, EETS, o.s., 192 (London: Oxford University Press, 1934), 2:601–8. All further citations are to this edition.

34. The poem's mention of Henry V (48–49) and the absence of explicit reference to his sudden and shocking death imply that he was still living when the poem was composed.

35. Pearsall simply assumes this commission (*John Lydgate,* 165), and Scattergood writes, "[T]here is no evidence to prove that this poem was commissioned by Humphrey, but it would be surprising if it were not" (*Politics and Poetry,* 146).

36. Pearsall, *John Lydgate,* 165–66.

37. Paul Strohm, *England's Empty Throne: Usurpation and the Language of Legitimation, 1399–1422* (New Haven, CT: Yale University Press, 1998), 192–93. This book is a tour de force of scholarship, brilliantly exposing the complex relationships between political power and textual culture during the fifteenth century. All the more surprising, then, is the author's unwillingness to see this complexity in Lydgate's work.

38. Ibid., 195.

39. Paul Bonenfant, *Du meurtre de Montereau au Traité de Troyes* (Brussels: Palais des Académies, 1957); Christopher Allmand, *Henry V* (London: Methuen, 1992), 128–50.

40. Henry himself seems to have understood this: the Norman chronicler Monstrelet states that on his deathbed Henry charged his councilors to preserve the Burgundian alliance. *Chronique d'Enguerran de Monstrelet en deux livres avec pièces justificatives, 1400–1444,* 6 vols., ed. L. Douët-d'Arcq, Société de l'histoire de France (Paris, 1857–1862), 4:110.

41. The fullest account of Jacqueline's turbulent life is by Richard Vaughan, *Philip the Good: The Apogee of Burgundy* (London: Longman, 1970), 31–49. See also Ralph A.

Griffiths, *The Reign of King Henry VI: The Exercise of Royal Authority, 1422–1461* (London: Ernest Benn, 1981), 68–93.

42. S. B. Chrimes, "The Pretensions of the Duke of Gloucester in 1422," *English Historical Review* 45 (1930): 101–3.

43. Vaughan, *Philip the Good*, 32–34.

44. Throughout this chapter, poetry is cited parenthetically in the text by line number or by book (or fragment) and line numbers.

45. Larry D. Benson, ed., *The Riverside Chaucer*, 3rd ed. (Boston: Houghton Mifflin, 1987). All further citations are to this edition.

46. Cf. David Aers, *Chaucer* (Brighton: Harvester Press, 1986): "Theseus transforms the *Consolation of Philosophy* into a *Consolation of Political Authority*. . . . Indeed, the present social order is naturalised, eternalised and given divine rather than human and historical foundations" (30–31).

47. Most critics date the *Siege* to 1421; see Johnstone Parr, "Astronomical Dating for Some of Lydgate's Poems," *PMLA* 67 (1952): 251–58. Simpson, "'Dysemol daies,'" prefers to date the poem after Henry V's death in 1422.

48. *Lydgate's Siege of Thebes*, 2 vols, ed. Axel Erdmann and Eilert Ekwall, EETS, e.s., 108, 125 (London: Kegan Paul, Trench, Trübner, 1911, 1930). All further citations are to this edition.

49. For Henry's campaigns from 1420 to 1422, see Allmand, *Henry V*, 151–82.

50. This is of course the Virgilian Dido; Ovid's Dido is an innocent victim, one of the numerous women consumed and destroyed by the male epic enterprise. Chaucer signals his awareness of these competing interpretations of Dido in book 1 of his *House of Fame*, which both indicts and excuses Aeneas's betrayal (293–432). The irony of Lydgate's use of Dido in his epithalamion likewise depends upon an awareness of both traditions. If you think of the Ovidian Dido, then Lydgate is eulogizing Jacqueline (she is an innocent victim, like Dido) while casting doubt upon Humphrey's role (to whom is Jacqueline faithful? Will Humphrey prove more worthy of that faith than Aeneas?). However, if you remember the Virgilian Dido, then Lydgate's comparison is less flattering and implies that Humphrey is making a mistake in getting mixed up with Jacqueline.

51. This comparison is more prescient than Lydgate can have intended in 1422: as Aeneas abandons Dido, so did Humphrey abandon Jacqueline in 1427 to marry one of Jacqueline's ladies-in-waiting, Eleanor Cobham.

52. Griffiths, *Reign of King Henry VI*, 68–93.

53. *Lydgate's Troy Book*, 4 vols., ed. Henry Bergen, EETS, e.s., 97, 103, 106, 126 (London: Kegan Paul, Trench, Trübner, 1906, 1908, 1910, 1935) (all further citations are to this edition). The comparison with Hector therefore does not reflect well on Jacqueline.

54. Strohm, *England's Empty Throne*, 193.

55. McKenna, "Henry VI," 151–53; Patterson, "Making Identities," 89–93. Sarah Gaunt, "Propaganda: Political Rhetoric and Identity, 1300–2000," in Taithe and Thornton, *Propaganda*, 27–39, cites one of the surviving copies of this genealogical diagram as an example of integration propaganda (32–33).

56. Patterson, "Making Identities," 93.

57. *Minor Poems of John Lydgate*, 2:613–22, lines 123–25.

58. Maurice Keen, "Diplomacy," in *Henry V: The Practice of Kingship*, ed. G. L. Harriss (London: Oxford University Press, 1985), 181–200.

59. *King Henry's Triumphal Entry into London*, in *Minor Poems of John Lydgate*, 2:630–48.

60. A detailed account of Henry V's entry survives in Taylor and Roskell, *Gesta*, 100–112. The order of stages in the two pageants is identical, and many of the same props were clearly used in both: e.g., the giant on London Bridge (Taylor and Roskell, *Gesta*, 102; Lydgate, *King Henry's Triumphal Entry*, lines 71–91).

61. Sarah Tolmie, "*Quia Hic Homo Multa Signa Facit:* The Royal Entry of Henry V into London, 23 November 1415," in *The Propagation of Power in the Medieval West: Selected Proceedings of the International Conference, Groningen 20–23 November 1996*, ed. Martin Gosman, Arjo Vanderjagt, and Jan Veenstra (Groningen: Egbert Forsten, 1997), 375.

62. This is not to say that the council could not derive some benefit from the pageant. The political support that London could offer the king was no less valuable than the customs revenue it provided to the royal coffers. Lydgate's poem records two brief prose speeches in which the mayor welcomes Henry to London, "other wyse called youre Chaumbre" (*Minor Poems of John Lydgate*, 2:632; cf. 2:647); this reminder of the special relationship between king and city was doubtless beneficial to both parties. Nevertheless, the pageant hardly portrays Lancastrian power in the figure of Henry VI as substantial and self-evident; to label the pageant as Lancastrian propaganda therefore misrepresents its illocutionary force.

63. Anne Middleton, "The Idea of Public Poetry in the Reign of Richard II," *Speculum* 53 (1978): 94–114. Some qualification is necessary because according to Middleton public poetry is "rarely occasional or topical, and it is indifferent on the whole to comprehensive rational systems of thought or of poetic structure" (95). However, in other ways, Lydgate fits Middleton's paradigm precisely: public poetry is "defined by a constant relation of speaker to audience within an ideally conceived worldly community, a relation which has become the poetic subject. In describing their mode of address, the poets most often refer to the general or common voice, and the ideal of human nature that sustains this voice assigns new importance to secular life, the civic virtues, and communal service. The voice of public poetry is neither courtly, nor spiritual, nor popular. It is pious, but its central pieties are worldly felicity and peaceful, harmonious communal existence. It speaks for bourgeois moderation. . . . This poetic voice is vernacular, practical, worldly, plain, public-spirited, and peace-loving—in a word, 'common,' rather than courtly or clerical, in its professed values and social allegiances" (95–96). This voice is only one among several in Lydgate's repertoire; however, it is the one that he consistently adopts when constructing the relationship between lords and the communities they govern.

5

"For al my body . . . weieth nat an unce"

Empty Poets and Rhetorical Weight in Lydgate's *Churl and the Bird*

James Simpson

Literary history necessarily works by principles of exclusion: literary historical narratives are generated, that is, by arguing that certain works are *not* fit for inclusion in a certain category or movement. The operations of exclusion are always at work in any literary history, given the human incapacity to take in more than a certain amount. The power of this exclusionary logic is, however, particularly strong in the historiography of Middle English literature, given the historical pressures to exclude and reject the whole period *en bloc*. British literary history began, that is, in the sixteenth century. This moment of cultural revolution, both political and religious, needed at once to define a national history, and to define it by excluding the period of greatest darkness, the later Middle Ages, when Roman pontifical power was at its height.

Such large-scale exclusion, however, cannot obliterate the past entirely. It must instead seek to isolate writers whose work can be taken as a prefiguration of the brilliant new present. This isolation always involves reinterpretation and sometimes involves positive rewriting of the old text so as to make it fit more squarely the demands of the present. In the case of the later Middle Ages, the figure consistently saved from the darkness, reinterpreted, and sometimes rewritten was Chaucer. Thus draconian legislation in 1542 that prohibited reading of almost all matter written before 1540 explicitly excepted the works of Chaucer.[1] Chaucer figured as a fully paid-up proto-Protestant by the third edition of Thynne's edition of Chaucer's *Works* in 1550, since by this time the *Plowman's Tale* had been fully incorporated into the *Canterbury Tales*.[2] And in 1570 John Foxe took Chaucer out of historical sequence to place him just before

Foxe's discussion of Luther, in the second edition of *Actes and Monuments*; here Chaucer was proximate to the greatest Reformation hero of all.[3]

Chaucer, then, proves the rule by exception. Once this work of isolating the exceptional figure is done, its corollary is also necessary, whereby the rule is confirmed by proving just how *un*exceptional all Chaucer's competitors were. In my view, this has been Lydgate's primary function in narratives of Middle English writing. Lydgate is most obviously Chaucer's competitor; in many ways Lydgate explicitly represents himself in precisely that way. From the middle of the sixteenth century, the comparison between the two poets is routinely made to Lydgate's detriment: he is pitched against Chaucer in a hopeless agon, which he is bound to lose. Lydgate proves the rule of medieval darkness and, in Lydgate's case, medieval dullness. He is doomed to imitate Chaucer but equally doomed to fail in the attempt. Lydgate generously provides grist for the exclusionary mill, and the bulk of Lydgate scholarship is generated by the logic of exclusion. Thus Lydgate's work is *not* rhetorically adept; *not* proto-Protestant; *not* humanist in any way; *not* imbued with any sense of historical distance and perspective; *not* feminist.

The foregoing is, at any rate, what I have argued at greater length in a recent book.[4] What, though, of more recent accounts of Lydgate? How has Lydgate fared in the historicist turn of scholarship over the last twenty or so years? Once we stop considering poetry from a relentlessly formalist perspective and consider instead the cultural work it does, how does Lydgate fare? Have the historicist decades been a new start for Lydgate studies?

The simple answer to that question is "no." On the contrary, the historicist turn has tended instead to work within the larger logic of Middle English studies, recycling the Chaucer-Lydgate comparison as contrastive: Chaucer is the historically alert, contestative poet, who contrasts with the inert, politically naïve and supine figure of Lydgate.[5] In this essay I test this account of Lydgate's relation with patrons, with reference to a short and largely ignored little text, *The Churl and the Bird*. From the evidence of this text, is Lydgate a Lancastrian sycophant?

I

Let me begin with a paradox. Political history tells us that Parliament, in the early decades of the fifteenth century, was extraordinarily outspoken. Powerful strands of literary history tell us, by contrast, that Lydgate and Hoccleve were extraordinarily subservient as spokesmen for the Lancastrian status quo. An obvious solution poses itself immediately: neither Lydgate nor Hoccleve

spoke for Parliament, but both were, instead, demonstrably in the pay of Lancastrian patrons. That resolution, while true, goes only some way to answer-
ing the apparent oddity of this situation of articulate parliamentary critique on
the one hand and sycophantic Lancastrian poets on the other. Both sides of the
paradox merit elaboration before we move to clarify a more persuasive resolution to this apparent contrast.

Throughout his reign, Henry IV was chronically short of money. The proportion of royal income derived from taxation, and therefore requiring consent of Parliament, had climbed by the early fifteenth century to more than
80 percent; it is no accident that in exactly these years the Commons of Parliament "enjoyed a greater influence over the business of central government
than at any time before the seventeenth century."[6] In the many parliaments of
Henry's reign, the function of the Commons was both to grant taxes and to
represent the grievances of the realm. This double function itself implies a relation between the giving of money and the king's receipt of words. The power
of the Commons in the early fifteenth century is also perceptible in their demand, made in 1401, 1404, and 1406, that the king bind members of his
council—the body of advisors in permanent service to the king—to do their
duty in an open oath taken in Parliament and that the king himself promise to
take their advice.[7] In their anxiety to repudiate Stubbs, twentieth-century historians hastened to deny that this represented any form of "premature constitutionalism,"[8] but it seems to me that such historians were themselves caught
in Stubbsian categories in making this denial. Certainly the Commons were
not promoting abstract ideals of parliamentary control; they were, however,
capitalizing on the weakness of the king to raise the binding power of their
own speech. Negotiation that broadens the base of consent usually emerges
out of political stand-off rather than from ideals alone.

This, then, is the situation in Parliament: a powerful and articulate source of
policy adroitly capitalized on financially weakened kings to raise the power of
its own voice. What of poets? Until recently the question has not been taken seriously: Lydgate and Hoccleve were negligible as political writers, given their
naïveté.[9] Recently, a much more sophisticated account has been proposed: Lydgate and Hoccleve were indeed Lancastrian propagandists, intently committed
to offering ideological support for early Lancastrian kings.[10] Their "dutiful
imaginings" were, however, frequently disrupted, given the impossibility of
their ideological program of supporting fundamentally illegitimate kings. They
"*try* to be as complicit as possible with every aspect of the Lancastrian programme," yet these arguments for "loyalty and continuity" cannot help exposing the unstable fissures of Lancastrian rule. In this they contrast with the

"Ricardian pattern," where poets "chide the monarch while assenting in the end to things he wants done."[11] Poets, unlike parliamentarians, are the victims of failed discursive ambition.

That this view of Lancastrian poets, with its Ricardian counterpart, is a new version of an old dichotomy in literary history does not in itself mean that it is wrong. I do, however, want to argue that it is implausible. This is a highly intentionalist account: Lancastrian poets *wanted,* but were helplessly unable, to legitimate the kings for whom they worked. They "produced poems which stumble constantly and even obsessively into referential difficulties they cannot afford to acknowledge. Condemned to ceaseless vigilance and interminable labour, their texts evince Herculean exertion in an impossible cause."[12] This reading acknowledges, that is, the disruptions and irregularities in Lancastrian poetry (i.e., the "referential difficulties") but contains them within an intentionalist barrier: the disruptions are there, but only because poets were unable to excise them. Against all the unavoidable evidence to the contrary, Lydgate's poetry stands firm in its maintenance of "official optimism."[13]

Being an intentionalist myself, I have no problem with the subtle intentionalism of the argument. I wish rather to question the location and therefore the nature of the intention.[14] This more recent account seems to me refreshingly and persuasively responsive to the disruptions in early Lancastrian poetry. Recognition of those disruptions is, indeed, central to the case that these Lancastrian poets were unable to govern all that disrupted "official optimism." Precisely *because* those disruptions and counterpositions are so evidently "there" in the texts, however, this interpretation threatens to tip over into an alternative, opposed account of Lydgatian intention. Once, that is, the pressure of the disruptions becomes so great, it becomes more plausible to attribute them to a differently located intention. It becomes more plausible, that is, to situate Lydgate in charge of these counterpositions. By this reading Lydgate addressed ideologically straightened kings in the way Parliament did: both poets and parliamentarians capitalized on weakened kings to advance the force of their own, perhaps distinct interests.

So my argument turns on the question of intention: Is it more plausible to attribute the disruptions and resistances in Lydgate's poetry to a failed intention that pits itself against an unmanageable historical environment? Or is it rather the case that the presence and force of the resistances are so unmistakable as to demand an alternative interpretation?

The obvious place to begin such an argument would be with the historical works, the *Troy Book* and the *Siege of Thebes.* Both these texts address themselves to two kinds of war, respectively external and civil, both of which were realities, or immediately potential threats, for Henry V and his successors. If Lydgate was holding out for "official optimism," these were appallingly bad choices of texts for translation: each plots the catastrophe that awaits the impru- dent exercise of war, both for losers and, more distressingly, for winners. In both narratives there are, indeed, no winners: the Greeks suffer a disaster in the aftermath of Troy no less catastrophic than that suffered by the Argives in Thebes. Kings and knights are represented as standing in the most urgent and serious need of good bureaucracies and courageous, learned counsel. These texts, no less than the other high-profile secular text translated by Lydgate, the *Fall of Princes,* relentlessly underline the truth that all political careers end in defeat, though here they end in catastrophe. Elsewhere I have delineated the path to catastrophe in both narratives;[15] in the context of the current argument, suffice it to say that if Lydgate's *intention* was to underwrite Lancastrian milita- rism, then his skills as a diplomat must be rated at zero. If such a low rating seems, as it does to me, implausible, then an alternative would be to relocate his intention. So far from promoting official optimism, these texts, it could be ar- gued, express consistent and reasoned opposition to both external and civil war. They promote not optimism but prudence in the face of history's treacherous- ness. The very few notes of "optimism," which are in any case restricted to pro- logues and epilogues, would more plausibly be interpreted as genuinely diplo- matic. They are plausibly acts of deference to powerful readers to whom the burden of these poems may well be acutely unwelcome.

It would, as I say, be possible to run my argument from those very high- profile texts. It would also be unmanageable in the space of this chapter. Let us instead sharpen and vary the front of the argument by looking to a much less high-profile text, Lydgate's *Churl and the Bird.* This text allows us access to Lyd- gate in less explicitly public mode, where the issue is less how to advise kings about war and more how to advise kings or lords per se. More than any other of Lydgate's texts, this is about the exercise of rhetoric itself. If we can argue from this small-scale yet concentrated example that Lydgate's intention is more plau- sibly one of checking patronal desire, we can argue the same for the higher- profile texts more confidently.

II

The Churl and the Bird is a short poem, 386 five-stress lines, in rhyme-royal stan- zas.[16] Its fabular narrative is delightful and relatively simple. A churl tends his garden, in which he regularly hears the beautiful song of a bird singing on a laurel tree. The churl captures the bird and constructs a pretty cage for her; the bird renounces her song, arguing that song and prison are ineluctably at odds. If he lets her go, the bird promises the churl, she will come to sing on demand. To this the churl replies that he will eat her if she refuses to sing. The bird shrewdly points out that the churl will not gain much by cooking her, since the bird has so little meat. If only she is freed, she will offer him three "wisdoms" that will be worth more than "al the gold that is shett in thi coofre" (161).[17] Once released, the bird resolves never to approach the fowler again but offers the three pieces of advice all the same: do not be too credulous; do not desire the impossible; and do not cry over spilt milk. As an apparently parting shot, she announces that the churl was a "verry natural foole" (225), since she, the bird, has a precious stone within her intestines, which ensures victory in battle, perpetual wealth, and universal harmony for its owner. The churl, needless to say, bursts into tears, at which point the bird delivers her real lesson: the churl has been too credulous; has desired the unpossessable; and has regretted that which has been decisively lost. The bird now delivers a genuinely parting shot, to the effect that it is a waste of time to teach idiots: "I cast me nevir hensforth, my lyvyng, / Aforn a cherl anymore to syng!" (363–64).

This little text was a great favorite throughout the fifteenth century and beyond: the *Manual of the Writings in Middle English* lists fifteen pre-1536 manuscripts in which it appears.[18] It was, furthermore, printed seven times between and including Caxton's first printing of 1477 and the Copeland print of c. 1565.[19] Although there is no explicit ascription to Lydgate in the poem itself, it often appears in collections of largely Lydgate material, such as Cambridge, University Library, MS Hh.4.12; Trinity College Cambridge, MS R.3.19; Leiden University Library, Vossius MS Germ. Gall. Q.9; and London, British Library, MS Lansdowne 699.[20]

Despite its popularity, hardly anything has been written about the poem. Dating it is impossible; although it is normally considered an early poem, there is no reason whatsoever that should prohibit a much later date: the *Horse, Goose and Sheep,* with which it has certain features in common, was certainly written after 1436.[21] As we shall see, it represents poets in a remarkably confident relation with patrons (of the kind found in, say, the *Fall of Princes*), which also might suggest a later date. Such scholarship as exists is largely restricted to the question of sources, an issue now convincingly resolved by Neil Cartwright. An earlier consensus was that Lydgate translated from some version of the "Countryman and the Little Bird" tale from the *Disciplina clericalis* of Petrus Alfonsus. Cartwright instead narrows down the source to a later generation of translations of the Alfonsus tale into Anglo-Norman, exemplified by the version of the story in the thirteenth-century Anglo-Norman debate poem *Le don-nei des amants.*[22]

As for literary criticism, there is very little. Derek Pearsall has two amusing pages on the poem in his *John Lydgate* of 1970, which neatly offer in small an example of the larger reception of Lydgate described above.[23] Pearsall begins by praising the poem but immediately contrasts it with its Chaucerian equivalent, the *Manciple's Tale*: Lydgate is "simpler and more straightforward, without the ironic undertones."[24] As if subliminally informed by the poem itself, Pearsall goes on to thematize Lydgate as the poet-churl in this way: "Lydgate is not markedly different from his usual self in this poem. He extracts every ounce of morality."[25] Lydgate, then, is like the poem's churl: "Ech thing drawith vnto his semblable," it being "convenable" a churl to bear "a mookfork in his honde" (260–64). And unlike the bird, who says she weighs less than an ounce (316), Lydgate is heavy, extracting every ounce of morality he can from the narrative.

The heavy, churlish work that Lydgate does is both rhetorical and herme-neutic, and so heavy is it that Pearsall finds himself wondering why the poem is such a delight. The answer is not only that the story is "neat." There are also "two other reasons": Chaucer and the French source. Chaucer "laid his hand lightly on Lydgate's handling of narrative and language," and given the source, Lydgate is "under less pressure to put on a performance."[26] Lumbering Lydgate, then, is heavy and inescapably himself (a churl), while the witty lightness of the bird is attributable to Chaucer's "light hand."

More recently, Helen Barr has read *The Churl and the Bird* in such a way as to translate its formal maneuvers into a language of social positioning. Her reading is a very exact replication of the newer, political readings of Lydgate's oeuvre characterized above. Barr sees the poem, that is, as tightly constrained by socially conservative intentions. Unlike the Chaucer's *Nun's Priest's Tale, The Churl and the Bird* "deliver[s] a lesson in social quietism," and "sanction[s] a conservative order of society as natural and God-given."[27] The prologue in par-ticular "endorse[s] social hierarchy"[28] and "attempt[s] to police the reading of the fable [Lydgate] translates."[29] The bird's teaching that everything has its rightful place applies specifically to the churl, a peasant identified with bodily appetites and incapable of apprehending any higher learning. The bird's "wis-doms" are examples of "unambiguous teaching which the churl is simply too stupid to comprehend"; her teaching is "insistently propositional and axiom-atic"; its use of the "present tense brooks no contradiction."[30]

Having argued that the "rhetorical social standings" of the animals and hu-mans in this text remain decidedly unscrambled,[31] Barr goes on, interestingly, to show how they are in fact very scrambled. The churl is the owner of a very courtly garden; he addresses the bird familiarly; the bird is a learned female animal instructing an obtuse male human; and her teaching is in fact about vacuity: if her story about the gem is false, then "why should we take the rest of her speech as authoritative?"[32]

The apparent contradictions of this reading are, as in the larger readings of Lydgate described above, contained within an intentionalist barrier: Lydgate wants to police the fable (that is his "declared aim"), but the disruptions are evidence of the difficulty he faced: "the faultlines are still visible."[33] Barr concludes by very tentatively suggesting that maybe Lydgate understood what had happened here: "perhaps," she asks, "the author was more alert to the social spillage than he lets on?"[34]

Questions of weight and emptiness inform both the readings of Pearsall and Barr. These metaphors of rhetorical and hermeneutic weight connect with the more recent account of Lancastrian political writing. Paul Strohm has brilliantly discussed the empty chest of Hoccleve's exemplum of John of Cancee in the *Regement of Princes.* The empty chest at once exposes the vacuity of the Lancastrian claim and offers Lancastrian kings a lesson in skilful management of that vacuity.[35] In what remains of this section, I want to focus on the rhetorical strategies of *The Churl and the Bird,* and I begin with themes of lightness and emptiness. If Hoccleve trains kings to deploy vacuity, I argue here that *The Churl and the Bird* also deploys emptiness to train Lancastrian readers; here, however, the poet is training the patron to recognize the impossibility of controlling court poets. For the startling surprise of this poem is, I argue, that court poets are empty and light; they are vacuous liars; they have nothing inside, no lessons but the indispensable lessons of rhetoric itself. The light bird here is Lydgate, while the obtuse peasant resembles no one more than the poet's patron. My reading, I need not stress, recognizes the evident disruptions of the poem but finds it implausible not to read those disruptions as strategic.

Pearsall, as we have seen, affirms that Lydgate "extracts every ounce of morality" in this small text. Certainly there are extended sequences of moral and/or prudential discourse: the bird's first *planctus* about the incompatibility of captivity and creativity (85–140); the bird's account of the foolishness of returning to a source of danger having once been captured (173–94); the three wise saws the bird delivers to the churl (197–217); the account of boorish stupidity in not having kept the precious bird whose innards contain a precious jewel (an account that is underwritten by proverbs about not casting pearls before swine), and the incapacity of a boor to act in any but a boorish way (253–80); and, finally, the mocking speech in which the bird delivers her final humiliation to the churl for having instantly ignored all her advice (299–364).

We might read all this as *the* advice of a poem whose narrative is wrung from within to deliver up every ounce of its moral content. Before we took that route, we might pause to recognize that the larger narrative is about advice *not* taken, ignored as it is by a fool. The bird itself makes the point more than once: "It were but foly with the for to carpe, / Or to preche of wisdamys more or lasse" (337–38). At the very least, we should recognize that the poem has implicit advice for its readers: they are not to be like the churl. Is that implicit advice, though, simply that we do not act as the churl: that we should not pay too hasty a credence to news, desire the impossible, and bewail the irredeemable? That we should not thus act is no doubt true, but anodyne. I propose instead that we apply the bird's first piece of advice to the poem itself. We should not be credulous, that is, about the poem's own advertised meanings:

> Yiff nat of wisdam to hasty credence
> To euery tale, nor to eche tidyng,
> But considre of reson and prudence
> Mong many talis is many grett lesyng.
> (197–200)

Apart from anything else, much of the bird's own advice turns out to be a lie. The first is that it cannot sing in captivity. It does sing, and very adroitly at that. Certainly the nature of the song changes. The initial scene is a *locus amoenus,* in which the bird sits atop a laurel tree and "did hir peyn most amorously to syng" (63); once captive, the genre of the bird's song changes from lyric to a prisoner's lament, but sing she does. The second lie is the promise that, once free, she will return every morning to sing "Vndir thi chaumbir or aforn thyn halle" (118). She makes this promise very explicit:

> Trust me weel I shal the nat disseive,
> Whoo that shal teche, of resoun he shal go fre.
> . . . .
> It sitt a mayster to have his liberte,
> And at large to have his lessoun,
> Have me nat suspectt, I meene no tresoun.
> (162–68)

As soon as she is free, of course, she instantly returns to the laurel tree and vows never to have more to do with the churl. This in itself a lie, since she does have more to do with the churl, by teaching him the three lessons.

And for the lessons themselves to work, the bird must tell a further lie, that she has the precious stone within her. She calls the churl a "verry natural foole" to have let her go, since she has within her a gem that weighs "a gret vnce" (234). She moralizes the churl's stupidity in having liberated her by reference to a model of ignorance frequently found in fables, that of casting pearls before swine. This topos is frequently used to figure the way in which the ignorant are incapable of perceiving the inner truth of narrative, even the inner truth of the apparently rough, non-pearl-like surface of Aesopian fable. Henryson, for example, uses the biblical reference (Matt. 7.6) to mock the stupidity of the cock who ignored the preciousness of the stone it rejects: the cock resists wisdom, "As dois ane sow to quhome men for the nanis / In hir draf troich wald saw the precious stanis" (146–47).[36] Lydgate's bird herself acts like a moralist offering the *moralitas* that definitively sums up the significance of the fable:

Men shuld nat put a precious margarite
As rubies, saphires or othir stonys ynde,
Emeroudes, nor othir perlis whihte
To fore rude swyn, that love draff of kynde.
(253–56)

This powerful, biblical reference turns out itself, of course, to be a decoy, a preparation for the knockout demonstration of churlish stupidity, which the bird goes on unhesitatingly to make once the churl bursts into tears at having lost the precious, inner stone.

The bird exploits, then, standard topoi of wisdom in fable writing as part of a fictional, lying, reasonably self-interested strategy. In itself this suggests that Lydgate does not "extract every ounce of morality," since the narrative generates a *surplus* that necessarily stands outside the boundaries of the moralizing narrative. This metapoetic *surplus* can only be constructed by a reader from the structure of the whole narrative. And it is in any case a *surplus* less to do with moralizing and more to do with the necessary deviations of fiction in the presence of the powerful.

More startlingly than that, the bird explodes the very premises of the fable tradition. Embedded within the fable tradition is the idea, that is, of embedding itself. The weighty, precious truth is *within*, despite an unpropitious surface; as Lydgate's own fables put it,

And, who that myneth downe lowe in the grounde,
Of golde and syluer groweth the mynerall;

Perlys whyte, clere and orientall
Ben ofte founde in muscle shellys blake,
And out of fables gret wysdom men may take.
(24–28)[37]

The startling, candid message of *The Churl and the Bird* is, instead, that there is
nothing inside. To underline the point, the bird says it twice, once before fooling
the churl about the nonexistent precious gem, and once after. Before, she per-
suades him not to cook her on the grounds that she weighs so little: "Thou shalt
of me haue a ful small repast" (152). And after the churl has been disabused of
his ridiculous desire to have this stone, the bird insists on her own vacuity:

In this doctryne I lost my labour,
To teche the sich proverbis of substaunce.
Now maist thou seen thi blynded lewde errour;
For al my body, peised in balaunce,
Weieth nat an vnce, rewde is thi remembraunce,
I to have moore peise closyd in myn entraile,
Than al my body set for the countirtaile.
(309–15)

Against the grain of the whole fable tradition, *The Churl and the Bird* strips the
surface down to reveal *nothing* within. The point of this demolition is to strip
any but a rhetorical content from the poet's advice. There is nothing here but
advice about listening carefully. To identify the "message" of the poem with its
stated morality, and to suggest that Lydgate "extracts every ounce" of morality,
is to fall victim to the bird's own warning against giving credence to "every tale
brouht to the of newe" (303). This is a text about the importance of rhetorical
process above sentential meanings. Equally, the bird's emptiness is also a warning against hoping for too much from court poets; once captive they can teach
us the art of listening, but no more. "Poets," Lydgate declares in his prologue
to *The Churl and the Bird,* "write wondirful liknessis, / And vndir covert kepte
hem silf ful cloos" (29–30). I suggest that the dialectic of keeping "vnder covert"
and exposure is in this text more complex and light footed than has previously
been acknowledged. On the one hand, Lydgate maintains a covert role by not
making explicit the burden of this poem as it applies to court patrons and poets;
on the other, he exposes the emptiness of the poet and the pathetic longing of
patrons that poets will offer up panacea and plenitude.

III

Why, an imagined interlocutor might ask, should we freight this poem with broadly "political" readings, readings that insist on the dangerous relations between poets and their powerful patrons? Who is to say that this is a poem about court poets and patrons? The simplest answer to that question is that Lydgate tells us so. In the *Debate of the Horse, Goose and Sheep,* for example, he says this about the social positioning and purpose of fable writing:

> Of many strange vncouth simylitude,
> Poetis of old fablis have contryvid,
> Of Sheep, of Hors, of Gees, of bestis rude,
> Bi which ther wittis wer secretly appreuid,
> Vndir covert tyrauntis eeke repreuid,
> Ther oppressiouns and malis to chastise.
>
> (580–85)[38]

So too, as we have already seen, he tells us in *The Churl and the Bird* that "poetes laureate / Bi dirk parables ful convenyent" write "wondirful liknessis, / And vndir covert kepte hem silf ful cloos" (15–30). By the same token, one could point to the self-conscious tradition of insular bird-poems that unquestionably broach the dangers of addressing the powerful. Lydgate evokes Chaucer's *Manciple's Tale,*[39] just as Skelton's *Speke Parott* cites *The Churl and the Bird* in its envoy. Skelton sends the poem off "to lordes and ladies," warning them to attend to the truth below the "wanton" surface, under which rests "Maters more precious than the ryche jacounce" (366).[40]

We need not settle for those answers, however. In the first place, the poem itself exploits rhetorical decorum in its presentation of the churl in particular, to suggest that he is more than a churl; and in the second, the poem's frame is explicitly political. Let me address each of these points briefly.

As I have already suggested, Lydgate disrupts the premises of fable writing in denying the reader any *inner* substance or kernel of truth. The truths of this poem are all, paradoxically, embedded on the outside, in the rhetorical surface. He also disrupts another fundamental premise of the fable tradition, that one keep one's station, know one's limits, and not over- or under-reach. The Cock's address to the jasp in Henryson's opening fable makes precisely these points: "Rise, gentill Iasp, of all stanis the flour, / Out of this fen, and pas quhar thow suld be; / Thow ganis not for me, nor I for the" (110–12). Now of course this principle of decorum is constantly broken by all sophisticated fable writers, since their point is that high, "gentle" wisdom is to be found in the dung-heap of literature. After all, in the *moralitas* to this very tale, Henryson berates the cock for having ignored the precious wisdom of the jasp. This constant dialectic of the importance and dangers of observing social propriety in fable literature accounts for the frequent shifts of literary style in that genre, as practiced by skilled authors such as Chaucer and Henryson.[41] A high, courtly style suddenly and pointedly obtrudes in the farmyard. That dialectic of literary decorum underwrites the social phenomenon whereby the socially low might shed light on the position of the socially elevated, and vice versa.

Lydgate does the same thing as Henryson and Chaucer, particularly in the description of the churl. Whereas Chaucer describes the low cock in high style in the *Nun's Priest's Tale* (2859–68), Lydgate does the reverse in his description of the churl. Here the socially low figure is described in terms that are both rhetorically and socially high. His garden is a paradisal *locus amoenus*. Unlike the sources, which simply have it that a *"vilein"* had, or went to a *"verger,"* making no mention of a laurel tree,[42] the garden of Lydgate's churl offers a perfect setting for the Apollonian bird, on the laurel tree at its center:

> Al thaleys were made pleyn with sond,
> The benchis turved with newe turvis grene,
> Sote herbis with condittes at the hond,
> That wellid vp ageyn the sonne shene,
> Lich siluer stremys, as any cristal cleene,
> The burbly wawis in ther vp boylyng
> Round as berel, ther bemys out shewyng.
> (50–56)

This is no peasant's utilitarian garden, just as the "chaumbir" and the "halle" (118) under which the bird promises to sing once liberated belong to no peasant. Neither does the cage imagined by the bird in which she might be trapped, "forged ... of gold, / And the pynaclis of berel and cristall" (92–93). The bird would, like the birds imagined in the *Manciple's Tale,* rather eat "wormes smale" than be fed with "mylk and wastelbred, / And swete cruddis brought to my pasture" (122–23). All these rhetorical mismatches imply that the churl of this poem is rather a figure for the wealthy patron. *The Churl and the Bird* insists on provoking its patronal readers to recognize that their real interest is *improper* identification with the churl.

However much, then, the bird insists on the ineluctable churlishness of the churl, and the fact that he can be nothing but himself, the rhetorical play of the poem as a whole relocates its action to court. And court, so the poem's frame implies, is no agreeable place. Unlike his source, Lydgate's fable is introduced by reference to the practice of old poets who wrote "liknessis and figures" under cover. Lydgate gives two examples of such figurative writing, one of which is drawn from a biblical example. He cites, that is, the fable narrated in Judges 9.9 in which the trees attempt to elect a king.[43] Each desirable nominee (in turn the olive, the fig, and the vine) declines the offer. Lydgate does not give us the whole story, which is recounted by Jotham, the youngest son of Gideon, whose sixty-eight brothers have been murdered in a power struggle in premonarchical Israel. Jotham's allegory is designed to expose the murderer of his brothers, his own brother Abimelech, whose monarchy is doubly illegitimate. Not only is he a usurper, but the system of the Israel in which he lives is not itself a monarchical system (his father Gideon had refused to become king). In Jotham's allegory (Judges 9.8–15) the olive, the fig, and the vine all decline the offer of kingship, as they do in Lydgate's version, refusing on the grounds that rulership would destroy their productivity. At this point the assembled trees nominate the bramble as their king, the bramble who threatens to burn "the cedars of Lebanon" if their election is in bad faith, which it clearly is. This, then, is a dark story of fratricidal energies and illegitimate rulership, like Lydgate's *Siege of Thebes*. It glances against, but remains elliptical about, violent narratives of courtly intrigue and a wholly illegitimate coup d'état. So far as we can tell, Lydgate added this prologue to his fable; such an unprompted addition would have been the act of an exceptionally, improbably maladroit courtly poet in Lancastrian England.

Both the rhetorical scrambling and the biblical frame of *The Churl and the Bird*, then, point to a courtly environment. Such an environment presses an interpretative choice upon us all the more insistently: if Lydgate wanted this to be a "docile" poem, then he has made spectacular blunders. The blunders are, indeed, so spectacular as to lead us to an alternative account of what he wanted to do. Surely blundering on that scale is implausible; a more probable account would be that Lydgate knew what he was about here. This, however, I concede, produces its own improbability, that patrons saw themselves as potential churls in the work of an "official" poet.

I prefer this improbability, for a variety of reasons. The poem itself can be read as a sympathetic but bracing account of the grief of power. Once trapped in its cage, for example, the bird produces a lament that grieves less for the weak than for the imprisoned powerful:

What vaileth it a leon to be a kyng
Off bestis all, shet in a tour of ston?
Or an egle vndir streite kepyng,

Callid also kyng of foules euerychon?
Fy on lordship whan liberte is gon!
Answer heer-to, and late it nat asterte,
Who singith mery, that syngith nat of herte?

(106–12)

The appeal of the court poet for discursive liberty is made, then, by ventrilo-quizing the courtier's own lifeless voice, trapped as it is in the deadening stric-tures of power. This implies a clear, jurisdictional distinction between poet and patron and a distinction from which the poet addresses the patron with re-markable confidence and candor. Once one admits that possibility, then the very high-profile works in the Lydgate oeuvre fall into line to back it up: *Troy Book,* the *Siege of Thebes,* and the *Fall of Princes* each, in its own ways, repre-sents poets or at least rhetorically practiced, prudential figures courageously ad-dressing aristocratic patrons and/or taking control of the reputations of those patrons.[44] Lydgate's poetry, in short, prompts us to imagine a wider range of re-lations between patron and poet than the simple opposition of propagandist/subversive offered by much New Historicist scholarship.

In conclusion, then, let us return to the problematic originally set: this is clearly a poem about the relations of court poets and their patrons. Disruptions in the relation between poet and patron are impossible to avoid. The lessons are primarily hermeneutic, and they are delivered primarily by means of evasion. The bird, indeed, wishes only for escape, and when she does so she takes care to mock her former patron as fit for nothing but the "muckfork." All this, of course, before Lydgate takes leave of his poem, instructing the text in an envoy to beseech his "maistir with humble affeccioun" to have mercy on "thi rude makyng" (380–82) and insisting that all has been said "vndir correccioun" of the master. Where do we locate the intention of this text? Is it with the poet who wants nothing more than to support a patron with "dutiful imaginings" but who cannot help exposing difficulties in that project? Or is it with the poet who constructs a subtle and penetrating account of patronal relations only to step back into deference in his envoy? Was Lydgate a terrible, heavy-handed fool? Or was he a light-footed poet, taking risks? Was he a churl, or a bird?

Notes

I warmly acknowledge the vigorous responses to earlier versions of this essay when deliv-ered as a paper at meetings at the University of Utrecht, the University of Victoria BC, and the New Chaucer Society Congress, 2002, in Boulder, CO. Larry Scanlon and Scott-Morgan Straker offered penetrating criticisms of the essay in draft, which I gratefully acknowledge.

1. T. E. Tomlins et al., eds., *Statutes of the Realm,* 11 vols. (London: Dawsons, 1810–28), 34 Henry 8, chap.1.1 (3:895).

2. For the history of Thynne's inclusion of the *Ploughman's Tale* in the *Canterbury Tales,* see Anne Hudson, "John Stow (1525?–1605)," in *Editing Chaucer, The Great Tradition,* ed. Paul G. Ruggiers (Norman, OK: Pilgrim Books, 1984), 59.

3. John Foxe, *The Acts and Monuments of the Christian Martyrs,* 4th ed., 8 vols., ed. Josiah Pratt (London: Religious Tract Society, 1877), 4:248–50. The interpolation does not appear in the first edition (1563). Foxe also printed Jack Upland as definite proof of Chaucer's Protestant convictions.

4. James Simpson, *Reform and Cultural Revolution, 1350–1547* (Oxford: Oxford University Press, 2002), chap. 2. The essay first appeared as "Bulldozing the Middle Ages: The Case of 'John Lydgate,'" *New Medieval Literatures* 4 (2000): 213–42.

5. A rare exception is Lee Patterson, "Making Identities in Fifteenth Century England: Henry V and John Lydgate," in *New Historical Literary Study: Essays on Reproducing Texts, Representing History,* ed. Jeffrey N. Cox and Larry J. Reynolds (Princeton, NJ: Princeton University Press, 1993), 69–107.

6. John Gillingham, "Crisis or Continuity? The Structure of Royal Authority in England 1369–1422," in *Das Spätmittelalterliche Königtum in europäischen Vergleich,* ed. Reinhard Schneider (Sigmaringen: Thorbecke, 1987), 59–80 (73).

7. See A. L. Brown, "Parliament, c. 1377–1422," in *The English Parliament in the Middle Ages,* ed. R. G. Davies and J. H. Denton (Manchester: Manchester University Press, 1981), 109–40.

8. Ibid., 134. For the larger repudiation of Stubbsian constitutionalism by twentieth-century British historians, see Christine Carpenter, "Political and Constitutional History before and after McFarlane," in *The McFarlane Legacy: Studies in Late Medieval Politics and Society,* ed. R. H. Britnell and A. J. Pollard (Stroud: Alan Sutton, 1995), 175–206.

9. For Lydgate and Hoccleve as politically naive, see, respectively, Derek Pearsall, *John Lydgate* (London: Routledge & Kegan Paul, 1970), 15, and Arthur B. Ferguson, *The Articulate Citizen and the English Renaissance* (Durham, NC: Duke University Press, 1965), 88–89.

10. The view most powerfully and eloquently expressed by Larry Scanlon, Paul Strohm, and Derek Pearsall. See Larry Scanlon, "The King's Two Voices: Narrative and Power in Hoccleve's Regement of Princes," in *Literary Practice and Social Change in Britain, 1380–1530,* ed. Lee Patterson, The New Historicism 8 (Berkeley: University of California Press, 1990), 216–47; Paul Strohm's generally admirable, not to say (for the notion of "Lancastrian" politico-literary culture) seminal *England's Empty Throne: Usurpation and the Language of Legitimation, 1399–1422* (New Haven, CT: Yale University Press, 1996), chap. 7, and his "Hoccleve, Lydgate and the Lancastrian Court," in *The Cambridge History of Medieval English Literature,* ed. David Wallace (Cambridge: Cambridge University Press, 1999), 640–61; and Derek Pearsall, "Hoccleve's Regement of Princes: The

Poetics of Royal Self-Representation," *Speculum* 69 (1994): 386–410. See now, however, an account of Lydgate's politics as, if not less collusive, not at all naive: Paul Strohm, "Lydgate and the Emergence of Pollicie in the Mirror Tradition," forthcoming. I am extremely grateful to Professor Strohm for having given me the chance to read this in typescript. Powerful correctives to the view of Hoccleve as Lancastrian propagandist are now available. See Ethan Knapp, *The Bureaucratic Muse: Thomas Hoccleve and the Literature of Late Medieval England* (University Park: Pennsylvania State University Press, 2001); Lee Patterson, "'What Is Me?': Self and Society in the Poetry of Thomas Hoccleve," *Studies in the Age of Chaucer* 23 (2001): 437–70; and Nicholas Perkins, *Hoccleve's "Regiment of Princes": Counsel and Constraint* (Cambridge: Brewer, 2001). See also James Simpson, *Reform and Cultural Revolution,* chap. 5.

11. Strohm, "Hoccleve, Lydgate," 654, 659.

12. Ibid., 661.

13. Ibid., 656.

14. For the necessity of incorporating some account of intention for this poetry, see also chap. 4 of this volume.

15. For Thebes, see James Simpson, "'Dysemol daies and fatal houres': Lydgate's *Destruction of Thebes* and Chaucer's *Knight's Tale*," in *The Long Fifteenth Century: Essays in Honour of Douglas Gray,* ed. Helen Cooper and Sally Mapstone (Oxford: Oxford University Press, 1997), 15–33. For the *Troy Book,* see Simpson, *Reform and Cultural Revolution,* chap. 3. The argument there is primarily devoted to the alliterative *Destruction of Troy,* but equally applicable in almost every respect to Lydgate's *Troy Book.*

16. All citations are from *The Churl and the Bird,* in *The Minor Poems of John Lydgate,* 2 vols., ed. Henry Noble MacCracken, EETS, e.s., 107, 192 (1911, 1934; reprint, London: Oxford University Press, 1997), no. 20, 2:468–85.

17. Throughout this chapter, poetry is cited parenthetically in the text by line number.

18. Alain Renoir and C. David Benson, "John Lydgate," in *A Manual of the Writings in Middle English, 1050–1500,* ed. J. Burke Severs and A. E. Hartung, 7 vols. (New Haven: Connecticut Academy of Arts and Sciences, 1967–), 6:1821–22, 2084–85.

19. A. W. Pollard and G. R. Redgrave, eds., *A Short-Title Catalogue of Books Printed in England, Scotland and Ireland and of English Books Printed Abroad 1475–1640,* 2nd ed., 3 vols., rev. W. A. Jackson et al. (London: Bibliographical Society, 1976–91), nos. 17008–14.

20. See Derek Pearsall, *John Lydgate (1371–1449): A Bio-Bibliography,* English Literary Studies 71 (Victoria, BC: University of Victoria, 1997), 80–84.

21. Ibid., 35.

22. Neil Cartlidge, "The Source of John Lydgate's The Churl and the Bird," *Notes and Queries,* n.s., 44 (1997): 22–24.

23. Pearsall, *John Lydgate,* 198–200.

24. Ibid., 198.

25. Ibid., 198.

26. Ibid., 199.

27. Helen Barr, *Socioliterary Practice in Late Medieval England* (Oxford: Oxford University Press, 2001), Afterword, 188–98. I am grateful to John Scattergood for drawing my attention to this valuable book.

28. Ibid., 189.

29. Ibid., 194.

30. Ibid., 192–93.

31. Ibid., 190.

32. Ibid., 194–96.

33. Ibid., 197.

34. Ibid.

35. Strohm, *England's Empty Throne*, 198–201. See also Sarah Tolmie, "The Prive Science of Thomas Hoccleve," *Studies in the Age of Chaucer* 22 (2000): 281–309.

36. Robert Henryson, *The Fables*, in *The Poems of Robert Henryson*, ed. Denton Fox (Oxford: Clarendon Press, 1981), 3–110.

37. John Lydgate, *Isopes Fabules*, in *Minor Poems of John Lydgate*, no. 21, 2:566–99.

38. John Lydgate, *The Debate of the Horse, Goose and Sheep*, in *Minor Poems of John Lydgate*, no. 23, 2:539–66. Nonmedievalist critics have no doubt of the political burden of such writing; see Annabel Patterson, *Fables of Power: Aesopian Writing and Political History* (Durham, NC: Duke University Press, 1991), 2, 45–47.

39. Compare the bird's declaration that she would prefer to eat "wormes smale" in the freedom of the forest rather than be fed dainties in a gilded cage (*The Churl and the Bird*, 85–140) with the Manciple's argument that birds naturally prefer the freedom of eating "wormes and swich wrecchednesse" to the delicacies of the gilded cage (the *Manciple's Tale*, in *The Riverside Chaucer*, 3rd ed., ed. Larry D. Benson [Oxford: Oxford University Press, 1987], 163–74).

40. See John Skelton, *The Complete English Poems*, ed. John Scattergood (Harmondsworth, Middlesex: Penguin, 1983), no. 18. Compare the "grett iagounce" (line 318) (not) embedded in the bird of *The Churl and the Bird*. This connection is pointed out by Patterson, *Fables of Power*, 49.

41. For a conspectus of fable writing in English the later Middle Ages, see James Simpson, "Beast Epic and Fable," in *Medieval England: An Encyclopaedia*, ed. Paul E. Szarmach, M. Teresa Tavormina, and Joel T. Rosenthal (New York: Garland, 1998), 111–12.

42. Compare the rhetorically spare presentation in *Le donnei des amants*: "Un vilein a un tens esteit, / Ki assez près d'un bois maneit, / Li quels aveit un bel verger / Ou sulent oiseus repeirer / E faire joie el tens d'esté, / Quant flur[s] e foilles s'unt mustré" (929–34). Gaston Paris, ed., "*Le donnei des amants*," *Romania* 25 (1896): 497–541.

43. Wyclif's wholly spiritual and frankly improbable interpretations of this biblical fable highlight, by contrast, the political slant of Lydgate's presentation. For Wyclif's discussion, see Kantik Ghosh, *The Wycliffite Heresy: Authority and the Interpretation of Texts* (Cambridge: Cambridge University Press, 2002), 25–28.

44. A position that has been well argued by Lois A. Ebin, "Lydgate's Views on Poetry," *Annuale Mediaevale* 18 (1977): 76–105. I give an account of the distinct jurisdictions of the late medieval clerical poet in *Reform and Cultural Revolution*, 98–101.

6

Civic Lydgate

The Poet and London

C. David Benson

One of the liveliest surviving short poems about life in medieval London is *London Lickpenny*. The fifteenth-century work, which survives in two later recensions, is a first-person account of a trip by a country visitor to the metropolis and the greedy selfishness he encounters there.[1] The traveler first goes to Westminster in search of justice from its various courts, only to be frustrated because, as the last line of each stanza, in some form, states: "for lacke of money, I may not spede." In addition to being disregarded because he is without wealth, the narrator also loses his hood in the press of the crowd. Leaving Westminster, he proceeds into the city of London itself, with its insistent cries of street peddlers touting such delicacies as "hot pescods" and "chery in the ryse" (67–68).[2] As he journeys through the city's shopping areas (Cheap, Candlewick, and Eastcheap), the visitor keeps being offered goods, foods, and services—from cloth to mackerel, from ribs of beef to songs "of Jenken and Julian" (81–94). But he is unable to take advantage of any of these because, as the stanza refrain continues to remind us, in London there is no success unless one has money. The cold cupidity of the city is starkly revealed on Cornhill, where amongst other "stolne gere" our protagonist sees for sale the very hood he had previously lost at Westminster, which he refuses to repurchase: "To by [buy] myne owne hode agayne, me thought it wrong" (103). After finally spending a penny on a pint of wine (though he remains hungry), the rural traveler, with relief and a prayer for London's reform, escapes from the city back into Kent.

London Lickpenny was long attributed to John Lydgate (perhaps originally by the antiquarian John Stow), though authoritative modern scholars have removed it from his canon.[3] In fact, the poem's most obvious resemblances are not to any of Lydgate's works but to moments at the beginning of another, earlier poem much concerned with London, William Langland's *Piers Plowman*. Both contain the mercantile streets cries of the metropolis and describe its extensive (and frequently dishonest) commercial activity, especially in respect to the retail selling of food and drink.[4] *London Lickpenny* also echoes the attacks in *Piers* against the abuses of the legal system: its line about the unwillingness of lawyers to speak a word without compensation ("he would not geve me a momme of his mouthe" [31]) echoes a similar line in the earlier poem (Pro.216).

That such a major London historian as Stow could identify Lydgate as the author of *London Lickpenny* is reason enough to reconsider the connections between the poet and the city. Lydgate and London is an association that has prompted little sustained attention.[5] Instead scholarship, with varying degrees of condescension, has tended to define three other Lydgates. First is the monkish Lydgate ("monk of Bury" is how he is identified by Stow and often by others), a cleric who at best displays a wide if somewhat automatic learning and at worst is prosaic when not downright driveling. A second, familiar Lydgate is the literary disciple of Chaucer, who is often judged to stumble badly as he attempts to hop behind his master. Finally, there is royalist Lydgate, the servile prince-pleaser who cranked out pieces on demand for the Lancastrian court. Each of these Lydgates contains a certain amount of truth, but in addition to a reflexive lack of generosity toward the poet's achievement, they downplay what Derek Pearsall has long stressed is the most distinctive quality of Lydgate's work: its extraordinary range of different kinds of writing, from long classical romances to utilitarian dietaries, from courtly love poems to a catalog of princes felled by fortune.

Now that Lydgate's critical time seems to have come round at last and we are being offered new ways to understand him (from Seth Lerer's infantilized poet to James Simpson's dark and often daring prophet), it may be appropriate to explore another, less dramatic, Lydgate: what we might call civic Lydgate. *Civic* in this essay refers specifically to the poet's writing about the idea and experience of the city, especially London. The concept shares the general thrust of Anne Middleton's influential idea of "public poetry," which she associates especially with Gower and Langland: "The voice of public poetry is neither courtly, nor spiritual, nor popular. . . . This poetic voice is vernacular, practical, worldly, plain, public-spirited, and peace-loving."[6] The poems that Lydgate wrote for and about London will demonstrate, if nothing else, that it is as reductive to limit him to a few social locales (the court or the monastery) as to a few literary forms. Of the many voices that Lydgate articulated in his poetry, the civic voice, specifically the voice of London, has not always been heard clearly. Part of the problem with civic Lydgate is that we know almost nothing for certain about the poet's experience of or residence in London. Lydgate's contemporary, the London bookman John Shirley (whose chatty headings to manuscript copies of the poet's works supply much of the external information we have about their occasions) identifies the capital as the site where several works were composed. The heading to *Virgo Mater Christi* even goes so far as to specify that Lydgate made the poem "by night as he lay in his bedde at London."[7] Yet little of Lydgate's London writing suggests the firsthand knowledge of the life of its streets found in *Piers Plowman* or *London Lickpenny*. Although the monk wrote for London, he was certainly not of London. He was a man of books, just as the French director Jean-Luc Godard is a man of films: their themes, style, and characters come more from deep absorption in their own medium than from life.

Stow's identification of Lydgate as the author of *London Lickpenny* is less surprising when we remember that the poet certainly did write two short, non-narrative poems that also take a satirical view of urban life and especially the victualing trades: *A Ballade of Jak Hare* and *Against Millers and Bakers*.[8] *Jak Hare,* though shorter than *Lickpenny* at fifty-six lines, is written in a eight-line stanza similar to the oldest recension of the latter and also uses a repeated refrain, in this case stressing the drunken, idle knave's ability to "plukke out the lynyng" of a bowl, tankard, pitcher, pot, or cup.[9] *Jack Hare,* unlike *London Lickpenny,* mentions no specific urban locations, though the statement that Jack is "a boy for Hogge of Ware" (5) alludes to Chaucer's Cook and thus suggests the London scene of the *Cook's Tale,* whose protagonist is a similarly reprobate reveler. *Jak Hare* is not a narrative but an unremitting litany of abuse directed against its hero's indolence, slovenliness, and dishonesty, as in the second stanza:

> This boy Maymond ful styborne of his bonys,
> Sloggy on morwen his lemes vp to dresse,
> A gentel harlot chose out for the noonys,
> Sone and cheeff eyr on-to dame Idylnesse,
> Cosyn to Wecock, brother to Reklesnesse,
> Wich late at eve and morwe at his rysyng
> Ne hath no ioie to do no besynesse,
> Saue of a tancard to plukke out the lynyng.
>
> (9–16)

Against Millers and Bakers, an even shorter (twenty-four lines), cleverer poem in eight-line stanzas (without a refrain), also does not specifically mention London, but the crimes and punishments as well as other institutions it so nimbly describes are precisely those that figure prominently in the city's surviving records (though they would also be appropriate to smaller towns in medieval England).[10] The poem begins dramatically ("Put out his hed" [1] and later "Put out his armys" [6]), with a seemingly heroic description of the central figure ("lyk a man vpon that tour to abyde" [2]) that is soon undercut by the undignified attack he suffers: "For cast of eggys wil not oonys spare, / Tyl he be quaylled, body, bak, and syde" (3–4). The second stanza reveals that the "bastyle" on which are displayed heads and arms is the municipal pillory and the figures exhibited there are not champions but "fals bakerys" (9–10). The poem then concludes with a third stanza suggesting that since such rogues are so often found there, the pillory ought to be the site for their communal observances:

> Let mellerys and bakerys gadre hem a gilde,
> And alle of assent make a fraternite;
> Vndir the pillory a litil chapell bylde. . . .
>
> (17–19)

The details of Lydgate's *Millers and Bakers* are glossed by the municipal statutes of medieval London, which decreed that those guilty of fraud involving the supply of food be sentenced to stand on the pillory, the raised platform that imprisoned the head and hands of malefactors in order to expose them to public humiliation and to eggs and other missiles. Deceit involving bread, the most basic foodstuff, was a special object of this punishment. John Stow's *Survey of London,* shortly before identifying Lydgate as the author of *London Lickpenny,* notes the establishment in 1401 of a pillory on Cornhill "for the punishment of Bakers offending in the assise of bread, for Millers stealing of corne at the Mill, for bawdes, scoulds, and other offenders."[11] In *Piers Plowman* mayors are urged to send to the pillory "Brewesters and baksters, bochiers and cokes," for they are the "men on this molde that moost harm werche" (3.79–80). In addition to the city pillory, Lydgate's *Millers and Bakers* also refers to another and more positive civic institution in London (and other towns): parish guild fraternities, which provided economic, religious, and communal benefits for their members.[12] Of course, what is principally mocked here is not fraternities in general but rather the particular members of this one (false millers and bakers) and the location of its chapel (under the pillory).

In his pioneering critical study of Lydgate, Pearsall commented that the
sharpness of observation and vigor of expression in *Jak Hare* and *Against Millers
and Bakers* "are enough to persuade one that Lydgate could have written that
masterpiece of fifteenth century low satire, *London Lickpenny* (though we must
accept that he did not)."[13] Lydgate's two poems, like *Lickpenny,* are indeed satiric accounts of urban activity: all three deal with ordinary people and the
clamor of commerce, consumption, and illegality in the big city. But there is a
major difference in perspective. *Lickpenny* views the city as an outsider and
from below, its country traveler is a victim of powerful institutions and mercantile practices, and he has nothing good to say about London. In contrast, Lydgate's two poems are written from a loftier, more complacent position in support of the municipal establishment. His principal targets are the slackers and
cheats who do not live up to their civic responsibilities, like Perkyn Reveler in
Chaucer's *Cook's Tale,* and he assumes that such malefactors should and will be
punished. Commercial abuses, including selling stolen goods, thrive unchecked
in *Lickpenny*'s London, but Lydgate's false bakers are sent to the pillory. Furthermore, there is no suggestion in Lydgate's poem of the wide-ranging criticism of the legal system that dominates the beginning of *London Lickpenny.* In
contrast to *Piers,* perhaps the most socially engaged London poem in Middle
English, and to *London Lickpenny,* Lydgate's short satirical works do not sym-
pathize with the poor against the rich or with the marginal against the official
but, as we shall see in Lydgate's other civic writing, support the hierarchical stability of an established community.

Lydgate's longest London work is *King Henry VI's Triumphal Entry into
London, 21 February 1432,* a 537-line poem in rhyme royal with two prose
speeches by the mayor.[14] The poem describes an elaborate civic procession
through the streets of the city (including pageants with miming actors at seven
different stations) to welcome back the ten-year-old Henry after his crowning
in Paris the previous December in an ultimately futile attempt to unite the
kingdoms of England and France. The title and subject of the *Triumphal Entry*
suggest a work of Lancastrian celebration like other poems Lydgate produced
on behalf of the boy-king, such as *The Title and Pedigree of Henry VI* and both
a *Roundel* and a *Balade* for Henry's 1429 coronation at Westminster.[15] Yet if its
protagonist is royal, the form of the *Triumphal Entry* points to Lydgate's monastic education, for, along with displays of classical learning, the poem expands
the biblical imagery of the original pageants, especially the use of the liturgy associated with Epiphany.[16] Moreover, despite its regal and religious elements, the
Triumphal Entry is a fundamentally civic work: having been commissioned by

municipal officials, it goes beyond dramatizing Henry as messianic ruler or indicating his road to personal salvation to insist upon his social obligations to
London and its citizens. The beginning and end of the poem present Henry as
a military and heavenly figure, but the heart of the *Triumphal Entry,* like the actual pageant it describes, casts him in a more domestic role as "a master of . . .
[the] traditional arts of home rule."[17]

The civic character of Lydgate's *Triumphal Entry* begins with its corporate
creation. In his Lydgate book, Pearsall assumed that the monk not only wrote
the poem but also helped to design the original pageants themselves, putting
him "in the position of an artistic director, or 'devisor,' who writes his own
souvenir programme."[18] Pearsall has since downgraded Lydgate's contribution
to that of a possible helper on the pageants, identifying John Carpenter, the
Town Clerk of London, whom from the first he recognized as the "producer"
of the event, as the "main organizer."[19] Henry Noble MacCracken first showed
the close similarity between Lydgate's poem and a surviving letter by Carpenter
describing Henry's entry, leading Kipling not only to agree that the letter was
the real source for the poem but also to conclude that "Lydgate probably did not
personally witness the civic triumph."[20] Lydgate's assistance (if any) in planning
the entry as well as his presence or absence at the event itself are now impossible
to determine and less relevant than the undoubted truth that his poem was only
one aspect of a complex civic undertaking. There is little evidence in this work
of the personal expression of a modern poet. Lydgate is instead writing on behalf of London and its values: he is a civic mouthpiece rather than a subjective
creator.

The *Triumphal Entry* records one event in the ceremonial history of London.
The specific entry it describes is part of an extensive tradition of civic pageantry
for royalty in the metropolis, which began well before Henry VI and continued
long after with a number of Tudor processions.[21] The entry of Henry VI was
neither unique nor private but a public, communal performance that occurred
throughout the city and involved many of its residents. The young king may
have been the protagonist of the event, but other Londoners also participated:
"the cite3enis thurh-oute the Citee / Halwyd that day with grete solempnyte"
(20–21). Henry was met at Blackheath and escorted into the city by municipal
officials (30–31), guildsmen from "euery craffte" (39), and even aliens (43–49).
Others located within the walls who took prominent roles were the actors who
mimed allegorical characters on the various pageant structures and the clergy
who formed a procession at St. Paul's (458 ff). As Kipling, citing Huizinga,
notes, such civic pageants were not limited to any one segment of society, high
or low, lay or clerical, but represented for medieval culture "one of its most seri-

ous modes of collective enjoyment, and a deeply felt assertion of communal solidarity."[22] All London is imagined to contribute to the *Triumphal Entry*.

Lydgate, whether present in person or not, made his contribution to this civic enterprise more as a recorder than as a creator, producing "a piece of mediaeval reporting, done at the request of the mayor and citizens."[23] Even if what he described were the inventions of others, his own work nevertheless had a lasting effect. The *Triumphal Entry* was copied into many London chronicles (such as that in British Library, London, MS Cotton, Julius B.II) and into more general histories such as Robert Fabyan's *New Chronicles of England and France*.[24] Lydgate's poem also influenced the form of subsequent royal entries. Apparently the pageant stages for Henry VI's entry had only brief written "scriptures" posted for spectators to read, but Lydgate's poem sometimes presents these as if they were actual speeches, an invention that seems to have inspired the dramatic verse spoken aloud by actors during the entry of Margaret of Anjou in 1445 (once thought to be by Lydgate) and thus the form of Renaissance entries.[25] Unlike Langland, Lydgate was not a voice crying in the London wilderness but a contributor to the municipal chorus.

Two important city officials were directly involved in the production of the *Triumphal Entry*: John Carpenter and John Wells. Carpenter, whose letter, as we have seen, was the primary and perhaps only source for Lydgate's poem, had long served as London's town clerk (1417–38). A close friend of Richard Whittington (three times mayor of London), Carpenter assembled the influential collection of city documents and precedents known as the *Liber Albus*. A couple of years before the 1432 entry, Carpenter had commissioned Lydgate to inscribe his *Danse Macabre* (a translation of the French mural text at the Church of the Holy Innocents in Paris) along with appropriate painting on a cloister wall at St. Paul's that was attached to a chapel in which Carpenter had recently built a chantry.[26] This was another multimedia, collaborative London project, though less public and communal than Henry's entry.

The other civic official behind the *Triumphal Entry* was the Lord Mayor of London for 1432, John Wells. In the one-stanza "Lenvoye" to the poem, Lydgate directly addresses Wells as "O noble Meir," asks pity for the literary failings of his "symple makyng," and concludes "that in moste lowly wyse / My wille were goode fforto do yow servyse" (531–37). The envoy suggests that if Carpenter provided the material for the *Triumphal Entry,* Wells may have actually commissioned it.[27] This assumption is strengthened by a digression (with no parallel in Carpenter's letter) in which Lydgate links part of one pageant— the fountains (or "welles") in Cheapside that were made to run with wine "in tokne of alle gladdesse" (322)—with the name of the mayor.[28]

O! how thes welles, who-so take goode hede,
With here likours moste holsome to atame,
Affore devysed notably in dede
Forto accorden with the Meirys name;
Which by report off his worthy ffame
That day was busy in alle his gouernaunce,
Vnto the Kyng fforto done plesaunce.

(342–48)

In addition to associating London's mayor with wholesome and pleasure-giving wells, another passage original with Lydgate in the *Triumphal Entry* offers a more direct encomium to the city. Just before the final envoy to Wells, Lydgate adds three stanzas that celebrate London in the most extravagant terms; he extols it as "Citee of Citees, off noblesse precellyng," which exhibits seven admirable, if somewhat general, virtues: "trewe menyng," "ffeythfull obseruaunce," "rihtwysnesse," "trouthe," "equyte," "stablenesse," and "vertue" (510–30). Despite its title, Lydgate's poem ends with civic rather than royal praise.

Throughout the *Triumphal Entry,* London is shown positively. There are none of the attacks on court and commerce found in *London Lickpenny* and certainly nothing of the disparagement of municipal authorities expressed in *Piers Plowman*. In Lydgate's poem we hear no shouts of rebellion or even sighs of alienation, but rather the official, public voice of London. In addition to a souvenir program, it is a promotional brochure. The *Triumphal Entry* is the opposite of *London Lickpenny* in both its route and ideology. It begins in Kent and ends in Westminster, instead of the reverse, and praises rather than satirizes the city, its institutions, and its citizens.

Lydgate's poem, like the city pageant on which it was based, not only welcomes Henry VI but also defines the proper relationship he should have with London. The encomium states that the capital was customarily called the "Kyngis Chambre" (530), and in both of his prose addresses to Henry, Mayor Wells refers to "your moste notable Citee off London, othir wyse called youre Chaumbre" (after 63 and 509). The alliance suggested by "chamber" is an intimate, domestic, loving one. Yet for all the affection shown to the king (and that is expected from him), the city also affirms the independence from royal control that it has struggled so long and so often to maintain. Henry does not enter London as a conqueror and take possession of it, nor does he long remain there (his major residences at Eltham and Westminster were outside the walls); rather, the king merely passes through the city, escorted by its officials and populace from before he crosses the Thames until he arrives at the abbey: "The Meire, the citezenis, abode and lefft him nouht, / Vnto Westmynstre tyl they hadde him brouht" (473–74). Then after Henry enters his palace at Westminster to rest, "The Meire, the citezenis, . . . / Ben home repeyred into hire citee" (494–95). The sovereign has been welcomed and feted, but for these citizens, London is not only "hire citee" but also their "home"—and it is from their perspective (and with their values) that the spectacle is described.

The most active figure, and the only one heard to speak during the entry, is not the king but the mayor, the elected representative of London (or, to be more accurate, of the city's merchant class). The mayor led the welcoming party at Blackheath, and Lydgate describes the commanding figure he cut there:

> Thanne with his sporys, he toke his hors anoon,
> That to beholde yt was a noble siht,
> How like a man he to the kyng ys goon
> Riht well cherid, off herte gladde and liht;
> Obeying to him as him ouht off riht.
>
> (57–61)

Although the last line declares that Mayor Wells is the king's obedient subject, the passage as a whole describes a more active figure: one who on horseback appeared a "noble siht" and who approached the king "like a man." The mayor also led the procession to Westminster, and, a week after the entry itself, he, in the presence of other London officials, presented the king with a gift of a thousand pounds and again addressed the monarch (496–509 and prose). Such gifts were a customary part of royal entries and certainly expected (Richard II's bitter dispute with London was occasioned by the refusal of such a gift), but the delay of a week seems meant to suggest the fiction that the money was the result of the city's free will and not forced. Hierarchy is, of course, observed (the mayor says in his prose speech that Londoners "in here moste lowly wyse" recommend themselves to "Youre Hyhnesse" with their "lytyll gyffte"), but the form of presentation implies that this is indeed a present, offered by an independent, if loyal and loving, mayor and city.

In addition to offering praise, the pageants and Lydgate's poem inform the king what he must do to ensure that London remains his chamber. The mayor's greeting to Henry at Blackheath gives thanks for the king's recent acquisition of the crown of France, but it ends with a more local request to God "to sende yow prosperite and many yeers, to the comforte off alle youre lovynge peple" (after 63).[29] The pageants that follow, and even more Lydgate's poem on them, emphasize the civic, bourgeois virtues of comfort and prosperity, which means good fortune in general and not just financial success, rather than the uncertainties of military glory and foreign conquest.[30] The first pageant site at the entrance to London Bridge does display a giant (apparently left from Henry V's entry after Agincourt),[31] standing on a tower as "a sturdy champeoun" with a sword upraised, "Alle fforeyn enmyes ffrom the Kyng to enchace" (72–77), but the second pageant, in the middle of London Bridge, has a more domestic message with three empresses (Nature, Fortune, and Grace), the last of whom brings "gladnes to citees and tovns" as well as lasting "prosperyte" (123–26). The gifts for the king offered by Nature, "strenth and myht" (150), may refer to martial accomplishment, but, even if that is so, they are more than matched by Fortune's gift of "lange prosperite" (149) and Grace's double gift of a long reign to Henry and justice ("equyte") to London: "Vertuously lange in thy ryall citee, / With septre and crovne to regne in equyte" (153–54).

The civic lessons of Henry's entry are clearest in the three central pageants, which were staged in the very heart of the city. Pageant three, on the top of Cornhill near the Church of St. Peter, is a tabernacle containing Dame Sapience and the seven liberal arts, on which is posted a written "scripture" (266) addressed to young kings on the importance of such wisdom and knowledge because they are judges: "Syth ye be iuges other ffolke to deme" (271). The fourth pageant, at the Conduit further down on Cornhill, is an even more explicit plea for the king to do justice, the chief domestic function of the monarch.[32] Giants and swords now give way to a child king surrounded by Mercy, Truth, and Clemence and by two judges and eight lawyers, with a "scripture" that refers to "equyte and riht" (299). Lydgate adds to Carpenter's account elements that further suggest the values of London's burgesses, such as mention of "prudent" Solomon (286) and a further reference to "prosperytee" (292). A quotation from King David is said by Lydgate, following Carpenter, to teach that "kyngis, princes, shulde aboute hem drawe / Folke that be trewe and well expert in lawe" (305–6). London urges Henry to act in a way that will ensure its own well-being. These two pageants, commending the law that was shown to be so corrupt in *London Lickpenny,* are located in the very part of the city (Cornhill) where the traveler saw his stolen hood and where so many other commercial abuses were punished by the pillory in medieval London.

The fifth pageant, at the Conduit in Cheap, not only puns on the name of John Wells, as we have seen, but also continues to show the king what he can and should do for London. Kipling argues that the details of this pageant "dramatize Henry's power to transform the city into a holy place," for it "appears to him now in the form of an earthly paradise."[33] Yet, however holy, this transformed London is very much a garden of *earthly* delights: this "Paradys" (310, cf. 363) has wells whose water has been turned into wine, as in Christ's miracle at Cana (312–13), and equally fabulous trees, "with leves ffresh off hewe, / Alle tyme off yeer, ffulle of ffruytes lade" (349–50). Enoch and Elijah appear in this pageant (367 ff), but so do the less spiritual Thetis and Bacchus (314–20): Cheap has become a "lusty place, a place of alle delycys" (308), whose wine, whatever its divine associations, "makith hertes liht" (318) because it is "a likour off rec-reacioun" (321), just as among its various fruits are those that "recomfort" (355) or "delyte" (361).[34]

Although positive in tone, these three central pageants set in the commercial heart of London do indirectly suggest some of the municipal problems found in *London Lickpenny* or *Piers Plowman*. Would the king be advised to maintain the law unless there was real concern about its corruption, or would London need to be imagined a paradise unless some had instead found it cold and rapa-cious? The *Triumphal Entry,* like the pageants on which it is based, shows London in splendor and fit for a king, but it is mindful that justice and prosperity are not inevitable, even for this "Citee of Citees," which is why it is so eager to welcome and instruct the new king.

Even though the *Triumphal Entry* describes a procession through the streets of London, there is no evidence that Lydgate knew much about daily life there. His knowledge of earthly cities probably came from his reading about famous ancient examples. In the encomium to London at the end of the *Triumphal Entry,* Lydgate notes that it was "In thy bygynnynge called Newe Troye" (512), alluding to the legend that the city, like Rome, was originally founded by de-scendants of Troy. A decade before the *Triumphal Entry,* Lydgate wrote a major poem on the fall of Troy and, later, a shorter one (by his standards) on the fall of Thebes. These two works recognize the potential that great cities always have for either success or failure; and, if the latter, not the petty crimes of *Jak Hare* and *Against Millers and Bakers* or even the institutional neglect and corruption in *London Lickpenny,* but the total ruin that results when kingly pride or ambi-tion risks the communal harmony, prosperity, and delight celebrated in the *Tri-umphal Entry.*

Lydgate's *Troy Book* is an expanded translation of Guido delle Colonne's fac-tual prose Latin history, *Historia destructionis Troiae.* The key civic episode in the poem, much developed by Lydgate, describes the rebuilding of Troy by Priam after its first destruction by Jason and Hercules (2.479–1066).[35] Priam summons workmen and artisans of all kinds to build a strong and magnifi-cently decorated city containing marble houses full of rich sculptures and wide streets covered by pathways and washed by piped water. "His new cite for to magnyfye" (2.788), Priam institutes jousts and other entertainments, including the first ever performances of comedy and tragedy. Lydgate describes at length how the latter were read from a pulpit by "an ancien poete" (2.868) while actors mimed the emotions expressed by his words: "So þat þer was no maner discordaunce / Atwen his dites and her contenaunce" (2.905–6). Having "brouȝt vn-to perfeccioun" his new city, Priam "Ful many day in this newe Troye, / With his liges lad his lyf in Ioye" (2.1058–61). Priam's Troy would seem a paradigm of the civic unity and splendor seen in the *Triumphal Entry,* but it also contains a warning for medieval London. Not satisfied to be "regnynge in quiete" (2.1064), Priam is stirred by malice to take vengeance on the Greeks, despite the opposition of his oldest son, Hector, who is described as desiring to remain "in quiete and in rest" because he is "so iust and so prudent" (2.1128–30). Hector represents the kind of ruler that London's pageant and Lydgate's poem wanted Henry VI to be, one concerned with the comfort of his city and prudent like Solomon in subordinating foreign adventure to domestic tranquility and justice. Lydgate's monkish learning in the *Troy Book,* which was undertaken as a royal commission from Henry V, results in civic, bourgeois lessons similar to those at the heart of the *Triumphal Entry.* The final destruction of Troy because of Priam's desire for chivalric honor and vengeance is a terrible warning to all cities, and especially "Newe Troye," of the fragility of even the most attractive earthly paradise.

Lydgate's second ancient poem, the *Siege of Thebes,* is associated with London by being ostensibly told to Chaucer's Canterbury pilgrims on their way back to the metropolis. After this contemporary prologue, the story itself begins with the building of another magnificent city. Although Lydgate briefly relates how Cadmus acquired the ample site of the future Thebes by the trick of cutting a bull's hide into strips (293–317), his principal narrative, taken from Boccaccio's *Genealogy of the Gods,* is about the actual construction of the city by Amphion (293–317, 194–292).[36] Amphion is a civic rather than a military leader. Described, like Hector, as "thys prudent Amphyoun" (201), he builds Thebes with "his swete song" (203), meaning that his "wordes swete, / That were so plesaunt fauourable, and mete" (229–30) caused those in the surrounding countries to volunteer to help him make "this Cite / Royal and riche" (238–39). The political lesson Lydgate draws is that the regal head should not "of disdeyn despyse" (264) the common "feet" upon which his support rests. Amphion's example demonstrates that Mercury's "soote sugred harpe" is more efficacious than "Mars swerd whetted kene and sharpe" (273–74); kind looks and speech, rather than riches, pride, or power, allow a king "Among his puple Hertes forto wynne / Of inward loue" (279–80): that is, to establish the kind of affectionate relationship advocated by the *Triumphal Entry* when it calls London the king's chamber. Unfortunately, Thebes, like Troy, does not continue the unity established by Amphion but is ruined by the greedy self-assertion of his successors. Lydgate's account of the building (and later ruin) of Thebes, as with Troy, celebrates values that are fundamentally civic rather than religious or chivalric: military force is questioned from the start in favor of communal effort, social harmony, and prudence, which are earthly, not heavenly, qualities.[37]

The *Triumphal Entry* was Lydgate's most prominent civic work (both because the event it describes involved the entire city and because of its contribution to later chronicles and entries), but the poet wrote poetry for other London spaces and occasions. The *Dance Macabre,* commissioned by John Carpenter for St. Paul's, has already been mentioned, and John Shirley's manuscript rubrics make other London attributions.[38] For example, Shirley writes that the *Legend of St. George* was "þe devyse of a steyned halle" that was "ymagyned by Daun Johan þe Munk of Bury Lydegate" at the request "of þarmorieres of London for þonour of þeyre broþerhoode and þeyre feest of Saint George" and that the antifeminist *Bycorne and Chychevache* was "þe deuise of a peynted or desteyned clothe for an halle a parlour or a chaumbre deuysed by Iohan Lidegate at þe request of a werþy citeseyn of London."[39] Exactly how Lydgate's verses were used in these displays is not certain, though it has been plausibly suggested that *St. George* was written to accompany wall paintings in the armorers' hall and that *Bycorne* was written on banners or a series of banners.[40] What is clear is that Lydgate's writings were part of public or semipublic displays or performances in London.[41]

During a period in the late 1420s that has been called "the apogee of his public career as a poet,"[42] Lydgate produced some of his most original and influential works, a series of seven "mummings." As the name suggests, mummings were pageants or dumbshows in which the actors, who may have formed a *tableau vivant* or mimed the action, remained silent (except perhaps for song), while a narrator described them.[43] As has been noted by others, Lydgate's mummings generally resemble his account in the *Troy Book* of how tragedy was presented in Priam's new city. In contrast to his limited role in the *Triumphal Entry,* Lydgate was apparently the creator as well as the recorder of these performances. There are earlier references to the form, but Lydgate's are the first scripts that survive, and his are the first, or among the first, to combine elements from a variety of sources, popular and elite, into a new kind of drama that directly influenced the Renaissance.[44] Some of Lydgate's mummings were written for the court, but others are more civic, performances not only given in London but also very much for and about London.

A Mumming at London, which, according to Shirley's heading, is "þe deuyse of a desguy sing to fore þe gret estates of þis lande, þane being at London," was intended for a national, not a municipal, occasion, probably the opening of Parliament in October 1427.[45] As is typical of the genre, the narrator directs the audience's attention to a series of actors (e.g., "Loo here þis lady þat yee may see" [1]), whom he then describes in detail. Although performed for an audience of all the "gret estates," the values of this mumming are practical and bourgeois, as we have seen in Lydgate's other civic writing. Dame Fortune is the central character of *A Mumming at London,* as in the poet's *Fall of Princes,* but even though she is introduced as the one who overthrew Alexander, Caesar, and other "prynces" whose tragedies will make up the later work (64–82), Fortune here turns out to be a much more manageable force, against whom the narrator brings on four other ladies, "Which shal hir power ouergoone" (134). In *A Mumming at London,* the vicissitudes of Fortune are defeated not by chivalric stoicism or Christian transcendence but by more optimistic and worldly agents: the cardinal or moral (as opposed to theological) virtues: Prudence, Righteousness (or Justice), Fortitude, and Temperance. The tone of the mumming is comic rather than tragic, emphasizing the sort of pragmatic, decent, and well-regulated communal behavior advocated by medieval London citizens in the rules of their craft and especially parish guilds.[46]

Both the first and last remedies against Fortune in *A Mumming at London* are those most directly related to the conduct expected of burgesses: Prudence (which we have seen Lydgate promote elsewhere in his civic poetry) and Temperance, which here means avoiding the social disgrace of the so-called tavern sins—gluttony, gambling, swearing, and rashness (297–309).[47] Righteousness and Fortitude may be aristocratic virtues, but Lydgate stresses their wider, communal significance. By the "scales of hir balaunces" (presumably a prop held by the actor), the former "sette hem alle in gouuernaunces" (175–76). She is Justice, dispensing "rightful doome" (180): one who favors neither "hyeghe estate, ner lowe degree" but "doope to bothen al equytee" (189–90), the impartial law missing in *London Lickpenny,* but, as "equyte and riht," recommended to the king, as previously noted, by the written scripture on the fourth pageant of the entry for Henry VI at the Conduit on Cornhill.[48] The third virtue, Fortitude, brandishes a sword like the giant on London Bridge during Henry's pageant, but her significance here is more philosophical and social than military, as seen by her association with "comune profit" (231), "communaltee" (236), "goode comune" (239), and "comune proufyte" (251).

The *Mumming at Bishopswood* was performed outside the city walls in Stepney,[49] but its audience was more narrowly municipal than that of *A Mum-*

ming at London: "þe Shirreves of London, acompanyed with þeire breþerne vpon Mayes daye."[50] As appropriate to May, the mumming is largely a celebration of the coming of spring in the poet's most flowery aureate diction. But amidst general claims, echoing values elsewhere in Lydgate's civic poetry, that the new year will bring "prosperitee" (33; cf. 81) to all estates as well as unity (50) and "prudent iuges" (52; cf. 64, 67), Lydgate directly addresses the London authorities in his audience, urging them, in lines reminiscent of *Piers Plowman*,[51] to fulfill their official responsibilities to the citizens and especially those most destitute:

> Beo faythfull founde in al vertu,
> Mayre, provost, shirreff, eche in his substaunce;
> And aldremen, whiche haue þe governaunce
> Over þe people by vertue may avayle,
> Þat noone oppression beo done to þe pourayle.
>
> (59–63)

Two other Lydgate mummings were specifically written for city guilds (the mercers and goldsmiths), perhaps the most widespread and important civic institutions in medieval London, given that they regulated both international and municipal trade, provided social and religious services to their members, and had influence on the government of the city (see n. 12 above). The guilds of the mercers and goldsmiths, though communal, were not a democratic cross section of London residents, or even representative of city guilds in general, but exceptionally wealthy and politically influential organizations. Both mummings were in honor of the Lord Mayor, William Eastfield, himself a mercer, and thus Lydgate was once again writing on behalf of the London establishment.

The *Mumming for the Mercers of London* was performed on Twelfth Night, January 6, 1429.[52] Its form is a letter about a journey by Jupiter's herald down from the heavens and across the face of the earth to London, mentioning a long list of exotic locales (Ethiopia and India as well as Parnassus), pagan gods (including Bacchus, who also appeared in the *Triumphal Entry*), classical and modern poets (Ovid and Virgil, Petrarch and Boccaccio), and allegorical ships painted with somewhat cryptic French mottoes. The poem flatters its guild audience with its learned allusions (even if Shirley's extensive and literal annotation—"Mars is god of batayle"—suggests such knowledge could not be assumed) and with its borrowings from French vision poetry, but perhaps most of all with the conceit that London and its mayor were the object of such a fabulous journey. The "certain estates" (101) on ships in the Thames, who at the

conclusion of the performance are said to want to visit the mayor, may have
been intended by Lydgate to allow the mercers to enjoy what Claire Sponsler
calls "an image of English [or perhaps, more accurately, London] centrality to
the mercantile world."[53]

A Mumming for the Goldsmiths of London, performed "affter souper" on
Candlemas, February 2, 1429, again in honor of Mayor Eastfield, is even more
explicitly a celebration of London than the *Mumming for the Mercers* and comparable to the encomium at the end of the *Triumphal Entry.*[54] The work begins
as if it were a religious epic with Fortune (here as narrator) introducing David,
the slayer of Goliath who was made king by Samuel: "þe chaumpyoun / Þat
sloughe þe tyraunt" (1–4, 12–13). But before the first stanza is over, our attention is directed away from the heroic and biblical to the local and familiar.
David, Fortune tells us, has come with the twelve tribes of Israel "to þis citee"
(London) with gifts "þe noble Mayre to seen and to vysyte" (5–7). London is
given nothing less than the Ark of the Covenant, whose bearers sing "With
laude and prys þe Lord to magnefye" (32). Even though religion and politics
were inseparable in the Middle Ages, the focus of the *Mumming for the Goldsmiths* is fundamentally civic. The gifts that David brings are called "boþe
hevenly and moral," but the following couplet is more specific: "Apperteyning
vn-to good gouuernaunce, / Vn-to þe Mayre for to doo pleasaunce" (19–21).
However heavenly and moral, these are practical gifts of municipal management, the same *buono governo* depicted in Ambrogio Lorenzetti's frescoes at
Siena's Palazzo Publico. David has come down "Frome his cytee of Iherusa-
lem" (22). Whereas this may refer to the celestial Jerusalem, the London to
which he arrives ("þis tovne" [25]) is the earthly metropolis in which the goldsmiths lived and worked, whose public well-being is promised: "Grace and
good eure and long prosperitee / Perpetuelly to byde in þis cytee" (27–28).

As with the mumming for the mercers, that for the goldsmiths flatters London and its merchant class by making it the destination of such an exotic and,
in this case, holy visit. The ark now bringing long prosperity to London is said
to be "more gracyous" than the Palladion that once guarded Troy (38–39) because God makes holy any place the ark resides (46–47). Later in the mumming London's historical association with Troy is recalled as the ark is called
upon to work its munificence:

Keepe and defende in þy proteccion
Þe Mayre, þe citeseyns, þe communes of þis tovne,
Called in cronycles whylome Nuwe Troye,
Graunte hem plente, vertu, honnour and ioye.

(67–70)

The recipients of the ark's protection are specifically civic (the mayor, citizens, and whole communality) and the benefits worldly, beginning with material comfort and ending with pleasure. As in the *Triumphal Entry,* London has become an earthly paradise.

The *Mumming for the Goldsmiths* ends by describing the civic leadership necessary to produce this Edenic London. The ark contains three specific gifts for the "noble Mayre" in the audience (74): "konnyng, grace, and might," which will enable him "to gouuerne with wisdome, pees and right / Þis noble cytee" and "lawes suche ordeyne" about which no one will complain (81–84). Lydgate's emphasis on the law is made clearer in the subsequent account of a written document said to be contained within the ark:

A wrytt with-inn shal vn-to you declare
And in effect pleynly specefye,
Where yee shal punysshe and where as yee shal spare,
And howe þat Mercy shal Rygour modefye.

(85–88)

As previously discussed, justice is a central motif throughout Lydgate's civic writing, especially in his *Against Millers and Bakers* and the *Triumphal Entry.* A mayor able to temper Rigor with Mercy is reminiscent of the pageant at the Conduit in Cornhill, which displayed a boy king surrounded by Mercy, Truth, and Clemency. The equitable justice that Londoners recommended to Henry VI during his entry is here a divine gift to their mayor.

The idea of justice in the *Mumming for the Goldsmiths* may seem as optimistic as some of Lydgate's other political lessons: judging is obviously no problem if one has a paper saying when to be strict and when lenient. The conclusion of the mumming may appear equally fatuous in promising the mayor that God will, by means of the ark, "Sette pees and rest, welfare and vnytee / Duryng youre tyme thoroughe-oute þis citee" (97–98). This is far from the civic corruption and conflicts of *London Lickpenny* and *Piers Plowman.* Lydgate's purpose here is to celebrate London, its guilds, and its mayor, not to attack them. He shows London as it ought to be, not as it is. Yet his vision is not wholly unlike that of the satirists, though he writes positively and they negatively: he dreams of laws about which no one can complain (but so does the author of *London Lickpenny*) and of the peace, unity, and charity so desired in *Piers Plowman.* Nor is Lydgate's civic poetry as naive as it may seem. As already noted in connection with the *Triumphal Entry,* why present an ideal unless to challenge reality? Is the poet telling us that justice will not come to London unless David arrives with the Ark of the Covenant? And how much confidence should the citizens of New Troy have in the ark when it is compared to the Palladion, whose theft caused the destruction of old Troy? For the ark, "bright as þe sonne beeme" (24)—undoubtedly the central prop of the mumming and an example of the goldsmiths' own work[55]—not only celebrates the prosperity of the city and its guilds but also lends support to *London Lickpenny*'s charge that success there comes only from money. Lydgate's civic writing is largely in praise of London, but it also includes, even if it denies a direct voice to, some of the grounds of contemporary criticism.

Notes

1. *Lickpenny* is quoted from John Stow's eight-line stanza version in British Library, MS Harley 542; see Eleanor Prescott Hammond, ed., *English Verse between Chaucer and Surrey* (Durham, NC: Duke University Press, 1927), 237–39. For the version of the poem from Harley 367 in seven-line stanzas, see Douglas Gray, ed., *The Oxford Book of Late Medieval Verse and Prose* (Oxford: Clarendon Press, 1985), 16–19.

2. Throughout this chapter, poetry is cited parenthetically in the text by line number or by book and line numbers.

3. In his *Survey of London,* Stow declares that *London Lickpenny* was "made by Lidgate a Monke of Berrie." John Stow, *A Survey of London,* ed. Charles L. Kingsford, 2 vols. (Oxford: Clarendon Press, 1908), 1:217. For a list of those who once accepted or rejected the poem as Lydgate's, see Hammond, *English Verse,* 237. No modern authority has believed it to be by Lydgate.

4. For the street cries, see William Langland, *The Vision of Piers Plowman,* ed. A. V. C. Schmidt, 2nd ed. (London: Everyman, 1995), Pro.226–30. All further citations are to this edition.

5. Walter F. Schirmer referred in passing to the "civic audience" of some of the mummings (*John Lydgate: A Study in the Culture of the XVth Century,* trans. Ann Keep [London: Methuen, 1961], 107), and Derek Pearsall noted that the poet received commissions from "kings, dukes and earles, but also from country gentlemen and countrywomen, and from London burgesses" and later linked Lydgate's mummings with his other "'London' poems" (*John Lydgate (1371–1449): A Bio-Bibliography,* English Literary Studies 71 [Victoria, BC: University of Victoria, 1997], 9, 31). For an ambitious redefinition of Lydgate's accomplishment, including his role as a poet for the London bourgeoisie, see James Simpson, "The Energies of John Lydgate," in *Reform and Cultural Revolution* (Oxford: Oxford University Press, 2002), 34–67, esp. 57–59.

6. Anne Middleton, "The Idea of Public Poetry in the Reign of Richard II," *Speculum* 53 (1978): 95–96.

7. *The Minor Poems of John Lydgate,* 2 vols., ed. Henry Noble MacCracken, EETS, o.s., 107, 192 (London: Oxford University Press, 1911, 1934), 1:288. We can choose to believe Shirley's claim or not, but Pearsall advises us that it is in the cloister at Bury that we

should expect Lydgate to have spent most of his time, except for the limited periods when he was studying at Oxford or was prior of Hatfield Broad Oak, though he may have occasionally stayed at the residence Bury maintained in London (Pearsall, *Bio-Bibliography,* 21–23, 30–31).

8. Another of Lydgate's satiric works, with a few parallels to *London Lickpenny,* is *A Ballade on an Ale-Seller,* which employs high rhetoric to make its low antifeminist points.

9. *Minor Poems of John Lydgate,* 2:445–48. All citations are to this edition.

10. Ibid., 2:448–49. All citations are to this edition.

11. Stow, *Survey,* 1:191. The Cornhill pillory, according to Stow, was placed on top of the Tun, formerly a municipal lock-up but by then a water conduit. A pillory certainly existed on or near the Tun before 1401. Evidence suggests that the Cornhill pillory was London's principal one, although there may have been others in the city. The relevant London Letter Books, Plea and Memoranda Rolls, and chronicles for the fourteenth and fifteenth centuries contain dozens of references to this punishment. In most cases the actual location of the pillory is not given (probably because everyone knew it), but when a place is mentioned it is almost invariably Cornhill. An early reference to the pillory on Cornhill (1318) is found in Letter Book E, fol. lxxxii, *Calendar of Letter-Books . . . of the City of London: Letter Book E,* ed. Reginald R. Sharpe (London: John Edward Francis, 1903), 96, trans. in Henry Thomas Riley, *Memorials of London and London Life in the XIIIth, XIVth, and XVth Centuries* [London: Longmans, 1868], 129). For two references to the Cornhill pillory in a fifteenth-year chronicle for years after the death of Lydgate, see *Chronicles of London,* ed. C. L. Kingsford (1905; reprint, Dursley: Alan Sutton, 1977), 187, 198. Cornhill, of course, is where the traveler in *London Lickpenny* sees his stolen hood offered for sale. As one of the principal markets in London, Cornhill was an appropriate place for the public display of commercial fraud. See David Benson, "*Piers Plowman* as a Poetry Pillory: The Pillory and the Cross," in *Medieval Literature and Historical Inquiry: Essays in Honor of Derek Pearsall,* ed. David Aers (Cambridge: Brewer, 2000), 31–54.

12. The general term *guild* denotes three different though related organizations: merchant guilds that regulated large-scale, often foreign trade; craft guilds that oversaw manufacture and retail sales; and parish guilds that gave spiritual and social support—though in practice the boundaries between the three types were not always clear. See Ben R. McRee, "Religious Gilds and Civic Order: The Case of Norwich in the Late Middle Ages," *Speculum* 67 (1992): 70 n. 2. Parish fraternities sometimes developed into craft guilds, but many remained primarily social, religious, and charitable societies; see Caroline M. Barron, "The Parish Fraternities of Medieval London," in *The Church in Pre-Reformation Society: Essays in Honour of F. R. H. Du Boulay,* ed. Caroline Barron and Christopher Harper-Bill (Woodbridge, Suffolk: Boydell Press, 1985), 13–37; and George Unwin, *The Gilds and Companies of London,* 4th ed. (London: Frank Cass, 1963). Lydgate seems to imagine a kind of craft guild of millers and bakers, but his identification of it as a fraternity and its possession of a chapel suggests a parish guild, which often maintained a priest to say mass for its living and dead members.

13. Derek Pearsall, *John Lydgate* (London: Routledge & Kegan Paul, 1970), 218.

14. *Minor Poems of John Lydgate,* 2:630–48. All citations are to this edition.

15. Ibid., 2:613–22, 624–30.

16. See Gordon Kipling, *Enter the King: Theatre, Liturgy, and Ritual in the Medieval Civic Triumph* (Oxford: Clarendon Press, 1998), 143–69; cf. Richard Osberg, "The Jesse Tree in the 1432 London Entry of Henry VI: Messianic Kingship and the Rule of Justice," *JMRS* 16 (1986): 213–32.

17. Kipling, *Enter the King,* 162.

18. Pearsall, *John Lydgate,* 171.

19. Pearsall, *Bio-Bibliography,* 34.

20. Kipling, *Enter the King,* 143 n. 59; cf. Gordon Kipling, "The London Pageants for Margaret of Anjou: A Medieval Script Restored," *Medieval English Theatre* 4 (1982): 25–26 n. 13. The letter is recorded in Letter Book K of the City of London, preserved in the Guildhall; see Reginald R. Sharpe, ed., *Calendar of Letter-Books of the City of London: Letter Book K* (London: John Edward Francis, 1911), 135–39. It is transcribed as appendix 3 to vol. 3 of *Munimenta Gildhallae Londoniensis,* 3 vols., ed. Henry T. Riley, Rolls Series (London, 1859–62), 457–64. Henry Noble MacCracken, "King Henry's Triumphal Entry into London, Lydgate's Poem, and Carpenter's Letter," *Archiv* 126 (1911): 75–102, who discussed the resemblances between Carpenter's letter and Lydgate's *Triumphal Entry* in detail, put the term *source* for the former in quotation marks and believed that a few elements in the latter came from Lydgate's personal experience. Kipling thinks that the "brother" to whom Carpenter addresses his letter was presumably the monk Lydgate himself (*Enter the King,* 142 n. 59).

21. The tradition began at least as early as Richard II's coronation in 1377 and includes Richard's formal reconciliation with the City in 1392 as well as Henry V's triumph after his Agincourt victory in 1415. See Kipling, *Enter the King,* especially his chronological index on 373–74.

22. Ibid., 3.

23. MacCracken, "King Henry's Triumphal Entry," 76.

24. For Cotton Julius B.III, see Kingsford, *Chronicles,* 97–116.

25. See Kipling, "London Pageants," 13. More than a century after Henry VI's entry, "the devisers of Edward VI's civic triumph in 1547 based their design upon this triumph" (presumably from copies of Lydgate's poem preserved in London chronicles), and it thus "became the only civic triumph ever to experience a revival." Kipling, *Enter the King,* 168 n.; cf. P. H. Parry, "On the Continuity of English Civic Pageantry: A Study of John Lydgate and the Tudor Pageant," *Forum for Modern Language Studies* 15 (1979), 224.

26. Pearsall, *John Lydgate,* 177–79; Pearsall, *Bio-Bibliography,* 27; Pearsall, "Signs of Life in Lydgate's *Danse Macabre,*" in *Zeit, Tod und Ewigkeit in der Renaissance Literature,* ed. J. Hogg, *Analecta Carthusiana* 117 (1987): 58–71. For an exciting new understanding of the *Danse,* see Simpson, "Energies of John Lydgate." For Carpenter's commission, see Stow, *Survey,* 1:327.

27. MacCracken, "King Henry's Triumphal Entry," 75.

28. Ibid., 90–91; Kipling, *Enter the King,* 164 n. 108.

29. The word *comfort* is not in Carpenter's English transcription of the mayor's speech (see *Munimenta Gildhallae* 3:458; cf. MacCracken, "King Henry's Triumphal Entry," 81).

30. Although there are other references to Henry's claim to the crown of France as well as to the crown of England (prose after lines 63, 93, 133, 397 ff., 487), the emphasis of the poem, especially at its core, is on the relationship of the king to the city.

31. Osberg, "Jesse Tree," 221.

32. See ibid., 226, 229; Kipling, *Enter the King,* 162.

33. *Enter the King,* 163; cf. 166–67.

34. Henry's heavenly journey is emphasized more in the final two pageants located near St. Paul's; see ibid., 167.

35. *Lydgate's Troy Book,* 4 vols., ed. Henry Bergen, EETS, e.s., 97, 103, 106, 126 (London: Kegan Paul, Trench, Trübner, 1906, 1908, 1910, 1935). All citations are to this edition.

36. *Lydgate's Siege of Thebes,* 2 vols., ed. Axel Erdmann and Eilert Ekwall, EETS, e.s., 108, 125 (London: Kegan Paul, Trench, Trübner, 1911, 1930). All citations are to this edition.

37. For recent, pessimistic political readings of the *Siege of Thebes,* see James Simpson, "'Dysemol daies and fatal houres': Lydgate's *Destruction of Thebes* and Chaucer's *Knight's Tale,*" in *The Long Fifteenth Century: Essays for Douglas Gray,* ed. Helen Cooper and Sally Mapstone (Oxford: Clarendon Press, 1997), 15–33; and Scott-Morgan Straker, "Deference and Difference: Lydgate, Chaucer, and *The Siege of Thebes,*" *RES,* n.s., 52 (2001): 1–21.

38. Pearsall calls Shirley's rubrics "an important source of information (and misinformation) for the dates and occasions of Lydgate's poems" (*Bio-Bibliography,* 17).

39. See *Minor Poems of John Lydgate,* 1:145; 2:433.

40. Pearsall, *John Lydgate,* 181, 180.

41. Shirley's heading to Lydgate's *A Procession of Corpus Cristi* says that what follows is "an ordenaunce of a precssyoun of þe feste of corpus cristi made in london. By daun John Lydegate," but it is not clear if he is saying that the procession or the composition of the poem took place in London; *Minor Poems of John Lydgate,* 1:35. Simpson notes other poems that Lydgate may have written for London burgesses: *Fabulae duorum mercatorum, Debate of the Horse, Goose and Sheep, Isopes Fabules,* and *Stans Puer* ("Energies of John Lydgate," 58). In Lydgate's *Pageant of Knowledge,* merchants are given their own separate estate; *Minor Poems of John Lydgate,* 2:724.

42. Pearsall, *Bio-Bibliography,* 28.

43. Glynne Wickham, *Early English Stages, 1300 to 1660* (London: Routledge, 1959), 1:191–207. For a radical rethinking of Lydgate's mummings, including the relationship of the London oligarchy to the crown, see Maura Nolan's essay elsewhere in this volume.

44. A mumming is recorded as early as 1377 during the reign of Richard II (Stow, *Survey,* 1:96; Wickham, *Early English Stages,* 1:197). On Lydgate's possible originality, see Wickham, *Early English Stages,* 1:207.

45. *Minor Poems of John Lydgate,* 2:682; all citations are to this edition. See Pearsall, *Bio-Bibliography,* 28.

46. See, e.g., Ben R. McRee, "Religious Gilds and Regulation of Behavior in Late Medieval Towns," in *People, Politics and Community in the Later Middle Ages,* ed. Joel Rosenthal and Colin Richmond (New York: St. Martin's Press, 1987), 108–22; and Gervase Rosser, "Workers' Associations in English Medieval Towns," in *Les métiers au Moyen Age: Aspects économiques et sociaux,* ed. Pascale Lambrechts and Jean-Pierre Sosson (Louvain: Université catholique de Louvain, 1994), 283–305.

47. In contrast to Chaucer's Criseyde, who confesses that she has been overwhelmed by events because among Prudence's three powers (to see the past, present, and future) she was never able to master the last (*Troilus and Crisyde,* in *The Riverside Chaucer,* ed. L. D. Benson, 3rd ed. [Boston: Houghton Mifflin, 1987], 5.743–49), Lydgate's narrator describes Prudence's triple powers and assumes that it is possible for humans to practice her foresight, declaring that "who þus dooþe" (161) will be defended "Ageyns Fortune goode and peruerse" (167). This is as optimistic and useless as the lessons at the end of the *Nun's Priest's Tale*: indeed, he who knows the future is protected, but *how* does any human achieve that knowledge?

48. Lydgate, *Triumphant Entry,* 299.

49. Schirmer, *John Lydgate,* 102–3.

50. *Minor Poems of John Lydgate,* 2:668. All further citations are to this edition.

51. E.g., Langland, *Piers Plowman,* 3.76–90.

52. See *Minor Poems of John Lydgate,* 2:695–98. All further citations are to this edition. For a detailed study of this mumming, see chap. 7 of this volume.

53. Claire Sponsler, "Alien Nation: London's Aliens and Lydgate's Mummings for the Mercers and Goldsmiths," in *The Postcolonial Middle Ages,* ed. Jeffrey Jerome Cohen (New York: St. Martin's Press, 2000), 239. Sponsler is among the recent critics, like Nolan, who see Lydgate's thought as more sophisticated than traditionally assumed; here and in the mumming for the goldsmiths she finds the poet confronting the xenophobic fears of Londoners and arguing instead for openness. Whether or not one accepts such a liberal, multicultural Lydgate, it is true that aliens were part of the delegation welcoming Henry at Blackheath during his entry.

54. *Minor Poems of John Lydgate,* 2:698–701. All citations are to this edition.

55. Wickham, *Early English Stages,* 1:201.

7

The Performance of the Literary

Lydgate's Mummings

Maura B. Nolan

In Trinity College Cambridge MS R. 3. 20 may be found a series of short poems by Lydgate that its compiler, John Shirley, introduced with variations of the term *mumming*—"the devyse of a momyng," "in wyse of mommers desguysed."[1] These include two performances before King Henry VI, at Eltham and at Windsor, and two spectacles in honor of Mayor William Eastfield of London, commissioned by the mercers' and goldsmiths' guilds. In his 1934 edition, *The Minor Poems of John Lydgate,*[2] Henry Noble MacCracken added to these four a further three "mummings"—those at Bishopswood, London, and Hertford—creating a minor canon of Lydgate's dramatic works, all of which can be dated between the years 1424 and 1430. These texts have been little discussed, despite (or perhaps because of) the fact that they occupy an anomalous place within both literary and dramatic histories of late medieval England; lacking detailed performance records, historians of the theater find the mummings intriguing but ultimately unrevealing, while literary critics have typically eschewed them in favor of Lydgate's more poetically ambitious texts, such as *Siege of Thebes* or *Troy Book*. But there is good reason for examining these poems more carefully. Because they stand at the intersection of genres and media—not quite "literature," nor yet "drama"—Lydgate's mummings challenge the assumptions from which both literary and dramatic criticism proceed.[3] They produce a serious temptation to speculate, to experiment with possible performance details and to reconstruct audience responses, even as the dearth of evidence for such performances enforces its own relentless logic of absence. Critical speculation about the mummings has tended to extrapolate in two ways, either drawing conclusions about the genre of "mumming" and its history or supplying details of performance that have no basis in textual evidence.[4] This is not to say that I do not recognize the need for what Paul Strohm has called "rememorative reconstruction"—the reassembly of the past in the present from the shards and bits of history, the defragmentation of what are necessarily disconnected and disparate shreds of medieval texts and textuality.[5] But it is precisely the *textuality* of Lydgate's mummings that is at issue here.[6] These are poems that insist upon their status as literary documents, as parts of a vernacular poetic tradition emerging—in large part due to Lydgate—as a privileged form of social commentary and aesthetic reflection. While the mummings are certainly iterations of cultural practice, as well as distillations of historical anxiety and crisis, they are first of all poetic texts, texts that actively solicit a kind of reading that begins with the words on the page and moves outward to encompass an entire intertextual network of sources, allusions, and contexts. As I will show, Lydgate takes up the mumming form (a mode of festive practice associated with London elites and their relationship to the king) and reproduces it in a new idiom—Chaucerian vernacular poetry.

While each of the seven texts MacCracken designated "mummings" uses a recognizably Chaucerian diction, and several directly draw from Chaucer's poetry, I will here consider only those four poems identified by Shirley—the single available contemporary witness—as "mummings." These include royal entertainments—the *Mumming at Eltham* and the *Mumming at Windsor*—and two performances for non-noble patrons, the *Mumming for the Mercers* and the *Mumming for the Goldsmiths*. I have limited my discussion to these texts for several reasons. First, as both Glynne Wickham and Derek Pearsall have noted, there are substantial differences between Shirley's "mummings" and the two poems he designates "disguisings," the entertainments at London and at Hertford. The latter are much longer works, presented in rhyming couplets; the "mummings" are all brief and in rhyme royal.[7] The *Mumming at Bishopswood,* though it is in rhyme royal, is exceptional in several ways; it is not described by Shirley as a "mumming," it does not take place at Christmas (the usual time of year for mummings), and it does not appear in Trinity College Cambridge MS R. 3. 20.[8] Further, as I will demonstrate below, all four "mummings" were written at a moment of cultural crisis; during a brief span of time—1428–30— in which English losses in France compelled the coronation of the youthful Henry VI in a massive propaganda effort to bolster the dual monarchy, an effort in which Lydgate was thoroughly involved.[9] Shirley's four "mummings," then, form a distinct group, linked generically and thematically, that demands closer analysis than it has typically received. I will argue in this essay not only that Lydgate's appropriation of the mumming form constitutes a genuine innovation, both literary and dramatic, but also that this innovation must be situated in relation to the very different audiences addressed by the two pairs of mummings, royal and mercantile. As I will show, the mercantile mummings effect a form of cultural *translatio,* bringing to an elite but non-noble audience the images, tropes and forms of aristocratic and clerkly culture: Chaucerian poetics, biblical exegesis, and classical and continental literary *auctoritee.* As such, they reflect the growing desire of the mercantile class for the cultural trappings of the aristocracy—and demonstrate the expansive capacity of both the mumming form and Chaucerian poetics to accommodate both class difference and national sentiment.

Mumming and the King: Eltham and Windsor

The most obvious—and most important—fact about the mummings at Eltham and Windsor is that they were performed before the king. In this, they are consistent with what is known about the cultural practice of mumming in England, a mode of performance for which there is very little evidence and that necessarily remains somewhat obscure, despite a number of attempts to define it as a popular folk custom with deep roots in the English past.[10] All such attempts are necessarily speculative; the first real evidence for mumming comes from very late in the reign of Edward III, when the word *mumming* begins to appear in written documents and the first extended descriptions of the practice occur.[11] Starting with a 1377 Christmas celebration for the young prince Richard, we find both descriptions of actual "mummings" and prohibitions of the practice, which continue to appear in the records throughout the fifteenth century.[12] According to the *Anonimalle Chronicle*'s recounting of the 1377 event, mumming appears to have been a festive, aristocratic holiday game that particularly concerned the relationship of London citizens to the king and his household: "En celle tenps les comunes de Loundres firent une graunte desporte et solempnite al iune prince, qare le dymaigne proschein avaunt la Purificacion de Nostre Dame a sayre et deinz noet furount vi^xx et x hommes degisement arrayes et bien mountez a chivalle pur moummere."[13] On this occasion, the mummers entered the castle and invited the prince to play at (loaded) dice; he made three casts and won a gold ball, a gold cup, and a gold ring. After his mother and the other lords in the household had cast and won gold rings, the prince called for wine and the evening ended with dancing, mummers on one side and the royal household on the other. Because the 1377 mumming is the first extended description of the practice, its elements—disguise, gift giving, game playing, and dancing—have long been identified as the standard characteristics of a familiar Christmas scenario.[14] On the basis of the recorded evidence, however, though it is clear that practices like wearing visors or masks and dice playing were relatively common, the term *mumming* appears to have been applied with some precision to occasions involving an address to the king. Sanctioned mumming, that is, involves the relation of non-noble persons—in particular, the London oligarchy—to the sovereign; mummers, however disguised, are Londoners paying homage to royalty. If the royal entry symbolically enacts the relationship of the king to the city, both signifying its submission to him and displaying its wealth and power, the mumming functions as a more private intrusion by the city into the king's household. The prohibitions that appear with such frequency during Richard's reign, and that typically issue from the mayor and aldermen, would seem not to be attempts to forbid the practice entirely, but (like sumptuary laws) restrictions upon who might be authorized to behave in a particular way. Mumming seems to have been a London practice that the London elite were determined to keep for themselves. And while it would surely be rash to suggest that the only mumming that occurred in England was that for which we have textual evidence, it remains the case that the practice emerged as a named activity at a historically specific moment and can be analyzed within quite particular parameters, without recourse to "folk custom" or popular tradition.

These conclusions are borne out by the evidence for mummings themselves. The mummings recorded during Richard II's reign are Christmastime entertainments performed by London citizens for the king, and at Christmas 1400–1401 a mumming was performed by men of London for the emperor of Constantinople, Manuel II, at Eltham.[15] All but a 1394 performance are identified by a source using the term *mumming,* although for a 1377 occasion the reference comes from a chronicle of a later date.[16] In the *Westminster Chronicle,* it is reported that at Christmas 1393 and 1394 Londoners visited the king at Eltham and Westminster; though on both occasions there was music, dancing, costumes (in 1393 the Londoners came with "glorioso apparatu" and in 1394 with "diverso apparatu"), and gifts (in 1393 a dromedary and a great bird, in 1394 a ship filled with offerings for the king and queen), the 1393 visit provided the occasion for a complicated negotiation of fines owed by the city to the king.[17] In every instance, mumming involves the appearance at court of Londoners at Christmastime, reenacting, in however attenuated a fashion, the visit of the Magi to the infant Christ before their earthly king.[18] As the 1393 visit makes clear, these occasions created a space for festive resolutions to political problems;

the powerful symbolism of the Epiphany visit lifted king and citizens out of the narrow world of city politics and into a more abstract and pleasing realm of serious play.

This portrait of mumming may seem far too narrowly drawn. But it has the advantage of delimiting a field of inquiry according to a vocabulary for which there is distinctive historical evidence. If it cannot be said that mumming was *always* a practice restricted to London and involving the king in some way, it must be noted that the reign of Richard II saw the development of a form of entertainment dedicated on *most occasions* to staging the relationship between the king and the London oligarchy. It required legislation not only because of the intrinsic potential of disguise to erase critical identity markers of class and status but also because it was a recognizably privileged form within which subordinates could negotiate, enact, and engage power relations.[19]

The Lancastrian kings seem to have been less welcoming to London mummers; after the usurpation, we find only one record of such a performance (and that took place almost immediately upon Henry IV's ascent) until Lydgate's mummings appear in the late 1420s—though there were prohibitions in 1404, 1405, 1417, and 1418.[20] It is not until the reign of Henry VI that evidence for the performance of mummings resumes. As in the case of the 1377 mumming before the young prince Richard, these performances take place before a youthful sovereign—and indeed, as soon as Henry VI is crowned records of mummings cease. There are also comparatively few prohibitions of mumming during his reign; Ian Lancashire records only two between 1419 and 1451 and none during the 1420s, when the series of mummings written by Lydgate was performed.[21] Of course, had Trinity College Cambridge R. 3. 20 not been collected and copied by John Shirley, there would be no record of any such performance during the 1420s, and a discussion of mumming during Henry VI's reign would look very different.[22] Since the mummings of the 1420s share a number of characteristics with the mummings of Richard II's reign—Christmas or Epiphany performance, costume, gift giving—one might expect to find that they similarly provide a structured and formal but intimate and private venue for the articulation of the relationship between the king and his subjects. And indeed, as the *Mumming at Windsor* and the *Mumming at Eltham* will show, Lydgate found the mumming form an ideal vehicle for Lancastrian propaganda.

The mummings at Eltham and Windsor are very short, very simple, and very direct. Both can be reasonably accurately dated; both took place at Christmas; and both are thematically appropriate for performance before the young sovereign. The *Mumming at Eltham* consists of twelve rhyme-royal stanzas describing the bringing of gifts (wine, wheat, and oil) from Bacchus, Juno, and

Ceres by "marchandes þat here be" (5).[23] The first seven stanzas culminate in the refrain "Pees with youre lieges, plente and gladnesse" and are addressed to the king; the remaining five are addressed to his mother Queen Katherine, with the refrain "Ay by encreese ioye and gladnesse of hert."[24] These conventional themes are elaborated in general terms, though the poem does contain topical references to the "rebelles, wheeche beon now reklesse" (24) and to the joining of the "hertes of England and of Fraunce" (33). The mumming was likely performed in 1425 or 1428, when Henry was at Eltham for Christmas;[25] the reference to "rebelles" favors the later date, when the dauphin and the French army had seriously threatened the English and the stability of the "two reavmes" (27) was in great doubt.[26] If the mumming form had provided Richard II and the London oligarchy with a means to negotiate and articulate the relationship between royal and civic authority, in the late 1420s the most pressing political question was not the role of London but the status of France. Despite the fact that merchants play a role in the Eltham mumming as mediators between the divinities Bacchus, Juno, and Ceres and the king—perhaps a gesture toward the civic origin of the form—the real issue addressed by the poem is the problem of double sovereignty, "two reavmes."

In its similar concern with the dual monarchy, the *Mumming at Windsor* is a companion piece to the *Mumming at Eltham*.[27] It is an extremely simple retelling in rhyme-royal stanzas of the conversion of King Clovis through his wife, St. Clotilde, his baptism by St. Remigius, and the miraculous appearance of the golden ampoule and fleur-de-lys. Its topicality is made perfectly clear; Lydgate describes how the ampoule and chrism are preserved at Rheims for the anointing of French kings and how "right soon" Henry VI will "resceyve his coroune" (85, 89). The date for the Windsor mumming is surely Christmas, 1429; Henry VI was crowned at Westminster on November 6 of that year and crowned at Paris on December 16, 1430.[28] The vision of the monarchy presented at Windsor asserts the divine right of Henry to rule by "just succession" (Lydgate refers to "succession" three times in eight lines); it is an openly propagandistic use of French traditions to buttress English claims. As J. W. McKenna has stated, "The very real though superficial interest which the Anglo-Gallic administrators showed in French royal history and traditions, and the use of those traditions in propagandist poetry and pageantry, testify to their determination that Henry VI's French antecedents should receive all possible publicity."[29] Indeed, at Christmas, 1430, Henry VI received from Anne, wife of the Duke of Bedford, a book of hours with a miniature of Clovis receiving the fleur-de-lys from St. Clotilde.[30]

The Eltham and Windsor mummings respond directly to the exigencies of the political situation in the late 1420s; their simplicity and brevity make clear that the question of the dual monarchy was the dominant issue at the English court. Lydgate more than earns his reputation as Lancastrian apologist in these poems; by adopting a form of court entertainment typically devoted to the negotiation of relations between the king and his subjects, he asserts the fundamental subordination of the French. The felt need for such an assertion, even at the English court, testifies to the degree of uncertainty caused by the changing fortunes of the war in France and by the youth of the king—and the mummings may be seen in this light as a combination of propaganda (directed outward) and flattery (directed to the king himself). This combination was designed to entertain and to reassure its audience; it takes up the familiar mumming form as a means of identifying the proper role for the king as receiver of gifts and sovereign lord. The *Mumming at Eltham* and the *Mumming at Windsor* make it clear that textuality alone does not confer the values of complexity and multivalence that, I will argue, distinguish the aesthetic of the mercantile mummings. Some cultural performances can indeed be analyzed in terms of topicality, as indices to the preoccupations and anxieties of a particular historical moment. Eltham and Windsor are functional texts, whose existence serves a specific purpose; they are illuminated by a historical understanding of the mumming form and its sedimented meaning, but they do not break away from or reshape either that form or its content.

Drama on Parnassus: Poetry and Performance

By contrast, the *Mumming for the Goldsmiths* and the *Mumming for the Mercers* present their audiences with the old form in a new context. In very different ways, the two performances stage the appropriation of multiple cultural traditions, forging an aesthetic synthesis of practice and textuality, I argue, that ultimately exceeds the limit of the form.[31] To illustrate this process, I turn first to the *Mumming for the Goldsmiths,* a performance similar to the Ricardian mumming in almost every way—it includes a procession of costumed folk bearing gifts, singing, and making music. But the gifts are for the mayor, not the king, and, as I will show, the sentiments expressed by the mumming betray not only an ambivalence about mayoral authority and a concern for such problems as legitimacy and succession but also a deep structural interest in the authority of dramatic representation. The *Mumming for the Goldsmiths* can be precisely dated to February 2, 1430, Candlemas Day, the feast of the Purification of Mary.[32] The kinds of political anxieties that provoked the propagandistic mummings at Windsor and Eltham are here displaced both temporally and figurally; instead of being a straightforward delivery of gifts, the mumming presents an elaborate and densely layered Old Testament scenario susceptible to both the simplest and the most exegetical of readings. By combining a royal form, a biblical theme, and a mercantile setting, Lydgate manages to produce a conservative document (and no doubt performance) with radical implications. Precisely because the text is written for an ephemeral occasion, however, those implications prove tantalizingly insubstantial, suggestive without in any way offering concrete challenges to the hegemonic standards that the mumming repeatedly invokes.

From the very beginning, the mumming is characterized by a mixture of registers. Shirley's headnote states that a herald called Fortune brings the mumming in the form of a letter. The use of a herald and the figuration of Fortune lend to the occasion a courtly air that fits oddly with the Old Testament note immediately sounded in the first stanza:

Þat worþy Dauid, which þat sloughe Golye,
Þe first kyng þat sprang oute of Iesse,
Of God echosen, þe bookes specefye,
By Samuel sette in his royal see,
With twelve trybus is comen to þis citee,
Brought royal gyfftes, kyngly him taquyte,
Þe noble Mayre to seen and to vysyte.

(1–7)

The sheer density of references in this stanza is belied by the simple visual image of the gift-bearing procession that it is designed to illustrate. Several themes are introduced here that will be woven together and elaborated over the course of the performance. First, the reference to Jesse, particularly in a mumming performed on the Feast of the Purification of Mary, recalls a series of well-known biblical texts that were associated with the Jesse tree image and the lineages of Mary and Christ. Isaiah 11:1—"et egredietur virga de radice Iesse et flos de radice eius ascendet" (Vulgate)—and Matthew 1:1–14 (which traces the lineage of Christ) were linked by commentators as prophecy and fulfillment. The flowering rod *(virga)* of Jesse became the pregnant virgin *(virgo)* in a powerful synthesis of Old and New Testaments, a synthesis exploited here to link the Feast of the Purification with secular homage to the mayor.[33] Second, the image of Samuel anointing David, from 1 Samuel 16, links succession to divine election, asserting that kingship must be ratified by anointment even when God has handpicked his candidate. This nexus of texts and images of divine lineage and succession is carried forward into the present by the action of the tribes carrying gifts to the mayor; the mayor acquires "royal gyfftes" just as David sits in his "royal see."

But the reference to Samuel necessarily recalls a moment of great doubt, the failure of Saul and the transfer of succession to the lineage of Jesse. Divine election covers a disruption in lineal descent caused by the inadequacy of Saul as king; Samuel's anointment represents the compensating earthly gesture necessary to accomplish the divine will. The *Mumming for the Goldsmiths* thus shares with the mummings at Eltham and Windsor an obsessive concern with lineage, succession, and hereditary right. But while the royal mummings were straightforward assertions of the legitimacy of Henry VI's rule in France, this mumming more subtly explores the parameters of such claims. Not only does Lydgate introduce a frame of reference—biblical exegesis—far more complex than the simple parade of pagan deities at Eltham or Windsor's miraculous story of conversion, but he also inserts a royal theme into a mercantile context. The idea of lineal succession is here applied to the mayor, an appropriation that allows the goldsmiths to flatter their mayor extravagantly while also presenting the right to rule as an acquired and negotiable status. In the first three stanzas of the mumming, the lineal relation of Christ and David is emphasized in order to suggest the mayor's place in the hereditary chain: like Christ, who "lyneally . . . came adowne" (11), the David figure in the mumming "is nowe descended" (16) to bring "gyfftes þat beon boþe hevenly and moral/Apperteyning vn-to good gouuernaunce" (19–20). As the recipient of these gifts, the mayor is both positioned within this divine succession and made to recognize the contingency of his power and authority; the gift confers both honor and obligation.

Thus far it seems clear that the substitution of the mayor for the king produces a different gift-giving dynamic. Gifts of gold (as in the 1377 mumming) or wine, wheat, and oil, even read allegorically, remain fundamentally simple homages and bespeak a simple relationship of obligation between lord and servant. A gift of writing—as Shirley tells us, "a lettre made in wyse of balade"—however, suggests a far more nuanced interaction between subordinate and superior. Lydgate brings to the traditional mumming a notion of literary patronage that implies that such cultural productions function both as vehicles for praise and honor and as serious engagements with questions of good governance and right rule. In the goldsmiths' mumming, this dual purpose is present from the beginning. The gift of the ark depends upon the capacity of the recipient to use it well:

> Þe arke of God, bright as þe sonne beeme,
> In-to þis tovne he haþe goodely brought,
> Which designeþe, *if hit be wel sought,*
> Grace and good eure and long prosperitee
> Perpetually to byde in þis cytee.
>
> (24–28)

The ark of God can signify grace, good fortune, and prosperity only if it is sought *properly*; it is a conditional gift that demands an active and engaged response. The nature of such a response is suggested by the next several stanzas, which outline and gloss David's behavior, both in the Old Testament and in the action of the mumming itself. First the Levites, the tribe specially designated as caretakers of the ark and its bearers here, are given a stage direction to "dooþe youre devoyre" and sing in honor of the Lord. Lydgate then turns to 2 Samuel 6, which describes David dancing before the ark as he enters Jerusalem, using the biblical text as theatrical scenario:

> Whylome þis arke, abyding in þe hous
> Of Ebdomadon, brought in ful gret ioye;
> For in effect it was more gracyous
> Þanne euer was Palladyone of Troye.
> Hit did gret gladnesse and hit did accoye
> Thinges contrarye and al aduersytee.
> Þeffect þer-of, whane Dauid did see,
>
> And fully knewe, howe God list for to blesse
> Thorughe his vertu and his mighty grace,
> Þat of gladdnesse Þey might nothing mysse—
> Wher hit aboode any maner spaace,
> God of His might halowed so Þe place—
> Wherfore Kynge Dauid, by gret deuocion,
> Maade of Þis ark a feyre translacion.
>
> In-to his hous and his palays royal,
> Brought by Þe Levytes with gret solempnytee;
> And he him-self in especyal

Daunsed and sang of gret humylyte,
And ful deuoutely lefft his ryaltee,
With Ephod gyrt, lyche preestis of þe lawe,
To gyf ensaumple howe pryde shoulde be withdrawe.

(36–56)

The exemplary lesson to be drawn from David's behavior is that a humble de-
meanor is appropriate to those in power; pride must be "withdrawe" in order
that the ark may be properly honored. Lest the mayor find the point too direct,
Lydgate suggests in the next stanza that the lesson is particularly meant for
"mynistres of þe Chirche" (59), though he makes sure to note that it applies as
well to "yche estate" (57). This simple exegetical reading of the passage from
Samuel, however, belies the complexity of Lydgate's choice of biblical text. Not
only is the incident of David dancing before the ark particularly fitting for the
Feast of the Purification, but it also constitutes a justification for dramatic representation itself.

A contemporary fifteenth-century translation of the popular typological
handbook *Speculum humanae salvationis,* the *Mirour of Mans Saluacioune,* provides a gloss to the passage that suggests its Marian significance:

And this assumpcioune of Marie was sometyme figurid
When in the Kyng Dauid house Gods Arc was translatid.
Dauid harped and daunced tofore thilk Archa Domini.

(3837–39)[34]

David here is a figure for Christ, who brings his mother to his house in a festive
procession just as David translates the ark to his Jerusalem palace. But David's
dancing references Christ in yet another way. The account in Samuel concludes
with David's wife, Michol, daughter of Saul, angrily reproving the king for his
exuberant and undignified behavior:

[R]eversusque est et David ut benediceret domui suae et egressa Michol filia
Saul in occursum David ait quam gloriosus fuit hodie rex Israhel disco-
periens se ante ancillas servorum suorum et nudatus est quasi si nudetur
unus de scurris [And David returned to bless his own house: and Michol
the daughter of Saul coming out to meet David, said: How glorious was the
king of Israel to day, uncovering himself before the handmaids of his servants, and was naked, as if one of the buffoons should be naked.]

(2 Samuel 6:20, Vulgate and Douay-Rheims translation)

In the *Mirour,* this passage is identified as a prefiguration of Christ's humiliation on the cross; David is scorned by Michol as Christ is scorned by the Jews.[35]
Other commentators understood the passage not only as a connection between
David's dancing and Christ's humiliation but also as a biblical justification for
certain kinds of medieval performance. As Lawrence Clopper notes, when Bernard of Clairvaux cites David's response to Michol, "I will play and make myself more vile," in a letter in which he provocatively compares monks to *jocula-
tores,* he not only suggests that worldly scorn constitutes the measure of the
success of devotional practice but also links David's dancing and playing with
the behavior of contemporary performers:

> In fact what else do seculars think we are doing but playing when what they
> desire most on earth, we fly from; and what they fly from, we desire? Like
> acrobats and dancers, who with heads down and feet up, stand or walk on
> their hands, and thus draw all eyes to themselves. But this is not a game for
> children or the theatre where lust is excited by the effeminate and indecent
> contortions of the actors, it is a joyous game, decent, grave and admirable,
> delighting the gaze of the heavenly onlookers. This pure and holy game he
> plays who says: "We are become a spectacle to angels and men."[36]

Like performers, monks are ridiculed and humbled by people in the world; the
monks, at least, will ultimately be exalted by God for their humiliation. Other
commentators made this connection as well. Bernard's association of worship
with performance similarly characterizes the discussion of 2 Samuel 6 in *Dives
and Pauper.* In a chapter immediately following the well-known defense of
"steraclis, pleyys & dauncis þat arn don principaly for deuocioun" (Com. 3,
Cap. 17, lines 13–14), Pauper cites David's dancing in order to legitimate "dauncis and songis" on holidays and feast days: "We fyndyn also in þe secunde book
of Kyngis, þe sextie chapitle [14–23], þat whan Dauyd schulde fettyn Goddis
hoche into Ierusalem Dauyd & al þe peple of Israel wentyn þerwith and pleyy-
dyn in al maner menstrasie & songyn & daunsedyn & sckepedyn for ioye and so
preysedyn & worschepedyn God."[37] In *Dives and Pauper,* Michol's reproof provides the necessary counterpoint against which a defense of festivity can be
mounted; David's dancing is truly devotional because it elicits scorn, unlike
"vnhonest dauncis and pleyys" that "steryn folc to lecherie & to oþer synnys"
(Com. 3, Cap. 17, lines 40–42). It is a commonplace that festive behavior exists
on the border of the licit and illicit; what Bernard and the authors of *Mirour*
and *Dives and Pauper* assert is that it also rests uneasily between the worldly and
the divine.[38]

Like Bernard and the *Dives and Pauper* author, Lydgate recognizes the fit between the story of David's dancing and contemporary medieval performing practices. He fully exploits the dramatic potential of the scene by restaging the translation of the ark; in this way, the mumming becomes a performance that contains its own authorization. Oddly, however, Lydgate truncates the episode, eliminating the critical role of Michol and her reproof and turning instead to generalized commentary on humility. Lydgate's omission of Michol's scorn effects a substitution of exegesis for acting, replacing the biblical dialogue—which reveals that David's true audience is God—with a didactic gesture toward the "mynistres of þe Chirche." In the simplest terms, Lydgate is merely being delicate with regard to the mayor, backing away from a direct suggestion that he should cast aside his mayoral robes and embrace Davidian humility. And it is surely right to see this mumming as an illustrative example of the muted and conventional quality of fifteenth-century political discourse; the mayor is given advice on good governance in the most flattering and favorable way possible. Yet the very layering of references, the subtlety of Lydgate's rhetorical maneuvering, demands a more nuanced reading. The *Mumming for the Goldsmiths* is patently meant to be read as well as performed; if in a crude way it simply represents an extravagant compliment to a man in power, it also presents itself to its audience as a text awaiting interpretation—awaiting the reader who will notice the absence of Michol's reproof. Lydgate's substitution of generalizing platitudes for the specific incidence of Michol's reproof must ultimately be attributed to a desire to subdue the tension between earthly authority and divine power evoked by the conclusion to the biblical episode. Michol, daughter of Saul, the king whom David superseded, taxes David with his kingly responsibility to maintain dignity *in the world*; David responds with a world-rejecting claim that he can be interpreted only by a higher power:

dixitque David ad Michol ante Dominum qui elegit me potius quam patrem tuum et quam omnem domum eius et praecepit mihi ut essem dux super populum Domini Israhel

et ludam et vilior fiam plus quam factus sum et ero humilis in oculis meis et cum ancillis de quibus locuta es gloriosior apparebo

[And David said to Michol: Before the Lord, who chose me rather than thy father, and than all his house, and commanded me to be ruler over the people of the Lord in Israel,

I will both play and make myself meaner than I have done: and I will be little in my own eyes: and with the handmaid of whom thou speakest, I shall
appear more glorious.]

(2 Sam. 6:22, 23, Vulgate and Douay-Rheims translation)

What Bernard gleans from this passage is that David's performance is directed
to God and interpretable only by God; similarly, he asserts, what appears to the
world as ridiculous behavior in the monks is understood by God as worship. In
Dives and Pauper, David's embrace of a "lowir degre" (Com. 3, Cap. 18, line 42)
is misread by Michol as the behavior of a "knaue" (138); what David explains is
that his performance is directed not to the people but to God, to whom it is utterly legible. But when Lydgate invokes the episode, he refuses the possibility of
worldly misreading; David's dance for the goldsmiths is glossed and unambiguous. And although David is described as having "ful deuoutely lefft his ryaltee . . .To gyf ensaumple howe pryde shoulde be withdrawe," the absence of
Michol's critique erases the possibility of conflict between devotion (represented
by dancing) and kingship.

Lydgate's portrayal of David functions differently from the mummings performed before Richard II. If in the earlier performances the distinction between
representation and the real was blurred until it nearly vanished—the king himself "playing" the role of king—here the artificiality of the procession stands
out in relief. King David's humility extends to his bringing gifts to the mayor of
London, "for þat meeknesse is a vertu feyre" (71); his figural status is clearly
marked and indeed highlighted. This insistence on figural interpretation is further exaggerated by Lydgate's use of Psalm 131 (Vulgate) as a linking device between the description of David's dancing and the proffering of the gifts. In a
remarkable enjambment, Lydgate combines secular and sacred history, chronicle writing and the singing of psalms, in a heavily overdetermined prayer for
the prosperity of London:

Nowe ryse vp, Lord, in-to Þy resting place,
Aark of Þyne hooly halowed mansyoun,
Þou aark of wisdome, of vertu and of grace,
Keepe and defende in þy proteccion
Þe Meyre, þe citeseyns, þe comunes of þis tovne,
Called in cronycles whylome Nuwe Troye,
Graunte hem plente, vertu, honnour and ioye.

(64–70)

Lest readers fail to note the translation, the manuscript includes a gloss to the appropriate lines in the Vulgate: "Surge domino in requiem tuam. Tu es archa sanctificacionis tue." Lydgate's use of these lines evokes not only the psalm itself but also the broader context of Marian devotion in which it was embedded. As one of the fifteen gradual psalms, Psalm 131 appeared in Books of Hours or primers as part of the Hours of the Blessed Virgin, making it familiar to both a lay and a clerical audience as a distinctively Marian text.[39] But as Eamon Duffy points out, even though "there is abundant evidence of very wide use of the primers among the laity," very few English translations of the text survive, a phenomenon he attributes to the "panic over Lollardy."[40] Paradoxically, then, it would seem that the Latin text of the psalm, which would have been recited by lay people at worship, may have been more familiar than the English translation that appears in the mumming. In this light, the Latin gloss to the passage would seem to address not merely a clerical audience but an educated lay readership as well.

As a performed text, the *Mumming for the Goldsmiths* is a complexly layered and stratified literary object, dense with allusion, which functions according to a double (if not triple or quadruple) logic all its own. The simplest narrative account of the action—a procession that retells the story of the translation of the ark by way of extravagantly complimenting the mayor—serves as a dominant hermeneutic that obviates more difficult (or dangerous) readings of the text and occasion. These alternative readings depend upon a sophisticated reading practice with its roots in biblical exegesis and secular poetics; they uneasily lurk just behind the screen provided by the ritualized gift giving that structures the occasion and delimits its meaning. In the passage quoted above, Lydgate truncates the psalm in order to insert references to the mayor, the citizens, and the commons of London, interpellating a secular audience as sacerdotal subjects. The psalm reads:

> Surge Domine in requiem tuam tu es arca santificationis tuae
> Sacerdotes tui induentur iustitia et sancti tui exultabunt.

> [Arise, O Lord, into thy resting place: thou and the ark, which thou has sanctified.
> Let thy priests be clothed with justice: and let thy saints rejoice.]
>   (Vulgate, Psalm 131, lines 8–9; Douay-Rheims translation)

Lydgate replaces "priests and saints" with "Mayor, citizens and communes," effecting what appears to be a secularization of the psalm as well as of the ark and its contents. But while "secularization" may suffice as a description of the *means* by which the work of the text is accomplished, it cannot stand as an adequate explanation of what that work might be. Not only does the mumming consistently imply that the secular world of the city may be comprehended as part of the sacred world of the psalm—thus the ark is "more gracyous" than the "Palladyone of Troye" (38–39) and "Nuwe Troye" is recast by David's entry as a kind of "New Jerusalem"[41] (69)—but it also uses that sacred world as a means of diminishing the standing of the mayor by invoking a higher authority. Lydgate's insistence on David's humility, his abdication of his "ryaltee," appears at first simply as a compliment to the mayor:

And for Þat meeknesse is a vertu feyre,
WorÞy Dauid, with kyngly excellence,
In goodely wyse haÞe made his repayre,
O noble Mayre, vn-to youre presence.

(71–74)

Here the mumming would seem to stage the submission of "kyngly excellence" to mayoral authority; just as David's dancing before the ark symbolically suggested the mayor's superior position (in performance, after all, David dances before the mayor), so too David's presentation of the gifts places the mayor in the traditional role of the king. But unlike the gifts that the Londoners brought for Richard II—gold balls and cups—David's present pointedly subordinates the mayor to the higher power of God:

Of purpoos put Þis aark to youre depoos,
With good entent, to make youre hert light;
And Þoo three thinges, which Þer inne beo cloos,
Shal gif to yowe konnyng, grace and might,
For to gouuerne with wisdome, pees and right
Þis noble cytee, and lawes such ordeyne,
Þat no man shal haue cause for to compleyne.

(78–84)

"Konnyng, grace and might" are the traditional attributes of the Son, Holy Ghost, and Father, mapped here onto the values of good governance, "wisdome, pees and right."[42] David's humility, which had seemed so fulsomely flattering to the mayor, is recoded here as meekness before the ark and its sacred cargo, a cargo that trumps the mayor's authority and places him in his proper relation both to God and to the goldsmiths. The subsequent stanzas specify the imperative of the gift; the mayor will receive a writ—analogous to the Ten Commandments—that reveals "Where yee shal punysshe and where as yee shal spare, / And how Þat Mercy shal Rygour modefye" (87–88). The purpose of the entire performance, it would seem, has been to deliver what Claire Spons-ler calls the "not-so-hidden message . . . that the goldsmiths expect the mayor to exercise his office effectively and fairly."[43] Indeed, the narrative arc of the mum-ming—minimal as it is—functions as a form of seduction; through flattery, it lures the mayor to accept, even if only ritually, advice and counsel from his sub-ordinates.

Such flattery, however, hardly needs the elaborate textual apparatus Lydgate has given it here. The detailed biblical scenario, with its exegetical links to the Purification of Mary and Marian devotion, might be understood as simply a pleasurable exercise in playmaking—as Lydgate's demonstration of what a literary monk could make of the traditional form of the mumming—but the particular themes that he chooses suggest a more complex motivation. The problem of succession that the reference to Samuel poses, the doubly sig-nificant "meeknesse" of David (as both exemplary humility before the Lord and symbolic submission to the mayor), and the embedded justification for per-formance contained in David's dance before the ark all gesture outward to the broader cultural context in which the goldsmiths produced their performance. Lydgate has appropriated the mumming both *for* and *from* the guild: on the one hand, he has produced a self-conscious imitation of royal occasions that be-speaks the ambitions of the mercantile class; on the other, he has used the mum-ming as a means of exploring the relationship of such occasions to a nexus of concerns characteristic of elite culture in the late 1420s. It might be argued, in fact, that the appearance of such concerns—questions of succession and right rulership—hardly testifies to Lydgate's intentions, so dominant were these themes during the entire Lancastrian period. But the self-referentiality of this particular mumming, its interest in justifying not only the authority of God and kings but also the very mode of representation through which that justi-fication is accomplished—performance—suggests that this text functions as more than an index to the fifteenth-century zeitgeist. The sheer density of the referential field in which the *Mumming for the Goldsmiths* is embedded belies the seeming simplicity of its propagandist aesthetic. What the mumming re-veals, in the end, is the degree to which representational forms—tropes, stories, images—contain deeply sedimented contents that cannot be erased or excluded once they have been invoked. David always recalls Samuel; his dancing always summons Michol's reproof. The sheer excessiveness of meaning created by

Lydgate's choice of images and his manipulation of authoritative texts in the *Mumming for the Goldsmiths* constitutes a refusal of the seeming simplicity of the mumming form and an insistence upon the value of poetic density. As I will show in my discussion of the *Mumming for the Mercers,* that value is both historical and social; it enables not only the exploration of such categories as sovereignty and authority but also the analysis of the historicity—the life and afterlife—of poetic excess itself.

―――――――

Even upon a cursory examination of Trinity College Cambridge MS R. 3. 20, the *Mumming for the Mercers* stands out from the surrounding texts and from Lydgate's other dramatic works. It is heavily glossed in Shirley's cramped hand; the annotations cover the margins of the poem and indeed rival it for the attention of the reader.[44] A closer look at the mumming reveals that it is rife with dense and difficult images drawn from classical mythology, contemporary geography, and the vernacular poetic tradition; figures such as Circe and Bacchus, places like Parnassus, and such poets as Ovid, Virgil, Petrarch, and Boccaccio are duly explained and contextualized by Shirley, who clearly feels that his audience will require a crib sheet to understand the text. The premise of the mumming is simple. Jupiter has sent a "poursuyant" (rubric, p. 695) from the East with letters for the mayor; having passed through Jerusalem, Libya, Ethiopia, "Inde," Mount Parnassus, Syria, and Egypt, the herald encounters three ships on his passage through the Mediterranean to England, each with an inscription in French. The first, which appears as he enters the great sea, is labeled "Grande travayle / Nulle avayle" (62–63) and contains a fisherman with empty nets. The second and third boats come into view as the herald arrives at the Thames; their labels comment further on the relationship between work and prosperity. The second states, "Taunt haut e bas que homme soyt, / Touz ioures regracyer dieux doyt" (83–84), retrospectively couching the fruitless labors of the first fishermen in a context of general thankfulness to God, while the third ship, filled with fish, reads, "grande payne / grande gayne" (90–91). The ships signal that the herald is nearing London, where he finds several vessels waiting, "hem to refresshe and to taken ayr," aboard which are "certein estates, wheche purveye and provyde," waiting to visit the "noble Mayr" (100, 101). Unlike the *Mumming for the Goldsmiths,* which animates the well-known narrative of David and the ark, the *Mumming for the Mercers* invokes a far less familiar set of allusions with which to engage its audience; the poem maps, along a spatial axis from East to West, a series of references to authorities and figures

("Petrark," "Jupiter") that represented the cultural capital of the aristocratic and royal elites. As Shirley's elaborate glosses show, Lydgate's mercantile audience would have approached these authoritative literary references as desirable but intimidatingly learned elements of aristocratic knowledge they wished to share. Certainly, as Claire Sponsler notes, the mumming dramatizes the assimilation of a messenger from a foreign land, the incorporation of the seeming alien into the domestic structure of power relations with the mayor.[45] But the "alien" here is in fact precisely that knowledge—of classical mythology and vernacular poetry—that a London mercantile elite might wish to learn and display.

Thus the *Mumming for the Mercers* can in part be understood as the attempt of a socially elite but non-noble group to identify itself as consumers of aristocratic cultural capital—and Shirley's glosses reflect an uncertainty about *his* audience's capacity to assimilate such material without aid. Richard Firth Green has argued that the tastes of this elite can be understood only in relation to aristocratic and courtly culture, suggesting that "it is the aristocracy, not the bourgeoisie, who are the *Kulturträger* of the fifteenth century."[46] The intimate relationship between the cultures of the merchant classes and the aristocracy can be seen in mercantile book ownership; far from revealing a "middle class" with literary productions specifically aimed at a middlebrow audience, records of book ownership show that London merchants were reading such fare as romances, Chaucer's *Canterbury Tales,* Gower's *Confessio Amantis,* and a variety of works by Lydgate—including courtly texts such as the *Complaint of the Black Knight,* the *Troy Book,* and the *Siege of Thebes.*[47] As Lee Patterson suggests, "English mercantile culture was largely confected out of the materials of other cultural formations—primarily aristocratic but also clerical—and lacked a center of its own."[48] In part, this diffuse quality was due to the mobility and variability of merchants and mercantile status; the famous example of Thomas Chaucer's rise to nobility provides only one instance of the fluidity that existed between the aristocracy and the merchant elite.[49] But an emphasis on the weakness of the boundary between noble and non-noble should not be taken to imply that London merchants lacked identity in the early fifteenth century. Sheila Lindenbaum has described the way in which, after the turbulent years of Richard II's reign in London, which included not only the Rising of 1381 but also the factional disputes of Nicholas Brembre and John of Northampton as well as the Good and Merciless Parliaments, the merchant elites reasserted both political and cultural control of the city. As a result, during the Lancastrian period, "there is a shift to heavily 'authorized' texts and stylistic uniformity," revealed not only in such official texts as the *Liber Albus* but also in manuscript compilations such as those of Shirley.[50] These phenomena—the investment of the merchant classes in aristocratic knowledge and modes of expression, and the assertion of identity concomitant with oligarchic control of the city—ultimately form the ground upon which any reading of Lydgate's "mercantile" mummings must stand. Thus the elaborately glossed display of erudition that constitutes the *Mumming for the Mercers* appears in this light as a synthesis of mercantile, aristocratic, and clerical discursive fields; not only does it present the mercers to themselves and to the mayor in the visual and linguistic codes of vernacular poetics and clerical learning, but it also interpellates its audience as educated consumers and practitioners of elite courtly culture.[51] The mercers' ambitions are made quite clear by Shirley, who states that the mumming was "ordeyned *ryallych* by þe worthy merciers."[52]

How to account, then, for the extended mapping of allusions along an East-West trajectory? The simplest answer would be that the conceit of the mumming—that Jupiter sends a herald from his mansion "ouer þe sonnes beem" (2)—demands a fanciful, but conventional, voyage from the furthest known reaches of the East to London. But Sponsler is correct to emphasize the sense of distance that the geographical description creates. It is, however, a distinctly *literary* geography, and any aura of strangeness it produces must be attributed to the determinedly didactic mission of the text, to the way in which it educates its audience in the tropes and figures of poetic culture both verbally and visually. This literariness is evident from the beginning, as the herald travels through "Ethyope and Ynde"; rather than encountering some exotic or strange person or object, he sees various dwelling places of the pagan gods and goddesses:

> Conveyed dovne, where Mars in Cyrrea
> Haþe bylt his paleys vpon þe sondes rede,
> And she, Venus, called Cytherrea,
> On Parnaso, with Pallas ful of drede;
> Smote on þe roche where þe Muses dwelle,
> Til þer sprange vp al sodeynly a welle,
>
> Called þe welle of Calyope,
> Mooste auctorysed amonges þees Cyryens—;
> Of which þe poetes þat dwelle in þat cuntree,
> And oþer famous rethorycyens,
> And þey þat cleped beon musycyens,
> Ar wont to drynk of þat hoolsome welle,
> Which þat alle oþer in vertu dooþe excelle—;
>
> (8–21)

The seeming split between "real" places—Ethiopia, India—and the mytho-
logical geography of "Cyrrea" and "Parnaso" is produced largely by the modern
cartographic imagination. Lydgate deploys a notion of place derived not from
mercantile encounter with the Other but from a set of unimpeachable medieval
authorities whose map of the world is here deliberately substituted for whatever
"real" experience of travelers and traders he might have known. Both Isidore's
Etymologiae (which elaborates Servius's commentary on Virgil) and Persius's
Satires describe the geography of Parnassus and its relation to the "hoolsome
welle" of the Muses; Lydgate would appear to have followed these authorities—
as well as Chaucer's *Anelida and Arcite*—not only in the *Mumming for the Mercers* but also in the *Mumming at Bishopswood* and the *Troy Book*.[53] Details in
each account vary, but the association of this particular landscape ("Parnaso"
and "Cyrrea") with the origins of poetry remains standard throughout.

     What is remarkable about the use of place and topography in the *Mumming
for the Mercers,* then, is less its evocation of the East than its mapping of a poetic
genealogy across place and time. The invocation of Parnassus instantiates a literary travelogue from classical rhetoricians to vernacular poets, beginning with
Tullius and Macrobius, moving through Ovid and Virgil, and culminating in
Petrarch and Boccaccio. Lydgate presents the mercers with an authorizing narrative that links the origins of poetry itself with the practice and performance
of mumming, clearly implying that just as Petrarch and Boccaccio, "Thoroughe
þat sugred bawme aureate / . . . called weren poetes laureate" (34–35), so too the
maker of this mumming has drunk from the "hoolsome welle" of Calliope.
Judging from Shirley's detailed gloss, readers and viewers were not expected to
be instantly familiar with these names: "Tulius a poete and a rethorisyen of
Rome. Macrobye an olde philosofre. Ovyde and Virgilius weren olde poetes,
þat oon of Rome, þat oþer of Naples afore þe tyme of Cryst. Fraunceys Petrark
was a poete of Florence. So were Bochas and Dante withinne þis hundreþe
yeere; and þey were called laureate for þey were coroned with laurer in token
þat þey excelled oþer in poetrye." What is "alien" and in need of familiarization
to Lydgate's audience is ultimately the store of cultural knowledge that authorizes and affirms elite identity in fifteenth-century England, a form of cultural
capital both displayed as a marker of the mercers' status and deployed as a didactic tool, part of a process of acculturation by which merchants may be integrated into the codes and practices that distinguish the elite.[54] Contrary to Lydgate's usual habit when authorizing himself as vernacular maker,[55] he makes no
mention of Chaucer or of English poetry more generally, suggesting that it is
precisely the relation between a foreign—classical or European—tradition of
eloquence and a native cultural practice—mumming—that this performance

stages. Indeed, Lydgate particularly seems to have avoided making a link between Chaucer and the classical tradition of eloquence, a connection that he himself had quite forcefully articulated a few years earlier, in the *Troy Book*:[56]

> And Chaucer now, allas, is nat alyve
> Me to reforme or to be my rede
> (For lak of whom slougher is my spede),
> The noble rethor that alle dide excelle;
> For in makyng he drank of the welle
> Undir Pernaso that the Musis kepe,
> On whiche hil I myghte never slepe—
> Onnethe slombre—for which, allas, I pleyne.
>   (3.550–57)

The elision of Chaucer from the *Mumming for the Mercers* represents both an insistence by Lydgate upon his unmediated relation to classical and European lines of poetic influence and an assertion of his own centrality to the didactic project of the text and performance. Chaucer may have "enlumined" the English language, but it is Lydgate who can effect a kind of *translatio* from European high culture to the mercantile sensibility embodied in the label "grande peyne / grande gayne."

This need for *translatio* produces the mode of excess and overdetermination in the *Mumming for the Mercers* revealed by Shirley's glosses. In contrast to the relatively simple *Mumming at Windsor*, for example, whose subject matter—the coronation of the king in uncertain times and in a foreign land—would seem far more likely to produce cultural anxiety and an excessive text, the *Mumming for the Mercers* is marked by repeated invocations of multiple authorizing narratives and modes of signification. Upon finishing his genealogical list of classical and European poets, Lydgate immediately turns to the Old Testament; leaving Parnassus behind, his herald passes through the Christian topography of Egypt, the Red Sea and the River Jordan:

> And thorughe Egypte his poursuyant is comme,
> Dovne descendid by þe Rede See,
> And haþe also his right wey ynomme
> Thoroughe valeye of þe Drye Tree
> By Flomme Jordan, coosteying þe cuntree,
> Where Iacob passed whylome with his staff,
> Taking his shippe, to seylen at poort Iaff.
>   (43–49)

Significantly, Shirley feels no need to annotate this stanza; its Old Testament reference is clearly legible to all. Lydgate has moved his audience through the alien landscape of poetic laureation to the landscape of the Christian past, a juxtaposition that acquires continuity through the fiction of the traveling "pour-suyant" but remains jarring nonetheless.[57] The effect Lydgate is aiming for, however, is a seamless integration of cultural systems; the appearance of the landmark River Jordan in the midst of this otherwise strange mythical world represents an attempt performatively to absorb the markers of aristocratic culture—classical figures and places, laureate poets and rhetors—into the mode of representation most familiar to a Christian mercantile audience, with biblical geography serving as a kind of gateway to Europe. This tactic is familiar to us from the *Mumming for the Goldsmiths,* in which the authorized secular narrative of London's Trojan origins is subordinated to and assimilated by the story of King David and the sacred ark, and it suggests a felt need on the part of both Lydgate and his audience for the synthesis of authorizing narratives and topoi—a need that reflects the uneasy fit between the classicizing drive of much vernacular poetry and the Christianizing impulse at the center of English medieval culture.

In this sense, the *Mumming for the Mercers* does work as a means of assimilation, a way of enacting the movement from classical to Christian to English, in which a contiguous map is drawn that leads inexorably to the mercers' own city. It is through this movement inward that Lydgate asserts on behalf of the mercers the right of the merchant elite to appropriate the central literary topoi of courtly vernacular culture. And by didactically displaying such cultural knowledge in a visual form designed for ease of consumption, Lydgate teaches his audience how to effect that appropriation themselves. In much the same way, Shirley's glosses substitute words for the ephemeral props and costumes that would have made legible the literary travelogue of the mumming, the movement from Parnassus to London, while his rubric—his invocation of the mumming as genre—operates in a similar fashion, making clear to the reader what would have been obvious to an audience: that this performance constitutes a redeployment of the practice of mumming, substituting for the king (its usual object of address) a figure from within the mercantile world itself, the mayor.

Lydgate's *translatio,* then, occurs on the level of both content (literary geography) and form (the mumming genre). What the mummings for the mercers and goldsmiths reveal is not merely the *function* of cultural performances (their response to crisis, their negotiation of difference, their ordering of a disordered world) but the *work* of specific literary texts in relation to an authorized landscape of such artifacts and texts—one that, for English merchants in 1429, bore marks of class status and privilege both alien and deeply desirable. To articulate the historicity of such texts requires us to embrace their status as poetry, to understand that our engagement with their "writtenness" or "literariness" does not undermine their status as artifacts of practice. It is not enough simply to note that Lydgate appropriates a form of address to the king in order to glorify the mayor; this merely illustrates the pride of the mercers and the goldsmiths in their political and economic clout. That pride is important, to be sure, as are the anxieties of such a group as they negotiate the demands of daily life in a mercantile world. But neither pride nor anxiety can fully explain the need for poetry. And it is that need—for David's dancing, for Parnassus, for Ovid, for Petrarch and Boccaccio—which the genre of the mumming translates and transforms. The literary world evoked by these texts, that is, constitutes their most genuinely historical element, their logic of excess revealing not the mere effect of an historical cause, not a simple social function, but a particular form hard at work to make and remake its own facticity—its own place in the past.

Notes

A version of this essay appears in Maura Nolan, *John Lydgate and the Making of Public Culture* (Cambridge: Cambridge University Press, 2005). All rights reserved. Used by permission of the publisher.

1. These lines are quoted from Shirley's rubrics for the *Mumming at Windsor* and the *Mumming for the Mercers,* in *The Minor Poems of John Lydgate,* ed. Henry Noble MacCracken, EETS, o.s., 192 (London: Oxford University Press, 1934), 2:691, 695. All further citations of the text and rubrics of the four mummings discussed in this chapter—*Mumming at Eltham, Mumming at Windsor, Mumming for the Mercers,* and *Mumming for the Goldsmiths*—are to this edition. For a complete treatment of Trinity College Cambridge MS R. 3. 20, see Margaret Connolly, *John Shirley: Book Production and the Noble Household in Fifteenth-Century England* (Brookfield, VT: Ashgate, 1998), particularly chap. 4, "MS Trinity College Cambridge R. 3. 20, Its Partners and Progeny," 69–102. I am grateful to the Masters and Fellows of Trinity College for permission to examine the manuscript.

2. *Minor Poems of John Lydgate,* 2:668–701. The only mumming that does not appear in Trinity College Cambridge MS R. 3. 20 is the *Mumming at Bishopswood,* which can be found in Bodleian Library, MS. Ashmole 59, another Shirley manuscript. For discussion of MS Bodley Ashmole 59, see Connolly, *John Shirley,* 145–69.

3. The standard position of Lydgate's mummings within dramatic and literary history is that provided by Glynne Wickham in his monumental history of the English stage, *Early English Stages, 1300–1600,* vol. 1, *1300–1576* (London: Routledge and Kegan Paul, 1959). Wickham suggests that Lydgate's theatrical works be seen as part of a narrative of the emergence of fully-fledged drama in England, arguing that Lydgate "[im-

posed] rudimentary form upon the heterogeneous secular entertainments of the minstrel troupes" (1:180). This narrative begins with folk drama—Lydgate "gave this folk-custom [mumming] a literary frame"—and moves from ritual to literature: "the ritual accompanying the giving of presents . . . was translated into a literary debate enacted before an audience" (1:207). Thus Lydgate's mummings acquire significance from their place in the history of secular drama, standing as, in Alan Renoir's words, "a landmark in the history of English drama," and illustrating the process by which quasi-religious ritual becomes recognizably literary performance; Alain Renoir, "On the Date of John Lydgate's 'Mumming at Hertford,'" *Archiv* 198 [1961]: 32–33. Elsewhere, Renoir cites Robert Withington's argument that "Lydgate used classical allegory in dramatic works about one hundred years before any other English author"; see Alain Renoir, *The Poetry of John Lydgate* (London: Routledge & Kegan Paul, 1967), 155 n. 19; Robert Withington, *English Pageantry: An Historical Outline* (1918; reprint, New York: B. Blom, 1963), 1:107. Wickham's narrative of the place of the mummings in dramatic history persists; see William Tydeman's reading of the mummings, which asserts that mumming was "a sophisticated survival of a pagan folk-ritual, or of the Roman Saturnalia, and a prerogative of the *bourgeoisie* rather than the nobility" (*The Theatre in the Middle Ages: Western European Stage Conditions, c. 800–1576* [Cambridge: Cambridge University Press, 1978], 73–74), and that of Marion Jones ("Early Moral Plays and the Earliest Secular Drama," in *The Revels History of Drama in English*, vol. 1, *Medieval Drama*, ed. Lois Potter [New York: Methuen, 1983], 213–91, esp. 237–42). The two most recent considerations of Lydgate's mummings do not challenge Wickham's thesis directly, though they shift the focus from literary history to cultural function. In her essay, "Alien Nation: London's Aliens and Lydgate's Mummings for the Mercers and Goldsmiths," in *The Postcolonial Middle Ages,* ed. Jeffrey Jerome Cohen (New York: St. Martin's Press, 2000), 237, Claire Sponsler argues that the mummings work in a Foucauldian sense as "ceremonial occasions . . . [that] provided arenas for the working through of such challenges [to hegemony], fostering a creative refashioning of recalcitrant and unpleasant socioeconomic realities." Similarly, Meg Twycross and Sarah Carpenter, in *Masks and Masking in Medieval and Early Tudor England* (Burlington, VT: Ashgate, 2002), 159, 160, 151, see Lydgate's mummings as "ceremonial" (though "problematical"), part of a tradition of courtly entertainment appropriated from the "popular urban custom of mumming." For Twycross and Carpenter, Lydgate's mummings are embedded within the broader context of medieval masking, a practice, they argue, derived in part from "home-grown popular customs" (15); despite their stated intent of critiquing the assumptions of early drama scholars about the "identity of all European folk custom and its roots in a pagan ritual past" (14–15), Twycross and Carpenter still assert the link between popular traditions and literary adaptations such as Lydgate's mummings. A brief discussion of Lydgate's mummings as part of a "London aesthetic" may be found in Lawrence Clopper, *Drama, Play and Game: English Festive Culture in the Medieval and Early Modern Period* (Chicago: University of Chicago Press, 2001), 161–65.

4. For an example of a speculative reading of the *Mumming at Windsor,* filled with suggestions for possible performance, see Suzanne Westfall, *Patrons and Performance: Early Tudor Household Revels* (Oxford: Clarendon Press, 1990), 34–37.

5. Paul Strohm, "Rememorative Reconstruction," *Studies in the Ages of Chaucer* 23 (2001): 3–16, esp. 8–11; see also Paul Strohm, "Shakespeare's Oldcastle," in *Theory and the Premodern Text* (Minneapolis: University of Minnesota Press, 2000), 132–48.

6. It would certainly be futile to argue that literary texts and dramatic performances had not been linked before Lydgate's mummings, and I am not doing so here. As any basic history of drama in England will show, scripted performances were occurring throughout the Middle Ages. But it is equally clear that the provision of a poetic text as script for a secular performance is a Lydgatean innovation; see Wickham, *Early English Stages,* 1:207. An important precursor to this coupling of text and performance may be seen in Richard Maydistone's *Concordia,* a 548-line Latin poem describing a 1392 procession by Richard II and Queen Anne through London; see Charles Roger Smith, ed., *Concordia facta inter regem Riccardum II et civitatem Londonie* (PhD diss., Princeton University, 1972) (Ann Arbor, MI: University Microfilms, 1972). The text is also printed by Thomas Wright in *Political Songs and Poems Relating to English History,* vol. 1, Rolls Series 14(London: Her Majesty's Stationery Office, 1859), 282–301. The *Concordia* is discussed by Paul Strohm in *Hochon's Arrow: The Social Imagination of Fourteenth-Century Texts* (Princeton, NJ: Princeton University Press, 1992), 107–11, and by Seth Lerer, "The Chaucerian Critique of Medieval Theatricality," in *The Performance of Middle English Culture: Essays on Chaucer and the Drama in Honor of Martin Stevens,* ed. James J. Paxson, Lawrence M. Clopper, and Sylvia Tomasch (Cambridge: D. S. Brewer, 1996), 59–76, 64–66. Kipling, in *Enter the King,* 11–21, discusses the 1392 spectacle as a "civic triumph" that uses the liturgy of Advent to effect a reconciliation between Richard and London after a protracted dispute.

7. See Wickham, *Early English Stages,* 1:204, and Derek Pearsall, *John Lydgate* (London: Routledge and Kegan Paul, 1970), 184. Shirley tells us that the *Mumming at London* was performed "to fore þe gret estates of þis lande"; it includes descriptions of Dame Fortune (drawn from the *Romance of the Rose*) and her defeat by the four cardinal virtues, each elaborately personified. The *Mumming at Hertford* is Lydgate's best-known dramatic work; it has been separately printed and recently performed. See Derek Forbes, *Lydgate's Disguising at Hertford Castle: The First Secular Comedy in the English Language* (Pulborough: Blot Publishing, 1998). The text stages a dispute before the king between rustic husbands and wives and includes references to the Wife of Bath and Griselda. In my book *John Lydgate and the Making of Public Culture* (Cambridge: Cambridge University Press, 2005), I discuss the two "disguisings" at length.

8. The *Mumming at Bishopswood* can be found in another Shirley manuscript, Bodleian Library, MS. Ashmole 59, and its date is unknown. It has been printed in *Minor Poems of John Lydgate,* 2:668–71, and in *John Lydgate: Poems,* ed. John Norton Smith (Oxford: Clarendon Press, 1966), 7–10 and notes. Shirley's rubric describes it as a "balade" made for the Mayday celebration of the "Shirreves of London"; it takes the form of a letter carried by Ver, daughter of Flora, goddess of "fresshe floures," that is filled with sage advice and hopeful sentiments.

9. Henry VI's dual coronations—in London and in Paris—produced a flurry of propaganda, both textual and dramatic, much of which Lydgate produced or was involved in producing. These include two poems in honor of the English coronation at Westminster in November 1429 (*Roundel at the Coronation of Henry VI* and *Ballade to King Henry VI upon his Coronation*) as well as verses to accompany the *soteltes*, or sugar sculptures, at the coronation banquet. All three texts emphasize the lineage of the young king—"descendid frome twoo lynes / Of Saynt Edward and of Saynt Lowys" (*Ballade*, 9–10)—and express hope that he will reign in wisdom and virtue. For the texts of these poems, see *Minor Poems of John Lydgate*, 2:622–30. Pearsall adds to these three *A Prayer for King, Queen and People*, which anticipates the coronation; see his discussion of the coronation poems in *John Lydgate (1371–1449): A Bio-Bibliography*, English Literary Studies Monograph Series 71 (Victoria, BC: University of Victoria, 1997), 29–30. Lydgate also wrote verses describing the pageants that welcomed Henry on his return from Paris; see *King Henry's Triumphal Entry into London, 21 Feb., 1432*, in Lydgate, *Minor Poems of John Lydgate*, 2:630–48. In chap. 4 of this volume, Scott-Morgan Straker makes the important argument that "propaganda" is a limiting notion for a poet as complex as Lydgate, showing in particular that the *Triumphal Entry* is as much instruction for the young king as propaganda on his behalf.

10. Beginning with E. K. Chambers's *The Medieval Stage* (Oxford: Clarendon Press, 1903), with its narrative of the folk origins of medieval drama, mumming has traditionally been understood as a folk custom that appears in the records at the moment it is appropriated by aristocrats and denied to the very persons with whom it originated. See, e.g., Enid Welsford, *The Court Masque: A Study in the Relationship between Poetry and the Revels* (Cambridge: Cambridge University Press, 1927); Meg Twycross, "My Visor Is Philemon's Roof," *Fifteenth-Century Studies* 13 (1988): 335–46; Tom Pettit, "Early English Traditional Drama: Approaches and Perspectives," *Research Opportunities in Renaissance Drama* 25 (1982): 1–30, and "Tudor Interludes and the Winter Revels," *Medieval English Theatre* 6, no. 1 (1984): 16–27. Pettit's articles usefully summarize the scholarship on the "lost tradition" of mummings; though he is quite critical of attempts to derive that tradition from more recent folk customs such as the Wooing plays or the Sword Dance, he ultimately concludes that popular Christmas customs were gradually elaborated to produce the sophisticated interludes of the Tudor period. In his *Medieval Theatre* (Cambridge: Cambridge University Press, 1987), Glynne Wickham wisely notes that if there were a lost tradition of mummings, "it is surely curious that no poet or diarist from Chaucer to Pepys should have even described such a play" (144), though he does ultimately assert that the mummer's play and other folk festivals have ancient origins. The most recent discussion of mumming appears in Twycross and Carpenter's *Masks and Masking*; building on the material appearing in Twycross's "My Visor," the book generally affirms the idea that mumming was a traditional cultural practice (see 82–100). The documentary evidence for mumming is summarized in Ian Lancashire's *Dramatic Texts and Records of Britain:*

A Chronological Topography to 1558 (Toronto: University of Toronto Press, 1984), which usefully indexes records of mummings and other performances. It should be noted as well that E. K. Chambers paved the way for all subsequent work on mumming; he provided a basic map of the evidence to be found in later scholarship like that of Twycross and Carpenter and that of Lancashire. See Chambers, *Medieval Stage,* 1:390–403.

11. Lancashire cites only one use of the term *mummer* before 1377, an incident in 1224 in which five Franciscans were confused with "mummers"—a record he classifies as "doubtful." Lancashire, *Dramatic Texts and Records*, p. 336, no. 1763. Excluding this record, the first use of the term in England appears in 1387, in an entry in the *Guildhall Letter-Book* (in French) prohibiting the practice; see *Calendar of the Letter-Books Preserved among the Archives of the Corporation of the City of London at the Guildhall,* ed. Reginald R. Sharpe (London: J. E. Francis, 1899–1912), H:322; cited by Lancashire, *Dramatic Texts and Records,* p. 176, no. 904; the original French reads: "ne nul voise pur mummer ne nul autre ieu ieuer oue visure ne en nulle autre estrange gise par quelle il ne poet estre connue sur pein denprisonment a volunte des mair et aldermans." Quoted by Twycross, "My Visor," 335. The term *mumming* would appear to have entered the English language from French, where it shows up in records slightly earlier. The *Dictionnaire de l'ancienne langue française,* ed. Frédéric Godefroy (Paris: F. Vieweg, 1888), 381–82, cites a number of fourteenth- and fifteenth-century appearances of the word or its variants, under the entries for *mome, momeor, momer,* and *momon*; the earliest use of the term it cites is in 1293, though the majority of references are to late-fourteenth-century and fifteenth-century sources, such as Monstrelet's chronicle. Charles d'Orléans mentions mumming twice in his verses; see *Poesies,* ed. Pierre Champion (Paris: Librarie Ancienne Honoré Champion, 1923), vol. 1, Ballad 88, pp. 128–29, and vol. 2, Roundeau 121, pp. 359–60. Susan Crane discusses the first of these, noting that the ballad was written to be read aloud during an interlude; see *The Performance of Self: Ritual, Clothing and Identity during the Hundred Years War* (Philadelphia: University of Pennsylvania Press, 2002), 141. See also n. 15 below for the use of the term in French in Maghfeld's Account Book in 1393. In an important book that appeared just as this article was being completed, Anne Lancashire, *London Civic Theatre: City Drama and Pageantry from Roman Times to 1558* (Cambridge: Cambridge University Press, 2002), 41–43, surveys the evidence for mumming in England; I have cited her work below where she introduces material not referenced elsewhere.

12. Beginning with a proclamation in 1334, Ian Lancashire records prohibitions that specifically mention mumming practices (masking and playing at dice in the earlier records, "mumming" itself in the later) in 1352, 1372, 1376, 1380, 1387 (January and December), 1393, 1404, 1405, 1417 and 1418. See Lancashire, *Dramatic Texts and Records,* nos. 888 (1334), 890 (1352), 894 (1372), 897 (1376), 900 (1380), 903 (January, 1387), 904 (December, 1387), 909 (1393), 913 (1404), 915 (1405), 921 (1417), and 922 (1418). All of the proclamations are dated November, December, or January, making it clear that the activity being outlawed is associated with Christmas; the 1418 prohibition is the most extensive: "No manere persone, of what astate, degre, or condicioun þat euere he be, duryng þis holy tyme of Cristemes be so hardy in eny wyse to walk by nyght in eny manere mom-

myng, pleyes, enterludes, or eny oþer disgisynges with eny feynyd berdis, peyntid visers, diffourmyd or colourid visages in eny wyse, up peyne of emprisonement of her bodyes." From *Letter-Book I,* fol. ccxxiii, in H. T. Riley, *Memorials of London and London Life, in the XIIIth, XIVth and XVth Centuries* (London: Longmans, Green, 1868), 669. For the 1417 prohibition, see Riley, 658. Cited in Lancashire, *Dramatic Texts and Records,* p. 179, nos. 921, 922.

13. *Anonimalle Chronicle,* ed. V. H. Galbraith (Manchester: Manchester University Press, 1927), 102–3. Cited in Lancashire, *Dramatic Texts and Records,* p. 160, no. 802. The passage is translated by John Stow in his *Survey of London,* ed. Charles Kingsford (Oxford: Clarendon Press, 1908), 1:96–97.

14. See Wickham, *Early English Stages,* 1:191–207, for a discussion of Lydgate's mummings in relation to gift giving and disguise as standard elements of the practice.

15. Lancashire, *Dramatic Texts and Records,* p. 129, no. 634; see also Edward Tyrrell and Nicholas H. Nicolas, eds., *A Chronicle of London from 1089 to 1483* (London: Longman & Green, 1827), 87. The event is described using the term *mumming* ("men of London maden a gret mommyng to hym of xij aldermen and there sones,") though the chronicle probably dates from later in the century; see Antonia Gransden's discussion of London chronicles in *Historical Writing in England,* vol. 2, *C. 1307 to the Early Sixteenth Century* (London: Routledge and Kegan Paul, 1982), 228–30. An earlier record, in French, that uses the term *momyng* can be found in the Merchant Taylors' accounts for 1400–1401 (Guildhall Library MS 34048/1, fol. 11r); payment is rendered "a le Guyhalle pur le Momyng a Nowelle." I quote the passage from Anne Lancashire, *London Civic Theatre,* 229 n. 43; it is also referenced by C. M. Clode, *Memorials of the Guild of Merchant Taylors of the Fraternity of John the Baptist* (London: Harrison & Sons, 1875), 62. Ian Lancashire cites this record as no. 912, p. 177. Clode suggests that the mumming took place at the Guildhall, but Anne Lancashire argues more plausibly that the Merchant Taylors' payment was a contribution to the mumming at Eltham (42).

16. In her discussion of the 1393 performance, Caroline M. Barron states in a note that "the mercers provided five men as mummers at a cost of 3, Mercers' Hall, Account Book 1347–1464, fo. 12. Gilbert Maghfeld lent the city chamberlain 40s for the mumming at Eltham at Christmas, Maghfeld Account Book fo. 35" ("The Quarrel of Richard II with London 1392–7," 195 n. 91). Portions of the Maghfeld Account Book were printed by Edith Rickert, "Extracts from a Fourteenth-Century Account Book," *Modern Philology* 24 (1926–27): 111–19; the relevant entry reads: "Item appreste pour le momyng al Roy a Eltham al feste de Noell xl s." Rickert dates the entry December, 1392, but as Barron shows, the mumming occurred in January 1393.

17. L. C. Hector and Barbara F. Harvey, eds. and trans., *The Westminster Chronicle, 1381–1394* (Oxford: Clarendon Press, 1982), 510–11 (1393) and 516–17 (1394). Lancashire, *Dramatic Texts and Records,* p. 129, no. 633 (1393) and p. 177, no. 910 (1393–94), cites the same text as the chronicle of John of Malvern, who continued Higden's *Polychronicon*; see *Polychronicon Ranulphi Higden Monachi Cestrensis,* ed. J. R. Lumby, Rolls Series 41 (London: Longman, 1865–66), 9: 278 (1393) and 281 (1394). However, Lumby mistakenly

identified the *Westminster Chronicle* as part of John of Malvern's continuation; see Hector and Harvey's introduction, xv and lxxv. See also Caroline M. Barron, "The Quarrel of Richard II with London 1392–7," 190–96. For a fascinating reading of the gift of the bird to Queen Anne, which Malverne describes as "mirabilem habentem guttur latissimum"—having a wondrously wide throat—as well as a general account of the rift between Richard II and the Londoners, see Strohm, *Hochon's Arrow,* 106–7.

18. To these four occasions (1377, 1393, 1394 and 1400–1401) might be added a fifth; Anne Lancashire notes that in the mercers' account books for 1395–96, payment is recorded for a royal mumming, though neither the time of year or location is specified. Lancashire does not indicate whether the records use the term *mumming* specifically. See Mercers' MS Wardens' Accounts, 1347–1464, fol. 19v, cited in Lancashire, *London Civic Theatre,* 42 and n. 41.

19. It was also a form that could easily be appropriated by persons less interested in the maintenance of social order. On two occasions we find records of mumming used to threaten the king, the first in 1400, when mummers attempted to assassinate Henry IV, and the second in 1414, when Henry V was threatened by Lollards disguised as mummers. Even if these accounts are inaccurate, they do indicate the extent to which the chroniclers at least saw the dangerous potential of mumming. For the 1400 incident, see John Capgrave, *Abbreuacioun of Cronicles,* ed. Peter J. Lucas, EETS, o.s., 285 (Oxford: Oxford University Press, 1983), 216; cited by Twycross, "My Visor," 338 n. 11. The date of the text is uncertain; Lucas concludes that it was written before 1461 and possibly begun before 1438 (xliii). It is clearly not contemporaneous with the events of 1400, however, and its use of the term *mumming* is consistent with a later date. Chambers, *Mediaeval Stage,* 1: 395 n. 1, noted the incident and cited several versions in various chronicle accounts; Lancashire, *Dramatic Texts and Records,* p. 285, no. 1510, similarly cites multiple accounts. For the 1414 attempt on Henry V, see Gregory's *Chronicle of London,* in *The Historical Collections of a Citizen of London in the Fifteenth Century,* ed. James Gairdner (London: Camden Society, 1876), 108; cited by Chambers, *Medieval Stage,* 1:396–97 n. 3. Lancashire, *Dramatic Texts and Records,* p. 129, no. 635, notes the event but dates it incorrectly to 1415. Paul Strohm discusses the incident briefly in *England's Empty Throne* (New Haven, CT: Yale University Press, 1998), 65, but points out that Gregory's *Chronicle* is "a highly unreliable source" (229 n. 6). However, he also notes that in the Exchequer Issue Rolls for February 1414, "payment is authorized for manacles 'for certain traitors recently captured at Eltham and elsewhere, and imprisoned.'" See PRO, E403/614/mem.12. The chronicle itself dates from a slightly later period; Gransden, *Historical Writing,* 230, asserts that it is "almost certainly by William Gregory, skinner, sheriff of London from 1436 to 1437 and mayor from 1451 to 1452." Gregory died in 1467, making it unlikely that he was composing the chronicle in 1414.

20. The 1400–1401 mumming is no. 634 in Lancashire, *Dramatic Texts and Records;* it was an entertainment by Londoners dressed as twelve aldermen and their sons in honor of the visit of Manuel II, Emperor of Constantinople. See Tyrrell and Nicolas, *Chronicle of London,* 87. For a full account of Manuel's visit, see Donald M. Nicol, "A Byzantine

Emperor in England: Manuel II's Visit to London in 1400–1401," *University of Birmingham Historical Journal* 12.2 (1970): 204–25, esp. 215. Anne Lancashire notes that a collection of contributions for this mumming appears in the mercers' accounts for 1400–1401 (Mercers' MS Wardens' Accounts 1347–1464, fol. 32v); see *London Civic Theatre,* 42 and n. 42.

21. Lancashire, *Dramatic Texts and Records,* p. 181, no. 935 (1437), and p. 182, no. 939 (1451).

22. The mummings also appear in British Library MS Additional 29729, a copy of Trinity College Cambridge MS R. 3. 20 made by Stow; see Julia Boffey and John J. Thompson, "Anthologies and Miscellanies: Production and Choice of Texts," in *Book Production and Publishing in Britain, 1375–1475,* ed. Jeremy Griffiths and Derek Pearsall (Cambridge: Cambridge University Press, 1989), 279–315, esp. 284.

23. Throughout this chapter, poetry is cited parenthetically in the text by line number or by book and line numbers. Richard Osberg notes the emergence in this mumming of classical figures, linking it to Maydistone's use of "Bacchus" in his description of the 1392 entry of Richard II, and to the appearance of Bacchus and Thetis in the 1432 entry of Henry VI; he also notes that Bacchus and Ceres appear, bearing wheat and grapes, in Pierre Gringore's pageants for the entrance of Mary Tudor into Paris on November 6, 1514; see "The Jesse Tree in the 1432 London Entry of Henry VI: Messianic Kingship and the Rule of Justice," *JMRS* 16 (1986): 213–32, 227 n. 29.

24. Queen Katherine is not named; Lydgate delicately addresses "yowe, Pryncesse, borne of Saint Lowys blood" (l52), and Shirley provides a gloss: "ad Reginam Katerinam, mother to Henrie yo. VI."

25. Scholars of the mummings have not agreed on a date for Eltham. In 1902 Rudolph Brotanek, *Die Englischen Maskenspiele* (Leipzig: Wilhem Braumüller, 1902), dated the poem 1427–28, based on what he saw as its reference to Henry Beaufort's abortive attempt at a crusade against the Hussites in those years. Brotanek's date was adopted by Withington, *English Pageantry,* 106–7, and Chambers, *Medieval Stage,* 1:397; again following Brotanek, Paul Reyher, *Les masques anglais* (Paris, 1909; reprint, New York: Benjamin Blom, 1964), 109, gives the more general date 1427–30. Walter Schirmer, *John Lydgate: A Study in the Culture of the XVth Century* (London: Methuen, 1961), 101, quotes Charles Kingsford in asserting that Lydgate had written mummings in 1424 and 1428, before arbitrarily assigning Eltham to 1424; no title for Kingsford's work is given and I have been unable to locate the reference. Pearsall, *Bio-Bibliography,* 29, notes that Henry was at Eltham for Christmas in 1425 and 1428, and suggests the latter date, given the cluster of mummings and occasional poems from 1428–32. Bertram Wolffe, *Henry VI* (1981; repr. New Haven, CT: Yale University Press, 2001), 37–38, asserts that Henry was at Eltham in 1426 and 1427 as well, citing the accounts kept by his chamber treasurer, John Merston and printed in *Foedera* (X, 387–88), which record payments to "Jakke Travaill & ses Compaignons" and "Jeweis de Abyndon" for "diverses Jeuues & Entreludes" for Christmas. I concur with Pearsall that the 1428 date is likely, but there is no conclusive evidence to date the mumming definitively.

26. See Ernst Jacob, *The Fifteenth Century: 1399–1485* (Oxford: Clarendon Press, 1961), pp. 243–47. Jacob points out that "from the battle of Verneuil [August, 1424] to the siege of Orléans [1428] is a period of minor action," lending support to the 1428 date for the Eltham mumming.

27. Richard Firth Green, *Poets and Princepleasers: Literature and the English Court in the Late Middle Ages* (Toronto: University of Toronto Press, 1980), 189, briefly mentions the *Mumming at Windsor* as one of Lydgate's "apologist" poems.

28. Pearsall, *Bio-Bibliography,* suggests the 1429 date as well.

29. J. W. McKenna, "Henry VI of England and the Dual Monarchy: Aspects of Royal Political Propaganda, 1422–1432," *Journal of the Warburg and Courtauld Institutes* 28 (1965): 155.

30. Ibid., 155. This image was particularly freighted with significance in 1429–30 not only because Charles VII had himself crowned at Rheims in July 1429 but because Henry VI was not able to be anointed at Rheims and had to settle for being crowned at Paris. See Jacob, *Fifteenth Century,* 248–50.

31. In chap. 5 of this volume, C. David Benson discusses these mummings, along with the *Mumming at London* and the *Mumming at Bishopswood,* in relation to their status as London performances that affirm civic values and covertly suggest criticisms of the city's focus on wealth.

32. Shirley's introduction states that "þe goldesmythes of þe Cite of London mommed . . . to þeyre Mayre Eestfeld, vpon Candelmasse day." According to Stow, Eastfield was mayor of London in 1429 and 1437 (John Stow, *A Survey of London,* ed. Charles L. Kingsford [Oxford: Clarendon Press, 1908], 2:173); Brotanek, *Die Englischen Maskenspiele,* 306, and Schirmer, *John Lydgate,* 107, assert that since neither the goldsmiths' nor the mercers' mummings mention the mayor being re-elected, the texts were likely performed in 1429, though the absence of such a mention does not conclusively point to the earlier date. Pearsall concurs that the 1429 date should be accepted; after 1433 or 1434, Lydgate had retired to Bury and his "laureate" period had passed (*John Lydgate,* 223; see also *Bio-Bibliography,* 29). Anne Lancashire has shown, however, that the date would have been 1430, not 1429, if the reference is to Eastfield's first term as mayor; Eastfield was elected on October 13, 1429, and thus Twelfth Night and Candlemas performances would have taken place in 1430. See Lancashire, *London Civic Theatre,* 121 and nn. 23–26.

33. For a discussion of the *Stirps Jesse* and one of its medieval commentators, Bishop Fulbert of Chartres, see Margot Fassler, "Mary's Nativity, Fulbert of Chartres, and the *Stirps Jesse:* Liturgical Innovation circa 1000 and Its Afterlife," *Speculum* 75 (2000): 389–434, esp. pp. 410–11.

34. *The Mirour of Mans Saluacioune,* ed. Avril Henry (Philadelphia: University of Pennsylvania Press, 1987) can be dated to approximately 1429 on the basis of the paper and hand of the manuscript; see Henry's introduction, 20. It is a close translation of *Speculum humanae salvationis* (SHS), a compilation of sources including the *Historia scholastica* of Petrus Comestor, Voragine's *Legenda aurea,* and Aquinas's *Summa theologica,*

which dates to 1310–14. *SHS* is a typological rendering of the life of the Virgin (which includes the life of Christ), giving three foreshadowing events for each incident narrated. Its popularity is attested to by the number of manuscripts—394—that have survived from the fourteenth and fifteenth centuries (Henry, *Mirour,* 10).

35. In a striking image, the anonymous translator compares Christ's crucified body to the strings on David's harp:

> Dauid in his harping prefigured Crist in this thinges,
> For Crist was stendid on the Crosse als in ane harpe ere the stringes.
> O Lord, how this faire harpe gaf a swete melody
> When Crist with doelfulle teres for vs cried myghtylye.

> (2719–22)

36. *The Letters of Bernard of Clairvaux,* trans. Bruno Scott James (London: Burns Oates, 1953), 135, quoted in Clopper, *Drama, Play and Game,* 56–57; see also Bernard of Clairvaux, *Lettere,* ed. Ferruccio Gastaldelli, in *Opere di San Bernardo,* vol. 6 (Milan: Fondazione di Studi Cistercenci, 1986), letter 87, 1:434–36.

37. *Dives and Pauper,* ed. Priscilla Heath Barnum, EETS, o.s., 275 (London: Oxford University Press, 1976), 297, Commandment III, Cap. Xviii, lines 31–35. Clopper discusses this text in *Drama, Play and Game,* 82–83, noting that the *Dives* author distinguishes between legitimate entertainments (legitimated by the Old Testament) and illicit recreation that leads to sin.

38. As Lawrence Clopper notes, the story of David dancing before the ark also appears at the end of *A Treatise of Miraclis Pleyinge,* where it serves as an example of the proper kind of "pleyinge": "Than, frend, yif we I wilen algate pleyen, pleyne we as Davith pleyide bifore the harke of God" (*A Treatise of Miraclis Pleyinge,* ed. Clifford Davidson [Kalamazoo, MI: Medieval Institute Publications, 1993], p. 114, lines 724–25). Clopper's reading of the *Treatise* suggests that its indictment of "miraclis pleyinge" refers only to "clerical parodies and *irrisiones*" rather than to vernacular mystery cycles; thus its use of the David and Michol example would be consistent with its indictment of a specific kind of playing rather than playing in general. For the standard reading of the text as antitheatrical, see Jonas Barish, *The Antitheatrical Prejudice* (Berkeley: University of California Press, 1981).

39. Eamon Duffy, *The Stripping of the Altars: Traditional Religion in England, 1400–1580* (New Haven, CT: Yale University Press, 1992), 210.

40. Ibid., 213. Duffy further notes that Lydgate had a particular affinity for translating material from the Little Office: "Lydgate, for example, produced verse translations of the calendar, the 'Fifteen Oes,' the Marian antiphons from the Little Office such as the 'Salve Regina,' and a number of popular devotions from the primer, like the indulgenced hymn on the five joys of Mary, 'Gaude Virgo Mater Christi'" (223).

41. The image of the city as a "New Jerusalem" had a long history in medieval culture, as Kipling points out in *Enter the King,* 15, citing Ernst Kantorowicz, "The 'King's

Advent' and the Enigmatic Panels in the Doors of Santa Sabina," *Art Bulletin* 26 (1944): 207–31. In England, both the 1392 reconciliation of Richard II with London, and Henry VI's 1432 entry exploited the image of London as "New Jerusalem"; see Kipling, *Enter the King,* 15–16, 143–44. C. David Benson notes, however, that the latter occasion mixed earthly with spiritual imagery, celebrating the fecundity of trees and the abundance of wine; see chap. 5 of this volume. So too the *Mumming for the Goldsmiths* mixes classical and Christian images of Troy and Jerusalem.

42. Clopper, *Drama, Play and Game,* 62, notes the correspondence of Lydgate's "konnyng, grace and might" to the Trinity. The three attributes of the Trinity were commonplaces in Middle English literature; Julian of Norwich expounds on the "myte, wisdam and love" of Father, Son, and Holy Spirit (*The Shewings of Julian of Norwich,* ed. Georgia R. Crampton [Kalamazoo, MI: Medieval Institute Publications, 1994], chap. 58, lines 2409–11). Further examples include *Piers Plowman,* B-text, passus 16, lines 30, 36, and the *Prioress's Tale,* 472 (where "Fadres Sapience" indicates Christ). I am grateful to Jill Mann for these references. Dante also refers to the "podestate, sapienza, amore" of the Trinity (*Inferno* 3.5–6). J. P. H. Clark traces the attribution to Augustine in "'Fiducia' in Julian of Norwich," *Downside Review* 100 (1982): 203–20.

43. Sponsler, "Alien Nation," 236.

44. Shirley's glosses have been printed by Aage Brusendorff, *The Chaucer Tradition* (Oxford: Clarendon Press, 1967), 466–67.

45. See Sponsler, "Alien Nation," in which she argues that the goldsmiths' and mercers' mummings may be read as allegories for the troubled relation of Londoners to alien merchants that work by deploying symbolic others—Easterners and Jews. Although I find this reading insightful in many ways, it depends upon somewhat doubtful textual evidence. Sponsler's assertion that the mummings stage otherness because they contain merchants from the East and Jews, while it does point to the interplay between outsider and insider, relies upon an identification of the characters in the texts that is far from certain. It is true that the main actors in the *Mumming for the Goldsmiths* are Israelites, specifically Levites. Although the fact that the historical Jews were expelled from England in the thirteenth century does suggest that Israelites would embody an "Other," this reading fails to account for the overwhelming *familiarity* of the Christian narrative of David and the Ark of the Covenant. As its appearance in the popular *Mirour of Mans Saluacioune* suggests, the story and the figure of David were well known, and would have signified not alterity but rather the incorporation of the secular into a dominant cultural and ideological narrative. Further, the easy fit between the exotic geography of the *Mumming for the Mercers* and the Orientalism thesis of Said cannot be sustained in the face of a careful textual reading. Sponsler's argument depends upon Wickham's speculation that the mercers are dressed as "Orientals," rather than on the evidence provided by the text itself; see Wickham, *Early English Stages,* 1:201 and 1:54. Unlike other medieval narratives—Middle English romances provide a good example—the encounter of Westerners with Eastern people is not staged by the *Mumming for the Mercers,* insofar as the

text (the only evidence available) records its dramatic action. In fact, though the ships are described as having "sayled ful fer towarde þe West" (80), they are identified as having *French* lettering on the sides—suggesting that the "East" is not very far away. Indeed, given the fraught nature of the relationship of England to France in 1429, the use of French phrases would surely have been a distinct gesture toward the French. The idea that French ships are sailing toward England to greet the mayor suggests the investment of London's mercantile elite in what C. David Benson has called (in reference to the 1432 royal entry) "civic, bourgeois values of comfort and prosperity . . . rather than the uncertainties of military glory and foreign conquest" (see chap. 5 of this book).

   46. Green, *Poets and Princepleasers,* 10. In using the term *aristocracy,* Green is referring specifically to the literature and practices of the court, rather than to some more generalized notion of "gentlemen" or "gentility"; it is in this narrow sense that I use the term as well. It is an important distinction because, as Sylvia Thrupp demonstrated, the dividing line between "merchant" and "gentleman" was a thin one; see *The Merchant Class of Medieval London* (Chicago: University of Chicago Press, 1948), 234–87, and n. 49 below. More recently, Rosemary Horrox has meticulously illustrated the fluidity of that boundary in the fifteenth century, suggesting that the "urban gentry" and the land-owning gentry were participants in a shared elite culture; see "The Urban Gentry in the Fifteenth Century," in *Towns and Townspeople in the Fifteenth Century,* ed. John A. F. Thomson (Gloucester: Alan Sutton, 1988), 22–44. A. I. Doyle has traced the production of manuscripts for courtly and noncourtly readers and shown that their tastes were very similar and that the distinction became more blurred over the course of the fifteenth century; see "English Books in and out of Court from Edward III to Henry VI," in *English Court Culture in the Later Middle Ages,* ed. V. J. Scattergood and J. W. Sherborne (New York: St. Martin's Press, 1983), 163–81. For a similar understanding of fifteenth-century "middle-class" literacy, see Malcolm Parkes, "The Literacy of the Laity," in *Scribes, Scripts and Readers: Studies in the Communication, Presentation and Dissemination of Medieval Texts* (London: Hambledon Press, 1991), 275–98.

   47. This abbreviated list is taken from the longer discussion in Carol Meale's "*The Libelle of Englyshe Polycye* and Mercantile Literary Culture in Late-Medieval London," in *London and Europe in the Later Middle Ages,* ed. Julia Boffey and Pamela King (London: University of London, 1995), 181–227. In particular, Meale cites several books that were owned by mercers, including such texts as the *Awntyrs of Arthure, Piers Plowman,* and the *Confessio Amantis,* as well as several by Lydgate: the *Complaint of the Black Knight,* the *Temple of Glass,* the *Serpent of Division,* the *Life of Our Lady,* and the *Siege of Thebes.* Some of the texts she cites—*Confessio Amantis, Troilus and Criseyde,* the *Siege of Thebes*— were owned by members of the mercantile class somewhat later than the period under consideration here, but I reference them to illustrate a general trend that began in the later fourteenth century and continued through the end of the Middle Ages. Parkes, "Literary of the Laity," 290–94, gives a number of examples of mercantile ownership, including the ownership of Trinity College Cambridge MS R. 3. 21 by a mercer, Roger Thorney.

This manuscript includes a number of works by Lydgate, and Margaret Connolly links it to the production of Shirley manuscripts such as Trinity College Cambridge MS. R. 3. 20; see *John Shirley,* 180–81.

48. Lee Patterson, *Chaucer and the Subject of History* (Madison: University of Wisconsin Press, 1991), 333. For further discussion of the development of "middle-class" culture, particularly in relation to literacy, see Janet Coleman, *Medieval Readers and Writers: 1350–1400* (New York: Columbia University Press, 1981). In describing a manuscript from the middle fifteenth century, Bodleian Library, MS. Tanner 346, Seth Lerer makes the point that "gentry readers sought to mime the structures of commission that granted authority to the patron" in aristocratic culture; see *Chaucer and His Readers: Imagining the Author in Late Medieval England* (Princeton, NJ: Princeton University Press, 1993), 84.

49. Sylvia Thrupp demonstrated the weakness of the dividing line between merchants and gentry, citing numerous instances of intermarriage and friendship between the groups, as well as examples of gentlemen who engaged in trade and merchants who became knights (*Merchant Class,* 256–78). In particular, she noted the habit of powerful London guilds of admitting members of the nobility to their ranks; the mercers admitted "over thirty members of gentle rank between the 1430's and the end of the century," and the goldsmiths admitted another man because he was "'a man of substance and in great favor with lords'" (256–57). She further noted the similarities between mercantile and gentle cultures in their attitudes to education and their choice of reading materials (247–48). To draw this line as finely as possible, Carol Meale, citing Felicity Riddy, uses the term *subculture* to describe the different "textual communities" at play in the late medieval English mercantile and aristocratic worlds. Meale, "*Libelle of Englyshe Polycye,*" 184; Felicity Riddy, "Reading for England: Arthurian Literature and National Consciousness," *Bibliographical Bulletin of the International Arthurian Society* 43 (1991): 314–32.

50. Sheila Lindenbaum, "London Texts and Literate Practices," in *The Cambridge History of Medieval Literature,* ed. David Wallace (Cambridge: Cambridge University Press, 1999), 285, 294–98. Lindenbaum's comprehensive discussion of mercantile culture focuses on its tendency toward uniformity and officialization during the fifteenth century; her emphasis is on the conservative qualities of cultural production during the period, rather than on the incoherences and inconsistencies that so fascinate Paul Strohm in *England's Empty Throne.* The two share the notion, however, that the fifteenth century saw a retrenchment from the experimentation of Chaucer (or indeed of John of Northampton) and toward more stable and uniform texts. For a brief reading of Lydgate's mummings that concludes that they are "politically conservative" and identifies them as political poems, see Lois Ebin, *John Lydgate* (Boston: Twayne Publishers, 1985), 86–91.

51. Christopher Baswell has brilliantly elucidated the way in which the mercantile culture of the late fourteenth century, in London and in Lynn, appropriated and deployed such aristocratic narratives as the founding of Rome by Aeneas; turning to manuscripts associated with the Rising of 1381, he demonstrates how "new and fractious urban agents might seek to imagine and consolidate communal identities under the aegis of an-

cient epic story" (17). See his "Aeneas in 1381," *New Medieval Literatures* 5 (2002): 7–58. Similarly, in his discussion of Shirley manuscripts, A. S. G. Edwards notes that they are typically down-market productions with up-market aspirations, showing how they "[offer] his audience glimpses into the life and more importantly the literary tastes of these great and good. . . . The most common element in a number of his rubrics is the stress on class." See "John Shirley and the Emulation of Courtly Culture," in *The Court and Cultural Diversity*, ed. Evelyn Mullally and John Thompson (Cambridge: D. S. Brewer, 1997), 309–17, 316.

52. Mary Rose McLaren has shown that the adjective *rially* appears in the London chronicles as a kind of shorthand to emphasize the majesty of various processions in honor of kings; according to her, it is a London term with a very particular resonance in relation to the monarchy. See her *London Chronicles of the Fifteenth Century: A Revolution in English Writing* (Cambridge: D. S. Brewer, 2002), 57–58.

53. See Isidore of Seville, *Etymologiarum sive Originum libri xx,* ed. W. M. Lindsay (Oxford: Clarendon Press, 1911), XIV, viii: 11–12, for the basic description of Parnassus, including its location near Cirrea and Boeotia; cited by John Norton-Smith in *The Poems of John Lydgate* (Oxford: Clarendon Press, 1966), 126 (notes to the *Mumming at Bishopswood*). The Bishopswood account reads:

> On Parnaso þe lusty muses nyene,
> Citherra with hire sone nowe dwellis,
> Þis sayson singe and þeire notes tuwyne
> Of poetrye besyde þe cristal wellis;
> Calyope þe dytes of hem tellis,
> And Orpheus with heos stringes sharpe
> Syngeþe a roundell with his temperd herpe.
> (99–105)

In the *Troy Book*, Lydgate imitates the invocations to books 2 and 3 of *Troilus and Criseyde* by calling on both Clio and Calliope, whom he describes as having their homes on Parnassus:

> But maketh Clyo for to ben my muse
> Wyth hir sustren that on Pernaso dwelle
> In Cirrea by Elicon the welle,
> Rennyng ful clere wyth stremys cristallyn
> And callyd is the welle Caballyn
> That sprang by touche of the Pegasee.
> And helpe also, O thou Calliope,
> That were moder unto Orpheus
> Whos dites wern so mellodyus . . .
> (Pro.40–48)

Lydgate's Troy Book, 4 vols., EETS, e.s., 97, 103, 106, 126 (London: Kegan Paul, Trench, Trübner, 1906, 1908, 1910, 1935). Here Lydgate repeats a common medieval mistake, also made by Chaucer (*House of Fame,* 522), in suggesting that Helicon is a well; as Norton-Smith points out in *John Lydgate: Poems,* Helicon was in fact one of the ridges *(iuga)* of Parnassus (126). Robert Edwards, in his edition of the *Troy Book* (*Troy Book: Selections* [Kalamazoo, MI: Medieval Institute Publications, 1998]) gives Persius's *Satires* as the source for the details of Parnassus, including the "welle Caballyn" (340, note to Pro.44), but it is clear that the basic outlines of Parnassian geography derived primarily from Isidore, who in turn repeats them from Servius's commentary on Virgil (*John Lydgate: Poems,* 126).

54. My conclusion here has been anticipated to a certain extent by Pearsall, who suggests in *John Lydgate* that the tastes of the "upper bourgeoisie" were being "created as well as satisfied" by such texts as the *Mumming for the Mercers* (73); see his discussion of the literary appetites of this class (71–76).

55. See, e.g., the well-known passage in the *Siege of Thebes* (39–57) that calls Chaucer "Floure of Poetes thorghout al breteyne" and the prologue to the *Fall of Princes,* (246–357), where Lydgate catalogs Chaucer's works and links him explicitly to Tully, Petrarch, and Boccaccio, all the while complaining that the Muses of Parnassus are sure to reject his call for help. *Lydgate's Siege of Thebes,* 2 vols., ed. Axel Erdmann and Eilert Ekwall, EETS, e.s., 108, 125 (London: Kegan Paul, Trench, Trübner, 1911, 1930); *Lydgate's Fall of Princes,* 4 vols., ed. Henry Bergen, EETS, e.s., 121, 122, 123, 124 (London: Oxford University Press, 1924–27). For a comprehensive, though not exhaustive, list of Lydgate's paeans to Chaucer, see Pearsall, *John Lydgate,* 80 n. 28.

56. *Lydgate's Troy Book.*

57. Once again, Lydgate reveals his debt to Chaucer in his use of the term *poursuyant;* according to the *Middle English Dictionary,* the first use of the word in English appears in the *House of Fame:* "That pursevantes and heraudes, / That crien ryche folkes laudes" (1321). Larry D. Benson, ed., *The Riverside Chaucer* (Boston: Houghton Mifflin, 1987), 364.

8

"Stable in study"

Lydgate's *Fall of Princes* and Duke Humphrey's Library

Jennifer Summit

The library of Humphrey, Duke of Gloucester, has been synonymous with the arrival of humanism in England. One of the first English libraries to include an extensive selection of works by classical and Italian humanist authors, it has earned Humphrey a reputation as "the first Englishman to show a lively appreciation of humanism" and the man who initiated "the history of the humanist book in Britain."[1] Humphrey's foundational bequests of books to Oxford University, in honor of which the Bodleian's rare books reading room still bears his name, have been credited with no less than leading England out of the Middle Ages; as his biographer announces, "[I]n the book-chests of Oxford lay the seeds of the English Renaissance."[2] But Humphrey's credentials as England's first Renaissance man have been harder to reconcile with the fact that he was also the patron of Lydgate's *Fall of Princes.* Except for the rare reader who has tried to find Lydgate also a Renaissance harbinger, most have tended to imagine the proto-Renaissance Humphrey and the author of the ultramedieval *Fall of Princes* as representatives of conflicting cultural forces and eras.[3] Thus Derek Pearsall argues that "Humphrey was touched . . . by the spirit of the Italian Renaissance and the reawakening of interest in classical literature, and his commissioning of a translation of the *De Casibus* is part of his admiration for anything that came out of Italy, but Lydgate responds only fitfully to the stimulus, and at almost every point reasserts . . . the medieval commonplaces upon which Boccaccio's work is so largely based."[4] In this reading, the *Fall of Princes* mounts a rearguard defense against the attempted progressivism of Humphrey's commission. Those elements that have long put off modern readers of the work—its endlessness, dry moralism, and repetition of exemplum piled upon exemplum—are assumed to have similarly put off the forward-looking Humphrey, who is imagined to have been sorely let down as a patron; where he wanted an aureate English Boccaccio or Petrarch, he got instead the leaden *Fall of Princes*.

Yet the idea that Humphrey and Lydgate were at odds over the *Fall of Princes* is belied by evidence of Humphrey's role in the work's composition. Humphrey not only commissioned the work but actively involved himself in its production, lending Lydgate books to use as sources and custom-ordering the envoys that constitute its most medievalizing feature. Indeed, the poem everywhere registers Humphrey's influence, as he repeatedly interjected himself into the writing process and apparently kept constant check on its progress, playing the role less of distant patron than of collaborator.[5] This essay reexamines the relationship between Humphrey and Lydgate—and, by extension, the categories of "Renaissance" and "medieval" that they have long sustained—by reconsidering the relationship between the textual monuments through which each is represented: Lydgate's *Fall of Princes* and Humphrey's library. Rather than seeing Lydgate's work in opposition to Humphrey's library and the impulses that created it, I consider the two as mutually dependent productions. In the reading that follows, I propose that Humphrey's library forms the general context for the *Fall of Princes,* which in turn supports—and even enables—the famous library's place in the world of fifteenth-century English thought and letters. If Humphrey brought humanist books into England, I argue, Lydgate's *Fall of Princes* didn't resist them so much as it attempted to make them meaningful within English contexts.

1431: The *Fall of Princes* and the Uprising

In Humphrey's own career as patron, the library and the *Fall of Princes* are congruent efforts. Lydgate received his commission in 1431, around the same time that Humphrey began to amass many of the most important books in his library. While Lydgate was busy writing, Humphrey commissioned a series of Italian humanists, beginning in 1433 with Leonardi Bruni, to oversee the copying and collection of books for his library, which grew steadily during this time.[6] By 1439, the year in which the *Fall of Princes* was finally completed, Humphrey was ready to make his first major gift of books to Oxford University.

If the *Fall of Princes* and the library occupied parallel tracks in the chronology of Humphrey's career as patron, they also sprang from the same historical impetus. Humphrey's patronage went hand in hand with—and was materially supported by—his political activities, and 1431 marks an eventful time for both. As Henry VI's uncle (being Henry V's youngest brother), Humphrey became Henry's lieutenant in England during a brief period when the young king was visiting France from 1430 to 1432. Lydgate, writing during this time in the present tense, pays tribute to Humphrey's performance in this capacity by celebrating the "Pes and quiete" that he maintained through "ful hih prudence" (1.380, 379),[7] but his words belie a period of threatened instability that occurred under Humphrey's watch. In spring of 1431 William Perkins or Maundvyll, under the pseudonym "Jack Sharpe of Wygmoreland," was found distributing handbills in the Midlands that pointed to a would-be rebellion unlike any that preceded it.[8] The bills themselves recycled many of the calls for religious disendowment advanced by Sir John Oldcastle in 1410.[9] But the conspiracy was discovered to go much further. Not stopping at religious disendowment, the plan was "totally to destroy the estate and person of the king," to disendow lay lords and to name Lollard successors—and thus, as one contemporary charged, "of ladds and lurdains [to] make lordes."[10] William Perkins planned to "take upon himself as a prince" and to replace the king's council with his own associates; Humphrey himself was to be replaced by one John Cook, a weaver from London.[11] Once the plot was uncovered, Humphrey acted swiftly and harshly to suppress it. Perkins and his co-conspirators were captured and spectacularly executed on May 17, but fear that more plotters remained at large drove Humphrey to organize a large-scale campaign against Lollards that resulted in a number of executions. Humphrey himself traveled widely during the spring and summer of 1431 to suspected centers of instability and signaled by his presence at several of the executions his personal interest in quelling the rebellion. The anti-Lollard campaign of 1431 inspired Lydgate to observe in the *Fall of Princes* that "in this land no Lollard dar abide," since Humphrey "sparith noon, but maketh himsilven strong" against heretics (1.400, 405).

The Jack Sharp rebellion represented a new level of threat to English political and social order. While earlier popular revolts counterbalanced demands for reform with support for the monarch, the rebellion of 1431 plotted the overthrow of the monarch and his councilors—and did so, moreover, during a potentially vulnerable moment for the monarchy, with the ten-year old Henry VI away in France and the nobility internally divided and sometimes at violent odds.[12] The king's response reflects the challenge that the rebellion posed to existing models of monarchal power and order when it charges the rebels with seeking

> gou[ver]naile in no wise be langyng vnto hem yat owen to be go[ver]ned, and not so to gov[er]ne; ye which sturyng and vsurpacion of oure roial

power, by ye lawe of this oure land is treson, ech resonable man may wel fele, yat in eschuyng of, chastisyng, and reddoure of oure lawes, yei in so doing . . . dispose hem to be out of subjection, obeissance, or awe of vs, and of oure lawe; and as God knoweth, neyere wolde yei be subgitt to His, ne to mannes, but wolde be louse and free.[13]

By putting men "[who] owen to be go[ver]ned" in the place of those who govern, Jack Sharp and the rebels wage an attack not only against the king but against "subjection," not just against the king's law but against God's. The rebellion itself fueled the emergence of what I. M. W. Harvey identifies as a "popular politics" in the mid-fifteenth century that fed on a growing sense of political clout within a group that identified itself as "the common people."[14] If the rebellion represented a "vsurpacion of . . . roial power," it was also a usurpation of literacy; in their sophisticated uses of bills, which included verse and other texts, Jack Sharp's rebels showed that they could use the tools of literacy for propaganda as effectively as the Lancastrians.[15] These were "acts of assertive literacy" like the broadsides of the 1381 rebels, of which Steven Justice observes: "they made their most important claim merely by *being* written documents that came (or claimed to come) from the hands of *rustici*."[16] The literacy of the 1431 rebels became their hallmark; thus contemporary Nicholas Bishop charges them with "wryt[ing] fals bulles and fals scriptures and gilful," and Humphrey alerts his agents to be on the lookout for "soweris of cedicions, disclaundrours, or trublulos langage, or talys."[17]

Humphrey's suppression of the would-be rebellion was generally held to have been a success. With the king's return from France approaching, he was able to parlay his political victory into a more material reward, convincing the council on November 20 to approve a substantial raise in salary to reward his efforts in "the taking and execution of the most horrible heretic and impious traitor to God and the said Lord king, who called himself John Sharp, and of many other heretical malefactors his accomplices."[18] If it revealed that Humphrey's political actions were never far removed from material self-interest, the raise also allowed Humphrey to pursue his literary interests by defraying, as his biographer observes, "the charges which he incurred as a patron of letters."[19] These charges saw an immediate upswing in 1431 to 1433, when he extended his sponsorship to Lydgate and initiated a major stage in the development of his library.[20] It is thus to Jack Sharp and his plot of 1431 that the *Fall of Princes* and Humphrey's library owe their common origin.

Humphrey's turn to literary patronage in the years following his lieutenancy did not represent a retirement from the public life but an attempt to extend his statesmanship from the level of practice to the level of theory. After the king's return from France, Humphrey resumed his earlier political role as first councilor but positioned himself to be closer to Henry VI and the centers of power in the court.[21] As Susanne Saygin suggests, Humphrey's patronage during this time could have been motivated by the practical desire to provide instruction to the young king in the arts of rulership.[22] But self-interest could not be far from those motivations. By offering himself as the source of such wisdom, Humphrey confirmed his indispensability to the monarch. He did so, moreover, by demonstrating the importance of books and reading to the maintenance of royal power. If the rebels used ephemeral literacy—in the form of bill posting—to make their case, Humphrey turned to monumental textuality, in the form of his library and the enormous *Fall of Princes,* as demonstrations of political might. Thus, through his patronage, he reasserted literacy as a tool of the ruler over the ruled. As I will argue in readings that follow, these interests shaped Humphrey's uses of humanism.

Whereas Shakespeare's Prospero asserts that "my library / was Dukedom large enough," Duke Humphrey conceived his library not as a retreat from political power but as an instrument of it.[23] In his effort to build an awe-inspiring library, Humphrey followed the example of Italian princes like Cosimo de Medici and Federico da Montrefeltro, Duke of Urbino, whose extensive libraries made the display of learning into an attribute of power.[24] Thanks to their examples, the library, marked by the extensiveness and richness of its holdings, became "a distinctive and characterizing element," as Armando Petrucci puts it, "of the new seignorial state then taking shape."[25] Humphrey's ambition to emulate his Italian counterparts in building a seigniorial library is reflected in his decision to employ as overseer of his collection the Milanese humanist Pier Candido Decembrio, whose brother Angelo authored a set of dialogues focusing on "the question of how a Renaissance prince and his courtiers and scholars should choose and use books."[26]

As well as offering an outward manifestation of his learning, Humphrey's book collecting was inspired by a practical desire to locate models of rulership from the classical past that supported his own political vision. The linchpin of his collection—and the work most often cited as evidence of Humphrey's humanism—is Decembrio's translation of Plato's *Republic,* which Decembrio purported to carry out in the duke's honor. In the letters that passed between them, Decembrio promises Humphrey that the work "will impart to you the form of a good and true prince," while Humphrey in turn finds Plato's prince a model of "wise statesmanship:" "Such is the dignity and grace of Plato," Humphrey writes in gratitude to Decembrio, "and so successful is your interpretation of him, that we cannot say to whom we owe most, to him for drawing a prince of such wise statesmanship, or to you for laboring to bring [this work] to light."[27] In the Fifth book of the *Republic,* which Decembrio translated and sent first to the duke to advertise the book's value, Plato famously formulates his model of the philosopher-king, when he has Socrates insist:

> Unless philosophers become kings in our cities, or unless those who now are kings and rulers become true philosophers, so that political power and philo-sophic intelligence converge, and unless those lesser natures who run after one without the other are excluded from governing, I believe there can be no end to troubles, my dear Glaucon, in our cities or for all mankind. Only then will our theory of the state spring to life and see the light of day, at least to the degree possible.[28]

Plato's philosopher-king dovetailed well with Humphrey's own persona as a learned statesman, which he attempted to project at home and abroad through his patronage. In Italy, where the mythology of the learned ruler was already familiar through other examples, humanists eagerly reflected back to the duke the terms of honor that he himself cultivated assiduously. The Venetian humanist Piero del Monte compared Humphrey to classical examples of learned statesmen like Caesar "who fought and judged by day, and wrote books by night." Similarly, Lapo da Castiglionchio dedicated his original treatise *Comparatio studiorum et rei militaris* to Humphrey, citing his fame as both a soldier and a devotee of "learning, eloquence, and the humane studies."[29] The image of Humphrey as scholar-prince was anchored by his library, whose fame spread in England as well as Italy. Oxford University's official letter of thanks for his bequest of books echoes the Italian humanists in comparing Humphrey to Caesar as both a soldier/scholar and founder of a great library: "Julius Caesar founded a library at Rome to preserve by books the fame of his conquest of the world," it reads. So, the letter claims hyperbolically (but not inaccurately), the library at Oxford "will be an everlasting monument of your fame."[30]

Lydgate's *Fall of Princes* needs to be read within this context of Humphrey's efforts to cultivate a persona as learned statesman. Like the others, Lydgate compares Humphrey to Caesar, who "natwithstandyng his conquest & renoun, / Vnto bookis he gaff gret attendaunce" (1.369–70). And further echoing his Italian counterparts, Lydgate praises his patron as a soldier-scholar who is "bothe manli and eek wis" (1.407), for whom "corage" and "studie" are congruent virtues:

His corage neuer doth appalle
To studie in bookis off antiquite,
Therin he hath so gret felicite
Vertuously hymsilff to ocupie,
Off vicious slouthe to haue the maistrie.
                    (1.393–99)

But Lydgate also adapts the classical and humanist figure of the soldier-scholar to the English contexts to which Humphrey's patronage responded. If Lydgate conceives Humphrey's literary activity in terms of the Benedictine injunction to "eschew idleness," as Pearsall notes,[31] he also identifies Humphrey's "maistrie" over "slouthe" in his study with his ability to "[make] hymsiluen strong" (1.405) against Lollard challenges in the state. Thus, while Humphrey's ruthlessness in quelling the Jack Sharp rebellion reveals his ability "to chastise alle that do therto tresoun" (1.413), his work in his study also leads to the more abstract and literary chastisement of "errour":

And to do plesaunce to our lord Iesu,
He studieth euere to haue intelligence;
Reedyng off bookis bryngith in vertu,
Vices excluding, slouthe and necligence,
Makith a prynce to haue experience,
To knowe hymsilff, in many sundry wise,
Wher he trespasith *his errour to chastise.*
                    (1.413–20, emphasis mine)

Chastising both treasonous Lollards and "errour" in himself, Lydgate's Humphrey offers the example of how statesmanship and reading are not only mutually supporting activities but two outcomes of the same activity—chastisement or *castigare,* an act of correction whose roots in humanist textual criticism Stephanie Jed has demonstrated.[32] By extension, Humphrey's ability to produce stability in the state begins with his ability to remain "stable in study" (1.389).

Lydgate's Libraries

If Humphrey's library anchors his personal mythology as scholar-prince, the *Fall of Princes* deserves to be called "a phenomenon of the library" (in Foucault's words), since it makes libraries its recurrent setting and touchstone.[33] Lydgate goes out of his way to establish the library as the scene of the work's composition. Whereas Boccaccio frequently refers to himself in the act of writing, Lydgate emphatically locates that act in a study or library, two terms he uses interchangeably: for instance, in a scene in which Boccaccio tells us only that "I was taking up my pen," Lydgate inserts details of location: "In his studi alone as Bochas stood" (6.1–2), and, a few lines down: "Bochas pensiff sool in his librarie" (6.15).[34] Thus Lydgate pictures Bochas not only in the act of writing but in a place where he is surrounded by books—a detail that figures importantly in Lydgate's vision of the work's composition and significance.[35] Libraries, Lydgate insists, are places to which writers are naturally drawn: "Poetis to sitte in ther librarie / Desire of nature, and to be solitarie" (3.3807–8). But despite being a place of solitude, Lydgate's library is not a retreat from the world but a setting of worldly action.

If Humphrey deserves praise because of his industrious literary activity ("Vertuously hymsilff to ocupie, / Off vicious slouthe to haue the maistrie"), Lydgate's Bochas locates that industry in the library. In the prologue to book 8, when Bochas finds himself succumbing to idleness, he is visited by the shade of Petrarch, who admonishes him, in a passage unique to Lydgate's version of the scene, "[Idleness] hath the drawe awey fro thi librarie" (8.101). Directing Bochas back to his library, Petrarch advises him to take example from "the book I maad of lyff solitarye," which "techeth the weie of virtuous besyness" (8.108–10). Petrarch's *Of the Solitary Life,* not mentioned by Boccaccio or Laurent, almost certainly refers to a book in Humphrey's library, and its insertion here could well have been directed by Humphrey himself.[36] It clarifies Lydgate's meaning in his observation about poets "in ther librarie" who desire "to be solitarie" by defining the kind of solitude that Petrarch describes as not a retreat from the world but an active engagement with it: "I mean a solitude," Petrarch writes, "that is not exclusive, leisure that is neither idle nor profitless but productive of advantage to many."[37] Solitude for Petrarch is a space of learning that proves itself in worldly application; thus he approvingly cites "examples of emperors and military leaders who liked solitude."[38] The "virtuous besyness" that Bochas learns to pursue in his library is of a piece with Lydgate's description of Humphrey's own library as a factory of virtue, a place dedicated to overcoming "slouthe and necligence," where "Reedyng off bookis bryngith in vertu."

Lydgate's ideas about libraries were shaped by his experience with two notable libraries of the fifteenth century: Duke Humphrey's library and the library at his monastery at Bury St. Edmund's. If Humphrey's library represents to many the dawning of a new kind of library, the Bury library, with its over two thousand volumes, helped to define the institution of the library for its time. As James Westfall Thompson argues, "[T]he fifteenth century was pre-eminently the time when separate library structures were being erected"—a shift from earlier habits of storing books in portable armaria or scattered in cloisters—and the Bury library played a key role in this development.[39] The first reference to the Bury collection as a "library" was by William Curteys, who was abbot from 1429–45, while Lydgate was a monk at Bury.[40] Curteys took an active interest in the monastery's library, reorganizing its book collection and archives, which had been formerly dispersed throughout several locations in the monastery, and bringing them into a central place that was designed and organized to facilitate efficient consultation of texts. Curteys's reform of the Bury library was enabled by the work of his illustrious predecessor, Henry of Kirkestede (also mistakenly known as "Boston of Bury"), who in the 1340s and 1350s compiled the *Catalogus de libris autenticis et apocrifis,* a massive bibliography that pioneered the method of organizing catalogs alphabetically by authors' names.[41] Kirkestede exercised a similarly pioneering influence over the Bury library, organizing the monastery's large collection according to the books' content, thereby producing "the earliest known system," as Richard H. Rouse and Mary A. Rouse observe, to use class-marks "to group books by category."[42] The Bury library that Lydgate knew defies generalizations like that of David Knowles when he observes that "the monastic library, even the greatest, had something of the appearance of a heap."[43] In contrast, the Bury library was a model of bibliographical organization that presumed active use.

Lydgate was thus present at one of the formative moments and places in the history of the medieval library. At Bury, Lydgate even played a role in the reorganization of the library by virtue of his close relationship with Abbot Curteys. Driven by what Rodney M. Thomson calls his "passion for record-making," the abbot ordered new copies of the monastery's cartularies, the records of the monastery's founding charters of privilege that formed the keystone of the monastic archive. Bury's charters had in fact been the object of popular rebellions themselves; in both 1327 and 1381, rebels sacked Bury's archives and burned many of its records, in violent challenges to the powerful monastery's control over local property.[44] At Curteys's request, the new cartularies were translated into Middle English verse by Lydgate himself, who signaled, in undertaking the project, his membership in the documentary structures of power against which the rebels chafed. Completed in 1440, soon after Lydgate completed the *Fall of Princes,* the resulting *Cartae versificatae* records miniature narratives of royal patronage that assert the interdependence between the monastery and the monarch. These reiterate the *Fall of Princes'* lesson that it is "onto pryncis gretli necessarie / To yiue exaumple how this world doth varie" and "To shewe thuntrust off al worldli thyng" (1.426–27, 429), as when the *Cartae versificatae* notes:

> In many a place of devyne scripture
> It is remembryd by ful contemplatyf,
> al worldly thyngis be variable and unsure
> $(221)^{45}$

And

> For ther may be no verray sykyrnesse,
> nor no felicite nor no perfyte glorye
> in worldly thynges, that bene ay transitorye.
> (222)

Where the *Fall of Princes* instructs rulers in vertuous behavior, the *Cartae versificatae* emphasizes rulers' reciprocal obligation to "holy chirche" and its institutions:

> For of old custom it longith unto kynges
> First holy chirche to meyntene and governe
> And for ther sogetys in al maner thynges
> for to prouyde and prudently discerne,
> to shewe themsylf lyk a clere lanterne,
> with lyght of verteu ther sogettys tenlumyne
> Both by example and vertuous doctryn.
> (223)

If, as the *Fall of Princes* asserts, "reedyng off bookis bryngith in vertu," the *Cartae versificatae* shows that the production of "verteu" relies on "the sentence of seyntys and of clerkys" (224), of which the monastery and its library are the guardians. Where monarchs are obliged to "maynteyne and governe" the church and its monasteries, those monasteries in turn produce and maintain the "vertuous doctryne" through which monarchs project their authority.

Lydgate's *Cartae versificatae,* then, produces a symbiotic relationship between monarch and monastery that bolsters the importance of the monastic library, whose importance Abbot Curteys was at that moment establishing. This argument about the utility of books to good rule is the flip side of Humphrey's library. Just as Humphrey built his library as a projection of political authority, the *Cartae versificatae* emphasizes the importance of monastic libraries in guarding the "vertuous doctryne" that rulers need. Together, they suggest that there is a greater continuity between the monastic library of Bury and the humanist library of Duke Humphrey than is appreciated by strict efforts to differentiate between—and in so doing, to oppose— "medieval" and "Renaissance" libraries and reading practices. Armando Petrucci and Pearl Kibre have found that Italian seignorial libraries during this time, while bearing a distinct humanist stamp, also maintained close ties to monastic libraries, which in many respects they attempted to emulate both in the scope of their holdings and in the institutional authority that they projected.[46] A similar connection exists between the libraries of Duke Humphrey and Bury St. Edmund's; as well as being two of the most extensive libraries of their day, the two share an ideological commitment to the library as a cornerstone of power.

The continuity between Humphrey's library and that of Bury St. Edmund's existed not only in function but also in content. Despite Humphrey's reputation as the first serious collector of classical texts in England, the Bury library included classical authors in great numbers, such as Cicero, Virgil, Horace, Ovid, and Juvenal.[47] It also contained a number of works by English Dominican friars such as Nicholas Trevet, Thomas Waleys, and Thomas Ringsted, whose presence in the collection indicates how the classics were read at Bury.[48] These authors were known for commentaries that adapted classical sources to Christian uses by submitting them to allegorical readings dedicated to extracting the "hidden meanings of the myths (*fabularum integumenta*)," as Trevet puts it in his commentary on Seneca.[49] In their zeal to produce Christian morals from classical texts, the friars have been criticized as bad classicists, whose tendency to "modernize" the classics was based in "a tight network of assumptions and instructions, given material form in the system of glosses, [that] bound them to the existing scholastic system of instruction, rather than to their historical place and time."[50] That tendency, so the traditional account goes, would be reversed by humanists who insisted on reading classical works in their original contexts. But the friars' classicism and the humanist classicism of Humphrey are in unlikely alliance; when it comes to extracting "hidden meanings" from texts, there is more in common than expected between the friars' search for Christian lessons in the classics and Humphrey's search for models of princely virtue. If, as Lydgate claims, Humphrey "hath gret ioie with clerkis to comune" (1.387), it is because clerks' literary training offers a lesson in how to extract, as the *Cartae versificatae* asserts, "virtuous doctryn" from "example."

"With clerkis to comune"

If Humphrey projected the *Fall of Princes* as a humanist enterprise, why did he employ a monk like Lydgate to produce it in the first place, rather than a humanist like Decembrio? While Humphrey admires Decembrio's language as "ancient and worthy of the ancients," the same could not be true of Lydgate, who continually proclaims his own lack of rhetorical skill. Lydgate observes that Boccaccio writes "with rethoriques sueet" (1.72) but declares that he himself is incapable of such rhetorical achievement: "havyng no colours but onli whit & blak" (1.465) (a claim appropriate to Lydgate, a member of the Benedictine "black monks"). In this, Lydgate makes the point that he writes not as a poet but as a clerk.[51] The distinction is crucial to the *Fall of Princes,* with its highly self-conscious reflections on the topic of writing. In a passage that is unique to his version, Lydgate describes the work of poets:

> Ther cheeff labour is vicis to repreve
> With a maner couert symylitude,
> And non estat with ther langage greeve
> Bi no rebukyng of termys dul and rude;
> What-euer thei write, on vertue ay conclude.
>
> (3.3830–34)

In his insistence that poets' meanings always conclude "on vertue," "what-euer thei write," Lydgate deliberately echoes St. Paul from Romans 15.4: "Whatever was written in former days was written for our instruction," a passage that became one of the key texts for medieval theories of allegoresis. Traditionally used to justify the recuperation of classical texts for Christian meanings, this doctrine suggested that meanings that seemed to point away from Christian truths could be interpreted allegorically in order to bring them into line with a Christian framework. In a similar vein, Lydgate insists that even when poets appear to use "rebuking of termys dul and rude," their true intention is not to "greeve" any "estat" but to produce virtue. Lydgate thus adapts Paul's model in the service of upholding the truths not of Christianity but of social order and the traditional hierarchy of the estates; but it will take a concerted reapplication of the monastic program of reading to do this.

As Lydgate asserts, clerks, trained as allegorical readers, are especially equipped to decode poets' "covert similitude" and to derive moral lessons from recalcitrant texts. Embodying this assertion, the *Fall of Princes* is created through the accumulation of poetic exempla followed by envoys, which are Lyd-gate's most notable innovation to his sources; those envoys gloss the exempla that precede them and uncover edifying moral lessons in line with Lydgate's charge to offer a work of instruction to princes. Thus, to cite an opening ex-ample that establishes the work's *modus operandi,* poets are responsible for fa-bles such as that of Saturn:

> These olde poetis with ther sawes swete
> Ful couertli in ther vers do feyne,
> How olde Saturne was whilom kyng of crete
> And off custum did his besy pyne,
> Off his godhed list for to ordeyne
> That he sholde, as off his nature,
> Echon deuoure as by his engendrure.
>
> (1.1401–7)

But having recounted this poetic fiction, Lydgate hastens to add that the story is a fable and thus should not be taken literally to refer to an actual king:

> To vndirstonde off poetis the process,
> Thei meene pleynli that this word Saturne
> Doth in it-silff nothyng but tyme expresse;
> And philisophres bere also witnesse,
> That as in tyme, foorth euery thyng is brouht
> So tyme ageynward bryngith euery thing to nouht.
>
> (1.1409–14)

Through Lydgate's gloss, a story of an unnatural king becomes a lesson about the circularity of time, a lesson that, as Lydgate attests, "clerkis recorde eek in ther writyng" (1.1415). Where poets write "couertli" and "with a maner couert symylitude," clerks "recorde" in clarifying language the virtuous lessons to be gleaned from those stories.

By aligning himself with clerks as a moralizing interpreter of poets, Lydgate establishes the project that will guide the *Fall of Princes.* Because Lydgate's training as a monastic reader prepares him to extract "covert" messages of Christian virtue from classical texts, he declares that he will emulate "these clerkis in writyng" who produce new writing from

Thyng that was maad of auctours hem beforn
Thei may off newe fynde and fantasie,
Out of old chaaf trie out ful cleene corne.
(1.22–24)

In this, Lydgate cites Augustine's famous model of allegorical reading as a process of separating "spiritual" corn from "literal" chaff, by extracting "the mystery" that is "covered in the wrapping of the letter."[52] For Augustine, the metaphor of the corn and the chaff illustrates the possibility of recuperating Christian meanings from non-Christian texts. But, as he did with Saint Paul, here Lydgate transforms Augustine's famous account of allegorical reading into a tool supporting of the secular authority of princes.

In so doing, Lydgate further transforms the chaff and corn model by insisting on the corn's newness; thus, as Larry Scanlon points out, he makes it less an anterior object of discovery than a product of "fantasie" or invention, a revision that allows clerks to approach their sources with "an almost unlimited latitude for innovation."[53] Lydgate claims precisely this latitude for himself in lines that open the *Fall of Princes'* prologue, which assert that writers must be willing to "make and unmake" their sources

In many sondry wyse,
As pottres, which to that craft entende,
Breke and renewe ther vesselis to a-mende.
(1.12–14)

With this potter metaphor, Lydgate presents the creative process as a form of renewal that involves a certain amount of destruction; the transformation of "old chaaf" into "ful cleene corne," he suggests, requires the use of force. In the *Fall of Princes* the main locus of that force is the envoy, a feature that Lydgate included at the special request of Humphrey, who charged him:

That I sholde in everi trajedie
Afftir the processe made mencioun,
At the eende sette a remedie,
With a lenvoie conueied be resoun,
And afftir that, with humble affeccioun,
To noble pryncis lowli it directe.
(2.148–53)

If breaking can be considered a form of amending, it is also germane to the form of "remedie" that Lydgate's envoys supply to his source texts. Humphrey's request for an envoy following every chapter significantly changes the tone of the work from its sources. Boccaccio conceived his own work less as a source of edification than as example to the "vicious" and "debauched" rulers of his age illustrating the tenuous nature of power; where he extracts lessons, he offers them as occasional breaks meant to leaven the otherwise relentless narrative of downfall: "In order that an unbroken succession of stories be not tiresome to the reader, I think it will be both more pleasant and useful from time to time to add inducements to virtue and dissuasions from vice."[54] But Humphrey's request forces Lydgate to turn each story into the basis of moral lessons for princes. Under that pressure, Lydgate constructs his envoys as a secular commentary that extracts moral meanings from his sources. But those sources are not always amenable to Humphrey's wishes—especially given the ambivalence toward princes that permeates Lydgate's humanist sources, including Boccaccio himself—forcing Lydgate to break and remake his sources in order to provide the kinds of moral stories Humphrey seeks.

"Reedyng off bookis bryngith in vertu"

When Humphrey lent Lydgate books from his library to incorporate into the *Fall of Princes*, it was with a clear agenda: to advance his self-fashioning as a scholar-prince and to extract edifying lessons in the arts of statesmanship. Humphrey's lendings are concentrated in one chapter of book 2. While it represents only a short portion of the vast *Fall of Princes*, the section offers a telling illustration of how books from Humphrey's library both shaped and were shaped by the *Fall of Princes*. Early in the second book of the *Fall of Princes* appears "A Chapitle / descryuyng how prynces being hedis of ther comountees should haue noble chaualrie true Iuges &c ther commounte to gouerne &c" (2.806). The chapter represents a noteworthy departure from Lydgate's sources. Boccaccio's original presents a chapter of a different nature, entitled "In Fastosam Regum superbiam"; despite his other departures from Boccaccio, Laurent is faithful in his treatment of this section, which he translates as "Contre les roys & princes orgueilleux." In Boccaccio and Laurent's versions, the chapter reminds kings that their power derives from the people, who maintain the right to deprive them of that power should they abuse it. Thus Boccaccio asserts, "To conspire against this kind of ruler, to take up arms, to deceive, to oppose this man is an act of greatness and, even more, of necessity. Scarcely any offering is more acceptable to God than the blood of a tyrant." In support of this assertion, Boccaccio cites examples of "extraordinary men" who "have dared the greatest deeds" in overthrowing tyrants; thus "Junius Brutus turned the Roman people against Tarquin the Proud, Virginius against Appius Claudius."[55] In his reading of Brutus and Virginius, Boccaccio follows a tradition in which these stories exemplify popular revolts against tyranny; they took an added resonance in Boccaccio's Florence, where they were held to champion republican freedom.[56] Boccaccio's citation of them here becomes one of those moments in his ideologically complex text in which, as David Wallace asserts, Boccaccio "shows a strong prorepublican, antityrannical bias in narrating histories of ancient Rome," reflecting his own allegiance to the Florentine republic.[57] Laurent translates the section faithfully while expanding it to catalog the moral failures of princes who are justly overthrown, before he concludes, following Boccaccio, "Il nest sacrifice a dieu tant aggreable comme est le sang du tyrant et maulvais prince pource que il corrompt les droitz diuins et humains."[58] And again, he cites, though also amplifies, the examples of "iunius brutus vng cytoyen de romme et cousin de la treschaste Lucresse" and "virgineus," who led "tout le people de romme contre appius Claudius," as examples of "aucuns qui ont ose entreprendre & acomplir tresgrans choses."[59]

In Lydgate's rendering, the chapter is dramatically revised in ways that reveal Humphrey's shaping influence on the *Fall of Princes.* In place of Boccaccio and Laurent's examples of the justified overthrow of tyrants and "maulvais prince," Lydgate offers an allegory of good government that is lifted from John of Salisbury's *Policraticus,* a book that Humphrey himself owned and almost certainly lent Lydgate for the purposes of this substitution.[60] Borrowing from John's well-known allegory of the body politic, Lydgate compares the nation to a human body in order to assert the interdependence of its parts:

> Hed, armys, bodi and ther fresshe visages
> Withoute feet or leggis may nat vaile
> To stonde upriht; for needis thei mut faile
> And semblabli suiectis in comountees
> Reise up the noblesse off pryncis in ther sees.
>
> (2.829–33)

Whereas in Boccaccio, and Laurent after him, the people rise up against princes, in Lydgate the people raise princes up as the legs raise up the body, an organic metaphor that not only stresses the interdependence of the body parts but insists on their mutual investment in the hierarchy of ruler over ruled.[61] It is surely apt that in John's source, Livy, the metaphor is invoked to quell a popular uprising.[62] As wielded in the *Fall of Princes,* the metaphor literally replaces an image of popular uprising with one that asserts the natural order of princely authority.

In keeping with his use of John of Salisbury, Lydgate similarly "amends" the stories of Lucrece and Virginia. Where Boccaccio and Laurent cite these stories to support popular revolts against tyrannical rule, Lydgate rounds out his "Chapter of Good Government" by retelling the same stories through alternative sources that can also be traced to Humphrey. As Lydgate recounts, he was first reluctant to retell Lucrece's story, since it had already been told by Chaucer ("sithe that Chaucer, cheeff poete of Bretayne, wrot off hir liff a legende souerayne" [2.979–80]), but, pressed by Humphrey, he complied with his lord's request:

> My lord bad I sholde abide,
> By good auys at leiser to translate
> The doolful processe off her pitous fate
>
> (2.1006–8)

What follows is a lengthy and faithful translation of Salutati's *Declamatio,* which tells the story of Lucrece's rape by Tarquin by focusing on its aftermath; first, in an address to Lucrece by her husband and father, urging her against the suicide that she threatens (2.1058–1211); next, in Lucrece's response, culminating in her suicide (2.1212–1330); and finally, in a description of Lucrece's vindication in the exile of the royal Tarquin and the establishment of the Roman republic.[63]

Humphrey's selection of the text for insertion into the *Fall of Princes* seems incongruous, particularly as an example of "Good Government" in the section that he so actively engineered. As written and received, Salutati's *Declamatio* is a story of supremely bad government; its author, the chancellor of republican Florence from 1375 to 1406, intended the narrative to illustrate the origin of *libertas Romana* as an example for Florentine republicanism by means of what Stephanie Jed reminds us is "humanist tradition which has celebrated Lucretia's rape as a prologue to republican freedom."[64] As reflected in Boccaccio's version, this tradition reads Tarquin's exile as a story of tyranny justly punished, a warning of the evils of tyranny, and a reminder of the power of the people to overthrow unjust rulers.

But as reread and glossed by Lydgate, the story is made to uphold a very different lesson. Following his faithful translation of Salutati's text, Lydgate reinterprets it as an example of the tragic aftereffects of bad governance; because of Tarquin's offense, Lydgate asserts, "Kynges [were] exiled for such mysgouvernaile" (2.1435). Whereas Salutati offered the story as a celebration of republican freedom, Lydgate offers it as an extension of his lesson, lifted from *Policraticus,* of the natural hierarchy of the kingdom and the evils that befall it when that order is violated. Republicanism is not the glorious end that justifies tragic means, then, but the threatening specter of a society out of order.

Lydgate advances this reading of Lucrece's story by pairing it with a retelling of the story of Virginia, echoing Boccaccio's and Laurent's linkage of the two stories. But again, rather than following Boccaccio or Laurent, he cross-references another source, "Titus Lyuyus" (2.1346). While Livy was a standard source of the Virginia story, I take Lydgate's reference to be to a specific book. Humphrey owned a magnificently illuminated copy of Livy that was translated by Pierre Bersuire; a gift from his brother John of Bedford, it was in Humphrey's library at the time Lydgate wrote this chapter.[65] Humphrey's desire for practical morality dovetails with Bersuire's stated aim in his translation of the work to use Livy's history as a store of exempla for royal readers; thus Bersuire writes in his prologue to King Jean le Bon, "Les Souverains doivent s'inspirer des exemples du anciens."[66] Following Bersuire, Lydgate offers the story of Virginia along with that of Lucrece as advice to "noble pryncis" on how to maintain their rule. Thus his envoy concludes:

> Noble pryncis, your resoun doth applie,
> which ouer the people ha[ue] dominacioun,
> So prudentli to gouerne hem and guie,
> That loue and dreed be trewe affeccioun
> Preserue ther hertis from fals rebellioun,
> Sithe to your hihnesse nothyng may more preuaile
> Than trewe subieccioun expert in the poraile.
>
> (2.1457–62)

True to Humphrey's request, Lydgate's envoy "remedie[s]" his sources by reinterpreting their meanings for the benefit of "noble pryncis." Thus Lydgate's envoy inverts the meanings of the stories of Lucrece and Virginia by offering them as lessons in how princes should maintain their "dominacioun" and "preserve" the people "from fals rebellion."

The reading process that Lydgate follows in this section of the *Fall of Princes* reflects the library settings with which Lydgate was familiar. If the selection of texts is dictated by Humphrey's library, Lydgate collates them in a way that is the literary outgrowth of innovations in library organization such as the class-mark system established at Bury by Henry of Kirkestede. Reading one subject across a variety of texts, he cross-references John of Salisbury's model of the body politic with Boccaccio's, and Salutati's stories of Lucrece and Virginia with those of Bersuire, and thus "corrects" his originals.

Lydgate's orientation as a reader might be glimpsed in illuminations and woodcuts that picture Lydgate at work: seated at a lectern before an open book that is surrounded by other books arranged on a circular platform, Lydgate does not read books singly but rather in groups.[67] This seating arrangement anticipates the readerly practice that Anthony Grafton and Lisa Jardine see manifested in the Renaissance "bookwheel," which enables readers to engage in a "centrifugal mode of reading" by which they "[consult] multiple volumes simultaneously."[68] If Lydgate's reading practice shares an intertextual focus with humanist practices of later ages, it also advances from specifically medieval methods of allegorical literacy. By replacing the republican lessons that Boccaccio and Salutati drew from the story of Lucrece with a commendation of princely rule, Lydgate could be following the model of his other source, Bersuire, who pioneered moral reading in his own *Ovid Moralised;* there Bersuire justified his practice of drawing Christian morals from pagan sources by asserting that "a man may, if he can, gather grapes from thorns, suck honey from a rock, take oil from the hardest stone, and build and construct the ark of the covenant from the treasures of the Egyptians. And Ovid says that it is allowable to learn from an enemy."[69] In a similar vein, Lydgate brings his monastic training into Duke Humphrey's library, and from the "old chaff" of Humphrey's sources he extracts the "ful cleene corn" of his envoys' lessons in statesmanship.

The Rise of Princes

To recall Pearsall's reading, with which this essay opened, I am arguing that Humphrey wanted more from Lydgate than an Englished *De casibus* motivated by "admiration for anything that came out of Italy." Rather, he directed Lydgate to incorporate humanist books into the *Fall of Princes* while actively transforming them, in the manner of a secular Bersuire, into propitious models of "Good Government." The "medievalizing" effect of Lydgate's treatment of his humanist sources, in other words, is entirely in keeping with the aim that

Humphrey embodied in his library, which was to assert literacy as a tool of royal authority.

Coming in the wake of the rebellion of 1431, Humphrey's interest in drawing literary lessons against the dangers of "fals rebellioun" is a topical one. The agents of Jack Sharp's rebellion threatened to "make lordes" out of "ladds and lurdains" and thus sought "gou[ver]naile in no wise be langyng vnto hem yat owen to be go[ver]ned, and not so to gov[er]ne" and thereby "dispose[d] hem to be out of subjection, obeissance, or awe" of royal rule.[70] In light of this threat, Lydgate's ability to produce lessons in "trewe subieccioun" is valuable indeed, as is his ability to transform stories of popular uprisings into exemplary tales supporting the natural hierarchy of ruler over ruled. If Lydgate accomplishes this transformation on a local level in his chapter "descryuyng how prynces being hedis of ther comountees sholde haue noble cheualrie true Iuges &c ther commounte to gouerne &c" in book 2, that accomplishment is consistent with other alterations that Lydgate made to his sources in the *Fall of Princes,* notably his elaborations on the theme that Lois Ebin calls "the story of the churl rising to power."[71] For example, Lydgate observes of the story of Spartacus:

> What thing mor cruel in comparisoun
> Or mor vengable of will & nat off riht,
> Than whan a cherl hath domynacioun!
> Lak of discrecioun bleendith so the siht
> Of comouneres, for diffaute of liht,
> Whan thei haue poweer contrees to gouerne
> Fare lik a beeste [that] can nothing disserne.
> (6.778–84)

Moreover, if the rebels of 1431 put Humphrey and his agents on the lookout for "trublos langage or talys," Lydgate shows how language and tales can be disciplined and remedied through a program of reading that brings them into line with the interests of rulers. In the end, this is what links the *Fall of Princes* with the literary project that is monumentalized in Humphrey's library. If both continually pay homage to books, they also teach and learn from one another how to remake them.

Notes

1. Roberto Weiss, *Humanism in England during the Fifteenth Century,* 2nd ed. (Oxford: Basil Blackwell, 1957), 69; J. B. Trapp, "The Humanist Book," in *The Cambridge*

History of the Book in Britain, vol. 3, *1400–1557,* ed. Lotte Hellinga and J. B. Trapp (Cambridge: Cambridge University Press, 1999), 295.

2. K. H. Vickers, *Humphrey, Duke of Gloucester: A Biography* (London: Archibald Constable, 1907), 422.

3. This is the reading of Vickers, *Humphrey,* 343–44; for a general discussion of the opposition between Humphrey's "progressive" humanist interests versus the "backward [ness]" of his "contacts with English authors such as John Lydgate," see Susanne Saygin, *Humphrey, Duke of Gloucester (1390–1447) and the Italian Humanists* (Leiden: Brill, 2002), 10. Alain Renoir, *The Poetry of John Lydgate* (Cambridge, MA: Harvard University Press, 1967), and Walter Schirmer, *John Lydgate: A Study of the Culture of the XVth Century,* trans. Ann E. Keep (1952; reprint, Berkeley: University of California Press, 1961), are virtually alone in seeing Lydgate as a proto-Renaissance figure.

4. Derek Pearsall, *John Lydgate* (London: Routledge & Kegan Paul, 1970), 224.

5. See E. P. Hammond, "Poet and Patron in The Fall of Princes," *Anglia* 38 (1914): 121–36.

6. Weiss, *Humanism in England,* 47–53.

7. *Lydgate's Fall of Princes,* 4 vols., ed. Henry Bergen, EETS, e.s., 121, 122, 123, 124 (London: Oxford University Press, 1924–27); all further citations are to this edition. Throughout this chapter, all poetry is cited parenthetically in the text by line number or by book and line numbers.

8. For a general overview of the Jack Sharp rebellion, see Vickers, *Humphrey,* 222–24, and Margaret Aston, *Lollards and Reformers: Images and Literacy in Late Medieval Religion* (London: Hambledon Press, 1984), 31–38.

9. Vickers, *Humphrey,* 223; Aston, *Lollards and Reformers,* 33.

10. "Letters from King Henry VI to the Abbot of St. Edmundsbury, and to the Alderman and Bailiffs of the Town, for the Suppression of the Lollards," ed. John Gage, *Archaeologia* 23 (1831): 342; Aston, *Lollards and Reformers,* 34.

11. Aston, *Lollards and Reformers,* 35.

12. For a discussion of the rebellion and its contexts, see Ralph A. Griffiths, *The Reign of King Henry VI: The Exercise of Royal Authority, 1422–1461* (London: Ernest Benn, 1981), 138–44.

13. "Letters from King Henry VI," 342.

14. I. M. W. Harvey, "Was There Popular Politics in Fifteenth-Century England?" in *The McFarlane Legacy: Studies in Late Medieval Politics and Society,* ed. R. H. Britness and A. J. Pollard (New York: St. Martin's Press, 1995). For an analysis of an earlier history of the "communes," see also Emily Steiner, "Commonalty and Literary Form in the 1370s and 1380s," *New Medieval Literatures* 6 (2003): 199–221.

15. On bill-casting such as the 1431 rebels practiced, see Wendy Scase, "'Strange and Wonderful Bills': Bill-Casting and Political Discourse in Late Medieval England," *New Medieval Literatures* 2 (1998): 225–47. One of the Jack Sharp bills "presented by John Sharpe to Humphrey duke of Gloucester" survives in British Library MS Harley 3775, fol. 120, and is edited by H. T. Riley in *Annales Monasterii St. Albani,* Rolls Series (London, 1870), 1:453–56.

16. Steven Justice, *Writing and Rebellion: England in 1381* (Berkeley: University of California Press, 1994), 24, 36.

17. Aston quotes Bishop from Cambridge University Library MS Dd. 14. 2. in *Lollards and Reformers*, 45; "Letters from King Henry VI," 343.

18. Vickers, *Humphrey,* 226.

19. Ibid., 227.

20. The *Fall of Princes* is generally dated between the rebellion in May 1431 and Henry's return from France in January 1432, on the strength of its present-tense references to Humphrey's lieutenancy and suppression of the Lollards. See Hammond, "Poet and Patron," 121–36.

21. See Saygin, *Humphrey,* 48–56, for an account of Humphrey's actions during this time.

22. Ibid., 63.

23. See William Shakespeare, *The Tempest,* ed. Stephen Orgel (Oxford: Oxford University Press, 1987), 1.2.109–10.

24. Weiss, *Humanism in England,* 58.

25. Armando Petrucci, *Writers and Readers in Medieval Italy: Studies in the History of Written Culture,* ed. and trans. Charles M. Radding (New Haven, CT: Yale University Press, 1995), 225.

26. Anthony Grafton, *Commerce with the Classics: Ancient Books and Renaissance Readers* (Ann Arbor: University of Michigan Press, 1997), 21.

27. Mario Borso, ed., "Correspondence of Humphrey Duke of Gloucester and Pier Candido Decembrio," *English Historical Review* 19 (1904): 513–14. Humphrey's response is translated by Vickers, *Humphrey,* 360.

28. Plato, *The Republic,* trans. Richard W. Sterling and William C. Scott (New York: W. W. Norton, 1985), 5.473d.

29. Vickers, *Humphrey,* 370, 373.

30. Rev. Henry Anstey, ed., *Epistolae Academicae Oxon.: Part I (1421–1457)* (Oxford: Clarendon Press, 1898), 177–79.

31. Pearsall, *John Lydgate,* 224.

32. See Stephanie H. Jed, *Chaste Thinking: The Rape of Lucretia and the Birth of Humanism* (Bloomington: Indiana University Press, 1989), 8–11 and passim.

33. Michel Foucault, "Fantasia of the Library," in *Language, Counter-Memory, Practice: Selected Essays and Interviews,* ed. and trans. Donald F. Bouchard (Ithaca, NY: Cornell University Press, 1977), 91.

34. Giovanni Boccaccio, *The Fates of Illustrious Men,* trans. Louis Brewer Hall (New York: Frederick Ungar, 1965), 137.

35. In another prologue in which Bochas falls asleep from weariness, Lydgate adds the gratuitous detail that he "Fill in a slombre lenyng on a cheste" (7.4), which locates him among the book chests that were the library's chief pieces of furniture. As Bergen notes, "Laurent does not mention a chest." *Lydgate's Fall of Princes,* 4:273.

36. See ibid., 4:196.

37. Francis Petrarch, *The Life of Solitude,* trans. Jacob Zeitlin (Urbana: University of Illinois Press, 1924), 291; see Douglas Radcliffe-Umstead, "Petrarch and the Freedom to Be Alone," in *Francis Petrarch, Six Centuries Later: A Symposium,* ed. Aldo Scaglione (Chicago: Newberry Library, 1975).

38. Petrarch, *Life of Solitude,* 282.

39. James Westfall Thompson, *The Medieval Library* (1939; reprint, New York: Hafner Publishing, 1965), 375–76. On the role of the Bury library in this development, see Rodney M. Thomson, *Archives of the Abbey of Bury St. Edmunds,* Suffolk Records Society 21 (Woodbridge, Suffolk: Boydell Press, 1980), 38–39.

40. R. H. Rouse, "Bostonus Buriensis and the Author of the *Catalogus Scriptorum Ecclesiae,*" *Speculum* 41 (1966): 489.

41. Henry of Kirkestede, *Catalogus de libris autenticis et apocrifis,* ed. Richard H. Rouse and Mary A. Rouse (London: British Library, 2004). See also Raymond Irwin, *The Heritage of the English Library* (New York: Hafner Publishing, 1964), 108; Rouse, "Bostonus Buriensis," 489–90.

42. Rouse and Rouse, introduction to Henry of Kirkestede, *Catalogus,* xlv.

43. David Knowles, *The Religious Orders in England,* 3 vols. (Cambridge: Cambridge University Press, 1948–55), 332.

44. Thomson, *Archives of the Abbey,* 38–39. On the sacking of the Bury archives in 1327 and 1381, see Rouse and Rouse, introduction to Henry of Kirkestede, xxix–xxxii.

45. The *Cartae versificatae* is reprinted in *Memorials of St. Edmund's Abbey,* ed. Thomas Arnold, *Rerum Britannicarum Medii Aevi scriptores,* Rolls Series 96 (Nendeln: Kraus Reprint, 1967), 215–37.

46. Petrucci, *Writers and Readers,* 211; Pearl Kibre, "The Intellectual Interests Reflected in Libraries of the Fourteenth and Fifteenth Centuries," *Journal of the History of Ideas* 7 (1946): 257–97.

47. M. R. James, "Bury St. Edmunds Manuscripts," *EHR* 41 (1926): 251–60; R. A. B. Mynors, "The Latin Classics Known to Boston of Bury," in *Fritz Saxl: A Volume of Memorial Essays,* ed. D. J. Gordon (London: Thomas Nelson & Sons, 1957), 199–217.

48. Pearsall, *John Lydgate,* 37.

49. Nicholas Trevet, "Commentary on Seneca's Tragedies: Extracts from *Prefatory Letters,*" in *Medieval Literary Theory and Criticism, c. 1100–c. 1375,* rev. ed., ed. A. J. Minnis and A. B. Scott (Oxford: Clarendon Press, 1988), 343. On the friars' production of commentary, see also Beryl Smalley, *English Friars and Antiquity in the Early Fourteenth Century* (Oxford: Blackwell, 1960), 35.

50. Anthony Grafton critiques this assumption in "The Humanist as Reader," in *A History of Reading in the West,* ed. Guglielmo Cavallo and Roger Chartier (Amherst: University of Massachusetts Press, 1999), 182.

51. For a reading of Lydgate's "writing like a clerk," see Seth Lerer, *Chaucer and His Readers: Imagining the Author in Late-Medieval England* (Princeton, NJ: Princeton University Press, 1993), chap. 1.

52. Augustine, *On Christian Doctrine,* trans. D. W. Robertson (Indianapolis, IN: Bobbs-Merrill Educational Publishing, 1958), 3.5.9.

53. Larry Scanlon, *Narrative, Authority, and Power: The Medieval Exemplum and the Chaucerian Tradition* (Cambridge: Cambridge University Press, 1994), 330.

54. Boccaccio, *Fates of Illustrious Men,* 2.

55. Ibid., 2; see *Lydgate's Fall of Princes* 4:172, for the original Latin.

56. See Ian Donaldson, *The Rapes of Lucretia: A Myth and Its Transformations* (Oxford: Clarendon Press, 1982), 8–10, 106.

57. Wallace goes on to make the point that Boccaccio's retelling of the Virginia story "sacrifices all interest in family pathos (father stabs daughter with a butcher's knife) in order to concentrate on the political struggle of the plebians against Claudius, an overweening *decemvir.*" See David Wallace, *Chaucerian Polity: Absolutist Lineages and Associational Forms in England and Italy* (Stanford, CA: Stanford University Press, 1997), 303.

58. *Lydgate's Fall of Princes* 4:174.

59. Ibid., 4:174–75.

60. See Pearsall, *John Lydgate,* 249; Wallace, *Chaucerian Polity,* 333; *Lydgate's Fall of Princes,* 4:172–75.

61. As Scanlon observes of John of Salisbury's use of the figure, "[T]he corporate fiction was always articulated from a position of social superiority." Scanlon, *Narrative, Authority, and Power,* 98.

62. See ibid., 99.

63. For the Latin version and a translation of Salutati's *Declamatio Lucretiae,* see the appendix to Jed, *Chaste Thinking;* for a close comparison between Salutati's and Lydgate's versions of the Lucrece story, see Eleanor Prescott Hammond, "Lydgate and Colluccio Salutati," *Modern Philology* 25 (1927): 49–57.

64. Jed, *Chaste Thinking,* 51.

65. This manuscript is Bibliotheque de Ste. Genevieve MS Francais, 777; see Vickers, *Humphrey,* 438.

66. Bersuire is cited in Jacques Monfrin, "Humanisme et traductions au moyen age," *Journal des Savants* (1963): 173. On Bersuire's use of Livy as a source of exempla for rulers, see M. J. Rychner, "Observations sur la traduction de Tite-Live par Pierre Bersuire," *Journal des Savants* (1963): 242–67, and Marie-Helene Tesniere, "Un remaniement du 'Tite-Live' de Pierre Bersuire par Laurent de Premierfait," *Romania* 107 (1986): 231–81.

67. On such lecterns built to hold multiple volumes, see John Willis Clark, *The Care of Books: An Essay on the Development of Libraries and Their Fittings, From the Earliest Times to the End of the Eighteenth Century* (Cambridge: Cambridge University Press, 1901), chap. 9. See the woodcuts of Lydgate that illustrate Wynkyn de Worde's *The p[ro]uerbes of Lydgate* (London, 1510) and Richard Pynson's *The testame[n]t of Iohn Lydgate monke of Berry which he made hymselfe* (London, 1520); a similar illumination illustrates the *Fall of Princes* in Huntington Library MS HM 268, fol. 18r, which pictures Lydgate and Duke Humphrey exchanging a book; they are seated in a library/study setting, and between them juts a circular reading desk holding several other books. The il-

lumination is reproduced as the cover image of Lerer, *Chaucer and His Readers.* Lerer discusses the image, in a different context, on 40–44.

68. Lisa Jardine and Anthony Grafton, "'Studied for Action': How Gabriel Harvey Read His Livy," *Past and Present* 129 (1990): 48.

69. Pierre Bersuire, "*The Moral Reduction*, Book XV: *Ovid Moralized*: Prologue and Extracts," in *Medieval Literary Theory and Criticism, c. 1100–c. 1375: The Commentary Tradition,* ed. A. J. Minnis et al. (Oxford: Clarendon Press, 1988), 367.

70. Gage, "Letters," 342.

71. Lois A. Ebin notes that the "change in point of view" that Lydgate makes in his revisions to his sources "is seen most dramatically in a conspicuous category of additions which he weaves into his source—the story of the churl rising to power." *John Lydgate* (Boston: Twayne Publishers, 1985), 67.

9

Lydgate, Hawes, and the Science of Rhetoric in the Late Middle Ages

Rita Copeland

In literary histories and critical studies of the English fifteenth century it has become standard to associate the theory of rhetoric enunciated in the works of Lydgate and Hawes with a notion of aureate poetics linked with service to the king and the state. But the association of their work with late medieval poetics should not obscure their place in the scientific or academic history of rhetoric. Lydgate's *Fall of Princes* and Hawes's *Pastime of Pleasure* present rhetoric within hierarchical schemes of the sciences, and their use of this scientific discourse allows them to modify the status and function of rhetoric as an art. In this essay I propose to consider these texts, and the problems they raise about eloquence, outside the standard framework of literary history, placing them instead in the long history of the disciplinary construction of rhetoric.

The history of rhetoric in the Middle Ages is in large part the history of its configuration within systems of knowledge. This view of rhetoric is not immediately familiar to us from internal histories of the discipline. But it was a view of rhetoric that would have been very familiar to medieval intellectuals, because classification of the sciences was the controlling discourse about knowledge in the Middle Ages. To organize knowledge into categories and branches was both to know it and to regulate it. More than modern academic cultures (at least those of Britain and North America), in which the division of knowledge into discrete categories is always institutionally immanent but is rarely itself an explicit object of discursive explanation,[1] medieval schools used the trope of scientific classification as a point of departure for virtually every kind of intellectual investigation. From the early medieval encyclopedias of Cassidorus,

Martianus Capella, and Isidore of Seville, which present knowledge as a series of (interlinked) disciplines according to the organizing principles of the seven liberal arts of the Stoic-Hellenistic scheme of logic, ethics, and physics, to the late medieval apparatus of the extrinsic and intrinsic prologues that introduce a text by first identifying its disciplinary affiliations and then describing the particular content of the art and the text, the hierarchies of the classification created an ever-visible macrostructure for any scientific inquiry.

As one of the central components of medieval curricula, the art of rhetoric would have been known and understood as much by its position within classifying schemes as by its internal features and parts. Perhaps the most important characteristic of rhetoric's fortunes in these systems is that its position among the sciences was remarkably unstable. To follow the progress of rhetoric in ancient and medieval knowledge systems is to witness the continuing repositioning and displacement of the science of discourse, its construction by and subordination to the institutional interests of competing disciplines, usually logic, politics, or ethics. Thus for a medieval writer, to change the role of rhetoric demanded not only saying something new about the art itself but repositioning it among the sciences.

Lydgate and Hawes describe scientific systems in which rhetoric takes on unusual prominence and, especially in the case of Hawes, occupies a disproportionate space in relation to the other arts. Why do these poets dilate upon rhetoric? The answer does not begin with their particular conceptions of the art. It begins, rather, with late medieval developments in scientific classification that reordered rhetoric's position in systems of knowledge and reconfigured its disciplinary role, and that thereby allowed such poets as Lydgate and Hawes to reconceive its function as an art. Accordingly, my discussion here moves from the broad terrain of Latin clerical discourse about the sciences, where I consider how the positioning of rhetoric among the arts indicates a certain ideological interest in restricting the disciplinary power of rhetoric, to what I see as a radical refiguring of rhetoric's place within systems of knowledge in the vernacular intellectual programs of Brunetto Latini, Dante, and Gower. In the civic ideology of Brunetto's *Trésor* and Dante's *Convivio*, and in Gower's adaptation of Brunetto's work in the *Confessio Amantis*, the role of rhetoric is transformed and elevated through a wholesale epistemological reordering of the sciences. I suggest that the prominence of rhetoric in the systems of Lydgate and Hawes derives from this radical vernacular "subtradition" of scientific classification. But the ideological purposes to which these later English poets put the new ascendancy of rhetoric were no longer continuous with the moral-political interests of their vernacular predecessors.

The traditional clerical cultures of medieval Latinity represented their own institutional interests through scientific classification. A classifying scheme offers a unifying picture of learning as an institution through images of the hierarchical relations of knowledge. Such hierarchies claim universality and stability through their very comprehensiveness. But as we see from one system of classification to the next, there is little that is actually stable about them; classifying paradigms are mechanisms of control and containment rather than authentic pictures of organic and internal stability.[2] Unifying systems work to conceal the struggles among disciplines to gain institutional hegemony. When we consider the history of a discipline, therefore, we must consider how the arrangements in which it is found serve to naturalize a particular order of political interests and conditions, such that these hierarchical relations appear inevitable.[3]

The interests of academic clericalisms, from monastic and cathedral school to university, can be seen in the kinds of control that systems of the sciences exert over the discipline of rhetoric. If rhetoric is about uses of language, or, as James Berlin has put it, "uses of language in the play of power,"[4] clerical Latinity, with its universalist claims, tends to suppress the notion that language may be a site of contemporary cultural contestation and even of resistance to authoritarian structures. In other words, the self-contained and politically insulated medieval schools do not actively recognize that the ancient rhetorical texts at the focus of curricular study are about public oratory and political debate. Thus most systems of classification tend to stress the abstract and instrumental aspects of rhetoric as argumentation. In Roman republican and even imperial treatments of rhetoric, the art is represented as the highest of the sciences, because it gives access to legal and political discourse.[5] But as Richard McKeon has shown, medieval academic discussions always subordinate rhetoric to whatever is the primary disciplinary interest, normally logic or theology.[6] Aquinas, for example, classifies rhetoric as a subdivision of logic, presenting it as one of the three forms (along with dialectic and poetic) of "inventive logic," which in its turn is a part of logic subject to the process of reasoning that arrives at probable proof.[7] The association between rhetoric and dialectic goes back at least to Aristotle's formulations in the opening of *Rhetoric,* where dialectic and rhetoric are presented as tools of all knowledge rather than as subordinate parts of any particular science. But medieval academic systems almost always stress the subordination of rhetoric to higher epistemological categories. Through the twelfth century, rhetoric is most commonly represented as a subdivision of the scientific category of logic. This earlier tradition is related not to Aristotelian notions of logic and its various tools but rather to the Stoic-Hellenistic threefold division of philosophy (knowledge or *scientia*) into logic (comprising rhetoric, dialectic, and sometimes grammar), ethics (comprising prudence, justice, fortitude, and temperance), and physics (comprising arithmetic, geometry, music, and astronomy). This is the scheme (more or less) that Isidore of Seville followed in the *Etymologiae* and that was adopted by Carolingian scholars such as John Scotus Eriugena and Martin of Laon. In his *Didascalicon* Hugh of St. Victor reproduces this system with some amplification, placing rhetoric, along with dialectic, as a subdivision of probable reasoning under rational argumentation, which is a part of logic.[8]

Other twelfth-century scholars introduced some variations in their placement of rhetoric and in so doing suggested new functions for the discipline. But the numerous attempts to classify it and to match its putative function to some real application serve to displace it further and expose the unreality of its value. Thierry of Chartres's extrinsic prologue to his commentary on the *De inventione* (composed sometime after 1130) designates rhetoric as "pars civilis scientiae maior"; borrowing from Cicero and late antique Ciceronian compendia, he states that eloquence and wisdom together constitute civil science, although he adds that eloquence plays the greater part in civil affairs. He also distinguishes rhetoric from logic, declaring that rhetoric is not to be considered the same as logic or part of logic because rhetoric uses the hypothesis, whereas logic uses the thesis.[9] But while his conception of rhetoric seems to return to a Ciceronian model of the art as part of the civil science of politics, Thierry actually undertakes his commentaries on the *De inventione* and *Ad Herennium* in the wake of the expansion of the dialectical curriculum in the cathedral schools of northern France. As John Ward has noted, the use of the *De inventione* as the main source of rhetorical doctrine allowed rhetoric to be separated from the political and judicial circumstances that defined its function in antiquity, so that it became instead a theoretical framework for the study of argumentative topics. The *De inventione* was thus appropriated during the twelfth century in the northern cathedral schools as a substitute of supplementary dialectic.[10]

The sense of unreality about rhetoric's function is even more apparent in the *De divisione philosophiae* of Dominicus Gundissalinus (fl. 1125–50). First Gundissalinus links rhetoric with dialectic and grammar as arts of speech in civil affairs *(civilis ratio),* grouping them under the Aristotelian category of practical science; moreover, he borrows wholesale Thierry of Chartres's discussion of rhetoric as *civilis ratio.*[11] But he also places rhetoric (along with poetic) under logic, drawing here on the Arabic tradition of classifying Aristotle's *Organon.*[12] The introduction of different epistemological schemes for classifying the sciences contributes further to the movement of rhetoric from one category to another. In addition to the Stoic-Hellenistic scheme of logic, ethics, and physics, the Aristotelian scheme of theoretical (or speculative), practical, and mechanical (or productive) sciences gained popularity with the gradual reappearance of the complete Aristotelian corpus. But the new Aristotelian scheme offers no firm fixture for rhetoric. Gundissalinus places rhetoric under both logic and practical sciences. Two other twelfth-century commentators, William of Conches and the anonymous author of the *Ysagoge in theologiam,* employ the Aristotelian scheme only to displace rhetoric from the practical sciences, inventing instead a new category, eloquence, which contains rhetoric, grammar, and dialectic.[13]

It is also apparent that the fortunes of rhetoric are sometimes tied to those of the whole trivium, while at other times rhetoric receives singular treatment. Two late-thirteenth-century Parisian masters, John of Dacia and Giles of Rome, divide the human sciences into mechanical and liberal; the latter are divided further into practical and speculative, and "auxiliary" (or "instrumental") to the speculative sciences is the category of rational sciences, which consists of rhetoric, logic, and grammar.[14] But elsewhere Giles recognizes the association specifically of rhetoric with moral science, concluding that it derives from both dialectic and politics.[15] Robert Kilwardby's *De ortu scientiarum* (ca. 1250) also places the trivium in a separate category of *artes sermocinales*; while the *artes sermocinales* are distinguished from the practical sciences, ethics, and mechanics, the two categories are related because actions and speech both produce effects.[16] But Kilwardby also admits rhetoric alone under ethics and civil science, because rhetoric is used in the negotiation of moral and political affairs.[17]

These many configurations suggest that rhetoric, as one of the language sciences, is valued as an instrument of reasoning; but its value is always defined and delimited by its subordination to a governing inquiry. It is subject to logic, subject to theology, subject to ethics. Where rhetoric's association with political discourse is recognized, this dimension of the art has little direct application in monastic, cathedral, and university clerical cultures. Rhetoric's power as an instrument of public debate is never realized in an institutional system that does not admit political challenge within its own ranks and in which contemporary uses of language do not constitute a sphere of political activity. In keeping with the institutional interests of Latin clericalism, disciplinary discussions represent rhetoric as little more than a textbook art. Thus rhetoric's application to civil science is always invoked in abstract and theoretical terms. As we see in Kilwardby, the political dimension of rhetoric is useful for showing the connections between various disciplinary categories and thus for affirming the essential unity and integrity of academic systems of knowledge as well as of the professional cadre that projects its universalist image through these systems.

Among vernacular intellectuals of the later Middle Ages, however, contemporary language use is a matter of urgent political interest. Brunetto Latini, Dante, and later Gower identify the production of knowledge with the interests of a particular time, place, and political community. The vernacular, although not in itself necessarily a politically inflected category, serves for them as the vehicle of such identification, and rhetoric becomes for them the scientific category that best expresses the aims of localism. In their hands rhetorical theory is a key articulation of the possibilities of applied political discourse; they imagine a rhetoric that is literally, not just formulaically, assigned to the service of civic discourse. But the means by which they revaluate the role of rhetoric is most significant: they return to the procedure of disciplinary classification, borrowing traditional academic paradigms of knowledge and reordering them to confer on rhetoric a new disciplinary prominence. Their radical transformations of these hierarchical systems belie academic claims to produce transcendent and universal categories that are somehow ideologically neutral. In representing the discipline of rhetoric, the vernacular paradigms of the sciences register new ideological interests in language as the primary instrument of social critique tied to immediate and local political practice.[18]

Brunetto Latini's revival of the Ciceronian notion of rhetoric as republican activity emerges out of the educational innovations of twelfth- and thirteenth-century Italian society. Both the *ars dictaminis* and *ars arengandi* (the art of speech making) represent practical, professional developments of academic rhetoric in the secular sphere.[19] The rise of rhetoric as a form of political analysis in Italian civic culture gives to Brunetto's own rhetorical projects their popularizing or broadly educative directive.[20] His encyclopedic *Livres dou trésor,* written in French during his exile in France during the 1260s, and his *Rettorica,* a Tuscan translation of the *De inventione* with a substantial didactic commentary, are the earliest vernacular prose treatments of classical rhetoric. The chronicler Giovanni Villani reinforces the Ciceronian notion of academic discourse translated into civic activity by recalling Brunetto as "a great philosopher and a consummate master of rhetoric, skillful both in oratory and writing. It was he who expounded Tully's Rhetoric and composed the good and useful book called the *Tesoro.* . . . [H]e was the master who first taught refinement to the Florentines and the arts of speaking well and of guiding and ruling our republic according to the science of politics."[21] As Marianne Shapiro notes, Villani constructs Brunetto's intellectual activity as rhetorical and hence civic practice.[22]

Brunetto's *Trésor* is a crucial originary text for the vernacular tradition of scientific discourse. It is the major precedent for Dante's project of the "vernacularization of culture" in the *Convivio*.[23] It is also one of the main sources of Gower's exposition of the sciences in book 7 of the *Confessio Amantis*. Book 1 of the *Trésor* presents a threefold division of the sciences into theoretical, practical, and logical (1.2–5), which is clearly a hybrid scheme.[24] But in the course of the treatise, Brunetto actually has little to say about logic, confining his schematic discussion of it to a brief section of the prologue (1.5). His interest is directed instead to the theoretical and practical sciences, suggesting the twofold *divisio scientiae* of theoretical and practical that was common in earlier periods.[25] Although the prologue promises an even treatment of theoretical, practical, and logical sciences, the emphasis actually falls on practical, with books 2 and 3 given over to the traditional subdivisions of *practica*, ethics, and politics. As a scientific category, logic is almost completely elided (2.1). Politics is divided into the mechanical arts and the *artes sermocinales*, grammar, dialectic, and rhetoric (1.4.6). In the prefatory remarks, grammar and dialectic receive only perfunctory attention, while rhetoric is introduced with a force that anticipates its comprehensive treatment in book 3 as the disciplinary partner of politics. Rhetoric is

> cele noble science ke nous ensegne trover et ordener et dire paroles bonnes et bieles et plaines de sentences selonc ce ke la nature requiert. C'est la mere des parliers, c'est l'enseignement de diteours, c'est la science ke adrece le monde premierement a bien fere, et ki encore l'adresce par les predications des sain homes, par les divines escriptures, et par la loi ki les gens governe a droit et a joustice. C'est la science de qui Tulles dit en son livre que celui a hautisme chose conquise ki de ce trespasse les homes dont li home trespassent tous les autres animaus, c'est de la parleure. (1.4.7) [that noble science that teaches us to discover, arrange, and deliver speeches that are good and beautiful and full of meaning, according to what the nature of things requires. It is the mother of orators, the instruction of writers; it is the science that directs the world firstly to proper action and that further directs it through holy preaching, through Holy Scripture, and through the law that governs men in righteousness and justice. It is the science of which Tully says in his book [*De inventione* 1.4.5] that that man has won a noble thing who excels men in the very thing in which we excel animals, and that is speech.]

The relationship of rhetoric to politics and to human law occupies most of book 3. This book is ostensibly about the science of politics, following on the treatment of the practical science of ethics in book 2 and of theoretical sciences in book 1. But the discussion of rhetoric takes up nearly 70 percent of book 3. Thus what is presented as an introductory section on rhetoric actually consti- tutes the bulk of the consideration of politics. But the logic of Brunetto's episte- mology justifies the overwhelming attention to rhetoric; he elevates the art from a subdivision of *artes sermocinales* to a position as the premier science of politics: "Et Tuilles dist que la plus haute science de cité governer si est rectorique, c'est a dire la science du parler; car se parleure ne fust cités ne seroit, ne nus establisse- mens de justice ne de humaine compaignie" (3.1.2). [And Tully says that the highest science of governing a city is rhetoric, that is, the science of speaking. For if there were no speech, there would be no cities, nor the establishment of justice or human community.] Brunetto's treatment of rhetoric elevates it, along with politics, virtually to the status of an epistemological category; he makes rhetoric and politics together almost a division of knowledge, rather than sub- ordinate elements of one of those divisions. The scheme of knowledge that emerges from the *divisio textus* of the *Trésor* is essentially that of theoretical sci- ences, practical sciences/ethics, and rhetoric/politics.

In the *Convivio* Dante also defines intellectual activity as an ethical project aimed at a communal benefit. He makes a very pointed case for using the ver- nacular as the vehicle of scientific instruction that can move an audience to wis- dom and virtue. This is the rationale behind the *Convivio*'s first tractate, with its well-known account of the impediments to learning, which represents one of the earliest critiques of the exclusionary apparatuses of academic clericalism (1.1).[26] The *Convivio* identifies vernacular poetry and its most characteristic Ro- mance genre, the *canso* or love song, with the office of moral philosophy; ver- nacular poetry can teach and reform and thus can encompass all problems of ethics, politics, and religion.

Because the job of vernacular speech is public discourse, its vehicle must be rhetoric. The *Convivio* is conceived through broadly Ciceronian rhetorical di- rectives.[27] The exposition of the sciences in book 2 creates a sovereign status for rhetoric in the system of the seven liberal arts, not by changing its hierarchical position but by magnifying its power. The *canso* that this book expounds opens with the line "Voi, che'ntendendo il terzo ciel movete, udite il ragionar ch'è nel mio core" (You who by understanding move the third heaven, hear the dis- course in my heart). The exposition proceeds to explain that the third heaven is the realm of Venus or love, and according to Dante's conceit its movers are the rhetoricians: "by the third heaven, I mean Rhetoric" (2.14.21–15.1). To explain this entails an exposition of the various sciences and their relationship to one another on analogy with a cosmic scheme of the heavens (2.13). Rhetoric has the greatest power of all the sciences to generate spiritual good; it leads to knowledge through charming persuasion (2.6.6), and, most important, it is the sweetest of the sciences, because its aim is to please (2.13.13–14). For this reason the third heaven, the realm of Venus or love, is compared to the science of rhetoric, for vernacular love poetry is Dante's chosen medium of public, ethical expression: the beauty of love poetry can, as he argues, move readers to wisdom and a knowledge of truth and persuade them to virtue. Thus rhetoric is also the mover of moral philosophy (2.14–15). The movers of the third heaven are Boethius and Cicero, the rhetoricians whose sweet discourse brought Dante to the love of his lady, Philosophy. Thus as the primary instrument of a vernacular intellectual project conceived in the ascendant interests of a civic ideology, rhetoric emerges from the shadows of logic to become the powerful mover of philosophy itself.

Book 7 of Gower's *Confessio Amantis* offers the most radical revision of the place of rhetoric in the system of the sciences. Gower used the *Trésor* as one of his sources for book 7, and while there is no evidence that he knew the *Convivio* directly, the *Confessio Amantis* is certainly the late-century English counterpart of Dante's program of wisdom and civic discourse modeled on the vernacular precedent of the *Trésor*. Like the *Convivio,* the *Confessio Amantis* repeatedly calls attention to its vernacularity, to its attempt to produce a learned tract on ethics, governance, and self-governance in a language that Gower identifies with the aspirations of a secular public. He offers a book in "oure englissh . . . for Engelondes sake" (*Prologus,* ll.23–24), tying the intellectual project to the ascendant interests of a vernacular state culture.[28]

Book 7 transfers these political concerns to an epistemological framework. It offers a scheme of the sciences based on the distinction between practical and theoretical knowledge. In his division of the sciences, Gower gives the three principal categories of knowledge as "theorique," "rethorique," and "practique." Rhetoric is elevated from its common position as a subdivision of a branch of science to the status of an epistemological category itself, along with theoretical knowledge and practical knowledge. As we know that book 7 is largely indebted to the *Trésor* for material and structure, it is not difficult to see how Gower arrived at his division of knowledge into theoretical, rhetorical, and practical. Gower seems to have seen the prominence of rhetoric in Brunetto's exposition and transformed it into an explicit principle of *divisio scientiae*: theoretical sciences (theology and natural history), rhetoric, and practical sciences (political ethics and governance). This exactly follows the lines of Brunetto's *divisio textus*: book 1 on theoretical sciences, book 2 on ethics, and book 3 on rhetoric and politics.

What Gower heard in the *Trésor* was the loud counterpoint of Brunetto's *divisio textus,* which elevates rhetoric to a sovereign science. Like the *Trésor,* the *Confessio Amantis* stages a transference of clerical science to a sphere of vernacular political discourse, drawing on English as well as Latin and Continental traditions of political complaint, estates satire, and advice to princes. And like Dante's restaging of Brunetto's encyclopedism in the hermeneutical drama of the *Convivio,* the *Confessio Amantis* traces a path from personal morality and the "singular profit" of *fine amour* to public and political morality, the "common profit" of political *caritas* that Amans is enjoined to seek. But in Gower's text, more clearly and radically than in Dante and Brunetto, rhetoric becomes the highest science, where vernacular or public political discourse is the highest aim. Even for the arch-conservative, antipopulist Gower, ethical discourse, a kind of public rhetoric, is the instrument of social critique. The word has more power than any other natural force:

> Bot yit the bokes tellen this,
> That word above alle erthli thinges
> Is vertuous in his doinges,
> Wher so it be to evele or goode.
> (7.1546–49)

Thus in the account of its place in the trivium, rhetoric is the sovereign discipline, served by both grammar and logic (7.1522–29).

Where rhetoric is the vital link between ethical discourse and political affairs, it emerges as the highest of the sciences. Brunetto, Dante, and Gower reimagine rhetoric in the terms of Ciceronian republicanism, as a form of public discursive activity. In these vernacular contexts, rhetoric generates broader intellectual discourse in its application to immediate political circumstances. When its social function is restored to it, rhetoric overshadows the other sciences. It would, of course, be sentimental to suggest that any of these vernacular authors imagine political rhetoric and public oratory in the unrestricted terms of democratic participation in civic or state governance; but it would be equally sentimental to suggest that Ciceronian republicanism was any more broad-based in its intended constituency. As Susan Noakes has suggested, Dante and Brunetto invent the audience that will participate in their civic rhetoric by creating the possibility of a vernacular intelligentsia, a literary and readerly meritocracy that offers a meeting ground between magnates and aspiring *popo-lani.*[29] Gower, interestingly, uses the mechanics of a vernacular public discourse to enforce the conservatism of a vertical social hierarchy that, for him, represents the only possibility of saving the state.[30] But Gower does invent a new audience through the elaboration of a vernacular rhetoric, breaking the boundaries not of class or economic status but of professionalism. Without unfixing the traditional vertical order of social power, he creates the possibility of a broader intellectual constituency by opening academic discourses to the existing arenas of political discourse. The Gramscian model of intellectual formation within emergent social groups has some applicability to the vernacular subtradition of rhetoric and science that I have described here: Brunetto, Dante, and Gower define a class of "organic intellectuals" within their respective vernacular communities, drawing on the ideas and strategies of the traditionally privileged clerical profession but shifting the authority for intellectual discourse to a newly empowered vernacular readership.[31]

This is the model of scientific taxonomy that enables and authorizes the elevation of rhetoric that we see in the work of Lydgate and Hawes. Many strains in late medieval literary culture contribute significantly to their representation of eloquence and the poet's role, but no other precedent accounts for their use of a disciplinary system in which rhetoric achieves such prominence. Other fifteenth-century treatments of the sciences, notably the anonymous *Court of Sapience* and Caxton's *Mirrour of the World,* offer hierarchical systems in which rhetoric occupies a very conventional position, receiving no greater attention or value than the other disciplines. I would suggest therefore that the remarkable prominence of rhetoric in Lydgate and Hawes looks back to the tradition of vernacular science that, as I have described it, begins with Brunetto Latini and is carried from its Continental context to English through the work of Gower. We can see Lydgate and Hawes as the late medieval continuators or beneficiaries of this tradition. Both poets deploy a scientific hierarchy in which rhetoric is the dominant discipline. But while they reproduce this structure in their magnification of rhetoric, the ideological imperative that they bring to this earlier system is entirely different from that of their vernacular predecessors. They do not reproduce the new function of rhetoric as a form of civic discourse that had earlier justified its new structural preeminence among the sciences.

Both these later poets understand rhetoric largely, or even primarily, in terms of poetics and assimilate the function of rhetoric to the power of poetic eloquence. Critical commentary on Lydgate and Hawes has naturally focused on their construction of an ascendant vernacular poetics.[32] But it is important to consider how they situate their conception of poetics within traditional discourses of the sciences, appealing to the disciplinary legitimacy of rhetoric to frame their revision of its function. In this respect Lydgate presents a somewhat more complex case than Hawes, because Lydgate seems to offer two versions of rhetoric. When he follows Boccaccio's *De casibus* via his immediate source in Premierfait's *Des cas des nobles,* he leans toward the public office of rhetoric in the person of the orator; but when left to his own devices, with no particular source to guide him, as in the prologue to the *Fall of Princes,* he blurs, as if by habit, any distinction between orators serving a public good and poets pleasing their kings.

In his treatment of rhetoric in book 6 of the *Fall of Princes,* Lydgate departs little from Premierfait's translation of Boccaccio's *De casibus.* In book 6 of *De casibus* Boccaccio appends to his account of the life of Cicero a virulent attack on the detractors of rhetoric and a praise of eloquence as a celestial gift and of beautiful speech as an instrument of reason and social order. Premierfait augments Boccaccio's theme by introducing at this point a scientific analysis of rhetoric along the scholastic lines of an extrinsic and intrinsic art. Lydgate follows Premierfait in this, and thus it is really Premierfait's contextualization of rhetoric in the order of the sciences that he reproduces. According to Premierfait's (and Lydgate's) account, the ancients divided philosophy into three parts, moral, natural, and rational, to the last of which rhetoric belongs. This is simply a renaming and reordering of the Stoic-Hellenistic division of philosophy into logic, ethics, and physics (e.g., in Premierfait-Lydgate, rational, moral, and natural). This division of knowledge is conventional (indeed, in fifteenth-century terms, rather old-fashioned), but it is interesting to speculate that Premierfait's decision to insert the scheme of the sciences in order to situate and justify his expatiation on rhetoric owes something to the spirit, if not the immediate influence, of Brunetto's *Trésor,* where rhetoric takes over the exposition of the sciences. It is also worth noting Lydgate's slight adjustment to Premierfait's description of rational science: where Premierfait defines it as the science "qui enseigne propre mesure et droicte facon de parolles ordonnees en argumens" (that teaches proper measure and the correct way of ordering speech in argumentation),[33] Lydgate describes it in terms that seem to echo Gower's view of rhetoric (and the subsidiary linguistic arts of grammar and logic) as the capacity through language to make moral choices: "And the thridde [part of the philosophy], raciounal, weel shewes / What men shal voide and what thing undirfonge, / And to that parti rethorik doth longe" (6.3295–97).

Rhetoric was thus dignified among the ancients, and Cicero translated the craft from Greece to Rome. He is remembered for "the habundance / Of elloquence stuffed with plesaunce" (3301–2). The intrinsic account of rhetoric offers a substantive, if conventional, survey of the five parts of rhetoric, in which Lydgate adds to Premierfait some matter on pronunciation (3341–53), significantly comparing rhetorical delivery with the tragic poetry of Seneca:

> Men in pronouncying mut folwe the mateer,—
> Old oratours kan bern herof witnesse,—
> A furious compleynt uttrid in distresse:
> This was the maner, as poetis do descryve,
> In his tragedies whan Senec was alyve.
>
> (6.3349–53)

Out of Boccaccio's defense of rhetoric Premierfait and Lydgate produce a scientific rationale for rhetoric's centrality among the sciences.

For Lydgate, however, this rationale is ultimately intelligible as an aesthetic value: rhetoric is important and useful because of its poetic charm and beauty, its "sugrid langage and vertuous daliaunce" (1.3467), its likeness to jewels and other "plesaunt obiectis to a mannys siht" (1.3486), and the profit that the orator brings to king and state by soothing and instructing with the melodious music of language. The identification of rhetoric with one of its parts, *colores* or figures and tropes, so that the whole art is resolved into a system of verbal decoration, is present in Premierfait. More important, it is the legacy of the twelfth- and thirteenth-century *artes poetriae,* which weighted rhetorical production in favor of style or *elocutio* and which imposed grammatical precepts of verbal ornamentation on their treatment of rhetorical categories.[34] It is not surprising that the late Middle Ages understands rhetoric largely in terms of poetic style; this is the inevitable product of the tension within rhetorical theory between the claims of argument and the claims of style, and the always strong pull in favor of style, of which the *artes poetriae* are a late and influential expression. It is rather more surprising that Brunetto, Dante, and Gower resist the pull toward poetic stylistics and situate rhetoric instead in a scientific system of ethics and politics. Dante's association of rhetoric with the charm of love poetry is only a pragmatic conceit (like his love poems themselves) for the attractive appeal of Philosophy.

Lydgate seems to be caught in this old conflict, pulled between the poetic and the political models of rhetoric. Rhetoric is sugared language, but it is also the oratorical proficiency that can move the will of a king to secure the good of the state. Lydgate manages the conflict by allowing the poetic to subsume the political. In the prologue to the *Fall of Princes* he locates his own work on a historical continuum of English poetry, in which Chaucer is the progenitor of English eloquence. The long account of Chaucerian poetics (246–357) leads to a brief disquisition on the historical prestige of poets who were in ancient times the favorites of kings:

> And these poetis I make off mencioun
> Were bi old tyme had in gret deynte,
> With kyngis, pryncis in every regioun,
> Gretli preferrid afftir ther degre;
> For lordis hadde plesance for to see,
> To studie a-mong, and to caste ther lookis
> At good[e] leiser upon wise bookis.
>
> (1.358–64)

Kings respond to the wisdom that poets proffer, a statement meant to set the stage for Lydgate's own appeal to his patron, Humphrey, Duke of Gloucester (372 ff). But the historical logic of the privileged relationship of poets to princes is exemplified by way of reference to Cicero and Caesar:

> For in the tyme off Cesar Iuluis,
> Whan the tryumphe he wan in Rome toun,
> He entre wolde the scoole off Tullius
> And heere his lecture off gret affecioun;
> And natwithstandyng his conquest & renoun,
> Unto bookis he gaff gret attendaunce
> And hadde in stories ioie and gret plesaunce.
>
> (365–71)

Here Lydgate conflates poetics and political oratory, invoking the authority of Cicero to substantiate the pleasure that poets' stories give to kings. Lydgate traces his own professional lineage from Chaucer back to Cicero and recasts Ciceronian rhetoric in the image of vernacular poetics.

We find a similar move in the scientific scheme of the *Court of Sapience,* where rhetoric is treated almost entirely in terms of stylistics and verbal ornamentation:[35]

> She [Dame Rhetoric] taught them all the craft of endytyng:
> Whiche vyces ben that shold avoyded be,
> Whiche ben the colours gay of that connyng,
> Theyr dyfference, and eke theyr properte.
>
> (1905–8)

The grammatical orientation of this picture of rhetoric is summed up in the invocation of Geoffrey of Vinsauf ("Galfryde the poet laureate" [1915]) as an authority for those who "wold conceyve the colours purperate / Of rethoryke" (1913–14).[36] Thus the poet's reference to Cicero (and to the broader field of legal rhetoric) is contained by the governing grammatical context:

> In Tullius also, moost eloquent,
> The chosen spouse unto this lady free,
> This gylted craft of glorye is content;
> Gay thinges y-made eke yf the lust to see
> Goo loke the *Code* also, the *Dygestes* thre,
> The bookes of lawe and eke of physyk goode;
> Of ornate speche there spryngeth up the floode.
> (1919–25)

Cicero and books of law give ornate speech, and rhetoric is subsumed by poetics. The *Court of Sapience* is unremarkable in its treatment of the sciences, and its presentation of rhetoric bears all the signs of late medieval theoretical convention. But Lydgate's *Fall of Princes,* with its emphatic positioning of rhetoric, carries forward the innovative scientific model of the earlier vernacular rhetorics, even as it exchanges the civic ideology that motivated those precedents for a much more conventional and parochial vision of stylistics that elides the poem's feeble efforts to reclaim a Ciceronian notion of political oratory. For Lydgate, the speech of an orator is no different in kind from poetic performance, as the allusion to Senecan tragedy to exemplify oratorical delivery suggests.

Hawes's account of the sciences in the *Pastime of Pleasure* propels rhetoric to an overwhelming preeminence. Written around 1505 while Hawes was at the court of Henry VII (and printed by Wynkyn de Worde in 1509), the poem may be said to have an equivocal historical consciousness. On the one hand, as A. S. G. Edwards and Seth Lerer argue,[37] it is an early modern text, composed with a view to print rather than to manuscript circulation. On the other hand, the poem is very much a late medieval product, a pilgrimage and quest poem and an allegory of knowledge framed in the genre of advice to princes.[38] But I would also suggest that the poem exhibits some of its strongest affinities with medieval vernacular tradition in its positioning of rhetoric among the sciences. Although the model of the sciences that it uses is the commonplace one of the trivium and quadrivium, in which the organization of disciplines is sequential rather than hierarchical, the sheer space given over to rhetoric in Hawes's account makes it the sovereign science in the *Pastime of Pleasure.* Compared to thirteen stanzas on grammar and six on logic, Hawes gives ninety-two stanzas to rhetoric. On his tour of the Tower of Doctrine, the hero Grand Amour goes *up* one flight of stairs from the chamber of Logic to the chamber of Rhetoric (652), a transparent allegory for rhetoric's precedence over its old disciplinary rival, logic.[39] Hawes's disproportionate attention to rhetoric should be seen not as a curiosity but rather as the last expression of a vernacular intellectual movement. Hawes has a direct precedent in Lydgate (who supersedes Chaucer for him as the poetic "master") and an indirect one in Gower's sources.

Like Lydgate—or probably because of Lydgate—Hawes reproduces the structural prominence of rhetoric that began with vernacular science of the late thirteenth century. But also like Lydgate, he assigns a function to rhetoric that is far removed from the notion of civic practice that first supplied the motive for rhetoric's elevation in vernacular systems of the arts. Hawes takes the assimilation of rhetoric to poetics to much more radical possibilities than we see in Lydgate. For Hawes, rhetoric is not simply poetics in the classroom sense of *artes poetriae,* or even in Lydgate's sense of luminous ornamentation.[40] He defines rhetoric in terms of the ancient philosophical mode of Macrobius, as the ability to speak fictively, to cloak literal truth in fair figures, just as the old poets used fiction *(fabula)* as a vehicle of philosophy. This is a central tenet of his doctrine of rhetorical invention:

> It was the guyse in olde antyquyte
> Of famous poets right ymagynatyfe
> Fables to fayne by good auctoryte
> They were so wyse and so inventyfe
> Theyr obscure reason fayre and sugratyfe
> Pronounced trouthe under cloudy fygures
> By the invencyon of theyr fatall scryptures.
>
> (715–21)

This idea of poetic fiction as truth cloaked under misty figures is actually a theoretical hybrid of poetics and hermeneutics, a defense of allegory. It is a philosophical model of poetry familiar from the Chartrian allegorists of the twelfth century and taken up again in Boccaccio's defense of poetry in the *De genealogia deorum gentilium* (14–15). In the *Pastime of Pleasure,* however, this common model of poetics takes a more complex form in its explicit linkage with rhetorical teachings of eloquence and especially of external ornamentation. Grand Amour kneels before Dame Rhetoric, asking her to imbue him with her eloquent power as he embarks on his exposition of rhetorical doctrine:

> Dystyll adowne thy lusty Rethoryke
>
> And depaynt my tonge with thy ryall floures. . . .
> And with thy power that thou me endue
> To moralyse thy lytterall censes trewe
> And clense awaye the myst of ygnoraunce
> With depured beames of goodly ordynaunce.
>
> (672–79)

It is now verbal ornamentation that carries the moral weight of rhetoric. Language, like a coat of paint (cf. "depaynt my tonge"), cloaks truth in luminous figures that have the power to moralize, that is, to expound the literal text morally. In this particular passage, I take the rather enigmatic line "To moralyse thy lytterall censes trewe" to mean that Hawes will use the powers of rhetorical color to expound, but also to veil, through moral allegory the virtues of rhetoric's own basic doctrines, Dame Rhetoric's "lytterall censes trewe." Rhetoric here has become allegory; and the job of allegory or *fabula* in its Macrobian sense is to hide truth from the uninitiated, to increase the gravity and prestige of philosophical truth by privatizing it. It should be remarked that Hawes's conflation of a technical rhetoric with the Macrobian notion of poetic allegory is a peculiar feature of his approach, not a theoretical commonplace. Boccaccio's discussion of the veils of poetic fiction, which is among the standard late medieval references for the theory of poetic allegory, makes in fact a very firm distinction between rhetorical invention and poetic fiction: "Yet, in truth, among the disguises of fiction rhetoric has no part, for whatever is composed as under a veil, and thus exquisitely wrought, is poetry and poetry alone."[41]

The idea of cloaking the "sentence under mysty figures" (932) is linked with the ennoblement and purification of truth and with the purification of language itself. Thus even Hawes's account of the political origins and public benefits of rhetoric is channeled into a defense of the refining order of figurative language: "Rethoryke she sayde was found by reason / Man for to govern well and prudently / His wordes to ordre his speche to puryfy" (691–93). The privatization of truth through its allegorical veiling becomes the chief objective of purified speech. The function of *elocutio* or eloquent style is to improve speech and thereby discriminate among audiences, dividing the rude from the refined, those who have not been initiated into the mysteries of veiled truth from those who have:

> The dulcet speche frome the langage rude
> Tellynge the tale in termes eloquent
> The barbary tongue it doth ferre exclude
> Electynge wordes which are expedyent
> In latyn or in englysshe after the entent
> Encensynge out the aromatyke fume
> Our language rude to exyle and consume.
>
> But what avayleth evermore to sowe
> The precyous stones amonge gruntynge hogges
> Draffe unto them is more meter I trowe.
>   (918–27)

But Hawes's assimilation of rhetoric to the Macrobian idea of poetic fiction as exclusive and privileged mystery does not prevent him from also trying to accommodate a Ciceronian narrative of the social origins of rhetoric. His account of *dispositio* (820–903) links the ordering of a text with the ordering of a society through the force of rhetoric. In a curious passage Hawes moves from the cloaking of truth by wise poets to another theme, the civilizing power of rhetoric that ushered in the rule of law and royal statecraft over a chaotic and lawless people:

> The fatall problemes of olde antyquyte
> Cloked with myst and with cloudes derke
> Ordred with reason and hye auctoryte
> The trouthe dyde shewe of all theyr covert werke
> Thus have they made many a noble clerke
> To dysnull [destroy] myschefe and inconvenyence
> They made our lawes with grete dylygence.
>
> Before the lawe in a tumblynge barge
> The people sayled without parfytnes
> Throughe the worlde all aboute at large
> They hadde none ordre nor no stedfastnes

Tyll rethorycyans founde Iustyce doubtles
Ordenynge kynges of ryghte hye dygnyte
Of all comyns to have the sовerainte.

(869–82)

The second stanza above, which describes the origins of rhetoric as a governing
order bringing law to a barbarous society, is strongly reminiscent of Cicero's
narrative of the birth of eloquence in *De inventione* (1.2.2). In Cicero's account,
the art of rhetoric was born when a man of eloquence emerged from among a
savage people and persuaded them to accept the rules of law and justice among
themselves. Thus rhetoric transformed a lawless people into a self-governing
society. Hawes's narrative is surely based on some version of the familiar Ciceronian legend, so comparable are the two; but the difference between them is
more telling. Cicero's is a republican fable, depicting a rhetoric that organizes
the people around self-governance. Hawes's, however, is a fable of royal power,
of the power of absolute sovereignty that rhetoric can bestow on the kings it or-
dains. The rhetoricians established justice and gave the enforcement of law over
to kings who embody its stability:

The barge to stere with lawe and Iustyce
Over the wawes of this lyfe transytorye
To dyrecte wronges and also preiudyce
And tho that wyll resyste a contrary
Agaynste theyr kynge by Iustyce openly
For theyr rebellion and evyll treason
Shall suffre dethe by right and reason.

(883–89)

In the same way that rhetorical doctrine has been combined with a Macrobian
poetics that seeks to conceal truth and conserve discursive knowledge in the
hands of an initiated elite, the fable of rhetoric's social origins has shifted from
a republican ideology in which eloquence is the tool of a self-governing people
to an ideology of royal absolutism in which rhetoric supports and justifies the
interests of state sovereignty.[42] It is thus thematically appropriate that the final
stanzas of this passage (890–903) return to the image of poets who distill aro-
matic liquors or words (892):

Clensynge our syght with ordre puryfyed
Whose famous draughtes so exemplyfyed

Sette us in ordre grace and governaunce
To lyve dyrectly without encombraunce.
                    (893–96)

The work of rhetorical *dispositio* orders the text and by extension the state. This business of rhetorical-poetic ordering is a secretive one, obscure and unintelligible to those rude dullards who "grope over where is no felynge / So dull they are that they can not fynde / This ryall arte for to perceyve in mynde" (901–3). The idea of a "royal art" of poetic mystery that must be guarded from its rude (uninitiated) spoilers is usefully overlaid on an idea of rhetoric that must be the preserve of royal power. A rhetoric understood on the model of the "veils of fiction" justifies its own exclusiveness and secrecy as instrument of both discursive and political control.[43]

This is the vehicle through which Hawes magnifies vernacular writing, tracing the progress of rhetoric as purification of language from Cicero in Latin to Lydgate in English (1161–76). Both Lydgate and Hawes inherit a uniquely vernacular model of rhetoric preeminent among the sciences precisely for its application to civic discourse; both convert this model into a vernacular rhetoric of poetic performance. Their rhetoric retains the scientific sovereignty it achieved in the earlier systems of classification even as it discards the social imperative that gave it such distinctive importance in vernacular scientific contexts. Lydgate and Hawes deploy the earlier disciplinary valorization of rhetoric to valorize their new conception of its function.

There is considerable historical irony in the fifteenth-century appropriation of rhetoric's earlier scientific prestige, for the vernacular poets of the fifteenth century return rhetoric to something of the private, elite control that it had in Latin academic environments. In academic configurations, of course, it is rhetoric's subordination within the scientific hierarchy that serves clerical interests, for language as contemporary political practice has little value (except as a threat) in an institutional system that claims to produce universal and transcendent categories of knowledge. Yet curiously, in the fifteenth-century vernacular context, the elevation of rhetoric has the same effect that its subordination had in Latin clerical contexts, that of delivering it into the control of a powerful elite. Represented as aureate poetics (Lydgate) and mystification of truth (Hawes), rhetoric is both magnified in prestige and delimited in function, lending itself readily to the service of the political elite, the king and the court. In their important studies of fifteenth-century poetry, Richard Firth Green and David Lawton have explored the social and aesthetic implications of poets' identification with the role of *orator regis*.[44] Green points out that the late-fifteenth-century term *orator regis* was technically reserved for those pol-ished Latinists whose oratory served the promotional interests of the king, es-pecially in international diplomacy. But he suggests that Hawes's deliberate conflation of rhetoric and poetics signals the emergence of vernacular poetry as a comparable form of royal public display. Lydgate's notion of the poet laureate in the service of princes shows this model of *orator regis* in an incipient form; as Lawton remarks in his discussion of the *Fall of Princes,* "The public writings of fifteenth-century English poets assist in the reification of kingship."[45] Both Lyd-gate and Hawes emphasize the value of rhetoric to enforce a state agenda, not to engender debate.

In this, of course, Lydgate and Hawes both anticipate and contribute to the High Renaissance notion of the court poet engaged in that most royal of rhe-torical functions, epideictic or demonstrative oratory, usually characterized as the genre of praise and blame.[46] Epideictic is the form of oratory most com-monly associated with the rhetoric practiced under the imperial absolutism of late antiquity, the so-called Second Sophistic. Late classical rhetoric, deprived of its deliberative or political function under the autocratic rule of the Caesars, turned increasingly to grand and florid display and, in its Roman form espe-cially, devoted its efforts to encomiastic tributes to the emperors. Rhetoric re-tained its earlier curricular and social prestige from the republican era, trans-ferring that prestige to a new and quite contrary function, that of aggrandizing imperial power. We see very much the same historical relationship between old disciplinary status and new social function in the rhetorical models of Lydgate and Hawes, so much so that it is not inappropriate to think of their practice as a "Second" Second Sophistic. Insofar as their epideictic poetics anticipate Re-naissance developments in oratorical and poetic careerism, this should not be at all a surprising analogy. But it is important to remember that their conception of rhetoric is not grounded in the humanist Ciceronianism of Poggio Braccio-lini or Traversagni. The magnification of rhetoric in Lydgate and Hawes is the product of a distinctively medieval scientific tradition, a vernacular science of discourse first imagined as a powerful tool of reformist activism. The elevation of rhetoric as vernacular public discourse in Brunetto, Dante, and Gower para-doxically enabled the disciplinary ascendancy of an exclusive and privatized rhetoric in fifteenth-century science.

Notes

This essay first appeared as "Lydgate, Hawes, and the Science of Rhetoric in the Late Middle Ages," in *Modern Language Quarterly* 53, no. 1 (1992): 57–82. Copyright, 1992,

1. In Anglo-American scholarship the exceptions are becoming more numerous. Influenced by French theorists of institutional relations such as Michel Foucault and Pierre Bourdieu, many British and American students of intellectual history and the history of science are developing and contributing to the field of "sociology of knowledge." For a survey and consideration of this field, see David R. Shumway and Ellen Messer-Davidow, "Disciplinarity: An Introduction," *Poetics Today* 12 (1991): 201–25. This issue of *Poetics Today* contains articles exemplifying a variety of approaches to the subject of disciplinarity. For the field of sociology of science, see Bruno Latour and Steve Woolgar, *Laboratory Life: The Construction of Scientific Facts,* 2nd ed. (Princeton, NJ: Princeton University Press, 1986).

2. Michel Foucault, *The Archaeology of Knowledge and the Discourse on Language,* trans. A. M. Sheridan Smith (New York: Pantheon, 1972), 224. Cf. Pierre Bourdieu and Jean-Claude Passeron, *Reproduction in Education, Society, and Culture,* 2nd ed., trans. Richard Nice (Thousand Oaks, CA: Sage Publications, 1990), 194–210.

3. I am paraphrasing here from the remarks of James Berlin on the historiography of rhetoric, in Berlin et al., "The Politics of Historiography," *Rhetoric Review* 7 (1988): 11.

4. Ibid., 6.

5. For further references and discussion of rhetoric's place among the sciences in Roman thought, see Rita Copeland, *Rhetoric, Hermeneutics, and Translation in the Middle Ages: Academic Traditions and Vernacular Texts* (Cambridge: Cambridge University Press, 1991), 14–18.

6. Richard McKeon, "Rhetoric in the Middle Ages," *Speculum* 17 (1942): 1–32; reprinted in *Critics and Criticism,* ed. R. S. Crane (Chicago: University of Chicago Press, 1952), 260–96.

7. Thomas Aquinas, preface to his commentary on the *Posterior Analytics,* in *Aristotelis libros peri hermeneias et posteriorum analyticorum expositio,* Leonine text, 2nd ed., ed. Raymundi M. Spiazzi (Turin: Marietti, 1964), 148.

8. Isidore of Seville, *Etymologicarum libri xx,* ed. W. M. Lindsay (Oxford: Clarendon Press, 1911), bk. 2, chap. 24; Eriugena, *De divisione naturae,* bk. 5, PL 122:870; on Martin of Laon, see John J. Contreni, "John Scottus, Martin Hiberniensis, the Liberal Arts, and Teaching," in *Insular Latin Studies,* ed. Michael Herren (Toronto: Pontifical Institute of Mediaeval Studies, 1981), 23–44; Hugh of St. Victor, *Didascalicon,* ed. C. H. Buttimer (Washington, DC: Catholic University of America Press, 1939), bk. 2, chaps. 28–30. See also the comprehensive survey by James A. Weisheipl, "Classification of the Sciences in Medieval Thought," *Mediaeval Studies* 27 (1965): 54–90. A recent study by Glending Olson, "The Medieval Fortunes of 'Theatrica,'" *Traditio* 42 (1986): 265–86, also provides important information on scientific classification.

9. *The Latin Rhetorical Commentaries by Thierry of Chartres,* ed. Karin Margareta Fredborg (Toronto: Pontifical Institute of Mediaeval Studies, 1988), 49–51.

10. John O. Ward, *"Artificiosa eloquentia* in the Middle Ages," 2 vols. (PhD diss., University of Toronto, 1972), 1:52–53, 242–46.

11. Dominicus Gundissalinus, *De divisione philosophiae,* ed. Ludwig Baur, Beiträge zur Geschichte der Philosophie des Mittelalters 4 (Münster, 1903), 16, 64.

12. Ibid., 71–73.

13. William of Conches, commentary on Boethius's *Consolatio,* 1, par. 1, ed. Charles Jourdain, "Des commentaries inédits de Guillaume de Conches et de Nicolas Triveth sur *La consolation de la philosophie* de Boèce," *Notices et extraits de manuscrits de la Bibliothèque impériale* 20, no. 2 (1862): 72–74; *Ysagoge in theologiam,* in *Écrits théologiques de l'école d'Abélard,* ed. A. Landgraf (Louvain, 1934), 70–73. See also the discussions in the important article by Gilbert Dahan, "Notes et texts sur la poétique au moyen âge," *Archives d'histoire doctrinale et littéraire du moyen âge* 47 (1960): 174, 178.

14. John of Dacia, *Divisio scientiae,* ed. Alfredus Otto, vol. 1 of *Johannis Daci opera,* Corpus Philosophorum Danicorum Medii Aevi 1 (Copenhagen: Gad, 1955), 34–44; for the scheme of Giles of Rome, see Dahan, "Notes et textes," 177 and 176 n. 20, reference.

15. Giles of Rome, *De differentia rhetoricae, ethicae, et politicae,* ed. Gerardo Bruni, *New Scholasticism* 6 (1932): 5–8. On Giles's views on rhetoric, see James J. Murphy, "The Scholastic Condemnation of Rhetoric in the Commentary of Giles of Rome on the *Rhetoric* of Aristotle," in *Arts libéraux et philosophie au moyen âge,* Actes du IVe congrès internationale de philosophie médiévale (Montreal: Institut d'études médiévales; Paris: Vrin, 1969), 833–41; and, more recently, see the important article by Ubaldo Staico, "Retorica e politica in Egidio Romano," *Documenti e studi sulla tradizione filosofica medievale* 3, no. 1 (1992): 1–75.

16. Robert Kilwardby, *De ortu scientiarum,* ed. Albert G. Judy, Auctores Britannici Medii Aevi 4 (London: British Academy; Toronto: Pontifical Institute of Mediaeval Studies, 1976), p. 10, § 5; p. 122, § 346; p. 224, §§ 657–60.

17. Ibid., p. 162, § 473.

18. The following discussion of rhetoric in Dante, Brunetto, and Gower is based in part on arguments in Copeland, *Rhetoric and Hermeneutics,* 181–84, 207–11.

19. The literature on *ars dictaminis* and the related *ars arengandi,* and their connection to academic training in law and rhetoric, is enormous. The best general overview of dictaminal literature is James J. Murphy, *Rhetoric in the Middle Ages* (Berkeley: University of California Press, 1974), 194–268, and Martin Camargo, *Ars dictaminis, ars dictandi,* Typologie des sources du moyen âge occidental 60 (Turnhout: Brepols, 1991); see also the essays in *Rhetorica* 19, no. 2 (2001), a special issue devoted to the *ars dictaminis.* Among accounts of the particular political environment that gave rise to these forms, see Helene Wieruszowski, "Ars dictaminis in the Time of Dante" and "Rhetoric and the Classics in Italian Education of the Thirteenth Century," in her collection *Politics and Culture in Medieval Spain and Italy* (Rome: Storia e Letteratura, 1971), 359–78, 589–628.

20. On rhetoric and political analysis, see Quentin Skinner, *The Foundations of Modern Political Thought,* vol. 1, *The Renaissance* (Cambridge: Cambridge University Press,

1978), 23–48. On Brunetto as popularizer, see J. K. Hyde, *Society and Politics in Medieval Italy: The Evolution of the Civil Life, 1000–1350* (New York: Macmillan, 1973), 91–93; Virginia Cox, "Ciceronian Rhetoric in Italy, 1260–1350," *Rhetorica* 17 (1999): 239–88; and most recently, Stephen J. Milner, "Exile, Rhetoric, and the Limits of Civic Republican Discourse," in *At the Margins: Minority Groups in Premodern Italy,* ed. Stephen J. Milner (Minneapolis: University of Minnesota Press, 2005), 162–91.

21. Quoted from the translation in Charles T. Davis, "Brunetto Latini and Dante," *Studi Medievali* 8 (1967): 422–23.

22. Marianne Shapiro, "On the Role of Rhetoric in the *Convivo,*" *Romance Philology* 40 (1986): 49.

23. Ibid. Dante's reference to the *Trésor* in the *Inferno,* bk. 15, pp. 119–20, suggests more than a link with the *Commedia*: Shapiro notes that "as far as the *Convio* is concerned, Brunetto's works instantiate an elaborate, conceptually articulated, Ciceronian civic rhetoric that has no commensurate Romance precedent" ("On the Role of Rhetoric," 49). Cf. also Davis, "Brunetto Latini and Dante," p. 441, on links between the *Trésor* and the *Convivio.*

24. Brunetto Latini, *Li livres dou trésor,* ed. Francis J. Carmody, University of California Publications in Modern Philology 22 (Berkeley: University of California Press, 1948).

25. Margaret T. Gibson, "The *Artes* in the Eleventh Century," in *Arts libéraux,* 121–26.

26. Dante, *Il convivio,* ed. Maria Simonelli (Bologna: Ricardo Pàtron, 1966).

27. Shapiro, "On the Role of Rhetoric," 60–62.

28. Throughout this chapter, poetry is cited parenthetically in the text by line number or by book and line numbers. The text of *Confessio Amantis* is taken from *The Complete Works of John Gower,* vols. 2–3, ed. G. C. Macaulay (Oxford: Clarendon, 1901), published previously in 1900 as EETS, e.s., 81–82. In the first recension of the text (1390), line 24, of course, contained an invocation to Richard ("A bok for king Richardes sake"), which Gower deleted in the second recension (1392), substituting "England" for "Richard." This redirection of attention from king to state has considerable impact on the significance of the poem, as it underscores the existing themes of public political activity.

29. Susan Noakes, "Hermeneutics, Politics, and Civic Ideology in the *Vita Nuova*: Thoughts Preliminary to an Interpretation," *Texas Studies in Literature and Language* 32 (1990): 40–59, esp. 53–54. Paul F. Gehl's study of Latin and vernacular learning in thirteenth-century Florence, "Preachers, Teachers, and Translators: The Social Meaning of Language Study in Trecento Tuscany" (which he has kindly shown me in typescript), demonstrates how Brunetto's *Reitorica* proposes an active rhetorical consciousness for its vernacular readership, a moral, reformist model of discourse that pushes beyond the purely literary usage of the Latin *ars dictaminis* to promote "a truly ambitious vernacular oratory" (54).

30. See Paul Strohm, "Form and Social Statement in *Confessio Amantis* and the *Canterbury Tales,*" *Studies in the Age of Chaucer* 1 (1979): 17–40.

31. See "The Formation of the Intellectuals," in *Selections from the Prison Notebooks of Antonio Gramsci,* ed. and trans. Quintin Hoare and Geoffrey Nowell Smith (1971; reprint, New York: International Press, 1983), 5–23.

32. Among recent treatments, see especially Lois A. Ebin, *Illuminator, Makar, Vates: Visions of Poetry in the Fifteenth Century* (Lincoln: University of Nebraska Press, 1988), chaps. 2 and 5; A. S. G. Edwards, *Stephen Hawes* (Boston: Twayne Publishers, 1983); Seth Lerer, "The Rhetoric of Fame: Stephen Hawes's Aureate Diction," *Spenser Studies* 5 (1984): 169–84; A. C. Spearing, *Medieval to Renaissance in English Poetry* (Cambridge: Cambridge University Press, 1985), 66 ff., 247 ff. On the social formation of the poet's function in the fifteenth century see Richard Firth Green, *Poets and Princepleasers: Literature and the English Court in the Late Middle Ages* (Toronto: University of Toronto Press, 1980), and David Lawton, "Dullness and the Fifteenth Century," *ELH* 54 (1987): 761–99.

33. The texts of Lydgate and Premierfait are taken from *Lydgate's Fall of Princes,* 4 vols., ed. Henry Bergen, EETS, e.s., 121, 122, 123, 124 (London: Oxford University Press, 1924–27). See 4:268 for the text quoted here from Premierfait.

34. See Paolo Bagni, *La costituzione della poesia nelle artes del 12–13 secolo* (Bologna: Zanichelli, 1968), 32–45. Cf. the discussion of this subject with reference to the fifteenth century and the Renaissance in Wilber Samuel Howell, *Logic and Rhetoric in England, 1500–1700* (New York: Russell & Russell, 1961), 75–76.

35. The text is taken from *The Court of Sapience,* ed. E. Ruth Harvey (Toronto: University of Toronto Press, 1984).

36. See James J. Murphy, "Caxton's Two Choices: 'Modern' and 'Medieval' Rhetoric in Traversagni's *Nova rhetorica* and the Anonymous *Court of Sapience,*" *Medievalia et humanistica* 3 (1972): 241–55.

37. Edwards, *Stephen Hawes,* 20–25; Seth Lerer, "Impressions of Identity: Print, Poetry, and Fame in Hawes and Skelton," chap. 6 of *Chaucer and His Readers* (Princeton, NJ: Princeton University Press, 1993).

38. On the particular pertinence to the early Tudor court of Hawes's use of the *speculum principum* genre, see Edwards, *Stephen Hawes,* 54–56.

39. Stephen Hawes, *The Pastime of Pleasure,* ed. William Edward Mead, EETS, 173 (London: Milford, 1928; reprint, Millwood, NY: Kraus, 1981). All further citations are to this edition.

40. Cf. the discussion by Howell that identifies Hawes's treatment of poetics primarily with the *artes poetriae* of the thirteenth-century grammarians (*Logic and Rhetoric,* 81–87).

41. Boccaccio, *De genealogia deorum gentilium* 14.17; trans. from Charles G. Osgood, *Boccaccio on Poetry* (Indianapolis, IN: Bobbs-Merrill, 1956), 42. See also Osgood's note on this passage (160).

42. Compare the treatment of this theme in Caxton's *Mirror of the World,* ed. O. L. Prior, EETS, e.s., 90 (London: Kegan Paul, Trench, Trübner, 1913), 36. "For the droytes

and lawes by whiche the jugements be made and that by rayson and after right ben kept and mayntened in the court of kynges of princes and of barons come and procede of Rethoryque."

43. The collaboration between poets and princes in the mystification of power is certainly not new with Hawes. Boccaccio's *Trattatello in laude di Dante* offers an account of the origins of poetry somewhat at variance with the one he gave earlier in *De genealogia*. The *Trattatello* recounts how

> various people in places began . . . to make themselves masters of the uneducated multitudes of their districts. . . . And they called themselves "kings," and appeared before the people with both slaves and ornaments, things unheard of among men before this time. . . . These things they could not accomplish satisfactorily without the collaboration of poets, who in order to amplify their own fame, to please the princes, to delight the princes' subjects, and to urge virtuous behaviour upon everyone (an appeal which would have had an opposite effect if framed in plain language) employed various and masterly fictions (little understood by dimwits today, let alone by the dimwits of that period), thereby causing to be believed that which the princes wished to be believed.

Trans. David Wallace, in *Medieval Literary Theory and Criticism, c. 1100–c. 1375: The Commentary Tradition*, ed. A. J. Minnis and A. B. Scott (Oxford: Clarendon Press, 1988), 493–94. Hawes, however, uses this model of poetic-princely self-mystification to elaborate a new theory of rhetoric, a theoretical conflation that does not occur in his most likely sources on poetics.

44. Green, *Poets and Princepleasers*, 174–77, and Lawton, "Dullness," 790–94.

45. Lawton, "Dullness," 789.

46. On humanist epideictic, see, e.g., John W. O'Malley, *Praise and Blame in Renaissance Rome: Rhetoric, Doctrine, and Reform in the Sacred Orators of the Papal Court, c. 1450–1521* (Durham, NC: Duke University Press, 1979); and Ronald G. Witt, *In the Footsteps of the Ancients: The Origins of Humanism from Lovato to Bruni* (Boston: Brill, 2000).

IO

"Hard is with seyntis for to make affray"

Lydgate the "Poet-Propagandist" as Hagiographer

Fiona Somerset

Henry MacCracken in his two-volume edition of Lydgate's minor poems is far from the first critic, and also far from the last, to attempt to treat Lydgate's "religious poems" and his "secular poems" in separation from one another.[1] Even if subdividing his materials into separate "religious" and "secular" volumes was merely the first convenient strategy that occurred to MacCracken, his choice illustrates a broader separation in our field, where religious and secular genres and modes are rarely thought of as readily comparable, even when written by the same poet—despite, or even perhaps because of, anomalous-seeming narratives that seem to straddle religious and secular categories, such as Chaucer's *Clerk's Tale* or *Man of Law's Tale,* or indeed his *Legend of Good Women.*[2] Yet Lydgate in particular is a poet whose "religious" and "secular" oeuvres cry out for cross-comparison—and for comparison, too, with a broader range of ostensibly "religious" or "secular" writings in the early fifteenth century, where competition over readerships and modes of reading is often staged over genre. Lydgate's hagiographical writings are a particularly fertile ground for such cross-comparison—though I certainly do not aim to examine all of his widely disparate writings about the lives of saints within a single essay.[3]

Lydgate's *St. Edmund and St. Fremund* has received little attention from critics interested in either of Lydgate's putatively separate spheres of achievement. Yet closer attention to this neglected work can contribute to both fields, complicating current debate over the political import of Lydgate's "propagandist" writings while giving a new dimension to recent ideological analyses of Lydgate's and other fifteenth-century hagiographical writings. Of late, medievalists who have used the concept of ideology in their analyses have often begun by ex-

plaining their use of it.[4] I should follow suit—not because I expect my readers
to be unfamiliar with the term but because its remarkable flexibility of definition and application, varying with the optimism or pessimism of the views on
human social activity of cultural and literary theorists who use it, will be helpful in positioning Lydgate's political writings. Most broadly, an ideology may
be viewed as a set of beliefs, values, assumptions, and/or ideas shared (or contested) within a society or among or between groups in a society. For some (and
it should be admitted that this is more of a caricature of views that have been
associated with Marx, Althusser, or even Adorno than a straightforward characterization), ideology has been seen as an illusion, a mystification of the real
that gives legitimacy to the actions of those with power in the society (though
the powerful will usually be as caught up in the illusion as those they oppress).
On this kind of account, literature reflects the dominant belief structure of a
society regardless of whether it is propaganda (and thus straightforwardly a vehicle of domination) or not (in which case it haplessly conveys ideology nonetheless).

   On the other hand, though, for others—especially those who think that any
"reality" is a social construct—ideology can be a more neutral and plural term.[5]
On this sort of account, all "reality" is ideological, in the sense that there is no
perception of the real separate from our culturally mediated ideas about it. Yet
it is still possible, indeed probably easier than on the first sort of account, to critique a given ideology. For no one ideology dominates absolutely. The dominant ideology of the ruling class (and indeed there may be more than one) is
subject to contestation by other, competing ideologies belonging to social groups
with assumptions, values, and beliefs of their own. On this sort of account, propaganda is the only sort of literature that merely reflects a dominant ideology,
and few works are unproblematically propagandistic according to this narrow
definition. Most literature is productive of ideology rather than merely its vehicle (though it remains necessarily its vehicle as well): literature engages di-
alogically in the articulation and contestation of the interests of particular social
groups. It can thus be a vital site of social critique and even a means of social
change—or at the very least, for those less optimistic or less interested in change,
a place where we can see writers sharing, endorsing, questioning, reinforcing,
and/or contesting the assumptions and values of their anticipated audiences,
both within and beyond the realm of their own intentions to convey some specific message.

   This last characterization of how writers engage with the views of their audiences is very much the sort of account that recent scholars of late medieval hagiography would provide, even though not all of them make explicit use of the

concept of ideology. As Coletti explains, summarizing recent conclusions, "[Fifteenth-century] authors sought to model [the saintly subjects of their narratives] in accordance with the values and aspirations of their well-to-do patrons even as they engaged social, religious, and political issues that were relevant both to communities of lay readers and to the fortunes of church and nation."[6] Hagiography, on this sort of account, provides readers with heroes who confront concerns like their own, whose characters and values resemble theirs (even if in a larger-than-life version) and whose actions (even if not their conclusion in martyrdom) demonstrate qualities to which the readers themselves aspire. Writers tailor their portrayal of saints to the aspirations of their readers as well as to their own concerns. Lydgate's role as just this sort of hagiographic ideologue to the nobility and gentry, and most especially for female readers, has been explored in detail by Winstead.[7]

But hagiography is not of course a genre that stands in isolation: it borders on (or even overlaps with) other genres in which Lydgate is equally at home, and whose ideological implications are equally worthy of exploration. The same sort of balance between flattering one's patrons and exhorting them to greater virtue that critics have found in fifteenth-century saints' lives is also a familiar feature of advice-to-princes literature addressed to the ruler of the realm and can similarly be viewed as a dialogic engagement with the assumptions and values of Lydgate's audience. Indeed, most recent criticism that focuses on Lydgate's *Troy Book* and *Siege of Thebes* seeks at least in part to debate whether it is flattery or exhortation that receives the greater weight of attention in these works.[8] Further, Lydgate's work as (in Pearsall's phrase) "poet-propagandist to the Lancastrian dynasty" has also been seen to include works of more immediate political import, such as the *Serpent of Division,* the *Title and Pedigree of Henry VI,* the *Roundel* and *Ballade* written for Henry VI's coronation, and *King Henry's Triumphal Entry into London, 21 Feb., 1432,* Lydgate's account of Henry's entry into London after his coronation in France.[9] Whether works such as these—or even the *Troy Book* and *Siege of Thebes*—can rightly be viewed as propaganda is a question ripe for debate, and recently addressed by James Simpson[10] and Scott Straker.[11] Their denials that Lydgate is engaging in propaganda will be productive if they result in closer attention to and more thoughtful analysis of Lydgate's political stances. Yet the conviction they aim to produce, that Lydgate is not a propagandist, should not lead us too swiftly to a concurrent certainty that Lydgate is not an ideologue. Just because a work is not "imperialist or propagandistic" does not mean that it is not political, or that it cannot at least in part further the king's interests.

The audience for Lydgate's historical and/or genealogical narratives, including the *Troy Book* and the *Siege of Thebes* but also, as I will show, *St. Edmund and St. Fremund,* would certainly have included members of the nobility
and gentry. Yet Lydgate's role in these writings is less that of a modeler of "gentil" behavior for these readers, as Winstead has argued is the case in several
fifteenth-century hagiographic works, than that of a regal ideologue. Dismiss-
ing the notion that this poetry is "propaganda" of the crudest sort should not
blind us to the ways that although these narratives of past events can accommodate advice and even criticism as well as admiration, their import is nonetheless
very much to the king's advantage. Poetry referring to a mythical or actual past
creates a narrative backdrop of past events and exempla against which the behavior of the current ruler and his court may be seen as normal, even if not exemplary. Even in cases where the past it presents is not one readers are anxious
to revisit, peopled neither by heroes who may be unequivocally admired nor by
efficacious advisors to those heroes, nonetheless such poetry tends prevailingly
to legitimate the current regime. This is so because the narrative field within
which the story is played out has already naturalized, in advance, whatever
might seem most problematic about contemporary rule.[12]

Like the *Troy Book* and the *Siege of Thebes, St. Edmund and St. Fremund*
seems concerned above all with regality, proper rule, and succession. What I
think it reveals is that Lydgate the Lancastrian ideologue, in the reign of Henry
VI, found that hagiography became the only possible articulation of regal ideology: the only plausible way to write Henry VI, as Lydgate had written his father, into history. For Henry V, the narrative backdrop that legitimized (even if
it also critiqued) his kingship in the *Troy Book* and the *Siege of Thebes* was classicizing and "secular". But for Henry VI, as the full disaster of his impending
personal rule became apparent—as I think it did toward the end of his minority in the early 1430s—the only genre within which his rule could be naturalized, the only source of possible exemplars, the only means of pursuing the
straitened advisorial ambition of protecting the regional interests of Lydgate's
own abbey, was a hagiography of saintly kings.[13] Thus, *St. Edmund and St. Fremund* is not merely, as it has typically been viewed, some sort of failed, disuni-
fied attempt at mixing genres between saint's legend and epic, prompted by Lydgate's aspirations to emulate Chaucer's literary saint's lives by adding rhetorical
flourishes to the sort of thing we find in the *South English Legendary.*[14] Instead,
St. Edmund and St. Fremund is Henry VI's *Troy Book*—or, especially if we agree
with Lee Patterson that the *Siege of Thebes* is yet more explicitly advice in the
form of history than the *Troy Book,* then *St. Edmund and St. Fremund*

is Henry VI's *Siege of Thebes*.[15] *St. Edmund and St. Fremund* naturalizes Henry VI's kingship through a hagiographic logic that we can see established elsewhere among Lydgate's religious writings—and also see contested elsewhere among his contemporaries by those with other ideas about sanctity, about the uses of narrative and of exemplarity, and about how to advise the king and mould the morals of readers more generally.

To begin to see how this is so, we should first review what evidence we have about Henry VI's rule, if rule it can be called—though the view of Henry VI's kingship that we can derive from Lydgate's *St. Edmund and St. Fremund* will in the end be most useful as a corroborating *part* of this rather scanty testimony, rather than something "literary" that stands apart from "historical context". Little (perhaps remarkably little) was written about Henry as ruler or prospective ruler during his reign. While much was written in subsequent years, little of it came from those who had known him. And all of this writing is of course politically motivated in one way or another.[16] Having inherited the thrones of both England and France as a baby, Henry was not much of a worry early in his reign. Concern focused instead on power struggles between members of the council established to rule during his minority: this is the context within which Lydgate's *Serpent of Division* was written.[17] Disquiet about Henry's kingship did become more apparent, however, as time went on. In 1428, when he was six, the ruling council gave his guardian and tutor Richard Beauchamp, Earl of Warwick, fairly conventional directions for his education; but by 1432, when Henry was ten, Warwick was appealing to the council for help in exercising authority over the king and protecting him from inappropriate influences.[18] According to Hardyng's *Chronicle*, Warwick asked to be released from his duties by 1436, when Henry was fourteen, despairing (says Hardyng, who is of course writing with the benefit of hindsight) at Henry's continuing simplicity and lack of discernment.[19] Concern must have reached new heights in 1437, when at fifteen Henry declared his majority, and may have peaked repeatedly in the years up to 1453, when Henry suffered a complete mental breakdown from which he may never have fully recovered.[20]

Just what role Henry may have played in the governance of the realm between 1437 and 1453 is a subject for historians to debate, probably endlessly, from the scant evidence offered by chronicles, letters, and records—most of the ones written subsequent to his reign strongly biased, of course, against Henry.[21] We may never be sure whether Henry was incapable of adult rule and easily influenced by those around him, or whether on the other hand he actively presided over the destruction of his father's legacy. But what we can note is a clear trend among all attempts at positive representation of Henry. Lydgate is not alone in his choice of genre and idiom. All those who wish to praise Henry, both during his reign and since, focus on his religious observances, his piety, his charity, his chastity.[22] Tellingly, no one ever remarks on his prowess in battle, his wise governance. Henry is a saint-in-waiting even from very early on in his reign, in 1437, when his determined preservation of his virginity from even the sight of women is remarked upon; and the descriptions of his patience during his later imprisonment and of his murder carry overtones of martyrdom.[23] After Henry's death, his grave was visited by pilgrims and miracles were attributed to him: like St. Edward the Confessor and St. Edmund, with whom Lydgate compares Henry in *St. Edmund and St. Fremund*—and like them, though even more so, the unfortunate ruler of a most unhappy reign—the genre within which Henry is remembered is that of hagiography.[24]

In *St. Edmund and St. Fremund,* Lydgate's ambitions for Henry's rule, and for the forms of advice that might be offered to him as ruler, have narrowed from the expansiveness of historical allusion that we see in his earlier secular "poet-propagandist" writings—where in the *Ballade to King Henry VI upon his Coronation,* written in 1429, for example, we see Solomon, David, Samson, Joshua, Judas Maccabeus, Alexander, both Julius Caesar *and* his murderer "Brutus Cassius," Hector, Fabricius, Zenocrates, Scipio, Clement, Titus, Trajan, Tiberius, Gratian, Justinian, Octavian, Constantine, Sigismund, and Henry V held up as models.[25] This mode of political historicizing brings in the past through allusion, but unlike the sustained narratives of the *Troy Book* or *Siege of Thebes* does not bring it to bear upon the king's present actions. Lydgate's choice of mode here was partly a matter of circumstance—for a child king, anything seems possible—and partly of occasion: a coronation is always a point of more or less pure potentiality and is hardly the place for any but the most ceremonial advice. In contrast to these exhortations absent of contemporary reference, I think that *St. Edmund and St. Fremund* engages with what Lydgate now knows of the king. Lydgate wrote the poem for Henry at the instigation of his abbot William Curteys to mark the occasion of Henry's lengthy visit to the monastery at Bury from 24 December 1433 to 23 April 1434: the work was probably completed after the visit, at Pearsall's guess some time between 1434 and 1436.[26] In this poem, Lydgate not only provides the most positive spin possible, through the saint/king exemplars St. Edmund, St. Fremund, and St. Edward the Confessor, on qualities of Henry's that are attested elsewhere—his unworldliness, piety, preference for contemplation rather than the business of governance, reluctance in war, compliance with the strong-willed, sanctimonious prudishness, and so on—but manages at the same time to offer pointed advice geared toward the future advantage of his abbey.

Lydgate's translation of the legend of St. Edmund is only one in a series of retellings of the Edmund legend, many of them associated with his abbey. Two prologues begin the work, the first promising St. Edmund's aid for Henry, the second outlining the topic of the work (St. Edmund) and the occasion of its commissioning for Henry VI (the royal visit). Book 1 recounts Edmund's early life and character and how he became Offa's heir and was crowned king of "East England," ending with a lengthy description of the excellence of his rule. In book 2 the jealous Danes Hyngwar and Ubba, seeking to revenge their father's death at the hands of a jealous courtier of Edmund's, attack England. Edmund wins an important battle but ends by appearing before Hyngwar as a prisoner, refusing to reject Christ, and being martyred: miracles follow. A prologue to book 3 introduces Fremund, and book 3 begins by recounting Fremund's saintly early life, just rule, hermitage (meanwhile Edmund is martyred), and calling to revenge Edmund as Christ's champion. With only twenty-four men Fremund slays forty thousand Danes; while giving thanks he is beheaded by a jealous duke (on whom he immediately miraculously revenges himself). Several miracles are then recounted, ending with a prayer to St. Fremund. Book 3's focus now returns to St. Edmund. Later, in 1013, the Danes return to England under Sweyn. They demand tribute, and St. Edmund miraculously gives Sweyn his "tribute" in the form of a fatal wound: never again do the Danes demand tribute. Six following miracles, among them the story of St. Edward the Confessor referred to below, further assert the martyr's qualities as a ruler and as protector of the franchise of the abbey and its environs. St. Edmund's remains are temporarily translated to London, then returned to Bury, with further accompanying miracles and a concluding promise of protection. A closing prayer asks St. Edmund to pray for Henry VI, and two envoys humbly ask the king to accept this work and protect the abbey. Three additional brief episodes in some manuscripts recount St. Edmund's miraculous resuscitation of three dead children; a final prayer reasserts St. Edmund's protection of his franchise.

Lydgate is the first to couple the legend of St. Edmund with that of St. Fremund within the same narrative.[27] We should not allow this innovation to be normalized too quickly, whether by Miller's suggestion that the double legend allows for a seamlessly serial chronology overall, or by Pearsall's and McKeehan's observations that the doubling resembles that found in popular narrative forms such as romances, in which sons often return to complete the work of their fathers, or by the fact that Lydgate did the same thing again in *St Alban and St Amphibalus*.[28] For the doubling of the legend is also one of the most important ways in which Lydgate inflects his hagiography with the genres of exemplary history, through a reduplicative series of comparisons that proliferate beyond the textual examples of Edmund, Fremund, and Edward the Confessor to Henry VI himself.

Thus the moment in the story at which St. Edward the Confessor honors the memory of St. Edmund in a visit to the abbey was always fraught with exemplary significance, as even the briefest description makes obvious: during Edward's visit the blasphemous Dane Osgothus is stricken down by St. Edmund for disdaining his legends, and Edward both suggests that the whole convent should pray for Osgothus's release and leads the prayers. Lydgate underscores Edward's and Edmund's mutual reinforcement here:

> This myracle is the more auctorysed
> That seynt Edward was ther-at present;
> Ouht off resoun to be mor solempnysed.
> For the holy kyng was so diligent.
>   (3.1296–99)

Yet in Lydgate's version the episode is made more exemplary still. For Lydgate, the purpose of Edward's visit is to give the abbey a large gift of land and confirm its franchise—an event recounted elsewhere but never before linked to the Osgothus miracle.[29] Further, Edward's and Edmund's mutual reinforcement recalls Lydgate's description, in his second prologue, of Henry's visit to the abbey: Henry "allone is [the abbey's] roial foundour, / Them to releue ageyn al wordly shoures, / Lyk as to-forn dide his progenitoures" (1.169–71), and because of Henry's conduct during this visit St. Edmund will show him special favor, granting him "in especial/ With Seint Edward to loue god and dreede" (1.183–84). Lydgate's exhortation for the future, too, conveyed in the final envoy addressed to Henry—"for kyng Edmundis notable reuerence / Beth to his chyrche dyffence and Champioun, / Be-cause yt ys off your ffundacioun!"[30]— means more than its bland surface would suggest in company with the trajectory of the preceding narrative.

That narrative presents a linked chain of martyr-king exemplars, each of whose refusal of a secular, martial model of kingship is compensated for both by God and by the next link in the chain. Thus Edmund could easily have achieved a military conquest over the church-threatening Danes (and that ease is Lydgate's invention) but instead chose martyrdom to avoid bloodshed.[31] Fremund, who had previously abandoned the governance of his own realm in favor of a career as a contemplative, emerges from his retreat to avenge his uncle Edmund's murder by miraculously defeating with only twenty-four knights an

army of forty thousand Danes bent on destruction of East Anglia and especially its churches and abbeys. Fremund is slain during his thanksgiving prayer;
but God allows him to avenge his own murder, and even forgive his murderer,
by means of a miracle involving corrosive blood. Edmund's most important
posthumous miracle, anticipated since the opening prologue (1.58–64), is his re-
tributive defeat of the next Danish encroachment through his murder of Sweyn,
who wishes to attack Christianity and encroach on Bury's franchise by imposing taxes. St. Edward on a visit to St. Edmund's donates land to the abbey, reaf-
firms its privileges, and endorses Edmund's sanctity by praying with the monks
for the release of the blasphemous legend-disdaining Dane Osgothus. In triumphal conclusion, Edmund's miracle-ridden retranslation to a newly built shrine
and church in Bury in 1095 uncannily resembles the circumstances of Henry's
visit, the event in the present from which the poem began.[32] Lydgate's narrative
creates a dynastic succession that is not patrilineal (for nephews succeed, rather
than sons); it is not even linear (for the dead return to intervene in succeeding
events, and the poem begins in and repeatedly reminds us of the present). It is
founded instead on the martyric furthering of God's will.

   This lineage of manifest merit does not resemble the manner of Henry VI's
accession to the throne, of course: if anything, it would appear to criticize it,
though this appearance is diminished by Lydgate's marked emphasis on Edmund and Fremund's rightful succession to their crowns and on their youthful
coronations.[33] Despite this surface dissimilarity, Lydgate's martyric lineage does
do ideological work for Henry. It provides Henry with an alternative spiritual
lineage with which to affiliate himself, one with greater honor perhaps than the
problematic Lancastrian succession. It also offers an exemplar for his own imminent personal rule that is both a covert alternative to that provided by his father and a manifold illustration of the swiftness of God's vengeance on those
who disrespect his martyrs—or Lydgate's abbey.

   Some of the regnal alternatives this poem occludes are clearer if we remember what the poem chooses to forget: that while historically the kings who
uphold the Bury St. Edmund's franchise and respect its liberties do include
St. Edward, they do not include Henry V. In the year before his death,
Henry V had called for a wide-ranging reform of the Benedictine order in
England, perhaps spurred on by the Carthusian prior of Mount Grace who was
a former Benedictine, Robert Layton, or perhaps more generally by the com-
plaints of "falsi fratres."[34] Henry wrote first to the abbot of Bury St. Edmund's,
Curteys's predecessor William Exeter, who demurred at Henry's request that
he summon a general chapter meeting, pointing out that the next meeting was
not due for a further two years and that in any case it should be the presidents

of the previous meeting who should convene it.[35] Undaunted, Henry wrote to those presidents, who summoned an extraordinary meeting at Westminster for May 1421, at which Henry delivered a speech to the monks and presented them with a list of proposed reforms. Even though the monks succeeded in delaying any action in committee until after Henry's death in the following year, it seems likely that his interference in Benedictine affairs was far from forgotten.[36]

No direct criticism of Henry V is visible within Lydgate's poem, as should scarcely surprise us: threats to the abbey's franchise come from Danes, thieves, those who dislike saints' legends, and, in the poem's most blatant presentism, Lollards. The exemplary Edmund during his reign is

> To alle religious protectour and support,
> To heretikes a yerde most mortal—
> Lollardis that tyme fond in him no confort,
> To holichirche he was so strong a wal,
> Hated fals doctryn in especial;
> And disdeyned of kyngly excellence
> To alle fals tonges to yeuen audience.
>
> (1.1012–18)

Regardless of whether Lydgate's references to Edmund's disregard for "fals doctryn" and "fals tonges" would have recalled for readers Henry V's undue attention to the reports of "falsi fratres" in 1421, Lydgate's attribution to Edmund of exemplary allegiance in the face of false reports is clearly affiliated with fifteenth-century discourses that sought to class any reformist anticlerical sentiment as a Lollard attack on the church. But Lollards, although they certainly have grave doubts about the exemplary value of saint's legends, cannot in Lydgate's day be so easily separated from the sympathies of the nobility and gentry. Nor can they, like Edmund's Danes, be sent back to Denmark.

Allegiances in Lydgate's England are less clear-cut than his account of the past makes them appear. Peter McNiven has presented a convincing case that in the reigns of Henry IV and V, ecclesiastical ideologues such as Thomas Arundel (or, I might add, Lydgate and Hoccleve) were quite successful in stigmatizing anticlericism among the secular ruling classes. Any opposition to the English church hierarchy, most particularly the wish to draw money from the church's endowments, was associated with Lollardy; and Lollardy was characterized as plotting the destruction of secular as well as spiritual institutions.[37] Yet such success was often hard-won, and several members of the nobility and gentry plainly had Lollard sympathies, or wishes to reform and/or draw funds from ecclesiastical sources, that they never abandoned.[38] Although Lydgate praises Humphrey, Duke of Gloucester, for his suppression of Lollards in 1431, for example, the Wycliffite *Dialogue between a Secular Priest and a Friar* (whose dedication and envoy claim it was presented to "Lord Glowcestre") makes of St. Edward the Confessor's exemplary value a matter for debate rather than self-assured assertion.[39]

The *Dialogue between a Secular Priest and a Friar* employs difficult philosophical language but makes it easy for lay readers to see who should be the winner: fourteen brief assertions by the friar are each in turn thoroughly refuted by the secular priest. The topics are drawn from the commonplaces of late medieval antifraternalism—half of the friar's assertions have to do with sin and the commandments, the other half with the friars' possessions and claims about voluntary mendicancy—yet the replies develop these topics in strikingly original directions. In claiming that this is the written record of a dialogue staged before "Lord Glowcestre," the dedication and envoy praise his acumen and leave it to him to determine the winner. Previously scholars have been fairly sure that the addressee was Thomas of Woodstock (d. 1397), whose Lollard sympathies are attested elsewhere. Yet once we have acknowledged that fifteenth-century ecclesiastical ideologues who present the gentry and nobility as strongly anti-Lollard should be read as engaged in the contestation of just that fact, while Lollards for their part were actively attempting to sway the nobility and gentry to their cause, then the suggestion that this dialogue might be an attempted appeal to Duke Humphrey's sympathies gains greater credence. And even if the dialogue had originally been written for Thomas Woodstock, this would not have been immediately evident to readers after his death: the sheer fact of the dialogue's survival into the fifteenth century would have superadded the implication—surely not unwelcome to its writer and readers—that Humphrey too was a potential sympathizer.[40]

As one of his arguments in favor of voluntary mendicancy, the *Dialogue*'s friar asserts that St. Edward had a vision of St. John, in which St. John appeared as a pilgrim and asked him for money. St. Edward gave St. John a ring, and the friar asserts that this legitimizes fraternal begging. The secular priest, the friar's opponent, interestingly does not reject hagiography, or the exemplary value of saints, wholesale. But he does insist on an alternative, allegorical interpretation of the story, which he grounds in the words of biblical saints. If St. Edward's vision contains any truth, he asserts, what it means is that St. Edward agreed with St. John that all earthly riches are worth nothing to the bliss of heaven and that each of us should behave like a pilgrim who seeks his resting place only in heaven, as St. Peter and St. Paul recommend. Like Lydgate's

St. Edmund and St. Fremund, the dialogue's resolution here urges a spiritual model of life in place of a more secular one. But the dialogue spiritualizes the sorts of monetary issues that in Lydgate's legend remain always material and even rather embarrassingly concrete. Its example complicates what Lydgate tries to keep simple.

Simplicity has its advantages. The advantages for Henry VI in accepting a new spiritual affiliation with St. Edmund, complete with the obligations to his own abbey that Lydgate attaches, in place of the complexities of his Lancastrian inheritance are well illustrated by the passage from which my title is drawn. Directly after recounting how the Danes' response to Sweyn's murder by Edmund was to leave England, Lydgate comments:

> And as myn Auctour in ordre doth deuyse,
> Neuer tirant durste putten assay
> Off seynt Edmund to breke the franchise,
> But he were punysshed withoute long delay.
> Hard is with seyntis forto make affray.
>
> (3.1108–12)

Never again did a tyrant attempt to encroach on Bury St. Edmund's franchise, but that he was punished by the saint without delay—as is illustrated by the immediately following story of Leofstan, a sheriff with no devotion to St. Edmund who disliked listening to his miracles and who was possessed by a fiend and struck dead for attempting to condemn a woman who had appealed to St. Edmund for sanctuary. No one can resist such an attack. Nor need Henry change his behavior in any way to gain this powerful support (and perhaps even serve as a posthumous instrument of God's power himself when his turn comes). The model of sanctity Lydgate urges mirrors Henry's known personal qualities and habits; with the aid of a little divine intervention, of a sort that Lydgate suggests it is only reasonable for him to expect, Henry will be more than adequate to the tasks of just governance and effective kingship.

To be sure, Lydgate does also exhort Henry to conform to a more traditional model of heroic kingship within the poem, even encouraging him, in the second prologue, to be like his father. "Forto rassemble by tryumphal victory / To his fadir, most notable of memory" (1.163–64), Henry should "in knyhthod" be "most marcial," have "with Arthour noblesse and hih renoun,/ And with Charlemayn . . . been egal" (1.180–82). The emphasis on St. Edmund's and St. Fremund's successions and coronations, too, irresistibly recalls Lydgate's various writings on these topics for Henry VI, and with them their similar mode of exhortation. And Lydgate vastly amplifies from his sources the description of Edmund's virtues in book 1 and early in book 2 in such a way that this part of the poem reads like a secular mirror for princes, singling out Edmund's governance of self, of the realm, and of his household for detailed description and praise.[41] Edmund himself is "An exaumplaire and a merour cler" (1.419). His realm, under his guidance, is "in oon [moral] ymage knet" (1.940, 949). And he is "merour of doctrine" (2.138) to his household, so that its members become "liht and lanterne / To alle uertuous how thei shal hem gouerne" (2.139–40).

These inflections with more secular models of kingship contribute to the poem's ideological work: the more Edmund is presented as a mirror for Henry, the more conventional-seeming the poem's exhortations for Henry's conduct, the better. Yet sooner or later, this poem subsumes all its secular inflections, all its worldly successes, into hagiography. Although the extended praise of Edmund's exemplary governance in books 1 and 2 would not for the most part seem out of place in a secular mirror for princes, it culminates in the refusal of a victory Edmund could easily have had, whose consequence is martyrdom. Even Fremund's later miraculous revenge with only twenty-four knights is just that: God's miracle, none of Fremund's own doing, and not the result of any human prowess. And the secular-seeming qualities Lydgate hopes for in Henry during the second prologue are to be conferred, not through any heroic activities, but through St. Edmund's intercession, "[b]e influence . . . fro the heuene doun" (1.179). Lydgate has found a way of including the aspirations for Henry VI's kingship that were also present in his earlier "poet-propagandist" poems—in which Arthur, Charlemagne, St. Edward, and Henry V all featured as models—but also of narrowing their range.

In return for accepting this narrowing of his potential field of action, Lydgate's *St. Edmund and St. Fremund* provides Henry with a way to imagine himself as a saint and hero in waiting, even before his personal rule begins. In this poem—and perhaps he is the first to do so—Lydgate has found the only genre within which Henry's character and actions can be compared with history in praiseworthy terms: in providing this model he may possibly have influenced not only future writers who describe Henry but Henry himself. Most enticing, for Henry, is the posthumous promise of the alternative lineage Lydgate offers. Each saint who has submitted himself to God's will in life, in Lydgate's narrative, becomes in death an invincible instrument of divine favor and vengeance, whose every whim is catered to by his subjects. There is little to distinguish Edmund's posthumous miracles from the actions of the most autocratic despot: since God wills it, Edmund can murder kings in their bedchambers, punish those who would steal even one jewel from his riches, strike down dead those who disrespect him, and scatter largesse upon those who pray to him; his monks are forever interceding for his favor. No secular mirror for princes would ever endorse such behaviors. But in Lydgate's poem they are acceptable from anyone who upholds the franchise and liberty from interference of the Benedictine abbey of Bury St. Edmund's and its surrounding region. Since Henry VI did, indeed, remain a friend to the abbey throughout his reign, we can only hope that Lydgate's remembered paradigm was a comfort to him in his unfortunate end.

Notes

I am grateful to the editors for comments on an earlier draft of this chapter.

1. See *The Minor Poems of John Lydgate*, vol. 1, *Religious Poems,* and vol. 2, *Secular Poems,* ed. Henry Noble MacCracken, EETS, e.s., 107, 192 (London: Oxford University Press, 1911, 1934).

2. Innovative recent work that attempts to draw closer comparisons between "secular" and "religious" genres and modes includes Jennifer E. Bryan, "Hoccleve, the Virgin, and the Politics of Complaint," *PMLA* 117 (2002): 1172–87; Catherine Sanok, "Reading Hagiographically: The *Legend of Good Women* and Its Feminine Audience," *Exemplaria* 13 (2001): 323–54, and "The Geography of Genre in the *Physician's Tale* and *Pearl*," *New Medieval Literatures* 5, ed. Rita Copeland, David Lawton, and Wendy Scase (Oxford: Oxford University Press, 2002), 177–201 (an intriguing exploration of medieval genre and ideology that I read only after completing this essay); Jocelyn Wogan-Browne, "'Bet . . . to . . . rede on holy seyntes lyves . . .': Romance and Hagiography Again," in *Readings in Medieval English Romance,* ed. Carol M. Meale (Woodbridge, Suffolk: Boydell & Brewer, 1994), 83–97; Larry Scanlon's work on both religious and secular exempla in *Narrative, Authority, and Power: The Medieval Exemplum and the Chaucerian Tradition* (Cambridge: Cambridge University Press, 1994); Ethan Knapp, *The Bureaucratic Muse: Thomas Hoccleve and the Literature of Late Medieval England* (University Park: Pennsylvania State University Press, 2001), esp. chap. 5, 129–57; and chap. 11 of this volume.

3. Lydgate's various hagiographical writings have typically been classed together by critics and treated homogeneously: the *Life of Our Lady* is commonly examined with the saint's lives, while prayers to saints are treated separately. See Walter F. Schirmer, *John Lydgate: A Study in the Culture of the XVth Century,* trans. Ann E. Keep (Berkeley: University of California Press, 1961); Derek Pearsall, *John Lydgate* (Charlottesville: University Press of Virginia, 1970); and Lois A. Ebin, *John Lydgate* (Boston: Twayne Publishers, 1985). While this approach is useful and probably necessary in a descriptive survey that aims to cover all of Lydgate's oeuvre, as these three writers do, it cannot help but obscure the sorts of generic affiliations I mean to examine here. Ruth Nisse's essay within this

volume (chap. 11), like mine, attempts to reconsider hagiography's position and importance within Lydgate's oeuvre, though her approach emphasizes stylistic and generic similarities among Lydgate's prayers, saints' lives, and the *Testament* while mine stresses ideological and generic commonalities between what have been called Lydgate's
"poet-propagandist" writings and his *St. Edmund and St. Fremund*. I thank Ruth for productive discussions during the process of writing our respective essays; we feel that our
approaches are complementary, even if our emphases differ. While new critical work on
Lydgate's saints' lives is beginning to emerge, *St. Edmund and St. Fremund* has previously
been examined only by Karen Winstead (as detailed below, nn. 7, 14).

4. See, e.g., Paul Strohm, *Hochon's Arrow: The Social Imagination of Fourteenth-
Century Texts* (Princeton, NJ: Princeton University Press, 1992), 6, where ideology is
"not . . . a set of inherently false and deliberately distortive beliefs, but more neutrally . . .
the entire set of socially imagined ideas by which people explain their lives and places in
a material order." See also Sanok, "Geography of Genre," 181 n. 12; and Gabrielle M.
Spiegel, *The Past as Text: The Theory and Practice of Medieval Historiography* (Baltimore:
Johns Hopkins University Press, 1997), 23 and 212 (quoted below in n.12). For a more
comprehensive list of ways ideology has recently been defined in a variety of disciplines,
see Terry Eagleton, *Ideology: An Introduction* (London: Verso, 1991), 1–2. Any account of
how genres do ideological work would seemingly need to begin by citing Fredric Jame-
son's *The Political Unconscious: Narrative as a Socially Symbolic Act* (Ithaca, NY: Cornell
University Press, 1981); yet his work is inspirational rather than foundational here. The
necessarily highly schematic account of ideology and its critique that follows is my own,
though I thank Andrew Cole for helping me see how best to cram the most necessary information into so small a space. This account may be augmented by consulting not only
the authors mentioned in passing (see, e.g., Karl Marx, *The German Ideology*, pt. 1, in *The
Marx-Engels Reader*, 2nd ed., ed. Robert C. Tucker (New York: W. W. Norton, 1978),
146–200; Louis Althusser, "Ideology and Ideological State Apparatuses (Notes toward
an Investigation," in *Lenin and Philosophy and Other Essays*, trans. Ben Brewster (London:
New Left Books, 1971); Theodor W. Adorno, *The Culture Industry: Selected Essays on
Mass Culture*, ed. J. M. Bernstein (London: Routledge, 1991); Antonio Gramsci, *Selections
from the Prison Notebooks*, ed. and trans. Quintin Hoare and Geoffrey Nowell Smith
(New York: International Publishers, 1971); and Stuart Hall, *Culture, Media, Language*
(London: Unwin Hyman, 1990); and Ernesto Laclau and Chantal Mouffe, *Hegemony
and Socialist Strategy: Towards a Radical Democratic Politics*, 2nd ed. (London: Verso,
2001), but also general introductory surveys by Raymond Williams, *Marxism and Literature* (Oxford: Oxford University Press, 1977), esp. 55–71 and 108–14; Eagleton, *Ideology*;
David Hawkes, *Ideology* (London: Routledge, 1996).

5. Never, perhaps, is the concept of ideology entirely neutral. Reflection on Clifford
Geertz's still-relevant remark in arguing for a neutral concept of ideology, that "No
one . . . would call himself an ideologue or consent unprotestingly to be called one by oth-

ers," may help to make this clear. See Clifford Geertz, "Ideology as a Cultural System," retrieved January 6, 2005, from http://xroads.virginia.edu/~DRBR/geertz.html.

6. Theresa Coletti, "*Paupertas est donum Dei*: Hagiography, Lay Religion, and the Economics of Salvation in the Digby Mary Magdalene," *Speculum* 76 (2001): 343. Coletti's study of the Digby *Mary Magdalene* is explicitly an investigation of hagiographic ideology, and it was one of the sparking points for my work on this chapter. Here she is summarizing the contributions to the study of Bokenham, Capgrave, and Lydgate made by Sheila Delany and Karen Winstead, but her remarks are relevant to a wider spectrum of newer work on late medieval sanctity (see among others the works cited in her n. 1).

7. See Karen A. Winstead, "Lydgate's Lives of Saints Edmund and Alban: Martyrdom and *Prudent Pollicie*," *Mediaevalia* 17 (1994): 221–41 (which addresses how Lydgate's *St. Edmund and St. Fremund* and *St. Alban and St. Amphibalus* address a lay readership among the gentry) as well as *Virgin Martyrs: Legends of Sainthood in Late Medieval England* (Ithaca, NY: Cornell University Press, 1997) (where chap. 3, 112–46, considers Lydgate and Bokenham's virgin martyr legends, mainly in the light of a female lay readership).

8. See, e.g., Lee Patterson, "Making Identities in Fifteenth-Century England: Henry V and John Lydgate," in *New Historical Literary Study: Essays on Reproducing Texts, Representing History,* ed. Jeffrey N. Cox and Larry J. Reynolds (Princeton, NJ: Princeton University Press, 1993), 69–107; Scott-Morgan Straker, "Deference and Difference: Lydgate, Chaucer, and the *Siege of Thebes,*" *Review of English Studies* 52 (2001): 1–21, and "Rivalry and Reciprocity in Lydgate's *Troy Book,*" in *New Medieval Literatures 3,* ed. David Lawton, Wendy Scase, and Rita Copeland (Oxford: Oxford University Press, 1999), 119–47; James Simpson, "The Other Book of Troy: Guido delle Colonne's *Historia destructionis Troiae* in Fourteenth- and Fifteenth-Century England," *Speculum* 73 (1998): 397–423, and "'Dysemol daies and fatal houres': Lydgate's *Destruction of Thebes* and Chaucer's *Knight's Tale,*" in *The Long Fifteenth Century: Essays for Douglas Gray,* ed. Helen Cooper and Sally Mapstone (Oxford: Clarendon Press, 1997), 15–33.

9. See Pearsall, *John Lydgate,* 169, for use of this term, associated especially with poems Lydgate produced for Henry VI's coronation.

10. Thus Simpson asserts in "The Other Book of Troy" that narratives of Troy based on Guido de Colonna's narrative rather than Virgil's are "in no way imperialist or propagandistic, not even covertly, not even when they try to be" (404); although the article is largely devoted to the alliterative *Destruction of Troy,* its arguments are meant also to apply to Lydgate's *Troy Book.* Simpson makes a similar argument about Lydgate's *Siege of Thebes* in "Dysemol daies."

11. Straker's essay "Propaganda, Intentionality, and the Lancastrian Lydgate" (chap. 4 of this volume) concentrates on some of the writings by Lydgate that have most often been termed "propagandist" (e.g., the *Triumphal Entry* and *Title and Pedigree*), although also on some that have not (e.g., *On Gloucester's Approaching Marriage*). I thank Scott for allowing me to read his work in draft.

12. My account here draws on Spiegel's analyses of the workings of ideology in the writing of history. Consider especially her remarks on royal historiography in *The Past as Text*:

> Historical writing is a powerful vehicle for the expression of ideological assertion, for it is able to address the historical issues crucially at stake and to lend to ideology the authority and prestige of the past, all the while dissimulating its status *as* ideology under the guise of a mere accounting of "what was." The prescriptive authority of the past makes it a privileged locus for working through the ideological implications of social changes in the present and the repository of contemporary concerns and desires. As a locus of value, a revised past holds out for contemporaries the promise of a perfectible present. (212)

While Spiegel's version of ideology is clearly less neutral and more closely allied to hegemony than Strohm's (on which see above, n. 5), its analysis of the rhetorical force of history seems compelling, whether that history is mythical, hagiographical, or more factually annalistic. I am also indebted to Maura Nolan's consideration of Spiegel's *Romancing the Past* in "The Art of History Writing: Lydgate's *Serpent of Division*," *Speculum* 78 (2003): 98–127. Clearly Simpson's account of Lydgate's secular historical writings deserves more extended attention than I have devoted to it here.

13. The very mixed success of attempts to provide Henry VI with more conventional advice-to-princes later in his reign might be read as corroboration of my claim here: consider Lydgate's own *Fall of Princes* (in which Humphrey, Duke of Gloucester, appears to have lost interest), or his unfinished *Secreta secretorum* translation, or the anonymous Vegetius translation *Knyghthode and Bataile* of c. 1457–60.

14. This is to summarize, though perhaps also to caricature slightly, the dismissals of the text by Schirmer, Pearsall, and Ebin. The only previous critic to have devoted extended attention to this legend's analysis appears to be Winstead, "Lydgate's Lives," who views it as an innovative experiment in hagiography directed toward lay audiences (but does not consider its address to the king). Winstead revises previous views partly by giving them a more positive cast than I do here.

15. See Patterson, "Making Identities."

16. On sources for the study of Henry VI's kingship, see the helpful recent introduction to previous assessments of the king by Keith Dockray, *Henry VI, Margaret of Anjou and the Wars of the Roses: A Source Book* (Stroud, Gloucestershire: Sutton Publishing, 2000), xiii–xxvii, 1–10. In addition to previous evaluations of sources cited by Dockray—Charles L. Kingsford, *English Historical Literature in the Fifteenth Century* (Oxford: Clarendon Press, 1913); Antonia Gransden, *Historical Writing in England*, vol. 2, *C. 1307 to the Early Sixteenth Century* (Ithaca, NY: Cornell University Press, 1982); B. P. Wolffe, "The Personal Rule of Henry VI," chap. 2 in *Fifteenth-Century England, 1399–1509: Studies in Politics and Society*, ed. S. B. Chrimes, C. D. Ross, and R. A. Griffiths (Manchester: Manchester University Press, 1972), 29–48, and *Henry VI* (London: Me-

thuen, 1981 [1983]); Ralph A. Griffiths, *The Reign of King Henry VI: The Exercise of Royal Authority, 1422–1461* (Berkeley: University of California Press, 1981); Roger Lovatt, "John Blacman: Biographer of Henry VI," in *The Writing of History in the Middle Ages: Essays Presented to Richard William Southern,* ed. R. H. C. Davis and J. M. Wallace-Hadrill (Oxford: Clarendon Press, 1981)—see John Watts, *Henry VI and the Politics of Kingship* (Cambridge: Cambridge University Press, 1996), and subsequently Christine Carpenter, *The Wars of the Roses: Politics and the Constitution in England, c. 1437–1509* (Cambridge: Cambridge University Press, 1997), and Helen Castor, *The King, the Crown, and the Duchy of Lancaster: Public Authority and Private Power, 1399–1461* (Oxford: Oxford University Press, 2000), who mostly shift attention from discerning Henry's character to investigating his role in royal policy. Contemporary with Henry, yet clearly motivated by political concerns, are correspondence between Warwick and the ruling council, in N. H. Nicholas, *Proceedings and Ordinances of the Privy Council,* 6 vols (London: Record Commission, 1834–37), vol. 3; a letter describing the king by Piero da Monte from 1437, in Johannes Haller, *Piero da Monte: Ein Gelehrter und Päpstlicher Beamter des 15 Jahrhunderts, seine Briefsammlung,* Bibliotek des deutschen Historischen Instituts in Rom 19 (Rome: Deutsches Historisches Institut, 1941), 42–46 (a translated excerpt appears in Griffiths, *Reign of King Henry VI,* 235; also in Dockray, *Henry VI,* 4); and *Johannis Capgrave Liber de illustribus Henricis,* ed. F. C. Hingeston, Rolls Series 7 (London: Longman, Brown, Green, Longmans & Roberts, 1858), dedicated to Henry VI (1–4) and including him among its subjects (125–39). Subsequent, but written by those with access to eyewitness information and contemporary accounts, are Hardyng's *Chronicle,* extant in versions presented to Henry VI and to his supplanter Edward IV (John Hardyng, *The Chronicle from the Firste Begynnyng of Englande,* Facsimile of London, 1543 edition, [Norwood, NJ: Walter J. Johnson, 1976] as well as versions of the *Brut* chronicle (Yorkist, and not used here), and Blacman's life of Henry VI (John Blacman, *Henry the Sixth,* ed. M. R. James, Cambridge: Cambridge University Press, 1919), written soon after Henry's death by a former chaplain of Henry's who claims to have consulted others who had known Henry; see also Lovatt, "John Blacman."

17. See Nolan, "Art of History Writing," for a compelling new analysis of this work.

18. These conventional instructions are summarized in Mabel E. Christie, *Henry VI* (New York: Houghton Mifflin, 1922), 47 (an instructively sentimental book); for an excerpt, see Dockray, *Henry VI,* 3; the Privy Council's instructions are printed in Nicholas, *Proceedings and Ordinances,* 3:296, 299. Warwick's later appeal to the council is printed in James Gairdner, ed., *The Paston Letters* (London: Chatto & Windus, 1904), 2:34–38.

19. Hardyng, *Chronicle,* fols. 220 r–v.

20. For a fairly detailed chronology of Henry's reign, see Griffiths, *Reign of King Henry VI,* xxi–xxiii.

21. On the sources, see n. 16 and the critics cited there; for quick surveys of previous debate in the field, see three of the most recent contributors: Carpenter, *Wars of the Roses,*

87–95; Castor, *The King, the Crown,* 45–50; and Dockray, *Henry VI,* esp. xli n. 19, xliii nn. 34, 35.

22. Piero da Monte praises the sixteen-year-old king for avoiding the sight and con-versation of women, for example (see n. 16), while John Capgrave praises Henry's piety, reverence, and foundation of Eton and King's College in 1441 (see Hingeston, *Johannis Capgrave Liber,* 131–33). Blacman records Henry's prayers and gives examples dating from childhood on of his chastity and piety (*Henry the Sixth,* 2, 7–9, 14–17). Subsequent accounts repeat these praises in similar terms.

23. On Henry's early chastity, see nn. 16 and 22; on his Christ-like endurance of im-prisonment and death, see especially Blacman, *Henry the Sixth,* 16–22.

24. On the cult of Henry VI, see John W. McKenna, "Piety and Propaganda: The Cult of King Henry VI," in *Chaucer and Middle English Studies in Honour of Rossell Hope Robbins,* ed. Beryl Rowland (London: Allen & Unwin, 1974), 72–88; on its longevity into the 1970s, see Griffiths, *Reign of King Henry VI,* 1; on late medieval English political saints more generally, see Simon Walker, "Political Saints in Later Medieval England," in *The McFarlane Legacy: Studies in Late Medieval Politics and Society,* ed. R. H. Britnell and A. J. Pollard (Stroud, Gloucestershire: Alan Sutton Publishing, 1995), 77–106.

25. *Minor Poems of John Lydgate,* 2:624–30; see lines 51–88.

26. On this visit and the writing of the poem, see Pearsall, *John Lydgate,* 26–27 and 280–83; Pearsall, *John Lydgate (1371–1449): A Bio-Bibliography,* English Literary Studies 71 (Victoria, BC: University of Victoria, 1997), 34, and for the conjectural dating, 51. See also Stephen Reimer's account of the circumstances in his introduction to "The Lives of Ss. Edmund and Fremund," retrieved 6 January 2005 from the Canon of John Lydgate Project Web site: www.ualberta.ca/~sreimer/edmund.

27. James I. Miller Jr. explains that the earliest extant version of the Fremund legend dates from the early thirteenth century; by the late thirteenth or early fourteenth century Fremund has become Edmund's nephew, but Lydgate is the first to incorporate Fre-mund's story into the narrative of St. Edmund in between Edmund's martyrdom and his posthumous revenge on the Danes. See James I. Miller, "Literature to History: Exploring a Medieval Saint's Legend and Its Context," in *Literature and History,* ed. I. E. Caden-head Jr. (Tulsa: University of Tulsa Press, 1970), 66–67.

28. See James Ivan Miller Jr., "John Lydgate's Saint Edmund and Saint Fremund: An Annotated Edition" (PhD diss., Harvard University, 1967), xxxi and 341–42; Irene P. McKeehan, "St Edmund of East Anglia: The Development of a Romantic Legend," *University of Colorado Studies* 15 (1925): 13–74, at 63–64; Pearsall, *John Lydgate,* 282. I have benefited from consulting Miller's thesis; it is a pity that his edition and his painstaking comparisons with its Latin sources were not published as he planned. Since restrictions on the use of Harvard theses prevent me from quoting from the edition without his permission, quotations will be drawn from the older edition, "S. Edmund und Fremund, von Lydgate, aus Ms Harl. 2278, mit den Varianten des Ms. Ashm. 46 (spätere Recen-

sion)," in *Altenglische Legenden,* ed. C. Horstmann (Heilbronn: Henninger, 1881), 376–445, and cited parenthetically by book and line number in the text. I have also consulted the as-yet incomplete hypertext edition by Reimer, "Lives of Ss. Edmund and Fremund." Although *St. Alban and St. Amphibalus* is obviously relevant to the study of *St. Edmund and St. Fremund,* I exclude it from consideration here in order to consider the latter poem's production for Henry VI without benefit of hindsight.

29. On the absence of any previous known link between Edward and the Osgothus miracle, see Miller, "John Lydgate's Saint Edmund," 347, 1280 n. In a separate article Miller explains the careful literary design of the section of the poem covering posthumous miracles of St. Edmund; James I. Miller Jr., "Lydgate the Hagiographer as a Literary Artist," in *The Learned and the Lewed,* ed. Larry D. Benson, Harvard English Studies 5 (Cambridge, MA: Harvard University Press, 1974), 279–90.

30. These lines are not numbered but appear on Horstmann, *Altenglische Legenden,* 440, at the end of the envoi to the king entitled "Regi."

31. On Lydgate's innovative depiction of Edmund's conquest as an easy battle, see Miller, "John Lydgate's Saint Edmund," 327, 371 ff. n.

32. Extensive rebuilding of the abbot's palace where Henry VI was to reside was necessary before his visit: see Pearsall, *John Lydgate,* 26, Reimer, introduction to "Lives of Ss Edmund." Lydgate in addition emphasizes the abbot Baldewyn's close ties with Edmund, as his former doctor (3.1408–16): a model perhaps for the developing relationship between Henry and Lydgate's own abbot William Curteys.

33. See 1.627–864, 3.281–322.

34. The first suggestion comes from the Croyland annalist, the second from Walsingham: for narrative accounts built on the chronicle sources and the records of the meeting, see William A. Pantin, ed., *Documents Illustrating the Activities of the General and Provincial Chapters of the English Black Monks, 1215–1540,* Camden, 3rd ser., 47 (London: Royal Historical Society, 1933), 2:98–100; David Knowles, *The Religious Orders in England,* vol. 2, *The End of the Middle Ages* (Cambridge: Cambridge University Press, 1955), 182–84.

35. For the letters (which are, however, fragmentary), see Pantin, *Documents,* 104–5.

36. For Henry's attempted reforms, see records of the proceedings in ibid., 105–34; as well as previous comments on the possible impact on Lydgate by Derek Pearsall, "Lydgate as Innovator," *MLQ* 53 (1992): 5–22, 18, and Patterson, "Making Identities," 93–95.

37. See Peter McNiven, *Heresy and Politics in the Reign of Henry IV: The Burning of John Badby* (Woodbridge, Suffolk: Boydell & Brewer, 1987), esp. chaps. 4 (63–78), 7 (118–35), and 9 (158–84). See also Margaret Aston, "Lollardy and Sedition, 1381–1431," reprinted with revisions in *Lollards and Reformers: Images and Literacy in Late Medieval Religion* (London: Hambledon Press, 1984), 1–47.

38. In addition to McNiven, *Heresy and Politics,* see K. B. McFarlane, *Lancastrian Kings and Lollard Knights* (Oxford: Clarendon Press, 1972), as well as several essays (e.g., those by Thomson, Jurkowski, Lutton, and Hope) in *Lollardy and the Gentry in the Later Middle Ages,* ed. Margaret Aston and Colin Richmond (Stroud, Gloucestershire: Sutton Publishing, 1997).

39. The *Dialogue between a Secular Clerk and a Friar* appears in Dublin, Trinity College MS 244, fols. 212v–219. The dialogue is the final item in this important Wycliffite manuscript, recently described by Ralph Hanna III, "Two Lollard Codices and Lollard Book-Production," *Studies in Bibliography* 43 (1990): 49–62, reprinted in *Pursuing History: Middle English Manuscripts and Their Texts* (Stanford, CA: Stanford University Press, 1996), 48–59. I am currently editing this dialogue along with three other Wycliffite dialogues for EETS. For further description of all four dialogues, see Anne Hudson, "A Lollard Quaternion," *Review of English Studies,* n.s., 22 (1971): 451–65, reprinted in Anne Hudson, *Lollards and Their Books* (London: Hambledon Press, 1985), 193–200.

40. For the suggestion that this same dialogue may have been owned and read among Lollard communities up into the sixteenth century, see Anne Hudson, *The Premature Reformation: Wycliffite Texts and Lollard History* (Oxford: Oxford University Press, 1987), 479, 486–89.

41. See especially the lengthy descriptive passage stretching from 1.858 to 1116. Pearsall, *John Lydgate,* 283, notices this passage's strong inflection with Lydgate's characteristic mode of statesmanlike secular advice, regardless of its hagiographic setting.

"Was it not Routhe to Se?"

Lydgate and the Styles of Martyrdom

Ruth Nisse

Bury's Male Virgin Martyrs

In his strange short poem *To St. Robert of Bury,* John Lydgate invokes the martyrdom of a boy supposed to have been murdered by the Jews of Bury St. Edmund's in 1181.[1] Lydgate, a monk of Bury, participates here in what Peter Brown has identified as the *Passio's* generic erasure of time: the hagiographer and his audience become eyewitnesses to the martyr's suffering in texts that "[record] the moments when the seemingly extinct past and the unimaginably distant future had pressed into the present":[2]

> Slayn in childhood by mortal violence,
> Allas! It was a pitous thing to see
> A sowkyng child, tendre of Innocence
> So to be scourged, and naylled to a tre;
> Thou myghtest crie, thou spak no word, parde,
> With-oute langage makyng a pitous soun.
>
> (9–14)[3]

Lydgate speaks here to the transformative power of piteousness, the basis of a child martyr's cult: "was it not routhe to see thi veins bleed?" (18). What stands out in this poem even more than the bloody spectacle, however, is Lydgate's emphasis on the martyr as *infans* as well as virgin, unable to speak or "pleyne" during his ordeal: "Thy purpil blood allayed with mylk whiht / Oppressid with turment koudest no woord seyne" (25–27). Although Lydgate makes it clear that Robert, now in heaven—"upon thyn hed a crown" (22)—can speak as an intercessor, the pathos-laden prayer focuses on his helpless pre-verbal, presymbolic age.

At the poem's end, Lydgate addresses the martyr in terms of his cult within the physical and spiritual space of Bury St. Edmund's:

> Have upon Bury thi gracious remembraunce
> That hast among hem a chapel & a shryne,
> With helpe of Edmund preserve hem from grevaunce,
> King of Estynglond, martyr and virgyne,
> With whose briht sonne lat thi sterre shyne,
> Strecchyng your stremys thoruh al this regioun.
>
> (33–38)

When the poet figures Robert hierarchically as a "star" to St. Edmund's "sun," he raises the possibilities of both a historical renewal of the abbey in a second founding virgin martyrdom and a personal, emotional renewal in his own fictive "eyewitness" account of the martyr's wounded body. Lydgate signals the historical specificity of the martyr's moment together with his eternal glory. By figuring himself poetically as the witness to the boy's agony, Lydgate in effect ventriloquizes the great Bury historian who penned St. Robert's *vita*, Jocelin of Brakelond, and thus seeks to participate imaginatively in the abbey's late-twelfth-century renaissance under Abbot Samson.[4]

In his outpouring of devotion, Lydgate nevertheless demonstrates the problematic uncertainties involved in representing a child victim. As Miri Rubin argues of Thomas of Monmouth's account of the killing of William of Norwich by Jews in 1144, such narratives fulfill expectations about Jewish cruelty but not contemporary theologians' understanding of Christian martyrdom.[5] "The medieval Church," André Vauchez writes, "never canonized a child or even a *iuvenis;* at the level of the local cult, young saints . . . were few, so strong remained the clerical prejudice which linked the *gravitas morum* with *senectus*."[6] Lydgate's little Robert is an extreme case: an unweaned *infans,* he cannot have died a martyr's noble death of willful self-sacrifice. The longing for death that makes the martyr in his or her final pronouncements here becomes entirely the desire of the hagiographer, who himself becomes the sacred drama's central figure. In this kind of cult, the writer in a sense appropriates the saint's own function by positioning his or her death within a context that confers meaning.

By finally situating Robert's comparatively recent "shryne" in relation to St. Edmund's, Lydgate fits the child's unknowable intentions to his abbey's culture of martyrdom. St. Edmund's legend had grown from his obscure origins as a ninth-century East Anglian king killed by the Danes; his cult was enhanced by means of Abbo of Fleury's hagiography (c. 985–87), Abbot Baldwin's translation of his miraculously preserved body to a new church in 1097, and the monks' subsequent viewings of his relics, such as the event of 1198 famously described in Jocelin's *Chronicle*.[7] In his prayer *To St. Robert*, Lydgate inscribes a new dimension of miraculous agency into St. Edmund's cult by claiming that the king ensures the authenticity of the infant's martyrdom: the "thy passioun" that ends the first four stanzas becomes "both your passioun" in a final unity of sanctity. As an interpreter of Bury's economy of sacred relics and texts, Lydgate shows his desire to return not only to the scene of martyrdom but to the scene of martyrology. The poet's concern here is with the writing of founding narratives at the intersection of historical and sacred time—that is, with the textual tradition that defines Bury St. Edmund's in relation to both the English nation and the church.

Lydgate's profound nostalgia in *To St. Robert* is not unlike the Prioress's in his "master" Chaucer's semi-ironic tale of ritual murder by Jews.[8] When, at the end of her Asiatic fiction of the "litel clergeon'"s murder, the well-fed Prioress harks back to England with "O yonge Hugh of Lincoln, slayn also / With cursed Jews, as is notable / For it is but a little while ago" (684–86), she too compresses time in a longing for monastic renewal through martyrdom's orgy of violence. As Joe Hillaby has recently detailed, the English cases of Jewish ritual murder, up to and including young Hugh in 1255, largely involved monastic ambitions for a patron saint or, at the very least, the building of a new shrine.[9] In their very different tones, Lydgate's prayer and the *Prioress's Tale* both address such issues of monastic prestige. Chaucer is primarily interested in the fictional possibilities of the child-martyr narrative and particularly of the psychology of the cloistered hagiographer. A long line of critics has explored the *Prioress's Tale*'s engagement with exegetical and liturgical models; Lee Patterson has recently characterized it as part of a monastic dialogue, met by the scathing "intertextual commentaries" of the satiric *Nun's Priest's Tale* and the respectably hagiographic *Second Nun's Tale*.[10] Lydgate, by contrast, removes the story further from any theological concerns with Jews, finding in its pathos an element that connects him to Bury's distant monastic politics and Latin literary traditions.

While the two texts draw an inevitable comparison, Lydgate is no naive sentimentalist, falling prey to Chaucer's acerbic joke. The poet's understanding of fifteenth-century decline, naturally embedded in his plea for a reinvigorated spirituality, is ubiquitous in both his religious and secular works. Little

St. Robert recalls that other crowned, inarticulate, and "pitous" infant, Henry VI.[11] Lydgate's imaginative projection back into the historical moment of 1180s Bury speaks to the contradictions within his monastic identity and authorial self-representation. As both monk and poetic "maker," Lydgate desires to emulate both the unspeaking innocence of the boy-martyr and the moving eloquence of the original *vita.*

It may seem bizarre to argue that Lydgate, the notoriously "prolix" court author of the gigantic *Troy Book* and the *Fall of Princes,* identifies, like the Prioress, with a childish ignorance of language; nonetheless, his later works reveal precisely a growing tension between courtly eloquence and contemplative silence. The aristocratic masculine ideal of the "poet laureate," with which Lydgate is so identified, gives way to the "laureat marter," the glory of Rome to Rome's exemplary victim.[12] As I'll argue later in this essay, in his *Testament,* a kind of last word, the poet attempts to fashion his own virgin martyrdom in the register of vernacular literary style.

In his vast literary oeuvre, Lydgate draws from and combines a heterogeneous set of courtly and devotional traditions. Of his major hagiographic works, *The Life of Saints Edmund and Fremund* and the later *Life of Saints Alban and Amphibalus,* Karen Winstead argues, "Lydgate's direct debts are not to earlier Middle English saints' lives, but rather to the tradition of learned, historically oriented Latin and French hagiography that evolved in English monasteries in the twelfth century."[13] In another assessment of the poet's approach to vernacularity, Christopher Cannon claims that Lydgate's "worldly" monastic style reveals how he creates a place for himself in a genealogy of poets laureate to all but the exclusion of the earlier Middle English devotional writers.[14] Unsurprisingly, then, it is in his representations of martyrdoms, radical interventions of sacred time into the worldly realm, that Lydgate puts the most pressure on the assumptions that underlie his literary affiliations.

By looking back to Jocelin, who was an actual eyewitness to little Robert's burial and the subsequent "signs and wonders . . . performed among the common folk" (16), Lydgate evokes a time when a local virgin martyrdom was still possible in England. Although little Robert's *vita,* of which only traces survive, presumably followed only one aspect of the early church's model of martyrdom—death at the hands of non-Christians—for Lydgate this is the most important as well as the safest.[15] The late antique martyr's typically scandalous narrative, the witnessing of his or her beliefs by refusing to submit to the demands of a hostile political authority, provides a matter of considerable anxiety for a hagiographer also enlisted as royal apologist.[16] Lydgate's hagiographies, needless to say, demonstrate his mastery of this genre of courtly tact.

In the *Lives of Saints Edmund and Fremund,* as in St. Robert's *vita,* the purity of the virgin male body violently cleanses the English realm of nonbelievers, whether pagans or Jews.[17] Lydgate composed this work for Henry VI after his visit to Bury in 1433–34, where the twelve-year-old king and his retinue were sumptuously entertained by Abbot William Curteys.[18] At the time that Lydgate presented his poem to the king in 1436, Henry was already known for his own strict chastity: as the papal representative Piero Da Monte noted in 1437, "[H]e avoided the sight and conversation of women, affirming these to be the work of the devil. . . . Those who knew him intimately said that he had preserved his virginity of mind and body to the present time, and that he was firmly resolved to have intercourse with no woman unless within the bounds of matrimony."[19] In recognition of the king's style of piety, Lydgate shapes his Latin sources to emphasize St. Edmund's virginal status. While the eleventh- and twelfth-century hagiographers had alluded to the saint's sexual purity, they celebrate him primarily as " rex et martyr." Abbo of Fleury's *Passio Sancti Eadmundi,* the first *vita,* ends with typical monastic praise of virginity as the highest virtue and attributes the miracle of Edmund's preserved body to his chastity; in Lydgate's interpretation, however, virginity is essential to Edmund's identity as "martir, maide, & kyng."[20] The poet is consistent in his praise of these "notable crownys thre" (50). Even as Lydgate translates his sources' portraits of Edmund as the perfect "christene prynce" (956) according to the model of Bede and his monastic descendants, he undermines the very idea of hereditary rule that naturally occupies such a central place in his Lancastrian political poems. In the *Lives of Saints Edmund and Fremund,* as Winstead stresses, Edmund's "noblesse" is a knightly engagement with the political world or "Rem publicam" (891) at all levels.[21] The saint's exemplary death, however, looks back to a different kind of Roman virtue, the "masculinized" femininity of the early virgin-martyrs.[22]

Despite his "hih prowesse" in battle (1.1027), St. Edmund, "King of Estyngglond," seeks martyrdom from the invading Danes Hygwar and Ubba rather than waging war. His ultimate goal, especially in Lydgate's account, is freedom for the East Anglian, and by extension all English, Christians:

Blood forto sheede he hath noon appetit,
And to been armyd he hath left his corage;
Affermeth platly and seith in pleyn language:
He moost desireth above al worldly good
For Cristis feith to deie and spende his blood.
And to ffranchise his kyngdam and contre,
He hath a corage, that he him-self alone,

So his peeple myht stonde at liberte,
To suffre deth meekly in his persone.
(2.640–48)

Edmund thus dies passive and violated, tied to a tree, "fulfilled with spynys thikke: / As was the martyr seynt Sebastyan," (2.763–64) and then beheaded. Lydgate's choice of associations is revealing:

Red by his sides the roial blood doun ran,
And ever to Jhesu he maade his orisouns.
Thus with the tryumphes of their passiouns
Blissid martirs, with crownes laureat
Cleyme hih in hevene to regne in ther estate.
Danys with arwes hookyd, sharpe, and grounde
Spenten ther shot fersere than liouns,
Most mortally, as wounde ay upon wounde
Renewid ageyn the deepe inpressiouns.
(2.768–74)

Edmund becomes one of "Cristis champiouns" (2.775) like the former soldier Sebastian, his "royal blood" exchanged for the kingdom of heaven. Like the virgin who through her martyrdom becomes a "bride of Christ"—Lydgate's own St. Margaret, for example—Edmund is a king whose worldly line ends with him so that he can "regne" with the saints.[23] The young man's virginity, furthermore, like that of the martyrs Agnes, Thecla, and Pelagia, in Ambrose's *De virginibus,* ultimately preserves his masculine "intactness" after his feminizing ordeal with the pagan "lions."[24] The saint's head, which helpfully calls out "her her her" to the Christians looking for him after the martyrdom, is miraculously rejoined to his body, leaving only a mark like a purple thread on his neck.

Edmund's death is avenged in book 3 of Lydgate's poem by his nephew Fremund, who becomes king until his own early martyrdom.[25] The poet takes the opportunity in this additional legend to interject a recuperative passage on royal descent, even though Fremund, like his uncle, remains a "maide duryng all his liff" (3.130). When he is crowned, Fremund is "As trewe enheritour by goddis ordyance, / Doun fro the stok off kynges descendyng / the pedegre by lyneal conveyyng" (3.297–99), terms almost identical to those Lydgate had used for Henry VI's English and French coronations.[26] Having been assured by an angel that he should take up arms against the pagans, Fremund defeats forty thousand Danes with an army of only twenty-four men before being murdered through treason: "Afforn ther face no paynym myhte abyde" (3.530).

Lydgate's treatment of virgin martyrdom in the *Lives of Saints Edmund and Fremund* illuminates his interest in little Robert as a new saint who provides historical continuity to the abbey's own sacred functions. Just as Edmund's and Fremund's deaths ultimately drive the pagans from East Anglia, the "holy boy's" martyrdom in Jocelin of Brakelond's *Chronicle* serves as a prelude to Abbot Samson's exile of the Jews from Bury nine years later. This purification of "the town of St. Edmund" was, Jocelin affirms, one of the "proofs of the Abbot's excellence."[27] By Lydgate's time, the sacrifice of Robert's "chast blood" recalls the expulsion of Jews from all of England and much of France as well. The renewal that little Robert's virgin martyrdom effects, then, is of the prestige of the abbey of Bury St. Edmund's within a larger nationalistic program. The boy's purity and integrity of body, like King Edmund's and the patron King Henry VI's, testifies to the purity of the monastery and the English *natio*.

The Monk's Laurels

Though Lydgate, as what Derek Pearsall has called the official "poet-propagandist" of the Lancastrian dynasty, was deeply concerned with national integrity, most recent critical assessments have demonstrated that the monk's Chaucerian poetics inevitably expose a self-defeating approach to the Lancastrians' ambitions.[28] As Paul Strohm has written of the "Lancastrian text" in general, its political inconsistencies produce only "a recipe for inevitable cognitive/aesthetic breakdown."[29] The fifteenth-century Chaucerian poets, finding the available rhetorical strategies insufficient to defend the Lancastrian central claim to the "double monarchy" of England and France, anatomize inability itself.[30] Lee Patterson traces the "anxiety and even the intuition of failure" in Lydgate's 1426 *The Title and Pedigree of Henry VI*, which shows the king's descent from "the stok riall / of St. Lowis," to the terms of the Treaty of Troyes itself. As Patterson argues, Henry V's 1420 peace sets up a self-contradictory "discourse of identity and difference" that defines England and France as distinct nations even as it confirms that the two crowns will "perpetually be togedyr in Oone and the same Persone."[31] James Simpson similarly reconsiders the *Siege of Thebes* as a celebration of the Treaty of Troyes, finding in Lydgate's glosses of the *Knight's Tale* a deeply pessimistic account of "the backward pull of history."[32] The ideas of English purity and identity that Lydgate celebrates in the *passiones* of his male virgin martyrs are, if ultimately irreconcilable with the incoherent discourses of the "double monarchy," a convenient means to sidestep genealogical questions altogether. The saints' lives constitute a parallel history governed by miraculous concepts of time and affinity in which blood spilled in martyrdom outweighs the blood of kings.

Lydgate's simultaneous late projects, the *Lives of Saints Edmund and Fremund* and the *Fall of Princes,* finished in 1438, reveal the extent of his divided allegiances. With Humphrey, Duke of Gloucester, as his patron, Lydgate exalts his long-held Petrarchan ideal of the laureate poet. The prologue of the encyclopedic *Fall* links a lengthy eulogy of "my maister Chuacer . . . off our language . . . the lodesterre" (1.246, 252), with praise for the "bothe manly and eek wis" (1.407) Humphrey as a figure who recalls the learned glories of "Cesar Iulius'" Rome: "For lordes hadde pleasance for to see, / To studie among, and to caste ther lookis / At good leiser upon wise bookis" (1.361–64).[33] As Seth Lerer writes of the nostalgia for an *auctor* of Chaucer's stature in the first decades of Henry VI's reign: "Lydgate's own propaganda and his pleas for patronage during this period articulate the fantasies of a writer needing to be that laureate."[34] Lydgate's "aureate" poetic style, the ornate Latinate rhetoric with which he and his contemporaries seek to imitate humanist models, also reaches its height in the *Fall of Princes.*[35] The *Fall* is a perverse vehicle for the laureate's fame, of course, since its seemingly endless amplifications of the *Monk's Tale* doom the prince's reputation to diminish as the poet's increases, a point Lydgate makes by including Richard II in *Of the Sodein Fall of Princes in Oure Dayes.*[36]

Lydgate completes the *Fall of Princes* with a distillation of his literary ideas in the form of an envoy to Duke Humphrey. Here, with formulaic protestations of modesty, Lydgate catalogs the great classical writers "Virgyle," "Ovyde," and "Dares Frygius" together with the modern "laureat" masters of "tragedyes olde," "Petrark," "John Bochas," and "Chauceer" (9.3401–27). When he at last inscribes himself into this august lineage, he invokes St. Edmund, a singular prince who escaped the poets' tragic narrative:

> But I that stonde lowe doun in the vale,
> So greet a book in Ynglyssh to translate,
> Did it be constreynt and no presumpcioun.
> Born in a vyllage which callyd is Lydgate
> Be olde tyme a famous castel toun;
> In Danys tyme it was bete doun,
> Tyme when Seynt Edmond, martyr, mayde, and kyng,
> Was sleyn at Oxne, be recoord of wrytyng.
>
> (9.3428–35)

Lydgate shuns his Chaucerian "laureate" legacy at the very moment of its fulfillment, identifying instead with the virgin martyr and his hagiographers. In
so doing, he significantly alters the valence of his "constraint" to write the *Fall*
at the Duke of Gloucester's "comaundement" (9.3304). The monk's name itself
disappears into the East Anglian landscape of towns that rise and fall at tyrants' commands; Lydgate abandons the "laureate" mutual fame of prince
and poet, leaving Humphrey to face his own impending spectacular fall of
the 1440s.[37] Unlike Chaucer's "manly" monk, who is so enamored of his "ex-
ametrons" that he never gets a chance to "seyn the lyf of Seint Edward," Lydgate keeps the conflicting assumptions of poetry and hagiography in dialogue.
At the end of his own monument to "tragedyes oolde," Lydgate counters its
theory of history with martyrdom's redemption of time.

In the *Lives of Saints Edmund and Fremund,* Lydgate's ambivalence toward
his Lancastrian patrons becomes especially pronounced when he attempts to
celebrate the impossible "double monarchy" of the unpromising adolescent
Henry VI. In the *Life of Our Lady,* his compendium of Marian legends written
during Henry V's reign, Lydgate had mourned "the Rhetorykes swete" (1.1623)
of Petrarch, Cicero, and "my maister Chaucer . . . / The noble Rhethor, poete of
Brytayne / That worthy was the laurer to have of poetrye . . ." (1.1628–31).[38] In
the likewise pious monastic context of *Edmund and Fremund,* by sharp contrast,
Chaucer is nowhere mentioned, his laurels subordinated to the "notable crowns
three" of St. Edmund: kingship, virginity, and martyrdom. With either aston-
ishing clumsiness or prophetic insight, Lydgate attempts to align these in high
exegetical style with Henry's two crowns, with the third—of martyrdom,
perhaps—awaiting him after his death:

> These thre crownys historyaly tayple,
> By pronostyke notably sovereyne
> To sixte Herry in fygur signefye
> How he is born to worthy crownys tweyne:
> Off France and Ingland, lynealy tatteyne
> In this lyff heer; affterward in hevene
> The thrydde crowne to receyve in certeyne,
> For his meritis, above the sterrys sevene.
>
> (1.65–72)

Through Lydgate's own circuitous reasoning and "aureate" rhymes, the double
monarchy itself emerges as an instrument of martyrdom.

In the *Lives of Saints Edmund and Fremund,* moreover, Lydgate's signature
rhyme of "laureate" and "aureate," which Lerer has analyzed in terms of the

poet's nostalgia for the golden age of the Ricardian court and its patronage of the Petrarchan laureate Chaucer, becomes metaphoric, assimilated to the power reversal inherent in martyrdom.[39] Unlike the glory and fame by which laureled Caesars and poets complement each other, the martyr—champion of the Roman arena—triumphs through his or her modest silence and endurance of pain.[40] Praying to Edmund himself for the words with which to translate his "holi lif" into English, Lydgate implores:

> Into my brest send a confortatiff
> Of sum fair language, tenbelisshe with thi liff!
> Send doun of grace thi licour aureat
> Which enlumynyth these rethoriciens
> To write of martirs ther passiouns laureat
> And causith also these fressh musiciens,
> Fals lust avoided of epicuriens,
> Of glorious seyntes the tryumphes for to synge
> That suffred peyne for Crist in ther levynge!
> (1.220–27)

Lydgate's aureate style remains in this classicizing, Dantean invocation but is governed by a new anti-Epicurean aesthetic; the virgin martyr "of Bury cheef patroun" is also his real patron, paying not with gold but with "licour aureate." Such a fundamentally conflicted set of images, in which the language to express physical pain becomes a balm to the poet's body, is appropriate to a hagiography so ideologically incoherent in its lavish praise for Henry VI. Of political necessity, the *Lives of Saints Edmund and Fremund* combines its author's wishes for Henry's resemblance to his father "by triumphal victory," "a palme of conquest," and even a place among the nine worthies (!), with the *vita* of a nonlineal and virgin king who renounces all war in favor of St. Sebastian's exemplary passive death. The "golden age" that Lydgate evokes in the poem is not that of the Ricardian or any other court but rather the founding miracle of Bury and its relics—the rejoining of Edmund's head to his body—and beyond that, the early church and the gory "triumphs" of its martyrs. Under the influence of his new "aureate licour," Lydgate looks back to a Rome where the real laurel crown went neither to Caesars nor poets but to Christian martyrs. In a rebuke to his former courtly self as well as his erstwhile Lancastrian patrons, the would-be Caesars Henry V and Humphrey, Duke of Gloucester, Lydgate inaugurates a new poetic project inspired by the power of suffering.

Lydgate's Virginity

In his last major work, known as the *Testament of Dan John Lydgate,* the author fully enacts a monastic poetics of martyrdom, combining the pathos of *Robert of Bury* with the ascetic renunciations of *Edmund and Fremund.* Associated in its manuscript tradition with Chaucer's *Prioress's Tale* and *Second Nun's Tale,* the *Testament* is, in a sense, Lydgate's auto-hagiography.[41] By virtue of its genre, of course, the *Testament* is supposed to be the poet's final statement before his death, and he affirms that he has no worldly heirs: "this hooly my entent / to make Iesu to be chief surveior, / Of my laste wille in my testament" (211–12).[42] Lydgate adds further urgency to the literary convention, however, by equating his confession with a martyr's self-defining declaration of faith.

The martyr with whom the monk of Bury finally identifies is neither the kingly Edmund nor the helpless Robert nor even the heroic Thomas à Becket, but rather Ignatius, the early second-century bishop of Antioch. Through Eusebius's history and his own letters, Ignatius is known for his intense fervor for martyrdom, which he duly received at the Emperor Trajan's orders.[43] Lydgate's *Testament,* however, draws on the late legends of St. Ignatius in the *Legenda aurea:*

> This name Jesu most profoundely doth myne;
> Marter Ignacius can beren therof witnesse,
> Amyd whos herte, be grace which is dyvyne,
> With Aureat letteres As gold that dyd shyne,
> His herte was graven, men may his legende se—
> (34–38)

According to Jacobus de Voragine's account, Ignatius's executioners asked him why he kept calling the name of Jesus throughout his tortures. "He replied: 'I have this name written on my heart and therefore cannot stop invoking it!' After his death, those who had heard him say this were driven by curiosity to find out if it was true, so they took the heart out of his body, split it down the middle and found there the name *Jesus Christ* inscribed in gold letters."[44] Lydgate had been fascinated by this most textual of saints throughout his poetic career; the *Life of Our Lady* includes a long passage on the martyrdom of Ignatius, describing Trajan's astonishment "Whan that he sawe his hert kytte atweyne, / And letters newe depicte in every veyne" (4.258–59); and he appears in a catalog of martyrs "clad in red" (41) in the third book of the *Lives of Saints Edmund and Fremund.*

Lydgate finds in this very literal story combining martyrdom and writing a way to recast the problem posed by *To Robert of Bury,* the struggle between eloquence and silence. In the *Testament,* the ideal of an aureate style is converted from courtly praise to perfect and eternal interior language and, finally, self-erasing *logos.* Once again echoing Dante and Chaucer in an invocation, Lydgate claims a contemplative's verbal incapacity with regard to Jesus's sacrifice:

> Ther is no speche nor language can remembre,
> Lettre, sillable, nor word that may expresse,
> Though into tunges were turned every membre
> Of man, to telle the excellent noblesse,
> Of blessed Iesu, which of his gret mekenesse,
> List suffre deth to make his servant fre.
>
> (57–62)[45]

Like the *infans* martyr Robert undergoing his crucifixion, the once-aspiring poet laureate is "withoute langage." Lydgate strikingly situates his inability to praise in the context of martyrdom's highest goal, the transformation of every torn body part into a tongue. As in Ignatius's *vita,* where the saint desires as much torture as possible, "limb being torn from limb and flesh from bone," the weight of language is measured by the accompanying degree of physical fragmentation.[46]

Lydgate reconciles his poetic identity with his desire for innocence by reenacting a kind of literary virgin martyrdom. Imitating his own poems on St. Edmund and little Robert, Lydgate focuses on themes of monastic and national renewal, although he seeks a repurification not of England but of his own English vernacular idiom. In this account, the poet's own "master" and literary father, the "laureate" Chaucer, occupies, in a sense, the place of the pagan or Jew who must either be killed off or converted in order to restore a legible identity. Lydgate negotiates this model's obvious connection between sexuality and rhetoric through the classic text on the subject, Augustine's *Confessions.* Eugene Vance analyzes Augustine's simultaneous "fall" into both sex and "the arts of language": "When puberty overwhelms [him] with 'dark concupiscence' of the flesh and 'unholy desire,' his eloquence becomes similarly perverted. Indeed from this moment forward, sexual desire serves in his narrative as an arch-metaphor for the perversions of language."[47] While Augustine's account of an adolescence spent in "a sizzling frying-pan of lusts" might seem an unlikely basis for his defense of innocence, Lydgate uses the church father's few nonsexual escapades and love of Latin rhetoric to imply rather than assert his own virginity.[48]

The *Testament* takes the form of a four-part reverie on Lydgate's sinful childhood and youth, which abruptly stops at the age of fifteen when he sees a crucifix bearing the command "Vide!" This is followed by a fifth part written in Jesus's voice from the cross, elaborating on what precisely to "behold." Fifteen is significantly the year before the age at which Augustine says that "frenzy gripped me and I surrendered myself entirely to lust"—a lust he relates intimately to his ambitions as a professional rhetorician, studying "literature and the art of public speaking."[49] It is also at "ful compleet fiftene yeer of age" (1.857), according to Lydgate's *vita* in *Edmund and Fremund*, that St. Edmund "was crowned at Bury kyng of this regioun" (1.855), the king who both preserved his chastity thereafter and abhorred "feyned lestnges and aduacioun, / kankrid mouthes and lippis destestable" (1.1020–21).

When Lydgate finally gets around to cataloguing his "many unbrydlyed passiouns" (613), they are pointedly nonsexual, including sudden changes of mood, coming to school late, and, in homage to Augustine, stealing fruit—and not just unalluring and tasteless pears:

> Ran in-to gardeynes, apples ther I stall;
> To gadre frutes, spared nedir hegge nor wall,
> To plukke grapes In other mennes vynes
> Was more ready than for to sey matynes.
> (638–41)

His more serious sins have to do with abuses of speech: even though he had already taken the "blak habite" (691) of a Benedictine, he describes himself "with tonge at large and brotel conscyence, / Ful of wordes, disordinat of language" (712–13) and further confesses, "To veyn fables I did myn eres dresse, / Fals detraccioun among was to me swete" (721–22). Together with Augustine, Lydgate claims that he "to sensualyte gave all the governaunce" (718); however, his is above all a sensuality of style.

Although Lydgate's rather strained and technical "virginity" is clearly a far cry from the otherworldly perfection of the church's virgin martyrs, it allows him, within this fictional frame, to confine his nonauthorial sinfulness to his "tender age" (408), a time that he formally associates with Chaucerian poetry. Childhood is springtime, which in the *Testament* is epitomized by the sexy style of the *Canterbury Tales*' General Prologue:

Whiche sesoun prikkes fressh corages,
Rejoiseth bestes walking in ther pasture.
Causeth byrdes to syngen in ther cages,
Whanne blood reneweth in every creature
Some observance doyng to nature.
. . . .
First Zepherus with his blastes sote
Enspireth ver with newe buddes grene,
The bawme ascendeth out of every rote,
Causyng with flowres ageyn the sunne shene
May among monthes sitt like a quene.

(297–301, 325–29)

If this "aureate" style functions as a temptation for the monk, Lydgate resists it,
concluding the Chaucerian section of the poem with a stern reminder of mor-
tality: "Men sen chyldren of byrth yong and grene, / Buryed withinne the yeres
fiftene" (373–74). Spring passes, he concludes, in order to show that "oure
dwellyng here is but a pilgrimage" (394), a devotional commonplace that nevertheless forecloses any other possible interpretations of the *Canterbury Tales.*

The *Testament,* as autobiography, is more notable for what it leaves out than
for what it includes—the entire period between Lydgate's conversion experience before the crucifix at age fifteen and his confessional return to that moment at around age seventy-five. The poem begs the question: What is the
status of Lydgate's long and extremely prolific career as the preeminent court
poet? Rather than reject his "laureate" period in a forthright retraction modeled on Augustine or Chaucer, he transforms these missing literary years into a
martyr's sacrifice. In the third section of the *Testament,* which he fashions as a
penitential psalm to Jesus, Lydgate transforms himself into a second St. Ignatius, facing the hungry lions in the emperor Trajan's arena:

Who shal yeve me leyser out to breke,
That thou Jesu mayst entren in myn herte
Ther to abyde more nere than my sherte
With aureate letres, grave there in substaunce?

(505–8)

Recalling his opening lines on Ignatius's engraved heart, Lydgate here turns
the author's desire for "leyser," the time necessary for reading and writing itself,
into the martyr's zeal for physical violation and death, a breaking out and in. In

his image of self-dissolution, Lydgate seeks to exchange the poet's laurels, the sign of his own courtly "aureate letters," for the martyr's metaphoric laurels, the ultimate sign of public authority reversed.

Lerer characterizes the Chaucerian Lydgate as "a fashioner of myth," who with his Latinate "aureate poetics" "conjures up a vision of a past world . . . the Edenic fantasy of the Petrarchan prospect."[50] If Lydgate's great temptation is a fantasy of direct descent from the Roman masters, he uses the form of the "laste wille" to end that line. In the *Testament*, the poet can renounce his Roman longings only by imagining himself as a martyred victim of Imperial Rome. Petrarch's celebrated statement upon receiving the laurel crown at Rome was that "since both Caesars and poets move towards the same goal though by different paths [body and spirit] it is fitting that one and the same reward be prepared for both . . . symbolizing the fragrance of good fame and of glory."[51] In response to this inaugurating discourse of late medieval and early modern court poetry, Lydgate finally submits both his spirit and body to the real fame and glory represented by martyrdom, the eternity of the saint's relics and *vita*. In the logic of the *Testament*, Lydgate's previous literary works become his sacrifice, the ephemeral, worldly things surrendered at the moment of death. In renouncing the assumptions about power relations between prince and poet that had underwritten most of his poetry, Lydgate also renounces the princes themselves. His initial gesture towards St. Edmund's martyrdom at the very moment of self-inscription as a "poet laureate" at the end of the *Fall of Princes* finds its conclusion in the self-erasure he effects in the *Testament* by transforming the act of invocation itself into a plea for Ignatius's inscribed heart.

Although he naturally focuses his Augustinian confession on his own life, then, Lydgate implicitly rejects the imperial claims of the Lancastrian double monarchy along with his role as its leading propagandist. By means of all these intertextual gymnastics, Lydgate styles himself a virgin-martyr, erasing the time between his last-minute conversion at fifteen and his new conversion sixty years later. In his interior "monastic renewal," he transforms his former Roman-masculine ideal of the Petrarchan laureate, the "Caesar of the spirit," into the feminine and adolescent heroics of the embattled, triumphant virgin. If the first sight of the crucifix preserves his bodily chastity, the second chastens his poetic identity as he prepares for death.

At the end of this aureate poem, Lydgate makes one final rhetorical move to change the meaning of his vernacular idiom to the "aureate letters" he prays to have etched inside his heart. In the final section of the *Testament*, Lydgate's autobiographical "I" disappears, replaced by Jesus's own exhortations to "behold" all the sights of the Passion in eighteen stanzas, each of which ends with the word *sacrifice*. In the last three stanzas, Jesus invites Lydgate and his readers to the "heavenly court" (879), "noon erthly palys wrought in so stately wyse" (895), a convention infused with new life by the poet's courtly past. The monk-author's martyrdom is at hand as his own voice is sacrificed along with the *logos*. The *Testament* ends as its genre demands, with the subject called to the silence of death.

Seen through the lens of the last stanzas of his last poem, Lydgate's vivid prayer *To Robert of Bury* makes more sense as a plea for another renewal of his abbey's glorious past. His apprehension of the helpless *infans* bleeding to death and making only a "pitous soun," returns the poet to a virgin purity of language that he similarly imagines in the *Testament*. By reliving the exact experience of Jocelin, Bury's greatest hagiographer, Lydgate assumes the authority of his predecessor's role. While his immediate understanding of the boy's suffering prepares him emotionally for his own sacrifice, Lydgate's own "pagan" elements, in the unfortunate absence of Bury's Jews, must stand in for the typical agents of martyrdom. Lydgate had executed his monastic masterpiece in the *Lives of Saints Edmund and Fremund,* undermining his weak royal patron in favor of his abbot, William Curteys, who had requested that he write the poem, and the "martyr, king, and virgin" Edmund himself. In the *Testament,* he turns the ideal of spiritual renewal inward, subjecting his Chaucerian poetics to the imperative of Jesus's bodily sacrifice.

Lydgate's late imagination of court and abbey in opposition proved to be oddly prophetic. By 1472, a year after the hapless Henry VI met his end in the tower, and twenty-three years after the poet's death, the last of the Lancastrians was being venerated as a royal martyr, with pilgrims flocking to his tomb at Chertsey Abbey.[52] While Lydgate's once-laureate fame is defined by his exclusion from the *Norton Anthology of English Literature,* where he is dismissed in an introduction as "a self-styled imitator of Chaucer" but not "the best of Chaucer's imitators," his metaphoric virgin-martyrdom is all but forgotten.[53] Henry, that most inept of monarchs, succeeded where the poet failed in winning the laurels, we may assume, because martyrdom always requires a body as well as a style.

Notes

I delivered a version of this essay at the conference "Suffering History": Martyrdom in Britain 1401–1570," sponsored by the Centre for Research in the Arts, Social Sciences and Humanities, Cambridge University. I would like to thank the conference's organizer,

James Simpson, and the other participants for their many helpful comments. I would also like to thank Fiona Somerset for our enlightening discussions of Lydgate's hagiographies as well as for reading my drafts and offering her always excellent advice.

1. *The Chronicle of Jocelin of Brakelond,* ed. H. E. Butler (Oxford: Oxford University Press, 1949), 16. For other accounts of the martyrdom, see H. Copinger Hill, "St. Robert of Bury St. Edmunds," *Proceedings of the Suffolk Institute of Archaeology and Natural History* 21 (1931–33): 98–107.

2. Peter Brown, *The Cult of the Saints* (Chicago, 1981), 81.

3. Lydgate, *To Robert of Bury,* in *The Minor Poems of John Lydgate,* 2 vols., ed. Henry Noble MacCracken, EETS, o.s., 107, 192 (London: Oxford University Press, 1911, 1934), 1:138–39. All further citations are to this edition. Throughout this chapter, poetry is cited parenthetically in the text by line number or by book and line numbers.

4. Jocelin of Brakelond's *vita* of Robert of Bury, which in his *Chronicle* he says he "set down elsewhere" (16), is now lost. Bale recorded it in his catalog, although he may simply have been following Jocelin; see *John Bale's Index of British and Other Writers,* ed. Reginald Lane Poole and Mary Bateson (Oxford: Oxford University Press, 1902), 276. I am assuming, however, that the text was still extant at Bury when Lydgate was writing. Jocelin's *Chronicle* is preserved in Bury's *Liber Albus,* together with the abbey's Customary and various other documents, now British Library MS. Harley 1005.

5. Miri Rubin, "Choosing Death? Experiences of Martyrdom in Late Medieval Europe," in *Martyrs and Martyrologies,* ed. Diana Wood, Studies in Church History 30 (Oxford: Blackwell, 1993), 153–83.

6. André Vauchez, *Sainthood in the Later Middle Ages,* trans. Jean Birrell (Cambridge: Cambridge University Press, 1997), 154.

7. *Chronicle of Jocelin,* 111–15.

8. Chaucer is not the first author to deal ironically with the idea of Jewish ritual murder: see, for example, the twelfth-century account of an accusation in Winchester in *The Chronicle of Richard of Devizes,* ed. John T. Appleby (London: Nelson, 1963), 66–69.

9. Joe Hillaby, "The Ritual-Child-Murder Accusation: Its Dissemination and Harold of Gloucester," *Transactions of the Jewish Historical Society* 34 (1994–96): 69–109. See also Gavin I. Langmuir, *Toward a Definition of Antisemitism* (Berkeley: University of California Press, 1990), 237–62.

10. Lee Patterson, "'The Living Witnesses of Our Redemption': Martyrdom and Imitation in Chaucer's *Prioress's Tale,*" *Journal of Medieval and Modern Studies* 31 (2001): 511.

11. Indeed, as Seth Lerer explains the age's thematic preoccupations with childhood, "For the better part of his minority and reign, Henry VI seemed more like the child than the father of his country." *Chaucer and His Readers: Imagining the Author in Late-Medieval England* (Princeton, NJ: Princeton University Press, 1993), 14–15.

12. Lydgate, *To St. Edmund,* 63, in *Minor Poems of John Lydgate,* 1:124–27.

13. Karen A. Winstead, "Lydgate's Lives of Saints Edmund and Alban: Martyrdom and Prudent Pollicie," *Mediaevalia* 17 (1994): 222.

14. Christopher Cannon, "Monastic Productions," in *The Cambridge History of Medieval English Literature,* ed. David Wallace (Cambridge: Cambridge University Press, 1999), 340–43.

15. For late antique definitions of martyrdom, see Jan Willem van Henten and Friedrich Avemarie, *Martyrdom and Noble Death: Selected Texts from Graeco-Roman, Jewish, and Christian Antiquity* (London: Routledge, 2002), and G. W. Bowersock, *Martyrdom and Rome* (Cambridge: Cambridge University Press, 1995), esp. 1–21.

16. For a discussion of just how skillfully Lydgate handles the politics of hagiography, see chap. 10 of this volume.

17. John Lydgate, *The Lives of Saints Edmund and Fremund,* in *Altenglische Legenden, Neue Folge,* ed. Carl Horstmann (Heilbronn: Henninger, 1881), 378–440. All further citations are to this edition.

18. Derek Pearsall, *John Lydgate (1371–1449): A Bio-Bibliography,* English Literary Studies 71 (Victoria, BC: University of Victoria, 1997), 34. See also the narrative of the royal visit recorded in Abbot Curteys's register: Craven Ord, ed., "Account of the Entertainment of King Henry the Sixth at the Abbey of Bury St. Edmund's," *Archaeologia* 15 (1806): 65–71.

19. Ralph Griffiths, *The Reign of King Henry VI: The Exercise of Royal Authority, 1422–1461* (London: Benn, 1981), 235. On the gossip that Henry's marriage to Margaret of Anjou remained unconsummated, see 255–56. For the Yorkist rumors that Prince Edward (b. 1453) was not Henry's son, see *An English Chronicle,* ed. J. S. Davies, Camden Society, o.s., 64 (London, 1856), 79–80.

20. Abbo of Fleury's *Passio* is in *Memorials of St. Edmund's Abbey,* 3 vols., ed. Thomas Arnold (London, 1890–96), 1: 3–25; the passage on Edmund's chastity is at 24. The Latin source for Edmund's early life is Geoffrey of Wells, *De infantia sancti Edmundi,* ed. R. M. Thomson, *Analecta Bollandiana* 95 (1977): 25–42. James I. Miller Jr. argues that Lydgate's source was the long anthology of Latin legends of St. Edmund found in MS Oxford Bodley 240, which he dates to the fourteenth century; see James I. Miller Jr., "Literature to History: Exploring a Medieval Saint's Legend and Its Context," in *Literature and History,* ed. I. E. Cadenhead Jr., University of Tulsa Monograph Series 9 (Tulsa, FL: University of Tulsa, 1970), 59–72. For an edition of this lengthy text, see Carl Horstmann, ed., *Nova legenda Anglie* (Oxford: Oxford University Press, 1901), 2:573–688.

21. Winstead, "Lydgate's Lives," 225–31.

22. Virginia Burrus, *"Begotten, Not Made": Conceiving Manhood in Late Antiquity* (Stanford, CA: Stanford University Press, 2000), 140–52.

23. On Lydgate's *Life of St. Margarete,* see Karen Winstead, *Virgin Martyrs: Legends of Sainthood in Late Medieval England* (Ithaca, NY: Cornell University Press, 1997), 122–29.

24. Burrus, *"Begotten, Not Made,"* 152. For a translation of *De Virginibus,* see Boniface Riley, O.P., *Ambrose* (London: Routledge, 1997), 71–116.

25. The Latin *vita* of Fremund, edited from MS Trinity College Dublin, B.2.7, is printed in Horstmann, *Nova legenda Anglie,* 2:689–98.

26. For example, *Henry VI's Triumphal Entry into London, 21 Feb. 1432,* written on the occasion of the king's return from his coronation at Paris: "The pedegree by iuste successioun, / as trewe cronycles trewly determyne, / Unto the Kyng ys now dessended doun / From eyther partye riht as eny lyne; / Upon whos heede now ffresshely done shyne / Two riche crounes . . ." (405–10). *Minor Poems of John Lydgate,* 2:630–48.

27. *Chronicle of Jocelin,* 45.

28. Derek Pearsall, *John Lydgate* (Charlottesville: University Press of Virginia, 1970), 69. Lee Patterson, "Making Identities in Fifteenth-Century England: Henry V and John Lydgate," in *New Historical Literary Study,* ed. Jeffrey Cox and Larry Reynolds (Princeton, NJ: Princeton University Press, 1993), 69–107. James Simpson, "'Dysemol daies and fatal houres': Lydgate's *Destruction of Thebes* and Chaucer's *Knight's Tale,*" in *The Long Fifteenth Century,* ed. Helen Cooper and Sally Mapstone (Oxford: Oxford University Press, 1997), 15–33.

29. Paul Strohm, "Hoccleve, Lydgate, and the Lancastrian Court," in Wallace, *Cambridge History,* 659.

30. See David Lawton's groundbreaking article, "Dullness and the Fifteenth Century," *ELH* 54 (1987): 761–99.

31. Patterson, "Making Identities," 89–93.

32. Simpson, "Dysemol daies," 33.

33. *Lydgate's Fall of Princes,* 4 vols., ed. Henry Bergen, EETS, e.s., 121, 122, 123, 124 (London: Oxford University Press, 1924–27). All further citations are to this edition.

34. Lerer, *Chaucer and His Readers,* 52.

35. Lydgate himself coined the English word *aureate.* On the literary theory of Lydgate's "aureate" style, see Lois Ebin, *Illuminator, Makar, Vates: Visions of Poetry in the Fifteenth Century* (Lincoln: University of Nebraska Press, 1988), 19–48. On the political weight of the term, see Lerer, *Chaucer and His Readers,* 21–56.

36. *Minor Poems of John Lydgate,* 2:660–61.

37. On Humphrey's arrest for treason and death in 1447, see Griffiths, *Reign of King Henry VI,* 496–97.

38. *A Critical Edition of John Lydgate's Life of Our Lady,* ed. Joseph A. Lauritis, Ralph A. Klinefelter, and Vernon F. Gallagher (Pittsburgh: Duquesne University, 1961). All further citations are to this edition.

39. Lerer, *Chaucer and His Readers,* 15 and 24–26.

40. See Burrus, *"Begotten, Not Made,"* 171–73; on the image of the martyr as gladiator, see Bowersock, *Martyrdom and Rome,* 41–57.

41. In British Library, MS. Harley 2383, the *Testament* breaks off at line 751 at 96v and is followed by Chaucer's two tales; it resumes at 108r. I would like to thank Anthony Bale for pointing me to this miscellany. In British Library, MS. Harley 2251, the fifth part of the *Testament* is included together with the two Chaucer texts. For more on these MSS, see Mary Godfrey, "The Fifteenth-Century Prioress's Tale and the Problem of Anti-Semitism," in *Rewriting Chaucer: Culture, Authority, and the Idea of the Authentic Text,*

1400–1602, ed. Thomas A. Prendergast and Barbara Kline (Columbus: Ohio State University Press, 1999), 93–115.

42. *The Testament,* in *Minor Poems of John Lydgate,* 1:329–62. See Julia Boffey, "Lydgate, Henryson, and the Literary Testament," *Modern Language Quarterly* 53 (1992): 41–56.

43. Eusebius, *The Ecclesiastical History,* trans. Kirsopp Lake (Cambridge, MA: Harvard University Press, 1953), 1:281–91; Ignatius's letters, written in captivity, are in Cyril C. Richardson, ed., *Early Christian Fathers* (New York: Macmillan, 1970), 74–120.

44. Jacobus de Voragine, *The Golden Legend,* trans. William G. Ryan (Princeton, NJ: Princeton University Press, 1993), 1:143.

45. See the prologue to the *Prioress's Tale* in Chaucer's *Canterbury Tales* and in turn its source, Dante's *Paradiso* 33.

46. Jacobus de Voragine, *Golden Legend,* 1:141.

47. Eugene Vance, *Mervelous Signals: Poetics and Sign Theory in the Middle Ages* (Lincoln: University of Nebraska Press, 1986), 18–19.

48. "Sartago flagitiosorum amorum." *Confessiones* III, 1; Martin Skutella, ed., *S Aureli Augustini Confessionum Libri XIII,* rev. ed. (Stuttgart: Teubner, 1996), 36.

49. "Vesania libidinis licentiosae . . ." *Confessiones,* II, 2; Skutella, *S. Aureli Augustini Confessionum,* 27; R. S. Pine-Coffin, trans., *Confessions* (Harmondsworth: Penguin, 1961), 44–45.

50. Lerer, *Chaucer and His Readers,* 44–45.

51. Petrarch, "Petrarch's Coronation Oration," in Ernest H. Wilkins, *Studies in the Life and Works of Petrarch* (Cambridge, MA: Harvard University Press, 1955), 309. See also Wilkins's detailed study of the event, "The Coronation of Petrarch," in *The Making of the Canzoniere and Other Petrarchan Studies* (Rome: Edizioni di Storia e Letteratura, 1951), 9–69.

52. See John W. McKenna, "Piety and Propaganda: The Cult of King Henry VI," in *Chaucer and Middle English Studies in Honor of Rossell Hope Robbins,* ed. Beryl Rowland (London, 1974), 72–88.

53. Stephen Greenblatt et al., eds., *Norton Anthology of English Literature,* 7th ed. (New York: W. W. Norton, 2000), 1:13. According to the introduction, Robert Henryson is "the best of Chaucer's imitators."

Contributors

C. DAVID BENSON is a Professor of English and Medieval Studies at the University of Connecticut. A founding editor of the *Lydgate Newsletter,* he is the author of *Public Piers Plowman* and other books and articles on Middle English literature.

RITA COPELAND is Professor and Chair of Comparative Literature at the University of Pennsylvania. She is the author of *Rhetoric, Hermeneutics, and Translation in the Middle Ages* and recently *Pedagogy, Intellectuals, and Dissent in the Later Middle Ages,* as well as many articles on the history of literary theory and rhetoric.

PHILLIPA HARDMAN is a Senior Lecturer in English at the University of Reading. She has edited *The Heege Manuscript*, *The Matter of Identity in Medieval Romance*, and *Medieval and Early Modern Miscellanies and Anthologies* and has written articles on late medieval English literature and its manuscript context.

ROBERT J. MEYER-LEE is Assistant Professor of English at Goshen College. He has published essays on Thomas Hoccleve and George Ashby and is currently completing a book entitled *Poets and Power from Chaucer to Wyatt.*

RUTH NISSE teaches English literature at the University of Nebraska–Lincoln. She is the author of *Defining Acts: Drama and the Politics of Interpretation in Late Medieval England.*

MAURA B. NOLAN is Assistant Professor of English at the University of Notre Dame, and author of *John Lydgate and the Making of Public Culture.* She has also coedited a book of essays with Jill Mann, *The Text in the Community: Essays on Medieval Works, Manuscripts, Authors, and Readers.*

LARRY SCANLON is Associate Professor of English at Rutgers, The State University of New Jersey. Formerly editor of *Studies in the Age of Chaucer*, he is also the author of *Narrative, Authority, and Power: The Medieval Exemplum and the Chaucerian Tradition*. He is currently completing a study entitled *At Sodom's Gate: Medieval Writing, Postmodern Theory, and the Regulation of Desire*.

JAMES SIMPSON is Professor of English and American Literature at Harvard University. He is the author of *Piers Plowman: An Introduction to the B Text*, *Sciences and the Self in Medieval Poetry*, and, most recently, *Reform and Cultural Revolution, 1350–1547*.

FIONA SOMERSET is Associate Professor of English at Duke University. She is the author of *Clerical Discourse and Lay Audience in Late Medieval England*, editor (with Nicholas Watson) of *The Vulgar Tongue: Medieval and Postmedieval Vernacularity* and (with Jill Havens and Derrick Pitard) of *Lollards and Their Influence in Late Medieval England*, and coeditor of the *Yearbook of Langland Studies*.

SCOTT-MORGAN STRAKER is an Assistant Professor at Department of English, Queen's University, Kingston, Canada. He is the author of articles on Lydgate and Chaucer.

JENNIFER SUMMIT is Associate Professor of English at Stanford University. She is the author of *Lost Property: the Woman Writer and English Literary History, 1380–1589*, and is completing a book project on the organization of reading and knowledge in medieval and early modern English libraries.

Index

Sharpe, Reginald K., 166n20
Shippey, T. A., 11n11
Shirley, John, 149, 159, 160, 161, 165n7,
    167n38, 167n41, 169–70, 173, 176,
    177, 186–91, 192n2, 194n7, 194n8,
    199n24, 200n32, 202n43, 203n47,
    204n51
Shumway, David R., 253n1
Sidney, Philip, 65–66
Siena, 162
Sigismund, emperor, 105–6, 108
Simpson, James, 26, 10n1, 10n2, 11n10,
    58n29, 59n38, 59n42, 123n7, 127n47,
    144n10, 145n15, 146n41, 146n44, 148,
    164n5, 166n26, 167n37, 167n41, 260,
    273n8, 273n10, 274n12, 285
Sir Gawain and the Green Knight, 5
Sir Thomas More, 34n27
Skelton, John, 78, 146n40
    Phyllyp Sparrowe, 32n13
    Speke Parott, 140
Skinner, Quentin, 103, 245n20
Smalley, Beryl, 229n49
Socrates, 212
Solomon, king, 156, 158
Somerset, Fiona, 296n16
Spearing, A. C., 92n2, 256n32
Speculum humanae salvationis, 179, 200n34
speech, 12, 22–23, 25–26, 30
    as dialogue, 25, 27, 62
    direct, 12, 22–23, 26
    indirect, 12, 22–23
    reported, 23
speech act theory, 103–6
Spenser, Edmund, 7, 36–37
    as English laureate poet, 54
Spiegel, Gabrielle M., 272n4, 274n12
Spitzer, Leo, 57n24
Sponsler, Claire, 162, 168n53, 185, 187, 188,
    192n3, 202n45
statesmanship, 207–31
Statute of Treason (1352), 83
Steiner, Emily, 227n14
Stepney, 160
Stow, John, 34n33, 147–50, 164n3, 165n11,
    166n26, 199n22, 200n32
Straker, Scott-Morgan, 56n9, 59n42, 123n7,
    167n37, 195n9, 160, 273n8, 273n11
Strips Jesse, 200n33
Strohm, Paul, 11n14, 57n26, 83, 91n1, 100,
    107, 115–16, 122n3, 126n37, 136,
    144n10, 145n14, 170, 194n5, 194n6,

197n17, 198n19, 204n50, 255n30,
    272n4, 274n12, 285
Stubbs, William, 131
Sweyn, 264, 266
syntax, 12–35. *See also* Chaucer, Geoffrey
    grammatical, 12, 14–22, 24–30
    —hypotactic, 16–17, 20–21, 25
    —paratactic, 16–17, 18–22, 26–29
    narrative, 14–16, 18, 20–30
    periodic, 14–15

Taithe, Bertrand, 124n19
Taylor, Frank, 126n30, 128n60
Taylor, Philip M., 124n19
tense, 12, 22
Tesniere, Marie-Helene, 230n66
theory (theoretical criticism), 3, 66–69
Thierry of Chartres
    Ad Herennium, 235
    De inventione, 235, 250
Thomas, duke of Clarence, 112
Thomas of Monmouth, 280
Thomas of Woodsrock, 268
Thompson, James Westfall, 215
Thompson, John A. F., 203n46
Thompson, John J., 199n22
Thomson, Oliver, 124n19
Thomson, Rodney M., 215, 229n37
Thorney, Robert, 203n47
Thornton, Tim, 124n19
Thorpe, William
    Testimony, 30
Thrupp, Sylvia, 203n46, 204n49
Thynne, William, 129, 144n2
Tillyard, E. M. W., 10n6
Tolkien, J. R. R., 4
Tomasch, Sylvia, 194n6
Trajan, 289, 292
translation, 9
Traversagni, 252
Treaty of Troyes, 108, 112, 117, 285
A Tretise of Miraclis Pleyinge, 201n38
Trevet, Nicholas, 217
Trigg, Stephanie, 36n10
trothe/trouthe, 47, 78–79
Tudor, Mary, 199n23
Tudor entries, 152, 199n23
Twycross, Meg, 192n3, 195n10, 196n11
Tyrrell, Edward, 197n15, 198n20

Ubaldo, Staico, 254n15
Unwin, George, 165n12